PROJECT FINANCING
Analyzing and Structuring Projects

PROJECT FINANCING

Analyzing and Structuring Projects

Carmel F. de Nahlik
WMG, University of Warwick, UK

Frank J Fabozzi
EDHEC Business School, France

World Scientific

NEW JERSEY · LONDON · SINGAPORE · BEIJING · SHANGHAI · HONG KONG · TAIPEI · CHENNAI · TOKYO

Published by

World Scientific Publishing Co. Pte. Ltd.

5 Toh Tuck Link, Singapore 596224

USA office: 27 Warren Street, Suite 401-402, Hackensack, NJ 07601

UK office: 57 Shelton Street, Covent Garden, London WC2H 9HE

Library of Congress Cataloging-in-Publication Data

Names: de Nahlik, Carmel F., author. | Fabozzi, Frank J., author.

Title: Project financing : analyzing and structuring projects / Carmel F. de Nahlik, WMG,
    University of Warwick, UK, Frank J. Fabozzi, EDHEC Business School, France.

Description: Hackensack, NJ : World Scientific, [2021] | Includes index.

Identifiers: LCCN 2020055775 | ISBN 9789811232398 (hardcover) |
    ISBN 9789811233173 (ebook for institutions) | ISBN 9789811233180 (ebook for individuals)

Subjects: LCSH: Corporations--Finance. | Capital investments. | Credit. | Loans.

Classification: LCC HG4026 .F335 2021 | DDC 658.4/040681--dc23

LC record available at https://lccn.loc.gov/2020055775

British Library Cataloguing-in-Publication Data

A catalogue record for this book is available from the British Library.

For any available supplementary material, please visit
https://www.worldscientific.com/worldscibooks/10.1142/12163#t=suppl

Desk Editors: Aanand Jayaraman/Lum Pui Yee

Typeset by Stallion Press
Email: enquiries@stallionpress.com

Printed in Singapore

To Chris, Serena and my sister Angela and all those
from whom I learned so much about project financing
and getting it right!

— Carmel F. de Nahlik

To the memory of my parents, Josephine and Alfonso Fabozzi.

— Frank J. Fabozzi

Preface

From its modern origins in the oil and gas industry and sophisticated leasing techniques, project financing has evolved into several different approaches and techniques that are widely used in sophisticated economies and in emerging economies by large companies and small, by governments and by small growing firms. In the 15 chapters in this book, we discuss the methods, structures and basics of instruments that can be employed to accomplish a successful project financing by addressing the three key elements of cash flow collateral/support structures, and risk management.

Following a detailed description of project financing in Chapter 1, we discuss the project financing process (Chapters 2–5), modelling and risk management (Chapters 6–8), public–private partnerships (Chapters 9 and 10), and project financing in practice (Chapters 11–15).

In discussing the project financing process, we explain in Chapter 2 how project management impacts project financing, describing the need to have a clear plan for a project and why such a document that describes this plan is the core to the success of a project. The documents that must be prepared (project plan and the offering memorandum) must communicate the essential information that stakeholders of a project need to know, is the subject of Chapter 3. In Chapter 4, we lay out the criteria for a successful project financing, starting with the different phases of a project and the considerations from providers of capital at each phase and then describe the key risk areas. The project financing process is the subject of Chapter 5.

Our coverage of modelling and risk management begins with Chapter 6 where the challenges in estimating the cost of a project are described. Chapters 7 and 8 cover financial models, the first covering the general principles and the second focusing on the unique aspects of financial modelling for different industries.

An increasing number of project financing transactions are part of an initiative used by governments for improving major project contracting, delivery and operation using a partnership process between the government and private sector. These project financing transactions are referred to as public–private partnerships. In Chapter 9, we describe these transactions, starting with a definition of public–private partnerships and the pros and cons of these transactions. Public–private partnerships in practice are the subject of Chapter 10, beginning with their different forms — pure concession agreements, design-build-operate-transfer and build-operate-transfer projects, design-build-finance-operate projects, and build-own-operate projects — and then describing the different types of projects for which public–private partnerships are formed — freestanding or commercial partnership, joint venture and services sold to the public. The thorny accounting issues associated with these transactions are also described in the chapter.

The last five chapters look at project financing in practice. Most projects have multiple core stakeholders and may have multiple owners. While many companies prefer absolute ownership and control of vital supply and distribution projects, as technology and services move around the world, jointly owned or controlled projects comprising partners with mutual goals, talents and resources are the norm. In Chapter 11, we explain the structures for jointly owned or sponsored projects. The objectives and considerations of project sponsors or a project company in connection with any construction financing, independent of the type of permanent financing, are explained in Chapter 12. In Chapter 13, we provide a general overview of trade financing, looking at the development of trade financing in terms of the instruments available including those used for pre-export finance, specific issues around supply chain financing, financing commodities, forfaiting and factoring and countertrade. Funding natural resource projects is covered in Chapter 14 using reserves-oriented financing. The same techniques that apply to a project financing of a new road, factory or gas development can also be used when contemplating corporate restructuring. In the final chapter in the book, Chapter 15, how techniques from project financing are used in corporate restructuring, asset sales, acquisitions and mergers are described.

Companion Book

Project Financing: Analyzing and Structuring Projects is less focused on the technical aspects of project financing, making it useful to a wider stakeholder group. In our companion book, *Project Financing: Financial Instruments and Risk Management*, we cover more technical aspects of project financing, focusing on the funding vehicles and risk management instruments. More specifically, we describe the different tools and techniques available to anyone who is engaged in providing funding or financial advice to a project. By project, we mean something of size and complexity (as opposed to the simpler project appraisal as taught at university's in finance courses under the topic "capital budgeting") but it is not limited to the mega projects.

Project financing is ultimately about applying three basic principles to a funding situation and from these three, all the other ideas flow. First, there needs to be a cash flow coming from the project that is capable of being captured by finance providers. Second, there needs to be a group of assets that can be segregated and contained by making sure they cannot be taken away by other parties, and thirdly there needs to be a risk envelope that is well understood and managed dynamically during the project's life. To do this, a network of contracts must exist to support the rights of the different stakeholders and their legal claims on the project.

In *Project Financing: Financial Instruments and Risk Management*, we examine all these aspects and provide some examples/min-cases of project structures and approaches. We begin and end with a case study of two projects that were standalone examples of project financing and controversial for different reasons at the time of their fundraising. Although these two cases are separated by almost 40 years, they demonstrate the influence of some of the modern flows of information and their pitfalls.

A Note on the Cases

The cases we chose were selected because they are relatively recent, but written over an extended period. In some instances this means that there may be ongoing situations such as legal or other investigations that may result in new information becoming available in the public domain. We have used our best endeavours to ensure information is correct as of 2020.

Acknowledgement

A major contribution to this book was provided by John Macgillivray (Managing Director of Project Planning and Management Ltd.) who authored Chapter 7 (Financial Models) and Chapter 8 (Financial Modelling for Different Industries).

About the Authors

Dr Carmel F. de Nahlik has advised many boards on governance, financial strategy and change projects. She holds degrees in Chemistry, an MBA, a PhD and a Master's in Online and Distance Learning as well as a PGCE for Higher Education. A former banker, now turned academic, she is the co-author of two books on project financing and one on banking, written for decisionmakers. Her international banking career was followed by an international consulting career and then a life as an academic. She has coached and mentored at board and senior government levels and resolved problems including politically sensitive financings. Carmel has taught at several universities in the UK and overseas and has designed and delivered executive education programmes focusing on project finance, project management, change, leadership and ethics and has participated in major change projects within large and small organisations. She is a Fellow of the Royal Society for Arts, a Member of the Association for Project Management and a former Council member of the Institute of Petroleum of Great Britain and Ireland and has held a number of nonexecutive director roles.

 **Frank J. Fabozzi** is a Professor of Finance at EDHEC Business School. Over the past 35 years, he has held various professorial positions at MIT, Yale, Princeton, Carnegie Mellon University and New York University. He is the editor of *The Journal of Portfolio Management*, the co-editor of *The Journal of Financial Data Science*, and a member of the editorial advisory board of *The Journal of Structured Finance*, *The Journal of Derivatives* and *The Journal of Fixed Income*. He has authored or coauthored numerous books, including *Equipment Leasing, Introduction to Securitization, The Complete CFO Handbook, Introduction to Structured Finance, Bond Markets, Analysis, and Strategies, Capital Budgeting: Theory and Practice*, and *Financial Management and Analysis*. He is a trustee of the BlackRock Fixed Income Board. Early in his career he was a consulting economist to the U.S. Army Corps of Engineers on water resource projects. He earned the designations of Chartered Financial Analyst (CFA) and Certified Public Accountant (CPA). He received his BA and MA in economics in 1970 from The City College of New York where he was elected to Phi Beta Kappa, and received a PhD in economics in 1972 from the City University of New York. In 1994 he was awarded an Honorary Doctorate of Humane Letters from Nova Southwestern University.

Contents

Chapter 1

An Overview of Project Finance

Introduction

The origins of project financing may be seen in such examples as merchant adventurers in the Middle Ages who invested in voyages, both in ships and cargo, in the expectation they would be repaid from the liquidation of the voyage proceeds. We can see the same approach today in conventional project financing and also in Islamic financing techniques where risks are shared by investors and funders in a project. The principles of project financing are also those that underpin other financial activities such as venture capital, trade finance, leveraged buyouts and other restructuring or financial engineering activities. Indeed, project finance can be considered a type of structured finance. So, although the term "project financing" has been used to describe all types and kinds of financing of projects, the term now tends to be more precise, as our definition shows:

> *A financing of a specific economic unit in which a lender is satisfied to look initially to the cash flows and earnings of that economic unit as the source of funds from which a loan will be repaid and equity serviced and to the assets of the economic unit as collateral for the loan within a specified risk framework.*

A key word in the definition is *initially*. While a lender may be willing to look *initially* to the cash flows of a project as the source of funds for repayment of the loan, the lender must also feel comfortable that the loan will in fact be paid on a worst-case basis. This may involve undertakings or direct or indirect guarantees by third parties who are motivated in some way to provide such support mechanisms.

Mission-critical to any project is its promoter or sponsor, and a project may have one or several sponsors. Construction companies act as sponsors to generate profits from the construction or operation of the project; operating companies sponsor projects to generate profits from fees for operating a facility and/or selling the product produced by the project. Some companies may do both with different entities set up as sponsors for each phase. Projects may also be set up to provide access to key resources or the processing or distribution of a basic product or service for a sponsor, or to ensure a source of supply vital to the sponsor's business.

The goal in project financing is to arrange a borrowing for a project that will benefit the sponsor and at the same time be completely "non-recourse" to the sponsor, so that there will be no impact on its financial statements, and in no way affects its credit standing. Indeed, project financing is sometimes called "non-recourse" or "off-balance sheet" financing. However, in today's world, regulators and accountants are taking an interest in the information asymmetries that may exist for stakeholders, including investors, in organizations when liabilities may "appear to disappear", so the "off-balance sheet" nature of project finance will be subject to change in future years. We discuss some of the changes in Chapter 5.

Lenders and borrowers may disagree as to what constitutes a *feasible project financing*. Borrowers prefer their projects to be financed independently and off-balance sheet. Lenders, on the other hand, are not in the venture capital business and are not equity risk takers. Lenders also want to feel secure that they are going to be repaid, preferably via more than one possible route, so either by the project, the sponsor or an interested third party. The challenge of designing a successful project financing to meet all stakeholder needs can be seen in these dilemmas. A successful project financing will include sufficient credit support through guarantees or undertakings of a sponsor or third party, so that lenders will be satisfied with the credit risk, while at the same time minimizing the recourse to the sponsor.

In practice, few projects are financed independently on their own merits without some form of credit support from sponsors. There is a popular misconception that project financing means off-balance sheet financing to the point that the project is completely self-supporting without guarantees or undertakings by financially responsible parties. This leads to misunderstandings by prospective sponsors who are under the impression that certain kinds of projects may be routinely financed as stand-alone self-supporting project financings. Such sponsors negotiate on the assumption that similar projects in which they have interests can also be financed without recourse to the sponsor, be off-balance sheet to the sponsor and be without any additional credit support from a financially responsible third party. Each project is different. Sadly, 100% loans to support a project (non-recourse to sponsors) that looks as though it would surely be successful based on optimistic financial projections are becoming very rare. Newer banking regulations pertaining to risks taken by banks and capital allocation to support different parts of the bank portfolio have also affected the appetite for non-recourse financing by banks (see Chapter 5).

From its modern origins in the oil and gas industry and sophisticated leasing techniques (indeed, where this book had its own origins), project finance has evolved into several different approaches and techniques that are widely used in sophisticated economies and in emerging economies by large companies and small, by governments and by tiny growing firms. This book discusses the methods, structures and instruments that can be used to accomplish a successful project financing by addressing the three key elements of cash flow, collateral/support structures and risk management.

The same focus on risk, cash flow and collateral can be seen in corporate finance and this is no accident. In the past boundaries were blurred between the two areas of banking and many people moved easily between the two functions. We show in later chapters how project finance techniques can be applied in situations often seen as belonging to corporate finance such as leveraged buyouts and employee-based incentive schemes. Project finance has come a long way since the first edition of this book and its origins but whatever the function title, the emphasis on cash flow, the management of assets and project risk are critical for successful financing.

1.1. Checklist for a Successful Project Financing

An independent economic unit that qualifies as a viable credit for project financing must usually meet the criteria, and have the characteristics, contained in the checklist shown in Table 1.1. However, not all the items listed are applicable to all project financings. Also, some of the criteria may be satisfied if the project has a guarantor willing to assume the financial exposure and the costs associated with some of the noted risks. On the

Table 1.1:   Checklist for a Successful Project Financing

Risk	Yes — Document Reference That Addresses It?	No — N/A Reason Why?
1 A credit risk rather than an equity risk is involved.		
2 A satisfactory feasibility study and financial plan have been prepared.		
3 The cost of supplies of product or raw material to be used by the project is assured.		
4 A supply of energy at reasonable cost has been assured.		
5 A market exists for the product, commodity, or service to be produced.		
6 Transportation is available at a reasonable cost to move the product to the market.		
7 Adequate communications are available.		
8 Building materials are available at the costs contemplated.		
9 The contractor is experienced and reliable.		
10 The operator is experienced and reliable.		
11 The project's management personnel are experienced and reliable.		
12 New technology is not involved.		
13 The contractual agreement among joint venture partners, if any, is satisfactory.		
14 A stable and friendly political environment exists; licences and permits are available; contracts can be enforced; legal remedies exist.		
15 There is no risk of expropriation.		
16 Country risk is satisfactory.		
17 Sovereign risk is satisfactory.		
18 Currency and foreign exchange risks have been addressed.		
19 The key promoters have made an adequate equity contribution.		
20 The project has adequate value as collateral.		
21 Satisfactory appraisals of resources and assets have been obtained.		

Table 1.1: *(Continued)*

Risk	Yes — Document Reference That Addresses It?	No — N/A Reason Why?
22 Adequate insurance coverage is contemplated.		
23 Force majeure risk has been addressed.		
24 Cost over-run risk has been addressed.		
25 Delay risk has been considered.		
26 The project will have an adequate ROE, ROI and ROA for the investor.		
27 Inflation rate projections are realistic.		
28 Interest rate projections are realistic.		
29 Environmental risks are manageable.		
30 Compliance with legislation such as US Foreign Corrupt Practice Act of 1977 (FCPA) and similar legislation.		
31 Protection systems are in place against criminal activities such as kidnapping and extortion.		
32 A commercial legal system is in place to protect property and contractual rights.		

Prepared by Frank J. Fabozzi and Peter K. Nevitt.

other hand, if a project financing fails to satisfy any of the applicable criteria, both lenders and sponsors will be apprehensive and should address the problem to resolve the risk exposure before proceeding. (Each item contained in the checklist is discussed in more detail in Chapter 3.)

1.2. Causes of Project Failures

The best way to appreciate the concerns of lenders about a project is to review and consider some of the common causes for project failures, which include the following:

- delay in completion of construction, with consequential increase in the interest expense on the construction financing component and delay in the contemplated revenue flow;
- capital cost overrun;

- technical failure;
- financial failure of the contractor;
- government interference;
- uninsured casualty losses;
- increased price or shortages of raw materials;
- technical obsolescence of the plant;
- loss of competitive position in the marketplace;
- expropriation;
- poor management;
- overly optimistic appraisals of the value of the collateral, such as oil and gas reserves; and
- financial difficulties within the host or sponsor country government(s).

For a project financing to be successfully achieved, these risks must be properly considered, monitored and avoided throughout the life of the project.

The Eurotunnel project and its financing presents an interesting case study that illustrates the failure to understand how project management issues can impact on a project financing, and to address some key risks involved in a new technology-based project financing. A short discussion of the Eurotunnel project appears at the end of this chapter. Throughout the book, we also include discussions of a number of other relevant examples of project financing transactions.

1.3. Credit Impact Objective

Sponsors or beneficiaries of projects with more complex financing packages have been influenced by several credit concerns including the following:

- a desire to manage the effects of restrictive covenants in an indenture or loan agreement which may preclude direct debt financing or leases for the project;
- the need to avoid the impact on stakeholders of an open-ended first mortgage;
- the requirement to treat any new financing for a project obtained by sponsors as a cash obligation that would dilute interest coverage ratios, and affect the sponsor's credit standing with the rating services; and

- the desire to restrict the direct liability of sponsors or third-party guarantors to a certain period of time such as during construction and/or the start-up period, thereby avoiding a liability for the project's remaining life.

These concerns expanded the use of project financing techniques from specialist domains, such as oil and gas, into new areas, such as the creation of special purpose vehicles to hold receivables using the "securitization" process and the asset-backed securities created sold in the financial market. However, following the failure of companies such as Enron, where liabilities were not transparent to stakeholders and the global financial crises wherein a few financial institutions required rescue packages, regulators and other stakeholders are re-emphasizing simplicity and transparency and refocusing on cash flow. We discuss this further in Chapter 5, as it impacts on the supply of this type of financing vehicle.

The credit impact arises because while the project cash flow is the primary source of repayment, sponsors may also be required to offer secondary support. If a sponsor cannot initially arrange long-term non-recourse debt for its project which will not impact its balance sheet, the project may still be feasible if the sponsor is willing to assume the credit risk during the construction and start-up phase, provided lenders are willing to re-examine the credit risk of the project after the project facility is completed and operating. Under such an arrangement, most of the objectives of an off-balance sheet project financing and limited credit impact can be achieved after the initial risk period of construction and start-up. In some instances, the lenders may be satisfied to rely on revenue produced by unconditional take-or-pay contracts from users of the product or services to be provided by the project to repay debt. In other instances, the condition of the market for the product or service may be such that sufficient revenues are assured after completion of construction and start-up so that lenders may rely on such revenues for repayment of their debts.

1.4. Accounting Considerations

Although historically the terms "project financing" and "off-balance sheet financing" may have been used interchangeably, while the project's debt may not be on the sponsor's balance sheet (but be footnoted), the project's debt will appear on the face of the project's balance sheet. In any event, one purpose of a project financing is to segregate or "ring fence" the credit risk of the project so that the credit risk of lending to either the sponsor or the project can be clearly and fairly appraised on its respective merits. The purpose is not to hide or conceal a liability of the sponsor from creditors, credit rating services, regulators or stockholders.

Financial reporting requirements are typically subject to International Accounting Standards Board and US Financial Accounting Standards Board rules under which sponsor entities and investors must report. Typically, significant undertakings of sponsor entities and investors must be shown in footnotes to their financial statements if not in the statements themselves.

Since project financings are concerned with cash flows and balance sheet accounting treatments, familiarity with accounting terms used to describe balance sheet reporting is important. Terms such as contingent liability, indirect liability, deferred liability, deferred expense, fixed charges, equity accounting and materiality are used to explain the appropriate positioning of entries in a sponsor's financial statements and footnotes. Two critical issues that arise in the project finance context are relatedness and consolidation. The tests for whether entities are related (and thus transactions between them may need to be disclosed) may vary locally, but the worldwide move towards accounting standards convergence has produced International Accounting Standard (IAS) 24, 27, 28 and 31.

Consolidation and joint venture reporting are the subjects of a joint project between the IAS and the US Financial Accounting Standards Board. This joint project led to three new reporting standards that became effective as International Financial Reporting Standard (IFRS) 10, 11 and 12. Further clarification was provided in 2012 around the definition of a special purpose entity and a single consolidation model and an exception of an "investment entity" included. IFRS 10 deals with consolidation, IFRS 11 with "joint arrangements" and IFRS 12 with disclosure relating to joint arrangements. The paramount principles include "fair value", a principle-based approach so that parties to a joint venture recognize their rights and obligations, especially concerning verifiability, comparability and understandability of the reporting of those arrangements by stakeholders. At the time of writing, a Post Implementation Review of the three new IFRS standards is underway to look at the standards as they work in practice is in phase 1 but has been affected by the COVID 19 virus epidemic.

In addition, IAS 11 (Construction contracts), IAS 37 (Provisions, Contingent liabilities and Contingent assets) and IFRS 6 (Exploration for and Evaluation of Mineral Resources) may need to be considered if relevant to a case.

These areas of relatedness and consolidation and disclosure are complex, interlinked with many others within a project financing. Although the details are outside the scope of this book, they should be addressed by advisers to ensure project revenue optimization and reporting compliance.

In general, accounting rules for reporting liabilities associated with a project finance structure are under continual review, as the accounting profession grapples with the problem of proper and fair disclosure and presentation of objective information to stockholders, lenders, rating agencies, guarantors, government agencies and other concerned parties.

1.5. Meeting Internal Project Appraisal Objectives

A large company can assemble a database of costs to evaluate new opportunities and that it can use for internally generated projects. However, this repository is not available to all companies as it requires resources and expertise. The use of cost estimation to manage project costs and overruns is becoming more widespread and so we include Chapter 6 on cost estimation. Most companies use one of three discounted cash flow methods — net present value, internal rate of return or modified internal rate of return (discussed in Chapters 7 and 8 on financial modelling) — to appraise the potential economic merits of projects. Therefore, project finance providers need to understand the nuances associated with each of these methods, especially about reinvestment and staged investments, and how target rates of return are set by sponsors for new capital investments. If a proposed capital expenditure will not generate a return greater than a company's target rate (often its weighted average cost of capital or risk-adjusted weighted average cost of capital), it is not regarded as a satisfactory use of capital resources. This is particularly true when a company can make alternative capital expenditures which will produce a return on capital that exceeds the target rate. If the net present value is highly sensitive to changes in key input prices, this may also be a marginal project.

Project financing has been used to improve the return on the capital invested in a project by leveraging the investment to a greater extent than would be possible in a straight commercial financing of the project, by using other interested stakeholders to support the debt through direct or indirect guarantees. An example would be an oil company with a promising coal property which it did not wish to develop because of better alternative uses of its capital. By bringing in a company which required the coal, such as a public utility, an indirect guarantee might be available in the form of a long-term take-or-pay contract which would support long-term debt to finance the construction of the coal mine. This, in turn, would permit the oil company's investment to be highly leveraged and consequently to produce a much higher rate of return for its stockholders.

1.6. Other Benefits

There are often other benefits resulting from segregating a financing as a project financing, that may have a bearing on the motives of the company seeking such a structure:

- dedicated credit sources may be available to the project that would not be available to the sponsor;
- guarantees may be available to the project that would not be available to the sponsor;
- a project financing may enjoy better credit terms and interest costs in situations in which a sponsor's credit is weak;
- higher leverage of debt to equity may be achieved;
- legal requirements applicable to certain investing institutions may be met by the project but not by the sponsor;
- regulatory problems affecting the sponsor may be avoided;
- for regulatory purposes, costs may be clearly segregated as a result of a project financing;
- the project may enable a public utility sponsor to achieve certain objectives regarding its rate base;
- investment protection in foreign projects may be improved by joint venturing with international parties, thus lessening the sovereign risk;
- a more favourable labour contract or climate may be possible by separating the operation from other activities of the sponsor; and/or construction financing costs may not be reflected in the sponsor's financial statements until the project begins producing revenue.

In some instances, any one of the aforementioned reasons may be the primary motivation for structuring a new operation as a project financing.

1.7. Tax Considerations

Specific tax benefits from any applicable tax credits, depreciation deductions, interest deductions, depletion deductions, research and development tax deductions, dividends-received credits, foreign tax credits, capital gains, decommissioning costs and non-capital start-up expenses may be very significant considerations in the investment, debt service and cash flow of most project financings. Care must be used in structuring a project financing to make sure that these tax benefits are both *usable* and *used if available*. Projects have run into problems when the key driver is tax-loss absorption or transfer or if assumptions about the absorptive capacity of the project to fully utilize the tax losses have been proved incorrect. If a project financing is to be housed in a new entity that does not have tax shelter benefits, it is important to structure the project financing so that any tax benefits can be transferred in so that the new entity is in a position to use such benefits to optimize cash flow.

1.8. Disincentives to Project Financing

Project financings are complex. The documentation tends to be complicated and thus add to fees payable, and the cost of borrowing funds is higher than conventional financing reflecting the greater risks. If the undertakings of several parties are necessary to structure the project financing, or if a joint venture is involved, the negotiation of the original financing agreements and operating agreements will require patience, forbearance and an understanding of partnerships. Decision-making in partnerships and joint ventures is never easy, since the friendliest of partners may have diverse interests, challenges and objectives. Problems can arise when the project champions (see Chapter 6) move on to new projects and working agreements are not fully documented, so good project management practice must apply. However, the rewards and advantages of a project financing will often justify the special problems which may arise in structuring and operating the project.

1.9. Principles Apply Regardless of Project Size or Context

Discussions of project financing sometimes tend to focus on large complex projects. This might lead one to the conclusion that the project financing principles discussed in this book have little application to smaller, more ordinary financings. This is not the case. The same principles used to finance a major pipeline, copper mine, or Channel Tunnel can be used to finance a cannery, a hotel, a ship or a processing plant.

Start-up companies in new and emerging business areas that are financed with risk capital in the form of equity present a different emphasis on the traditional rules for project financing. One example is the rapid development of the internet and electronic data transfer systems that have given rise to e-commerce business opportunities that can result in a few cases of very large growth potential and future profits. Since the risk for investors is very high, these are usually equity financed since the risk profile of the project cash flows would not qualify these projects for debt finance. More can be found on this in Chapter 4.

The time horizon of sponsors of many venture capitalists may be limited to the time it takes to go to the public markets or to find a buyer, so key exit decision dates must be clearly specified from the initial negotiations.

1.10. Building Blocks of Project Financing

Before reviewing various specific project financings, it is necessary to discuss the building blocks of project financing. First, the project needs to generate a strong cash flow. Then there needs to be an adequate equity cushion underpinning any project debt. Debt instruments include notes, debentures, bonds, subordinated notes, term debt secured by a particular asset, non-recourse debt, limited-recourse debt, warrants, options, tax-exempt industrial revenue bonds, capital leases, operating leases, service leases, bank loans, short-term notes and commercial paper. This debt may be unsecured or secured by a particular asset, full recourse, limited recourse or non-recourse and may or may not have additional features such as warrants or options. This debt, in turn, may be restructured or combined with derivatives, such as interest rate swaps and options, and currency swaps and options. The debt is supported by the financial viability of the project, as well as the equity commitment and any direct guarantees, contingent guarantees, indirect guarantees and implied guarantees. Projects may be structured using subsidiaries, unrestricted subsidiaries, special purpose corporations, nominee corporations, jointly owned corporations, general partnerships, limited partnerships, joint ventures and trusts. These borrowings, guarantees and entities can be combined in a variety of ways to produce a viable project financing package that services its debt and equity.

When considering a project financing package, sponsors and advisers would normally also review financial structuring methods used in other industries to generate ideas for new structures transferable between industries or from one country to another country, recognizing differences in laws and tax consequences.

1.11. Reconsidering Decision-Making

Economists, psychologists and other social scientists have revisited the ways we look at decision-making and this particularly applies to areas of project finance. While in the past, the model of rational decision-making underpinned the creation of large revenue generating projects and their associated financing decisions and structures, even though Herbert Simon proposed the concept of bounded rationality in a series of research papers starting in the late 1940s. Today, we admit the importance of behavioural drivers and the increasing importance of behavioural finance approaches. Thus, we can sometimes see, with hindsight, that certain projects were doomed to problematic existence because the underlying decisions were not rational, but were overlaid by drivers resulting from the personal needs of the decision makers.

A theoretical example of this might be a vanity project conceived by a chief executive wanting to leave a legacy or create a lasting monument. Another example might be complex structures inserted into project financing by bankers who might be considering their own personal remuneration and performance targets, rather than the overall financial logic of the transaction.

As we look at the governance of organizations and the turnover of staff in key roles, we can observe the mismatch between long-term project timescales and short-term involvement by individual stakeholders. Consequently, as we look forward to the next decades of successful projects that will reshape the world in which we live, it makes sense to recall that decisions are made by individuals with decision-making frames influenced by the project and their personal goals. As we assess and approve such long-term projects as a financial community, interrogating and auditing those decisions as an ongoing quality control process can ensure that the project contributes to a positive future, and not one with sovereign debt crises, increased taxes and so on, as the price for poor decision-making.

Project finance and specifically the private finance initiative implemented through public–private partnerships (discussed in Chapters 9 and 10) has received poor press comments in traditional heartland areas such as the UK when private finance initiative projects to build new hospitals or refurbish government buildings have resulted in hospital wards being closed and what appear to be unreasonable charges under the operating and maintenance contracts. This detracts from the important contribution that the project finance community makes to continued sustainable economic prosperity. In today's world of the instant sound bite, decisions are more open to debate and public scrutiny. Corporate social responsibility applies to financiers, meaning that all stakeholders in the project finance community need to be ever more mindful of the basis for and the short and longer-term consequences of decisions made.

1.12. Case Study: Eurotunnel — A Disaster for Lenders

We conclude this chapter with a case study on the Eurotunnel, a binational project formed by the UK's Channel Tunnel Group and France's France Manche S.A. The Eurotunnel project may seem a curious choice since it is not a recent project, it was completed more than 20 years ago. However, it allows us to consider the longer-term view of a project that was at times both a success and a disaster. Many projects are signed, and then begin a lengthy construction process, followed by operation. Press reports will offer snapshots that are biased by the prevailing view of the stakeholders. Those involved in the early phases of a project will move on to other roles and responsibilities. One of the only ways to judge a project's success is to consider it over its entire lifetime as some projects have difficult beginnings and then turn out to be successful and the reverse, the dream project, can also turn into a nightmare. This is also why in Chapter 2 we stress the importance of capturing and learning through a "lessons learned" phase, that relates to the whole project over its lifetime and not just its different phases.

This offers two major challenges to project finance best practice: understanding the history and path that has caused the success or failure and ensuring lessons are learned; and building the reference database of projects like those discussed in Chapter 6 for optimal cost estimation.

The 31-mile link under the English Channel between the UK and France was one of the most expensive projects in the world. It was the third attempt at a "Chunnel" and came after the second had been cancelled by an incoming UK government afraid of a huge increase in the capital budget for the project — a long-tunnel project in Japan had just been completed with a cost overrun of 100%.

The primary project sponsors, the UK and French governments, had different opening positions. The UK government under then Prime Minister Margaret Thatcher, took a view that no public money would be committed to the project.

A competition (quite normal for government projects or projects over a certain size under competitive tendering rules) was held so that various groups of engineers, designers, and construction companies and financial backers presented their approaches to a panel representing the two governments, with a winning design chosen in 1986. More recent developments support long span bridges, such as Øresund between Denmark and Sweden, as a tunnel alternative, but at the time the preference was for an underground tunnel, viewed as least disruptive to one of the world's busiest shipping lanes.

Financed by an initial consortium of over 200 banks and supported by a 55-year concession awarded in 1986, it was a project where the original timeline for the construction phase, the overall cost and the level and timing of start-up revenues were found to be underestimated The proposed project financing failed our checklist (see Figure 1.1) on many grounds, any one of which should have caused rejection.

Thus, in May 1987, in the equity prospectus, construction was expected to be completed by May 1993. In 1990, construction was estimated to be completed by May 1994. Actual completion occurred in December 1994. In the 1987 budget, total cost to build and open the tunnel was estimated to be £4.9 billion. In 1990, the estimate was raised to £7.5 billion. The actual cost was £9.7 billion, and the project was opened in 1994 with the first year recording a loss of £925 million, including substantial interest charges.

Some of the cost overrun was because of "unknown unknowns" where the geological substructure was found to be different from that expected and tunnelling progress was slower. Projects can encounter unexpected hazards, even though in today's world, better geophysical and geological data mapping systems can offer better risk management, but large projects must have adequate contingency funds in place so that

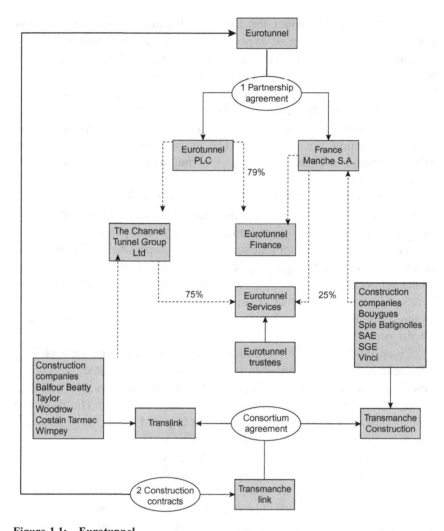

Figure 1.1:   Eurotunnel

Prepared by Frank J. Fabozzi and Peter Nevitt.

work can continue, especially with new (tunnelling) technology as in this case.

The Eurotunnel project suffered stakeholder conflicts of interest in several areas. One was that the project owning company during the construction phase (Transmanche Link) was created by the construction contractors to issue a construction contract to those contractors (i.e. themselves). The project structure is shown in Figure 1.1.

The political agenda meant that finalization and signature of the project financing became a matter of national pride (and pressure) even though the construction budget was not finalized and the rail equipment not finally specified at the time the project was syndicated for funding. Such political pressures are not uncommon in large infrastructure projects.

One example of apparent inconsistencies in the project management that led to problems for the financial package was that the equipment specification aspect was revisited during the construction period, with a cost increase to the project of £1 billion for fire safety on the rail shuttle cars. Yet, on 18 November 1996, the 21.42 train from Coquelles in France caught fire and the overall fire systems failed (compounded by human error), shutting down the system for six months, with a further fire on a shuttle train in 2008.

In addition, successive British governments failed to upgrade the rail connection from London to Folkestone at the entry to the English side of the tunnel, whereas the French established their TGV express trains from the Coquelles portal to Paris. So, traffic feeding into the tunnel and derived revenues were affected by collateral projects outside the control of the main one. The fast rail connection, known as HS1, is now in place from London, having opened in 2003 and reopened in 2007, following a relocation of the London terminal to St Pancras.

Finally, the competition (the ferry companies) retaliated, competing with Eurotunnel on many fronts, including price and convenience. (Ironically, in 2012, Eurotunnel acquired the ferries and assets of one competitor, SeaFrance, and began operating a ferry service on the Dover–Calais route, albeit under a different brand. This acquisition was referred to the Competition and Markets Authority and in 2015, this ferry operation closed.)

The investing public were invited to buy shares in the project as it launched in 1987 with the promise of free travel (depending on the size of the investment) in the first round. As the costs mounted, the equity holders were the first to suffer, closely followed by the bankers. Each renegotiation was costly, given the large numbers of bankers involved and a secondary market opened for Eurotunnel debt, selling at a substantial discount. By 2006, a plan to convert half of the debt into 87% of the equity was floated and rejected, with the company entering the protection of the French bankruptcy court for six months in August 2006. A final restructuring in 2007 led to a new injection of capital. An exchange offer by a new company, GET SA, offered a mixture of shares and warrants for 93% of the share capital of Eurotunnel PLC/SA and debt was more than halved with some senior debt partly repaid so that the debt burden could become more manageable.

Now more than 20 years old, Eurotunnel also owns 51% of the ElecLink Project that involves building an electric interconnector between France and the UK via the tunnel. The restructured Eurotunnel, known as Getlink, following a recent reorganization, has paid increasing dividends since 2010. The majority of the shares are held by US investors and individual shareholders account for just 10% of the equity.

Although matters are much improved for the Eurotunnel project, it offers lessons about financing large projects. However, have the lessons really been learned? Chapter 2 looks at project management and how an understanding of this systemic approach can help all stakeholders in a project financing.

Chapter 2

How Project Management Impacts Project Finance

Introduction

Systematic co-ordination and control of resources and logistics are vital for a smooth and successful completion of a project. Project management as a separate and defined skillset is relatively recent and the promotion of professional project managers and indeed programme managers (those managing a set of associated projects) has been assisted by organizations such as the Project Management Institute (PMI) and the Chartered Association for Project Management (CAPM) both of which have developed formal qualifications. While construction companies have long experience in managing projects, more recently governments and public sector bodies have realized that accountability for public money requires a more professional approach and this has led to qualifications such as PRojects in Controlled Environments (PRINCE 2) and Managing Successful Programmes (MSP) in addition to those offered by the aforementioned associations with expectations that staff in organizations bidding for publicly funded project monies will hold these qualifications and that the project will operate within a formal governance framework associated with these qualifications.

In this chapter, we look at how the provision of finance intersects with the project management process, offering opportunities to all sides. We also consider stakeholder management, critical to success for projects as we will see in the example at the end. This is not an exhaustive treatise on project management for reasons of space, but there are many additional resources available for those interested in project and programme management.

Inside a programme or linked series of projects (such as the US Space Programme), the Programme Office is looking to coordinate activities across the various projects and make economies of scope and scale across all of the projects. A good Programme Office can function very efficiently and deliver this but a change in scope can affect other projects within a programme especially when certain resources may be in relatively short supply. A programme manager or director inside a large multinational company will be one of a handful of very senior people probably just below board level. A project manager or director inside the same company may well have control of a project worth billions of dollars. These are very different to the so-called project managers popularized on television programmes such as "The Apprentice" and the term "project manager" or "programme manager" is often misunderstood and misused, especially by the junior staff at financial institutions who consider that this is the point where trivial questions can be answered. This can cause unnecessary and unhelpful friction inside a project. One way to manage it is to have designated points of contact in the various organizations through which communications flow.

2.1. Project Management and the Project Life Cycle

Project management focuses on three main factors: scope, time and cost and the interrelationship between these three, as well as the trade-off with quality, as shown in Figure 2.1.

These factors will flow from the business plan and in turn shape the detail of the project: the breaking down into smaller subprojects (the work breakdown schedule); milestone setting; a critical path analysis for project completion; regular risk assessments and a regular project review with communication back to stakeholders.

The scope of the project will set its boundaries that will in turn contain the resources for which financing is provided through debt and equity. A feasibility study for a project should not be funded as part of the overall project financing but represent an equity investment by the project sponsors. There are several reasons for this: funding the feasibility study shows that the sponsors are serious about the project and are prepared to

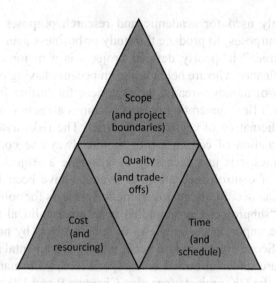

Figure 2.1: **The Interrelationship of Scope, Cost, Time and Quality in Project Management**

Prepared by Carmel F. de Nahlik and Frank J. Fabozzi.

make a significant upfront investment. If the feasibility study shows that the project is not viable then it is for the sponsors to review their investment selection and decision-making processes and it is a risk most appropriately borne by the shareholders. For smaller projects, especially start-ups, there may be a request to refinance the cost of the feasibility study with the argument that it has been expensive and has consumed resources. The counterargument for this is one that many small project companies, especially natural resource based or high-tech based companies are reluctant to hear — that they will need to share the project and share the risks from the early stages. As we will see in detail in the next chapter, the feasibility study requires the maximum amount of investment to get the best quality information available in order to make the best decision about the project's future. Feasibility studies (and business plans) at the larger end of project financings will do this as a matter of course, not least because the sponsors will have access to databases of high-quality information. For smaller newer companies, especially those using new technology, or start-ups, there is a real temptation to do this on a very small budget, and in some cases to use students (with access to data that should be only used for academic and research purposes and not for commercial purposes) to produce the study or business plan.

"Scope creep" in poorly defined projects is a major headache for providers of finance who are held to ransom because having put in significant amounts of money already, the argument for further funding for a completed cash flow generating project becomes attractive when viewed against the alternative of crystallizing a loss. The risks associated with such an "escalation of commitment" should always be considered and sadly sometimes it is just necessary to terminate a project because the scope is out of control once all other avenues have been investigated. Scope creep can occur in large governmental projects for political reasons where other "subprojects" are bundled in to meet political agendas and this raises the importance of reviews of such projects by neutral expert third parties. Scope creep can also occur when governmental stakeholders in a project are under-informed or inexperienced, with many examples coming from the UK projects (see also Chapters 9 and 12). In such projects, there may be political reasons for the choice of stakeholder groups represented in the project and that may not reflect competence requirements to make some of the decisions.

An example might be the decision to locate the restroom facilities in a multi-bed ward in a public hospital that is being financed through the private–public partnership (PPP) scheme. Individual private rooms with bathrooms would be considered more expensive so it is already a lower-cost option. Sitting round the table to make the decision could be representatives from the contractor, the health authority, the hospital administration, a consultant representing clinical excellence and a nurse. The contractor is interested in increasing the contract's size, the health authority and the hospital administration would be interested in minimizing the contract size, an engaged consultant clinician would have a view (but may be more focused on clinical work rather than budgets). Finally a nurse represents point of delivery care and the people who are going to have to manage the day-to-day traffic of patients from their beds to the restroom site. The nurse and his or her colleagues are not the only people who are going to live with the consequences of the decision but also the stakeholders with the least power in this decision since they can be overruled by everybody. In our example the decision is made to minimize costs and locate the restroom area further away from the hospital ward leaving the nurse and his or her colleagues to deal with the consequences of patients having further to travel and more opportunity for accidents. Money is saved in one budget but is deferred to be spent in others. These hidden budgetary ownership issues need to be fully understood by project managers and by providers of finance.

Once the scope of the project is signed off then changes to it will require the completion of change orders and this can reopen the door for contract price negotiations. We could see that the aforementioned example might have originally included the restrooms some distance away, that that was the scope approved and a more inclusive review committee might then have queried whether this was the best location with the change order costs then becoming a major factor.

A less obvious impact of change in scope can cause significant damage to subcontractors to a project where such changes can be cata-strophic. Perhaps a piece of equipment has been specified for a project and the design drawings shared with the subcontractor. On the basis of this, the subcontractor has gone out to look for funding to build the tools to produce the machinery. Changes here might threaten a company's financial future if they are not supported with payments (and they are not always). More on this in a later section of this chapter.

Setting the cost of a project from the beginning and delivering to that cost budget or indeed below budget is the goal of every project manager. Circumstances can cause this to be an ideal rather than the reality even with good risk management practices. In Chapter 6, we consider cost approaches used today through reference costing and databases using dif-ferent forms of cost estimation. Just as defining the scope of the project can affect the costs, so a failure to define the costs carefully can affect the scope if cost-cutting measures need to be employed to remain within budget. From the financing point of view, in the event that a transaction is syndicated (see Chapter 5), changes in costs that will require unforeseen additional financing will need to go back to the syndicate for a further vote. If other circumstances have changed then this opens the door for unhappy participants to try and negotiate an exit requiring very diplomatic skills on the part of the lead bank and a delay to decision-making. This in turn can hold up the project, impacting on the timeline.

Banks that specialize in particular industries or countries may have a very good idea of project costs at an aggregate level but may not under-stand the different costs as they break down to individual work packages. The use of experts can offer some comfort to providers of finance but sometimes events may cause costs to behave in unexpected ways. Changing the scope of a project also requires a detailed look at the differ-ent cost behaviours before approval is given. Not all costs increase in a linear manner (some are stepped), so this needs to be carefully examined for inclusion in the project model (see also Chapters 7 and 8).

Scheduling a project by considering the sequencing of various work packages and their interdependencies and an understanding of the critical path analysis through the project allows lenders to see how progress is occurring and relate that to resource consumption, including financial drawdowns. International competition laws apply to many large contracts, especially those in the public sector with a requirement to go out to international tender for a percentage of the contract value. This can cause significant delays to a project start-up and may even require the contractors to absorb the cost of educating local suppliers in order to meet the specification for local content. For development projects, the inclusion of a substantial percentage of local content may be a part of the project tender so that local industry is encouraged. There is also the potential for a close encounter with unacceptable ethical practices whereby certain local companies are favoured by important government officials and are used as conduits to channel project monies to certain individuals. With increasing transparency and scrutiny, providers of finance can also face difficult discussions with legislators if they are seen to have been party to these types of arrangement.

Setting milestones for a project with key deliverables at those points offers a positive approach to project management that all parties need to be cautious about the "unknown unknowns" that can interfere. One PPP project in the UK encountered problems and delays because a colony of rare reptiles was discovered; more likely scenarios, especially in countries where there have been a number of different civilizations, revolve around the discovery of antiquities and a subsequent need to complete an archaeological excavation. Pinch points, where timing, may be critically affected can also include weather windows such as the monsoon season or major religious events that may impact on logistics or working practices.

Following an operational performance testing phase, the project may be handed over to its owners. This can be linked to a move to limited recourse financing if financial completion tests (linked to operational completion tests) are met.

Changes to any part of the project need a review of the work breakdown schedule, the project management system, the cost, the timing and the critical path. All of these processes and records are dynamic and need to be reviewed and updated and communicated on a regular basis. In a project loan, the concept of "materiality" in terms of the scale of any changes will be defined so that small changes do not require discussion and voting. Debates around what constitutes materiality in a loan agreement can thus be lengthy since both sides are looking for control and damage limitation.

2.2. The Different Stages of the Project and How Finance Fits in

Figure 2.2 shows the links between the different types of finance at different stages of a project's lifespan. It also shows how and why it is important to think through the different areas of finance and how they

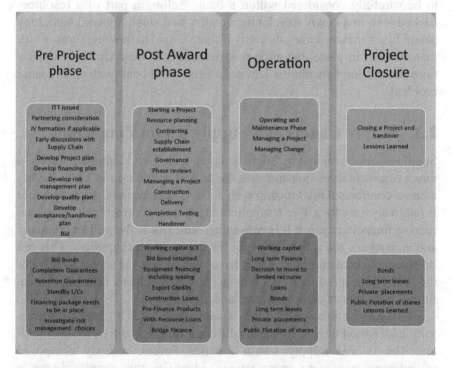

Figure 2.2: The Different Phases of a Project and How the Project Management Process Intersects with Project Financing

Note: The pale grey boxes are project management activities; the darker grey, the related project financing activities.

Prepared by Carmel F. de Nahlik and Frank J. Fabozzi.

interlink from the beginning and the development of the project plan and can explain to those who are new to project financing how the different types of financing fit together. Managing this financing structure inside the project organization and inside the bank group requires all the project management skills that we have discussed in the previous paragraphs.

If there is a problem with any of the transition points, the smooth management of the project can grind to a halt. This is why the choice of banks within a financing group for a larger project is really critical. Historic practices of either "selling down" or using a "participation" route to engage "client banks" can cause problems irrespective of whether the sale is on a recourse or non-recourse basis, not least from a reporting point of view and the need to provide adequate asset allocation to meet central bank and other regulatory expectations. The ethics of this practice needs to be carefully considered within a bank. Selling a part of a resource-backed loan in a newly developing country to a small regional bank may sound like it makes sense especially if there is said to be some form of risk management in place, but such risk management may also have limitations around implementation leaving a very small bank with a very large problem.

2.3. Supply Chains and Supply Chain Financing

Suppliers can be ranked by "tier" or layer, with Tier 1 suppliers having a direct contractual relationship with the project company and Tier 2 having a direct contractual relationship with a Tier 1 supplier and so on. While it is relatively easy for a Tier 1 supplier to take their contract to the bank and receive financing against it because the credit risk is the project company and its backers, the problems begin for the lower tier suppliers. This can be especially challenging if, as we have seen earlier, the scope, the cost or the time elements of a project change. As supply chains internationalize, further elements of complexity are added.

Like project financing, Supply Chain Finance (SCF) is not a universally understood term — it means different things to different stakeholders. The Global Supply Chain Finance Forum, a body composed of industry sponsoring organizations, identifies two supply chains: a Physical Supply Chain (PSC) responsible for managing and delivering the transformation of raw materials or services into a finished product or bundle of services from (a) supplier(s) to a buyer and/or end user and a linked Financial Supply Chain (FSC) that underpins the process.

Traditionally there have been three key areas of SCF: buyer centric (including reverse factoring and confirming); supplier centric (including receivables finance, receivables purchase and factoring) and; inventory centric (usually inventory finance and purchase order finance).
These are further refined into[1]:

Receivables purchasing:

- Receivables discounting
- Forfaiting
- Factoring
- Payables finance.

Loans or advance based:

- Loan or advance against receivables
- Loan or advance against inventory
- Distributor finance
- Pre-shipment finance.

Linked to this is a finance-enabling framework matching data and payments called a "Bank Payment Obligation", discussed in more detail in subsequent paragraphs.

Although the increased automation of contracting, invoice and payment approvals and business-to-business networks have offered cost saving opportunities to complex supply chains, there are also risks that cannot be ignored including that of a need for caution to avoid any latent money laundering activities.

SCF is essentially about financing the different parts of the cash-to-cash cycle for an enterprise. This cycle is shown in Figure 2.3, also illustrating how long funds can be tied up in this cycle and the vulnerability of an enterprise that is not making commodity parts, so this SCF is looking within a supplier company! These vulnerabilities will be affected by the specific properties of the resources supplied, so for example, there may be minimum production run sizes (rather than making to order) or particular times when resources are available (seasonality). For delivery into a supply chain using a "just in time" approach, this may force the supplier to hold higher than expected inventory levels. Any changes after

---

[1] From the Global Supply Chain Finance Forum website. http://supplychainfinanceforum.org.

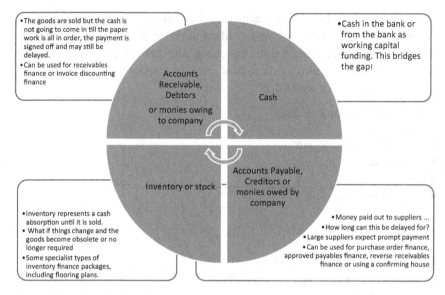

Figure 2.3:   The Cash to Cash Cycle

Prepared by Carmel F. de Nahlik and Frank J. Fabozzi.

the production run that may affect goods supplied will have financial implications as the inventory could be redundant. There may also be minimum shipment sizes (perhaps related to container sizes). In these cases, it may make sense to try and negotiate some form of early acceptance of the goods or contractual co-ownership of the surplus inventory to enable payment.

These transactions may not be immediately visible to the providers of project funding as they are operating at a higher level, but some knowledge about policies, etc., as a minimum can be useful for risk management of the larger project.

The basic formula to determine working capital is as follows:

$$\text{Working Capital} = (\text{Accounts Receivable} + \text{Inventory})$$
$$- (\text{Accounts Payable} + \text{Cash})$$

Looking at this in more detail we can see that if amounts are in balance there may still be a timing gap, or both an amount gap and a timing gap may require the provision of external funding. Even though there have been some governmental and supra-governmental efforts of lobby for invoices to be paid within 30 days, a dispute of any type can cause payment to be extended and some firms may still be relying on their own large internal legal departments to face down smaller companies that may need to pay for any form of legal claim, adding to costs and reducing their margin of profit. Payment completion is a blend of two questions: solvency (can the buyer pay?) and intention (will the buyer pay?) and as such is subject to internal political processes.

It may not be unusual for cash to be tied up in this cycle for a long period of time: we can think of the supplier of specialist parts to a factory, where a bigger production run makes better cost sense, but the movement to the project company may be on a just in time schedule. So here the accounts payable may be settled in 40 days, with inventory taking a further 30–90 days to allow for shipping time and then accounts receivable taking another 40 days. As this company prices the contract, it will be allowing for 140 days including a margin of safety (say 10 days) for external funding to support the work and the associated other costs such as labour, overheads etc.

Having so much money tied up in a contract explains the demand for SCF, but the quality of the receivables (the most common form of financing) and the strength of the small and medium-sized enterprise (SME) financials determine how financeable they are. Banks have less appetite for smaller entities and so this business is shifting to a new form of capital provider, the peer-to-peer business lender (P2P). Investors are driven to seek higher returns in the present era of low interest rates and financing. What appears to be self-liquidating transactions of this type can offer higher returns. Various platforms offer risk ratings for categories of receivables and investors (who need be pre-qualified by completion of a form of risk tolerance questionnaire by the platform) can purchase receivables at a discount or participate in pools of such receivables. Platforms generally only offer a service matching facility and independent due diligence is recommended, but for many non-professional investors, it is difficult and expensive to access the data needed. Banks are also developing their own SCF platforms to integrate with client e-invoicing systems and payment systems and global standards provided by bodies such as the International Chamber of Commerce (ICC) are also assisting in the growth of this rapidly developing area of finance.

Obviously judicious use of a global supply chain can confer additional tax benefits but this is a very specialized area and expert advice should be sought.

Another aspect of SCF is the so-called Bank Payment Obligation (BPO) mentioned earlier. This is used as part of the SWIFT payment system to facilitate SCF activity and is an irrevocable conditional undertaking to make a payment issued between banks. It has been adopted by the ICC and is governed by their rules. BPOs may be used instead of letters of credit for buyer finance under a Purchase Order (rather than an invoice). For BPOs to work there needs to be full transparency between the customers and the bank and excellent tracking of the movement of goods.

Figures 2.4 and 2.5 show how the various aspects of SCF fit with the different activities in the larger supply chain for a project and gives the reader a process map for project financing elements that will also explain how the different parts of this book fit together. Figure 2.4 shows the activity from the perspective of the project manager and the project finance package provider. Figure 2.5 removes the perspectives and concentrates on the activities associated with each phase.

Historically product groups supporting these instruments might have been found in banks that specialized in international trade but they have diminished in importance in recent years and many trade finance groups have closed, with a loss of the corporate memory relating to problem solving in disputes. Negotiating documents associated with some of these

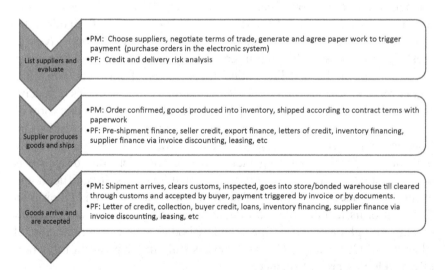

Figure 2.4:   Project Management, Project Finance Elements and the Project Supply Chain

Prepared by Carmel F. de Nahlik and Frank J. Fabozzi.

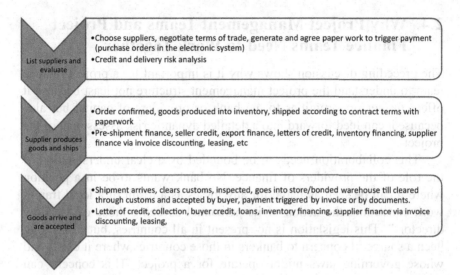

List suppliers and evaluate
- Choose suppliers, negotiate terms of trade, generate and agree paper work to trigger payment (purchase orders in the electronic system)
- Credit and delivery risk analysis

Supplier produces goods and ships
- Order confirmed, goods produced into inventory, shipped according to contract terms with paperwork
- Pre-shipment finance, seller credit, export finance, letters of credit, inventory financing, supplier finance via invoice discounting, leasing, etc

Goods arrive and are accepted
- Shipment arrives, clears customs, inspected, goes into store/bonded warehouse till cleared through customs and accepted by buyer, payment triggered by invoice or by documents.
- Letter of credit, collection, buyer credit, loans, inventory financing, supplier finance via invoice discounting, leasing,

Figure 2.5: The Supply Chain in Action
Prepared by Carmel F. de Nahlik and Frank J. Fabozzi.

financial products, especially used for more remote and less technology focused economies, is a painstaking process and since payment is not made until there is complete satisfaction with everything, can be seen by some stakeholders as "blocking payment" and unsympathetically so it is also important to shield staff from aggressive clients.

SCF is an emergent area of finance and its intersection with project financing and project management usually lies in the area of provision of raw materials and services to enable cash flow generation, but it may occur in other places too.

Worth noting is the emergence of the controversial reverse factoring of invoices. Normal factoring is used by suppliers to generate cash using invoices that are sold to a third party for a discount. Money arrives early, but less of it. In the past, factoring entities have been said to "cherry pick" the invoices, choosing those most likely to be paid and rejecting those that may be more problematic to collect. In reverse factoring, the factoring company pays off the supplier early and is repaid by the buyer at a later date, at a premium reflecting a carrying cost. While on the surface, this looks like a win–win strategy for all members of the supply chain, and a short-term deal, there are reported instances of reverse factoring "morphing" into something looking more like short-term finance of just under a year.

2.4. Why Project Management Teams and Project Finance Teams Need to Work Together

The preceding discussion shows why it is important for a project finance team to understand the project management structure not least because it offers further opportunities to the bank or providers of capital but also because it can feed forward into a detailed dynamic risk assessment of the project.

This collaboration needs to be bounded by a clear understanding of the role of the providers of finance. No bank wants to be in a position where it can be seen as liable for any losses as a result of a legal framework construing the action of its personnel as being those of "shadow directors". This legislation is not present in all countries, but it has long been a source of concern to bankers in those countries where it exists and whose governing laws might operate for a project. This concern can explain why when things may not be going well for a project, the project team may be taking a back seat to a legal team at meetings and the trust that has been built up between the borrower and the providers of finance can appear to fall away.

Managing this collaborative relationship is not straightforward, not least because larger complex projects may often experience external events (as well as internal ones) that cause stress on the project and may require changes to scope, timescale and costs. Just as many companies may change the project team once the project moves into an operating phase, so banks may also change the team reflecting a different risk profile once the project is finished construction and commissioning.

An understanding of project management as it works inside a particular project organization can add value to a relationship between the providers of funds and the project sponsors/developers/operators. A sharing of a common language can build trust between various stakeholders and that can be useful when considering the management and resolution of minor challenges rather than reverting to the contract and attendant costs.

Not all stakeholders are equal, and the power and influence of different stakeholders will change throughout the life of a project. Good project management normally requires identification of key stakeholders at different stages — lists of the stakeholders can be lengthy but if they have little power or influence then it may just be necessary to keep them informed. There are many useful ways of looking at identifying different stakeholders in different boxes at various points in a project but above all they need to be re-considered dynamically, not as flat static maps. Stakeholder mapping workshops are very common in large projects and providers of finance might compare their own maps with those of the project managers as similarities and differences which shed light on perceptual anomalies and allow better communication between the two groups to ensure the project runs smoothly.

2.5. Lessons Learned and Sharing Them

At the close of a project, best practice suggests that a meeting is held to determine lessons learned and how those lessons will be shared inside the organization. Does this happen in practice?

There are several other factors to consider that will impact on the behaviour of individuals and project teams as a project draws to a close. The first of these is what is going to happen to the individuals next? If they are already assigned to another project, then this will be the focus of their energy. The closing project is over, and the new project is about to start so naturally this is where thoughts will be directed. The second of these requires good recordkeeping throughout the project's life. Again, there is a dilemma: a written record of something that has taken place is a document that can be subpoenaed by a lawyer in the event that negotiations reopen about rebates or refunds on the contract or issues arise about ongoing operations and maintenance. So, a tension exists between best practice and risk management. As a result, lessons learned meetings will very often be short because the attention span within the room is focused elsewhere and will show a bias towards positive lessons rather than the more useful "things we could do differently next time".

A compilation of lessons learned can offer a powerful source of intangible resources to a company especially one that aspires to be a learning organization. In turn, this can offer a potential route for enhanced survival by providing the data to allow decisions to be made that can avoid expensive failures in the future. But a repository of lessons learned is only valuable if those lessons learned are disseminated. Rather like some quality reports, filing them does not communicate their contents for continuous improvement.

Bankers do not generally have a "lessons learned" meeting at the end of a successful financial close and still less at the end of the final repayment of a project loan for two related reasons: first of all, the pipeline of transactions will mean that there will be instant pressure from another transaction and secondly because the career span of a banker in a project group will normally be much shorter than the life of the project. The impact of these personnel changes on a project may be substantial in terms of incurring hidden costs. If there are incomplete file notes to backup decisions made and incoming bankers to a project team who believe that they have insufficient time to read the files in order to understand the transaction, the easy solution is to ring up somebody on the project team and ask for a quick "heads up" on the transaction. Not only is this unprofessional but it can also lead to misunderstandings and indeed the development of inaccurate perceptions of what is going on inside the project. It also takes time from the project management team that should be spent managing the project. Nevertheless, this phenomenon has been increasing over recent years and does not reflect well on the perceptions of project finance team members by project managers. One way to manage this is to have a really clear and comprehensive summary sheet in the file and to update this regularly.

The major changes in the banking system, staff turnover and varying focus on project financing as an area of interest for individual banks contributes to a loss of intellectual capital inside those organizations. As a result, it is not uncommon to see mistakes in transactions from a decade ago being repeated or indeed structures from earlier transactions passed off as something just invented. This leaves an interesting stakeholder group in possession of these key data — the lawyers, who then become the keepers of the "project memory". Intervention by this stakeholder group can not only be very helpful but also comes with additional costs, usually passed on to the borrowing entity and can be a source of avoidable friction.

In an ideal world, how would data collection from the lessons learned activity work? First of all, the meeting needs to set an appropriate tone that focuses on the lessons and not the blame. In some organizations, lessons learned meetings have been reported as focused on scapegoating members of staff for errors with senior members of staff often declining to take responsibility for their actions. So, the "no blame" ground rule has to be seen to work by staff members in order to expose potential weaknesses in the project management and then consider how they might be addressed in future. One easy suggestion is to consider that any records of this meeting do not name individuals other than as attendees. Secondly, the meeting needs to be scheduled as soon as possible after the project is closed, or even after each stage is closed to ensure that material that is fresh in the minds of the project team members can be captured for the future. If it is delayed, then attendances can be affected by job moves, new roles and key voices will be lost. This could be achieved by incentivizing or even mandating attendance. Thirdly, enough time needs to be allowed for a thorough discussion of any issues. Independent and skilled chairing of the meeting can facilitate this, but a standard agenda can restrict the data collected. Finally, an action plan relating to the lessons learned makes a logical conclusion to the meeting and of course, the action needs to be seen to be taken!

2.6. Case Study: Green Energy in the Kingdom of the Thunder Dragon

The Kingdom of Bhutan is one of the most remote countries in the world, located high in the Himalayas. It is landlocked and bordered by Tibet in the north, the Indian states of Sikkim in the west and Assam, West Bengal and Arunachal Pradesh in the south and east. Bhutan has remained independent for centuries and is situated on the ancient Silk Road. Originally a Buddhist theocracy, the current ruling family reunited the country and established relations with the former British Empire during the 19th century. Relations with India, the other major local power, have been sensitive. Following India's independence, Bhutan agreed to let India offer protection and in 2007, a mutual treaty was signed to forbid either country allowing territory to be used to prejudice the security of the other. There is also a disputed border with China. A year after a treaty with China was signed in 2016 and agreed a continuation of border surveys and further discussions about the undelineated border, Chinese troops began to build an all-weather road through parts of west Bhutan in one of the disputed areas. Indian troops became involved and both sides withdrew. Border issues escalated again in June 2020 when Bhutan applied for a grant for the Sakteng Wildlife Sanctuary in the eastern part of the country from the United Nations Development Program's Global Environmental Fund and this was blocked by China, with a follow up diplomatic note claiming Sakteng for China. This new dispute, following on from the Sakteng grant case, illustrates further the position of Bhutan as the "jam in the sandwich" between the two major regional powers.

In 2008, Bhutan transitioned from an absolute monarchy to a constitutional monarchy with the change of head of state to its present King.

It is perhaps best known for pioneering the metric of Gross National Happiness. The country is very biodiverse as a result of its spectacular topography and conservation of the environment is very important in Bhutan. It has a relatively small population (less than a million) spread across a large land area with communities often remote from major towns. Road building and other infrastructure are both difficult and expensive to complete, and the windows of opportunity in the different climate zones are limited. Travel across the country during the rainy season is both slow and arduous even on the new tarmac roads. The economy is based on agriculture, forestry, tourism and the sale of hydroelectric power to India, the country's largest export, and Bhutan is expected to benefit geopolitically from the move towards renewable or "green" energy. The country is improving its standard of living but the Asian Development Bank (ADB) reported 8.2% of the population living below the national poverty line in 2017, which led to the introduction of the first Sustainable Development Goal as "No Poverty".[2]

Bhutan has been a member of the ADB since 1982 and the ensuing years have reflected the ABD's active involvement in the country's development. In 2019, the ADB reported a debt service ratio of 15.8% for Bhutan (defined as total debt service payments of each economy, which comprise principal repayments (excluding short-term debt) and interest payments on outstanding external debt, as a percentage of exports of goods and services).[3] In 2014, there was around 84% of outstanding rupee debt related to hydropower from previous Indian-sponsored power projects with perceptions of asymmetry concerning the costs and contracts.[4] The ADB has funded or co-funded 204 projects either in Bhutan or including Bhutan as a participant from 1985 to date, totalling US$924.12 million.[5]

Part of the support from ADB has been assisting the country in restructuring its industry and important sectors of the economy (as well as road and infrastructure projects). The Bhutan Electricity Act of 2001, established the Bhutan Electricity Authority as the body responsible for licensing tariff setting and monitoring, and paved the way for the establishment of the Bhutan Power Corporation in 2002 with the responsibility

---

[2] ADB website for poverty in Bhutan.
[3] ADB website dataset on debt service outlook as of 2020.
[4] South Asian Network on Dams Rivers and People, (SANDRP) website.
[5] Main ADB page on Bhutan.

of transmission to India and inside Bhutan, and distribution. In 2008, the Druk Green Power Corporation (DGPC) was formed by merging three existing hydropower power corporations: Chhukha, Basochhu, and Kurichhu, completed in 1980, 2005 and 2002, respectively. While the two earlier projects had been completed through grants and loans from the Indian government, Basochhu was supported by the Austrian government. DGPC provides 15% of power from its plants to the government as a royalty and cross-subsidizes local power prices through the exports of power to India. DGPC is indirectly owned by the Bhutanese Government.

The Dagana Dzhongkhag area is in the temperate zone that has wet summers and cool dry winters and in an area mostly covered by forest. It is one of the remotest districts in Bhutan and is served by the Dagachhu River that ultimately drains into the Brahmaputra in India.

The project has two components: clean power for regional trade and renewable energy access for the poor. In order to look at the project, a Technical Assistance report was prepared by the ADB and the Bhutan Power Corporation and funded by the Japan Special Fund. (Bhutan has enjoyed warm diplomatic relations with Japan since 1986 and the Imperial family have made several visits. Japan also contributed aid for disaster relief against glacial lake outburst floods.) The other important international contributor was the Austrian Development Agency that offered a series of euro-based funding contributions on its own account and on behalf of the European Union to support the Bhutanese in the inclusion of this project under the Clean Development Mechanism (CDM) with technical and engineering assistance and the transfer of knowledge.

In spite of Bhutan's power surplus at the time, the drawdown on power in India during the winter months has meant that even households with access to electricity have to resort to the more hazardous fuel sources such as kerosene or wood burning. (Historically fire has been a major hazard in Bhutan and many of the spectacular buildings have been recreated more than once over the centuries as a result of fire.) Dagachhu is one of the poorest and remote parts of Bhutan and for the local population this project would herald a significant change in their standard of living.

The plan was for a 114 megawatt (MW) run of river hydropower plant to be constructed. Stories from local stakeholders collected at the time included the benefit to local women who no longer had to collect firewood each day or travel to produce kerosene for lighting, no longer needed to cook and rear children in potentially health harming conditions since they now had access to cheap, clean and stable electricity supplies. The roads and telecoms that formed part of the project meant that emergencies could be dealt with in an easier way than sending messengers to the nearest telephone, often hours away. Journeys by bus that took a day could now be undertaken in three hours and the quality of life improved. Prior to the project, school attendance was affected by the distances, lack of transport and lack of boarding facilities.[6] Better bus services for children to take them to school and remove the need for an hour's walk as well as better school facilities would also contribute to better education outcomes further raising living standards.

As an early consideration, disruption to the local community though inevitable was not significant; land acquisition was for additional access to roads and the ADB required a mandatory and transparent resettlement plan to be prepared and implemented. From this it can be seen that most of the land belonged to the government, but some private lands were to be affected. Twenty-five households were affected (145 people). While no structures were part of this, farmland in the form of crop land and fruit trees (and thus an important part of the livelihoods of the community members) were and the level of detail in the plan is such that 3.1 acres of paddy fields, 8.16 acres of maize and 188 orange trees were mentioned. (Oranges are the major fruit crop, after replacing cardamom.) Ultimately the compensation was in the form of a land-for-land exchange but with some cash paid to recognize the immediate loss of harvestable crops. This process took over a year and included active participation of the affected people, the Bhutanese government (through changes to land registration and compensation processes) and the wider communities in a series of long meetings of all stakeholders. A monitoring process was put in place and a grievance escalation process established. The process was successful and completed by 2008.

One of the challenges the project faced in the early stages was a legacy issue. Bhutan had signed an agreement with India to develop hydropower and promote cross-border power trading, but this did not recognize a need for Bhutan to be able to use private sector foreign direct investment in projects. Bhutan itself had very limited domestic capital

---

[6]Information obtained from the case study section at the end of the following report "Future Carbon Fund: Delivering Co-benefits from Sustainable Development," ADB, 2017.

available for any project and was reliant on bilateral assistance from India and the negotiation of export tariffs for power that also fell under the assistance programme. In order to offer alternative approaches, the ADB supported the Government of Bhutan in putting together an institutional framework and policies to permit private investment and participation in projects, not least power projects. The Sustainable Hydropower Development Policy of 2008 paved the way for PPPs and was a catalyst in the structural change to produce DGPC as a holding company for such projects. Alongside this went a simplification of processes and clearances associated with such foreign investment, and this too formed a part of the development policy. Dagachhu was not only a flagship project for Bhutan but also for the ADB promoting cross-border power trading inside Asia. The second part of this legacy issue was to do with power resale in India.

The first project documents were produced in 2005 and were for a 126 MW run of the river project to be developed by a joint venture between DGPC and the Tata Group of India Power Company, a privately owned Indian company forming part of the giant Tata group. This was incorporated as a special-purpose vehicle, with partners being a second local company and subsidiary of DGPC, the Dagachhu Hydro Power Corporation (DHPC) and the Tata Power Company. Another Tata subsidiary, Tata Power Trading Company, signed a long-term power purchase agreement (PPA) that would increase each year.[7] There is a benefit sharing clause in case the Indian offtaker can sell power at a higher price in the local Indian market than the base cost in the Power Purchase Agreement (PPA).

The project was split into two components: the main power project and a related rural electrification project for internal distribution to seven districts within Bhutan. International procurement by competitive bidding was adopted with national competitive bidding for the civil works coming in at less than US$1 million. An engineering, procurement construction (EPC) contract was put out to local tender for the civil works, with several of the parties to the project operating their own procurement methods, including the Austrian Export Credit Agency. Detailed cost estimates and cost breakdowns were also prepared. However, two issues arose during the project execution: one set was the result of the unexpected geological condition encountered once the project began, resulting in a need for

---

[7]Details of this released into the public domain differ but it appears to be 25 years in duration.

additional reinforcement. The second resulted from a large escalation of labour and material costs and adverse foreign currency movements. Additionally, the original first-ranked bidder for the civil works was changed to the second-ranked bidder following the discovery of financial irregularities associated with one of the shareholders.

Ultimately the project was 16.5% over budget and the ADB offered an additional financing of US$35.1 million through a supplementary long-term ADF loan. The related rural electrification component of the project that was financed by ADB grant funding was completed at US$31.7 million, just under the budget of US$32.9 million and was successful in bringing power to a larger number of homes than originally planned. While originally the project was expected to be completed by December 2012 (i.e. within four years of ADB approval in 2008), the turbines were only released for commercial operation in February and March 2015 and loan closings ran between 2014 and 2015 (Tables 2.1 and 2.2).

The project was commissioned in March 2015 and is fully operational. It is the first hydropower project completed under Bhutanese management, rather than the historic projects managed by Indian companies. The ADB loans run for 30–32 years with a minimum five-year grace period and are made to the Government of Bhutan for onward lending to

Table 2.1:   Dagachhu Power Plant Construction Costs

Item		Amounts in US$ Million	
		Appraisal Estimate	Actual Cost
Civil works		80.2	103.4
Electromechanical		59.2	84.2
Infrastructure: Roads and distribution lines*		13.9	14.3
Project management		8.6	8.2
	Subtotal	**161.9**	**210.2**
Interest during construction		14.4	18.5
Export credit guarantee		5.1	5.9
	Subtotal	**19.5**	**24.4**
Contingencies		**20.1**	
	Total	**201.5**	**234.6**

Note: *Excludes related transmission costs of US$5.6 million, supported by the Bhutan Power Corporation.
Prepared by ADB. Completion report for project 37399-013 dated August 2017, p. 3.

Table 2.2: Dagachhu Power Project Financing

Item	Plan Amount $ Million	Equity Share %	Actual Amount $ Million	Equity Share %
Equity				
DGPC	18.0	23	19.6	24
DGPC (through ADB hard-term ADF* loan)	29.0	36	29.4	35
National Pension and Provident fund of Bhutan	12.0	15	12.4	15
Tata Power Company	21.0	26	21.5	26
Subtotal	**80.0**	**100**	**82.9**	**100**
Debt				
ADB (OCR** loan)	51.0		51.0	
ADB (additional hard-term ADF loan)			35.1	
National Pension and Provident fund of Bhutan	15.0		11.5	
Austrian Export Credit Agency	55.5		54.1	
Subtotal	**121.5**		**151.7**	
Total project cost	**201.5**		**234.6**	
Debt-equity ratio	60:40		65:35	

Note: *ADF = Asian Development Fund; **OCR = Ordinary Capital Resources.
Prepared by ADB. Completion report for project 37399-013 dated August 2017, p. 4.

the project companies. The project was registered as the world's first cross-border CDM project through the United Nations Framework Convention on Climate Change in 2010 and DHP has signed a certified emissions reduction purchase agreement with ADB (the latter acts as a trustee of the Future Carbon Fund) to permit the sale of carbon credits generated from the plant. In July 2013, the project was recognized for an award by the Development Impact Honours Program of the United States Department of the Treasury. Subsequent projects in Bhutan have built on this model and the ADB conducted a rigorous "lessons learned" exercise and rated various aspects of the project to ensure capture of key learning and its incorporation into future projects. The single major uncertainty for all of Bhutan's hydropower projects is the shrinking of the glaciers that feed the rivers and hence provide the flow for run of river or dam-based hydropower projects as a result of climate change effects.

Chapter 3

From Project Plan to Offering Memorandum: What Core Stakeholders Need to Know

Introduction

In the previous chapter, we identified the need to have a clear plan for a project and this document is core to its success. Writing good business plans or project plans is not easy and the plan is built up over time, tested and rewritten and adjusted as the project proceeds. However, the business plan and its related document, the offering memorandum, give providers of funding the information needed to make the best decision possible at that time. Sometimes they are viewed as a single document, cast in stone at that point, so all parties need to liaise to ensure that they are updated regularly and the update communicated to all parties.

The business plan is the document that the project sponsors will produce in order to justify the project and to explain it to various stakeholders. As such, it needs to be coherent and include the best quality data available. Business plans can sometimes look as if they were prepared for a (not very good) student assignment and be incomplete and include unsupported claims. They can reflect the emotional investment of the sponsors, especially for projects that include new sponsors or what are seen as higher goal outcomes, such as a project to solve a local problem and increase living standards. Alternatively, they may focus on the micro detail and be overly long and complex to decipher.

43

The business plan opens the door to a discussion with potential suppliers of capital and needs to be credible and robust. Business plans are discussion documents and as such should be challenged. Providers of finance will do their own due diligence on the plan and will challenge assumptions made.

Once the business plan has been established as representing a viable project to attract investment, and external funders are approached, it can become the basis for an offering memorandum.

To make an informed decision in response to a borrower's proposal, the would-be provider of funds need to have adequate information about the investment or loan and the returns they may expect. Just as for an initial public offering or share issue, a project financing requires an offering memorandum that fully describes the project and outlines management's policies and plans. One of the primary purposes of hiring a financial adviser is to receive professional assistance in preparing the offering memorandum in a form and substance that will appeal to providers of finance.

The offering memorandum, which may also be called the financing memorandum, proposal or prospectus, is a more developed version of a term sheet that outlines the basic terms of the deal on offer (see Table 3.1). The purpose of this document is to provide lenders and equity investors with the information needed to make a preliminary decision to commit funds to the project. As such it is an important selling tool that can clearly demonstrate the planning ability and general competence of management to financial stakeholders and lenders.

The offering memorandum should be signed off by the sponsors, who warrant the accuracy of its contents, and be realistic, with attainable financial projections. Loan covenants and ratios should closely track these projections and demonstrate clearly that the project company can service its debt and equity in line with expectations.

Cash is king. Lenders are primarily concerned with cash flow that will cover debt service over the project's life and over the loan's life, with an adequate margin of safety. Examples of this margin might be a 2:1 debt service over the project's life and 1.5:1 over the loan's life.

The offering memorandum should contain the following information as a minimum.

Table 3.1: Summary of Terms

Amount:

Type of financing:

Use of proceeds:

Drawdown dates:

Final maturity and average life:

Interest rate:

Commitment fee:

Definitions:

Financial covenants:

- Required prepayments
- Optional prepayments without penalty
- Restrictions on refinancing
- Optional prepayments under certain circumstances
- Optional prepayments with penalty protective covenants
- Working capital
- Short-term debt
- Long-term (funded) debt
  - Senior
  - Subordinated
- Lease obligations

Protective covenants:

- Dividends, other stock payments and repurchases of stock
- Guarantees and other contingent liabilities
- Supply and purchase contracts
- Mortgages, liens, charges and other encumbrances
- Sale and lease-back transactions
- Change of ownership and assignment of interests
- Cross-defaults, common terms and inter-creditor agreement implications for this transaction

Governing law

Prepared by Frank J. Fabozzi and Peter Nevitt.

3.1. Proposed Financing and Summary of Terms

The offering memorandum opens with a one-page summary (often called the term sheet) which briefly describes the proposed financing. This is followed by a summary of terms for each type of financing requested containing the information shown in Table 3.1, and briefly described as follows:

- the amount, timing and purpose of the financing;
- the type of financing requested (such as unsecured debt, equipment leases, secured debt, subordinated debt, convertible debt, debt with warrants);
- a description of the security to be offered;
- the proposed interest rate;
- the proposed currency;
- the proposed final maturity, repayment schedule and average life; and
- a brief description of the proposed covenants to be included in the loan agreement.

3.2. Protection for Providers of Capital

3.2.1. *Capitalization*

Based on the most recent balance sheet, the section on capital structure shows the project company's existing and/or *pro forma* capitalization using the format contained in Table 3.2. The offering memorandum describes all proposed long-term debt and lease obligations as shown in Tables 3.3 and 3.4, respectively. It provides a breakdown of existing and proposed short-term bank lines and, if applicable, indicates usage by month for the recent years. The memorandum also states and explains any contingent liabilities or guarantees and gives a complete breakdown of equity ownership, including the percentage ownership of officers, directors and other major stockholders, with an emphasis on the ownership by key project stakeholders and financially strong stockholders or shareholders. It explains the dividend policy while debt remains in place.

3.3. The Project Company

The project company section will summarize important background information regarding the project company (such as its date and state of

Table 3.2: Existing and *Pro Forma* Capitalization

	(Dollars in Millions)			
	31 December, 20--		31 December, 20--	
	Actual		*Pro Forma*	
Short-term debt	US$		US$	
Long-term debt	US$	%	US$	%
Senior				
Subordinated				
Preferred stock*				
Common stock				
Surplus				
Retained earnings				
Total long-term capital	US$	100%	US$	100%
Senior long-term debt/total long-term capital				
Long-term debt/total long-term capital				
Total debt/total long-term capital + short-term debt				

Note: *At liquidation value.
Prepared by Frank J. Fabozzi and Peter K. Nevitt.

incorporation and organization) and include names, locations and proposed lines of business for the project. If the project company is already in existence, the offering memorandum briefly states and explains any recent financial results, as well as management's plans and expectations for the coming years.

3.3.1. *Products/Markets*

This section should describe the project company's product(s) or service(s) and the market(s) for each including a discussion of historical and projected growth in the markets served. If the project company has been in existence, sales and pre-tax profits by major products for the past five years are shown using the format contained in Table 3.5. The memorandum should describe any plans for major new products or services and the project company's research and development programme.

Table 3.3:   Schedule of Long-Term Debt*

(Dollars in Millions)

Long-Term Debt	Year-End before Proposed Issue	Repayments									
		Year 1	Year 2	Year 3	Year 4	Year 5	Year 6	Year 7	Year 8	Year 9	Year 10
Description of existing debt (mortgage notes and so on)											
Sub-total											
Proposed issue											
Total											
Ending current portion											
Ending L–T portion											
Interest expense:											
Short-term debt											
Long-term debt											
Total											

Notes: *As a continuation of the schedule, provide the following information on each of the company's existing long-term debt obligations.
1. Interest rate and final maturity.
2. Source of the financing.
3. Major protective covenants.
Prepared by Frank J. Fabozzi and Peter K. Nevitt.

Table 3.4: Schedule of Lease Obligations

(Dollars in Millions)

| | Finance Leases[1] | | | | | | |
| | Minimum Annual Rental Payments | | | | | Next Five Year Period | Next Five Year Period |
	Year 1	Year 2	Year 3	Year 4	Year 5		
Type of asset leased							
List groups if appropriate:							
Total							
Present value of finance leases:							
Average interest rate used to compute present value:							

| | Other Leases[2] | | | | | | |
| | Minimum Annual Rental Payments | | | | | Next Five Year Period | Next Five Year Period |
	Year 1	Year 2	Year 3	Year 4	Year 5		
Type of asset leased							
List groups if appropriate:							
Total							
Total rentals payments							

Notes:

[1] Long-term, non-cancellable leases whose original term constitutes a substantial portion (75%+) of the useful life of the underlying asset.

[2] Cancellable leases and non-cancellable leases whose original term does not constitute a major portion of the useful life of the underlying asset.

Prepared by Frank J. Fabozzi and Peter K. Nevitt.

Table 3.5:   Breakdown of Sales and Profits

(Dollars in Millions)

	Net Sales										Pre-Tax Profit Contribution									
	Year 1		Year 2		Year 3		Year 4		Year 5		Year 1		Year 2		Year 3		Year 4		Year 5	
	US$	%	US$	%	US$	%	US$	%	US$	%	US$	%	US$	%	US$	%	US$	%	US$	%
Half year-ending (month and day)																				
Product, division or subsidiary																				
Total		= 100%		= 100%		= 100%		= 100%		= 100%		= 100%		= 100%		= 100%		= 100%		= 100%
Less:																				
Corporate overhead																				
Other unallocated expenses																				
Interest (total)																				
Taxes																				
Net income																				

Prepared by Frank J. Fabozzi and Peter K. Nevitt.

3.3.2. *Marketing*

This section discusses the project company's marketing strategy and outlines how it plans to sell and distribute its products or services and how they will be priced. It analyzes the company's customers and any concentration of sales volume among them. It highlights any current or anticipated sales contracts, including take-or-pay contracts, take-and-pay contracts or similar arrangements. This section may often be written with input from a recognized third-party expert or include an expert report.

3.3.3. *Competition*

This part of the memorandum describes the nature of competition in the project company's industry and names the major competitors with, if available, the market share enjoyed by each. It elaborates on the company's projected position in the industry, examines the strengths and weaknesses of competitors and anticipates competitor responses to this project. Independent expert industry trade growth and government data should be included, if appropriate, to define the company's position in the market.

3.3.4. *Manufacturing and Production*

This section explains the location, nature, physical size, capacity and utilization of the project company's existing and proposed manufacturing and/or production facilities and whether they will be owned or leased. Proposed capital expenditures for the next five years and a brief description of the company's manufacturing methods and costs, sources, availability and cost of the raw materials and/or components used together with any existing or proposed supply contracts for raw material, feed stock and energy form a picture of the cash flow dynamics of the project. This section is also where the company's status under federal, state and local environmental and safety regulations is detailed.

3.3.5. *Management/Personnel*

Stakeholders need to see an organizational chart of the project and its sponsors with brief biographies for key members of management, indicating relevant salary and bonus arrangements. Brief biographies of the company's directors, both executive and non-executive indicating their outside affiliations are also critical in showing the calibre of the management and board. Full disclosure of detailed information about project staff including directors and managers is required by lenders prior to any signature, so any difficult issues should be raised and addressed with appropriate legal guidance, if necessary. The size of the proposed project's labour force and its nature (for example, the level of skills, unionization, strike history, current contracts) offers insights into future cost containment.

3.3.6. *Business Risks*

Best practice in project management includes a risk analysis, covered further in Chapter 5. Conventionally this includes a list of the major business risks faced by the company together with an analysis of probability, impact and mitigation steps taken or proposed by the management team, including insurance. Any pending litigation that may affect the sponsor companies should also be discussed here.

3.3.7. *Historical and Other Financial Information*

If the project company or its guarantors have an existing operating history, a summary of the project company's audited income statements, balance sheets, sources and uses of funds statements as suggested in Tables 3.6–3.9, respectively should be included. Definitions for suggested ratios are shown in Table 3.10. An explanation of any abrupt changes or sustained deterioration in the financial statistics (for example, abrupt declines in sales and earnings, large increases in receivables or inventories unaccompanied by increasing sales and so on) needs to be included with the data. Pin-pointing problems, indicating what actions the company has taken or is taking to resolve them, demonstrates awareness of important issues and a desire for transparency to potential stakeholders. Similarly, any important acquisitions or disposals during the past five years, need to be clarified, including income statements and balance sheets for any acquired or disposed company for the three years prior to acquisition or disposition and the price and form of the transaction can be helpful. A description of

Table 3.6:   Historical (Projected) Consolidated Income Statements

| | (Dollars in Millions) | | | | |
| | 31 December | | | | |
	Year 1	Year 2	Year 3	Year 4	Year 5
Sales					
Cost of goods sold					
Selling and advertising expense					
EBITDA					
Depreciation and depletion					
EBIT					
General and administrative expenses					
Interest earned					
Interest paid					
Other expenses (classify if material)					
Taxes (other than federal)					
EBT					
Federal income taxes[1]					
Tax credit available					
Tax credit used					
Income before extraordinary items					
Extraordinary items					
(describe the specific items)					
Net income					
Distribution of profits					
Limits: debt to equity ratio					
cover ratio (periodic)					
cover ratio (loan life)					
from profits					
Gross dividend					
Dividend tax					
Retained earnings					
Number of shares used for per share calculations[2]					
Earnings per share[2]					
Dividends per share[2]					
Return on total assets[3]					
Return on long-term capital[3]					
Return on equity[3]					

Notes:

[1] Distinguish between current and deferred income taxes. Disclose treatment and amount of investment tax credit and tax loss carry (back) forward credit, if applicable.

[2] Should be adjusted for stock splits and stock dividends.

[3] See Table 3.10 for definitions of these ratios.

Prepared by Frank J. Fabozzi and Peter K. Nevitt.

Table 3.7:   **Historical (Projected) Consolidated Balance Sheets**

| | (Dollars in Millions) | | | | |
| | 31 December | | | | |
	Year 1	Year 2	Year 3	Year 4	Year 5
Assets					
Investments property, plant and equipment (gross)					
Accumulated depreciation					
Property, plant and equipment (net)					
Current assets					
Accounts receivable					
Inventory					
Operating cash					
Sub total					
Sinking funds					
Escrow account					
Total					
Liabilities and stockholders' equity					
Stockholders' equity					
Equity					
Reserves					
Currency adjustment					
Sub total					
Long-term liabilities					
Long-term debt (less current portion)					
Other liabilities					
Deferred taxes					
Sub total					
Current liabilities[1]					
Tax outstanding					
Current portion long-term debt					
Creditors					
Dividends					
Sub total					
Total					
Quick ratio[2]					
Current ratio					
Receivables turnover					
Inventory turnover					
Short-term debt/current assets					
Short-term debt/current liabilities					
Working capital ratio[2]					

Notes:
[1] Should be broken down by specific account.
[2] See Table 3.10 for a definition of this ratio.
Prepared by Frank J. Fabozzi and Peter K. Nevitt.

Table 3.8:   Historical (Projected) Consolidated Cash Flow Statements

		(Dollars in Millions)			
		31 December			
	Year 1	Year 2	Year 3	Year 4	Year 5
Operations					
Revenues					
Operating costs					
Marketing					
Increase in working capital					
Interest earned					
Interest paid					
Tax					
Fees					
Net cash from operations					
Investing					
Capital cost					
Abandonment					
Scrap					
Net cash from investing					
Financing					
Equity					
Loans					
Loan repayment					
Loan prepayment					
Dividends					
Net cash from financing					
Changes in cash					
Beginning cash					
Ending cash					

Prepared by Frank J. Fabozzi and Peter K. Nevitt.

the project company's financial policies (that is, dividend policy, capital structure policy, return on investment objectives and similar policies), management information systems, operating capital budgeting and long-range financial planning procedures and details of any existing loan and/

Table 3.9:   Historical (Projected) Comparative Data

	(Dollars in Millions)				
	31 December				
	Year 1	Year 2	Year 3	Year 4	Year 5
Income before taxes					
Taxes					
Net income					
Total interest[1]					
Imputed interest on leases[2]					
Interest coverage:[3]					
Before-tax					
After-tax					
Interest and rental coverage:[3]					
Before-tax					
After-tax					
Depreciation					
Other non-cash items					
Cash flow/long-term debt[3]					
Long-term debt/net property, plant & equipment					
Net tangible assets/long-term debt[3]					

Notes:
[1] Interest on short-term and long-term debt.
[2] Imputed interest on finance leases. If this data is not available, use 1/3 of total annual rentals.
[3] See Table 3.10 for a definition of this ratio.
Prepared by Frank J. Fabozzi and Peter K. Nevitt.

or significant lease agreements offer insights into the requirements and patterns of fund flows and should align with availability within the current year's operating budgeting and long-range financial planning procedures.

    If information is available, compare the project company to major competitors in terms of projected sales volume, margins and returns. Also, compare the company's projected capitalization and related ratios (see Table 3.7) to those major competitors. If the intent is that the project loan will be supported by a guarantee or long-term contract from a sponsor, then that support needs to be clear and robust by demonstrating the power of the sponsor's financial strength from the following information

Table 3.10: Formulae for Calculating Various Ratios for Industrial Companies

Fixed Charge Coverages:

Interest coverage:
Before-tax
$$\frac{\text{Total interest expense} + \text{Before-tax income}^1}{\text{Total interest expense}}$$

After-tax
$$\frac{\text{Total interest expense} + \text{Net income}^1}{\text{Total interest expense}}$$

Interest and rental coverage:

Before-tax
$$\frac{\text{Total interest expense} + \text{Imputed interest on finance leases}^2 + \text{Before-tax income}^1}{\text{Total interest expense} + \text{Imputed interest on finance leases}}$$

After-tax
$$\frac{\text{Total interest expense} + \text{Imputed interest on finance leases}^2 + \text{Net income}^1}{\text{Total interest expense} + \text{Imputed interest on finance leases}}$$

Net tangible asset/long-term debt
$$\frac{\text{Stockholders' equity} - \text{Intangibles} + \text{Long-term debt}}{\text{Long-term debt (excluding current portion)}}$$

Liquidity ratios:

Cash flow ratio
$$\frac{\text{Net income}^1 + \text{Depreciation}^3}{\text{Long-term debt}}$$

Working capital ratio
$$\frac{\text{Current assets} - \text{Current liabilities}}{\text{Long-term debt}}$$

Quick ratio (acid test)
$$\frac{\text{Cash} + \text{Marketable securities} + \text{Receivables}}{\text{Current liabilities}}$$

Returns:

Return on total assets
$$\frac{\text{Net income}^1}{\text{Total assets}}$$

Return on long-term capital
$$\frac{\text{Interest on long-term debt} + \text{Net income}^1}{\text{Long-term debt} + \text{Stockholders' equity}}$$

Return on equity
$$\frac{\text{Net income}^1}{\text{Stockholders' equity}}$$

Notes:
[1] Adjusted for the effect of non-recurring items.
[2] Average implicit interest rate times present value of leases. If data are not available, substitute 1/3 total annual rentals.
[3] Other non-cash items should be added.
Prepared by Frank J. Fabozzi and Peter K. Nevitt.

either included within the financing memorandum, or indicating whether it is available upon request:

(1) annual reports and pertinent regulatory filings for the past five years;
(2) if applicable, consolidating financial statements for the past five years, preferably audited;
(3) interim reports for the current year;
(4) the most recent interim or other proxy statements or other announcements issued to shareholders; and
(5) any recent prospectuses for equity or debt issues.

Similarly, if the project loan or lease will be supported by the collateral value of the project or equipment being financed, appraisals of the project or equipment should be included, as well as the value of the project upon completion and a forecast of the used equipment value at various dates after being placed in service.

3.4. Plans and Forecasts

Lenders and investors expect to see income statements, balance sheets and cash flow statements forecast over the expected life of the project. The forecasts should incorporate the proposed financing and should preferably be displayed at six-month intervals. The formats contained in Tables 3.6–3.8 are suggested. They should provide statistical data for the forecast period using the format contained in Table 3.9. The forecast should be broken down by major divisions or subsidiaries. Detailed assumptions should accompany the forecast and include a scenario analysis with a high and a low case and sensitivity analysis as explained in Chapter 7.

Alongside this, a detailed explanation of the use of the proceeds from the proposed financing, including mention of where the proceeds are to be used for construction of a facility. This needs to breakdown the projected cost(s), the amount of the initial investment, the estimated future investment (and timing, preferably under several scenarios), and the earnings and cash flow the investment is expected to generate. The facility or facilities being financed should be described in detail, so it can be evaluated against suitable alternative technologies and the contractor should be identified along with any special arrangements with the contractor discussed.

Providing a detailed description of the company's activities during and after the project and the project company's future direction as well as any plans for major changes in the organization, management or operating policies and an outline of future capital requirements and plans for financing such requirements allows investors and lenders to see evidence of a sustainable future and give confidence.

3.5. Secrets of Successful Business Plans

A good business plan is an investment in a project's future and when prepared in large organizations can benefit from the corporate memory and previous projects. Such plans are usually subject to rigorous internal challenges and assessed against corporate scenario plans. For the less well-capitalized sponsor, the resources will need to be purchased with money from a tight budget. Many plans fail because there is insufficient rigorously researched data sitting behind the request for funds. Consequently, a good business plan should have the following attributes:

- be brief but comprehensive;
- use the best authenticated data available, not out-of-date material from the web;
- include evidence-supported verified material about the sponsors. A number of high-profile examples in recent years showed phantom PhDs, research and experience. Misrepresentation in a business plan not only makes suppliers of funds question the economic value of the project but also injures the reputation of any institution that then produces an offering memorandum based on it;
- be supported by the sponsors readiness to answer questions and visit any potential financial participants. Many projects may have a corporate video to support their request for funding;
- be realistic in the scope and scale of the project and its returns and debt horizons. Gone are days when shipping bankers were prepared to lend high asset percentages, skew the repayment to lower amounts for a five-year period and gamble on a take-out financing once the ship had demonstrated its cash flow earning potential. These higher risk deals are associated with higher bank capital allocation under most banking frameworks and thus more expensive for institutions;

- associated with the last point, if the lending horizon of banks seems to be five years and the project has a seven-year life, there may be a temptation to "massage" the numbers so the project pays back its debt within five years. Good diligence by a lender should spot this risk; and
- not to expect debt finance providers to take second place to equity investors by allowing dividends to be removed from project cash flows too early. Waterfall accounts, debt service reserve accounts and dividend recapture provisions (see Chapter 7) can assist with this.

3.6. Each Case is Different

All of the aforementioned information outlined will not be required in every case. However, a presentation that follows this systematic and comprehensive approach will contribute to the successful arrangement of a project financing.

In many project financings, the company will be newly established and have no past operating history, and in such cases heavy emphasis on the projected financial statements and rationale for the financial outlook is essential. In such instances background information and the operating history of the key sponsor and/or guarantor is appropriate, including all of the information described previously.

3.7. Potential Future Liabilities

Most project agreements with host governments, landowners or communities now include an expectation that the site will be restored to its original condition and projects may need to include those future costs as a part of the financial appraisal. Communities are becoming less likely to bear these costs, especially if the clean-up or restoration exercise may require specialist technical knowledge. Many Western brownfield sites (that is industrial and commercial properties that have been either abandoned or underused, but can be prepared for reuse) have required a clean-up operation before a new project can be started. The removal of asbestos, which requires specialist know-how, is just one exemplar hazard. Older buildings, constructed when different safety measures or insulation standards existed, need to be removed in a manner safe for all stakeholders. From examples in the

North Sea, where abandonment costs were once a distant issue and then in the 1990s became a financial reality, expectations have now been formalized in accounting standards and also recognized by fiscal authorities.

The problem for sponsors is that quantifying the termination costs of a venture including removal, restoration and clean-up costs can be difficult to estimate at the start of a long-term project. Nevertheless, it is imprudent to ignore them and provisions should be made and adjusted once these costs are estimated and included as a part of any project appraisal or re-appraisal process.

3.8. Case Study: When the Deal isn't as Described on the Tin

In the Winter of 2013, the World Wildlife Fund (WWF) published a report of a joint initiative with the charity CARE Internationals to promote conservation and sustainable fishing in Mozambique.[1]

In 2014, Credit Suisse (CS), WWF and McKinsey published a report on "conservation finance" — a new asset class seen as a partnership between NGOs and banks to support conservation efforts.[2] Rather than the historic harvesting of fish by foreign vessels (with payments to the local government), the local ownership of the marine resource and its management and harvest could capture more of the value chain inside a country and also manage sustainability of fishing stocks by controlling the way that fishing was conducted (essentially larger hole sizes in nets to allow juvenile fish to escape and breed).

In 2013, the Government of Mozambique adopted the Strategic Plan for Development of Tuna Fishery by forming a new government-owned local company, Empresa Mocambicana de Atum SA (EMATUM). Mozambique has a long coastline and foreign firms were actively fishing in its waters.

Mozambique is a country that has had a long-term internal struggle and though independence from Portugal was granted in 1975, a bitter civil war persisted until 1990 and election results were disputed, culminating in another outbreak of hostilities in 2013, and leading to a further peace settlement in 2014, so "steady state" nationhood is comparatively recent

---

[1] *World Wildlife Magazine*, Winter, 2013.

[2] See the Credit Suisse website for the latest environmental responsibility policies.

and groups linked to the parties to the internal struggle are now in power. Mozambique intends to develop its significant gas reserves but this has been delayed by a large number of LNG projects coming on stream around the world, making the development less economically attractive.

Much of the early part of this case study is not in the public domain, but there is an agreement on a number of facts. In 2013, the Government of Mozambique decided to borrow money from two banks — CS International and VTB Capital PLC, a subsidiary of VTB, the former Bank for Foreign Trade or Vneshtorgbank and now the sixth largest Russian Bank. It is 60% owned by a Russian state agency. The purpose of the loans were to support three sets of activities: vessels and equipment to support the Exclusion Zone (the Proindicus transaction); the development of a tuna fishing fleet (the EMATUM transaction); and maintenance and repair facilities to support these two sets of vessels (the MAM transaction). To simplify a complex story, much of which is still not in the public domain, the EMATUM transaction (as one part of this) used seven-year loan notes, issued by a Netherlands BV as a special purpose vehicle, would be backed by a sovereign guarantee from the government of Mozambique and were issued in US dollars. The final total amount was US$850 million, for EMATUM, provided by CS International and a five-year $540 million facility supplied by VTB, with a six-year term loan for $372 million (later increased to $622 million) for Proindicus. The notes carried a yield of 8.5% and Mozambique carried a credit rating of B+. This was the first international issue for Mozambique and as such attracted interest from many investment funds because of the generous return in times of low interest rates and the novelty value, so the notes were fully subscribed, though unlisted. The MAM and Proindicus transactions were not notified to the noteholders.

EMATUM was a brand new state-owned company with no listed board of directors when the loan was made. Indeed, the prospectus was said to have been three pages long with no commentary on the sovereign guarantor. At the time of issue, estimates were provided that suggested that Mozambique was catching 200,000 tons of tuna with a price of US$10,000 (the price of top-grade Japanese sashimi tuna). In 2013, the national fisheries office reported foreign and national vessels had caught 6,000 tons. The 2016 estimate of fishing revenues of US$224 million that was stated in the strategic plan, has not been met and some experts believe tuna stocks are falling further in the Indian Ocean.

The new funds were to be used to purchase 24 fishing boats, three trimaran patrol boats and equipment for a land co-ordination centre together with IP and support. The disbursements of loan funds appear in at least one case, to have been against an invoice for the full contract price with no further breakdown. The National Commercial Code of Mozambique anticipates a greater breakdown than provided to enable appropriate audits to be conducted. The supply contract was with an Abu Dhabi-based entity linked to a French shipyard, both owned by a Lebanese entrepreneur with substantial shipping interests.

It seemed that not all the material was delivered and that which was available was not operational for various reasons given by both the contractor and the Mozambican counterparties. Certainly, the contractor and associated parties had taken an expanded role, but it is unclear whether this is because of inexperience on the part of the local counterparty.

The land grant and permits needed for the co-ordination centre and fish storage facilities seem not to have been completed. Training of staff to support the project and maintenance of equipment also appears not to have been carried out.

At the same time, it was suggested that a significant portion of the original loan may have been used to purchase military hardware as a part of the state defence budget rather than the fishery-related equipment specified, though this statement is unconfirmed and denied by the contractor. If this was so, the change of purpose was not advised to investors, an issue since investment funds and other corporate investors have asset restriction policies often precluding investment in armaments (as well as gambling, alcohol and tobacco related products or companies). Much of the detail of the specification of the ships, equipment and support services that were delivered is shrouded in confidentiality agreements pertaining to national security and awaits unravelling.

The first challenge emerged when the first debt principal repayment was not made (interest payments were made by the government though the origin of the funds is unclear). EMATUM realized a loss of US$25 million in 2014. The US dollar income of Mozambique is largely reliant on oil and gas and the fall in the world oil price affected the country's dollar income. To avoid a formal default, the debt was "reprofiled" and the notes were repackaged by CS and VTB Capital, exchanged and rescheduled in an agreement dated April 2016, when the obligation was formally assumed by the Republic of Mozambique with a 10.5% coupon and a bullet-style maturity date of 2023. The prospectus was 132 pages long and the new notes rated B3 by Moody's.

However, an analysis of disclosure in the EMATUM prospectus revealed the existence of the two further loans (US\$622 million and US\$535 million) that had been made to Mozambican state entities through the same banks as part of the larger transaction to support coastal defence requirements, again guaranteed by the state. This new and larger contingent liability was not reported to bodies such as the G19, the International Monetary Fund (IMF) and other donors that were supporting the economy of Mozambique. The 2013 Budget Law set a maximum limit on government guarantees issued of US\$6 million, so increases in debt of the scale represented by these three transactions will damage the prospects of the country attempting to move out of the poverty trap, as funds to service this external dollar debt will not be available for other infrastructure and domestic projects. There are also further reports of another US\$221 million loan from another country's interior ministry. Assistance from the IMF and the 13 other donor countries was suspended in April 2016 when the additional debt was revealed. A court ruling suggested that the Budget Monitoring Committee in Mozambique ruled the loan and the subsequent restructuring illegal.

A change in government has led to greater cooperation with agencies attempting to clarify the situation. However, the resulting structural problems in the Mozambican economy in servicing these debts, coupled with the over reliance on oil and gas revenues (not due to flow until 2020 at the earliest) has led to a further default and investigations are ongoing. A comprehensive external audit by a specialist investigator raises further questions and indicates many areas of opacity. Debt rescheduling talks are ongoing but there are still questions about the legality of some of this debt.

In December 2017, but only disclosed publicly in May 2018, a partnership agreement between the newly renamed Tunamar (formerly EMATUM) and the former founder of the Blackwater Security Group was signed. The tuna boats were said to be expected to start fishing in 2019 but the fate of the debt remained unclear at this point, other than reports that discussions continue.

In March 2019, three Mozambican officials and five "business executives" (three of whom were the Credit Suisse bankers involved in this transaction) were indicted in the US in a fraud and money laundering case that suggested they had personally benefited from a diversion of some of the funds raised by this and two other transactions. The three ex-bankers were charged with facilitating bribe payments to the Mozambique officials and bypassing the internal controls at the bank. A further nine suspects were detained in Mozambique in August 2019.

A further restructuring in late May 2019 of the 2013 bonds saw investors exchange the existing bonds for new paper accruing from July 2019 and maturing in 2031. The coupon is 5% up to 2023 rising to a reported 9% from 2023 till final maturity. This compares with a flat 5.875% in the (unimplemented) 2018 rescheduling agreement.[3]

Credit Suisse maintained that the loan is valid, despite the claims that it was not officially sanctioned. New systems have been reportedly put in place so this cannot happen again. Further lawsuits, including one from VTB, relating to the validity of the debt will be heard in London in 2020–2021 following the breakdown of arbitration attempts.

The lessons that can be learned from this simplified version of a very complex and secretive saga by taking the loan at face value and viewing it as a commercial transaction are as follows:

- Querying an investment decision based on a sparse business plan.
- A little investigation would immediately have raised red flags about the scalability of the proposed venture — the jump in size of the tuna fishing activity was just not feasible, the fish prices were based on top quality sashimi, not those obtained by nearby fleets or on the market.
- Traceability and transparency expectations from investors also mean that an offering of this type needs to be able to demonstrate that the funds are being spent on the purpose disclosed to the investors. If this money has been spent on armaments, this is inappropriate. If, as the contractor suggests, the funds were spent on patrol boats without the armaments to stop and arrest vessels, then the spirit of the original purpose could be argued to have been honoured, even though an analyst might question how effective the patrols might be. National defence budgets are not usually financed in this separate manner, but as a part of the national budget and disclosed as such.
- Transparent project management is also expected, so staged payments against clearly achieved objectives rather than the reported few large disbursements do not give investors comfort, especially within the context of a struggling economy.
- Although it has been argued that there was/is a government guarantee, the value of that needs to be viewed in the context of no foreign

---

[3]"Mozambique: First Ex-Ematum Interest Payment under New Deal", *Further Africa*, 19 March 2020.

currency reserves to meet obligations. The guarantee should have been notified to the Central Bank and to the IMF — indeed this is likely to have been a conditions precedent to the loan, so how systems failed is unclear, though the government has now assumed responsibility in the restructuring.

- Foreign currency loans are always a source of risk, and especially so if debt is being serviced before foreign currency earnings come on stream.

- Inappropriate technology and training that has been alluded to in some of the reports can also mean that many of the assets purchased are not available for cash flow generation through resale and may even be incomplete or poorly maintained.

- A return to the three parts of any project financing — cash flow, assets and the risk envelope — reveal that in this case, the cash flow forecasts were very over optimistic, the assets reportedly too technically complex and certainly of limited secondary value as support for loans of this size and the risk envelope was very poorly understood.

- Nevertheless, NGOs continue to try and support fishery projects with limited success. It also seems that the government has decided to allow access to non-national boats through a series of tuna fisheries partnerships with implications for sustainability of all fish stocks, not just tuna.

- Finally, involvement in a scheme that is not legally sound can mean severe financial penalties and even jail time for bankers.

Chapter 4

Criteria for Successful Project Financing

Introduction

In this chapter, we begin by looking at the different risk phases of a project and the considerations for providers of finance at each phase. Then we examine the key risk areas identified in the checklist for a successful project financing in Table 1.1 in Chapter 1.

If we think of a project as a stream of cash flows coming from a group of ring-fenced assets owned by a group of sponsors who have divided and agreed to share all of the project's risks, we can see that risk assessment and risk management are a key part of any decision to embark on a project. We begin by looking at risks for common project phases and the implications of those risks for providers of finance.

4.1. Risk Phases

Project financing risks can be divided into three major groupings reflecting key time frames for a project in which the elements of credit exposure assume different characteristics (see Figure 4.1):

- engineering and construction phase;
- start-up, which may be classed as a "pre-completion" phase; and
- operations according to planned specifications, which may generate cash flow after "project completion".

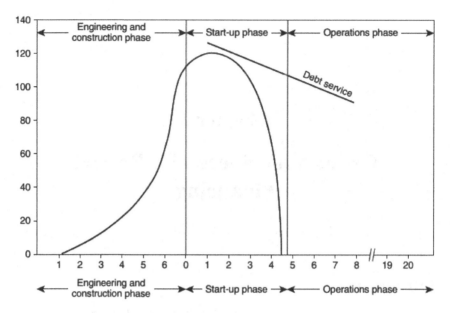

Figure 4.1:   Risk Phases in a Project Financing

Prepared by Frank J. Fabozzi and Peter K. Nevitt.

Different guarantees and undertakings from different partners may be used in each time frame to provide the credit support necessary for structuring a project financing. The term "project completion" is used to designate a point at which the project is considered strong enough to stand on its own feet, and guarantees and support mechanisms fall away so as to leave the lenders and equity holders reliant solely on the project cash flows to generate loan repayments and investor returns.

In order to have a viable project, therefore, the sponsors need to complete a thorough feasibility study. Organizations are often reluctant to invest a significant amount of capital in feasibility studies because if the project is not eventually undertaken, then the cost of the study must be written off. It is a balancing act: on the one hand, a feasibility study needs to be well researched and accurate to provide information to aid in decision-making, but, on the other hand, organizational stakeholders and specifically shareholders can object to an investment in what can become a significant write-off for them. A good feasibility study will include a commentary on different risks to support a sound case for the investment decision.

4.1.1. *Engineering and/or Construction Phase*

Projects generally begin with a long period of planning and engineering. Equipment is ordered, construction contracts are negotiated and actual construction begins. During this phase, it is also important to remember that projects will require working capital, most likely in the currency of the country in which the project is located. After construction begins, the amount of financing at risk begins to increase sharply as funds are advanced to purchase material, labour and equipment. Interest charges on loans to finance construction also begin to accumulate, but at this point there is no certainty that the project will be completed and thereby generate any cash flow. In the engineering/construction phase, lenders will be looking for support from sponsors or other third parties to increase the likelihood that any funds loaned are repaid.

4.1.2. *Start-up Phase*

Project lenders do not regard a project as completed when construction has been completed. They are concerned with whether or not the plant or facility will operate in line with the costs and to the specifications which were planned when the financing was arranged. Similarly, when project finance is applied to services, lenders need to be sure that the services can be delivered in line with the specifications detailed in the original financing. A project that fails to produce the product or service in the amounts and at the costs originally planned, or to sell at the prices that were projected, may prove the feasibility study and the cash flows on which it is based to be unsound and raise the prospect that there may be insufficient cash to pay expenses, service debt and provide the projected return to equity.

Project lenders regard a project as acceptable only after the plant or facility has been in operation for a sufficient period of time to ensure that the plant will in fact produce the product or service at the price, in the amounts and to the standards assumed in the financial plan that formed the basis for the financing. This start-up risk period may run from a few months to several years.

4.1.3. *Operations According to Specification*

Once the parties are satisfied that the plant is running to specification, the steady-state operating phase begins. Revenues from the sale of the product produced or service performed should be sufficient to service debt, interest and principal, pay operating costs and provide a return to sponsors and investors. Once the appropriate experts are satisfied that the project is generating stable cash flows in line with projections, it is said to have met its "completion test" and a completion certificate is issued; at that point the project may move into the non-recourse phase where guarantees from sponsors fall away and the servicing of debt and payment to equity investors arises exclusively from the project's cash flows. Not all projects switch to a non-recourse mode. Some sponsors may be prepared to pay a premium at the beginning of a project for the possibility of subsequent non-recourse financing. However, as the project progresses, they may choose to continue to guarantee debt service payments so that even though the project could potentially meet a completion test, and shift to a limited or non-recourse basis, that test is never requested. Why might this be?

In order to shift to a non-recourse financing basis, lenders need to receive a lot of sensitive information about the specific project, and in a highly competitive industry context, sponsors may be reluctant to release that information to third parties even under confidentiality agreements.

4.2. Different Lenders for Different Risk Periods

Some projects are financed from beginning to end with a single lender or single group of lenders, but in some cases different lenders or groups of lenders may provide funds during different risk phases. An example of this might be specialist export support schemes that will be limited in the time period for which they are available.

Some lenders like to lend for longer terms and some prefer short-term lending. Some lenders specialize in construction lending and are equipped to monitor engineering and construction of a project, some are not. Some lenders will accept and rely on guarantees of different sponsors during the construction, start-up or operation phases, and some will not. Some lenders will accept the credit risk of a turn-key operating project, but are not interested in the high-risk lending during construction and start-up. Lenders also have various geographic, industry and other limits in their portfolios so their ability to engage in different projects will depend on an institutional asset allocation strategy.

Interest rates will also vary during the different risk phases of project financing and with the different credit support from sponsors during those time periods. Short-term construction lenders are very concerned about the availability of long-term "take out" financing by other lenders upon completion of the construction or start-up phase and will insist that the take-out lenders be present from the outset of the construction financing, with both groups paying particular attention to the events that will trigger the movement between the two financing phases.

4.3. Review of Criteria for Successful Project Financing

Table 1.1 in Chapter 1 shows a checklist for planning and structuring a successful project financing. A discussion of each of the topics on that checklist follows. Some items are combined and and this is noted in the section header.

4.3.1. *Credit Risk Rather Than Equity Risk is Involved*

A credit risk should be involved in lending to the project rather than an equity risk or a venture capital risk. Lenders are not in the business of taking equity risk even if compensated as equity risk takers as discussed in the subsequent paragraphs.

Following the banking crises in the first decade of the new century, central bank regulators and specifically the Basel Committee on Banking Supervision amended the capital requirements for banks by increasing the amount of capital required to underpin different classes of bank assets. In the case of project loans, a bank takes a higher level of risk in return for a higher reward. The Basel III Capital Accord Standards continue an upward trend in terms of bank capital that regulators require to underpin more risky bank assets. The need to tie up bank capital in this way is likely to restrict the amount of lending available for leveraged project financing deals in the future and has already had an impact on project finance groups and a fall in the numbers of banks in the market.

The question of whether a credit risk or an equity risk is involved usually arises in connection with the adequacy of the underlying equity investment in the project, and the risks assumed by the sponsors and interested parties. For example, for a $200 million project, 10% equity would be $20 million, which may represent a sizeable equity investment by the sponsor. It is natural for sponsors to want to leverage their equity investment with as much debt financing as much as they can, but the higher the leverage, the higher the risk for the sponsors and the lenders and bondholders. Commercial lenders advance funds only to the extent that they are comfortable that projected cash flows will be adequate to meet debt service requirements with a margin for risk. They expect to see a significant equity contribution as a cushion underneath the debt and also as a tangible example of commitment by the sponsors.

Lenders may sometimes be compensated for riskier projects with higher interest rates but there are limits. They are not expected to assume risks that go beyond conventional lending risks. Some specialist lenders provide high risk loans for start-up situations, but would expect to be compensated by a share of the ownership and/or profits, as well as interest on their loan. This blend of debt and equity has been used in the oil industry, and examples can be seen in the early development of the North Sea. Linked to this approach, project financings and start-up companies often use a layer of debt superior to equity in the case of a future bankruptcy, but junior (subordinated) to senior debt. This subordinated debt has a high interest rate and may have an equity feature such as warrants for common stock or conversion rights for common stock. This type of debt is sometimes referred to as *mezzanine financing*.

When such subordinated high-risk financing takes the form of public or privately placed bonds rather than bank debt, the bonds are typically rated below investment grade to reflect the added risk. Very high risk reward bonds are sometimes referred to as high-yield bond, speculative-grade bonds or junk bonds.[1]

The equity in a project financing not only comes mostly from the sponsors, but may also come from other stakeholder sources directly interested in the project such as end users, off-takers, suppliers, operators, contractors, or government or other agencies.

4.3.2. *Feasibility Study and Financial Projections*

Assumptions used in the feasibility study must be realistic. Detailed cash flow projections should be prepared, and matrices of results should be produced, using different revenue and cost assumptions including the sensitivity of the project to changes in one or more key input variables.

---

[1] See Chapters 6 and 7 of the companion volume to this book, *Project Financing: Financial Instruments and Risk Management*.

Worst-case scenarios must be considered, and contingency plans prepared (see Figures 4.2–4.6).

The feasibility study should cover all applicable points suggested in this chapter and will reflect the professional ability of the project sponsors, the degree of commitment, and the financial and other resources they assign to the project.

Key conclusions drawn from the feasibility study should be independently verified and confirmed by well-recognized external consultants. Lenders may commission their own external consultants as well to review the entire project and provide independent opinions, with the costs borne by the project sponsors.

The feasibility study, financial projections and any supporting consultants' studies must confirm that the product, commodity or service that represents the project's cash flow generating capability can be produced at the costs contemplated, and sold at the prices and profit margins contemplated.

Conservative projections of the project's assured internally generated cash flows must be prepared and justified by appropriate independent

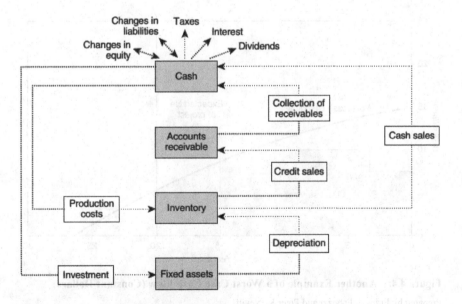

Figure 4.2: Cash Flow from Production

Prepared by Frank J. Fabozzi and Peter K. Nevitt.

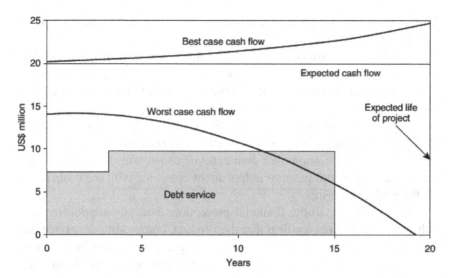

Figure 4.3: Comparison of Expected Cash Flow, Best Case and Worst Case (Constant Dollars)

Prepared by Frank J. Fabozzi and Peter K. Nevitt.

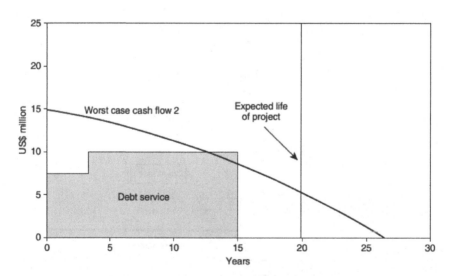

Figure 4.4: Another Example of a Worst Case Cash Flow (Constant Dollars)

Prepared by Frank J. Fabozzi and Peter K. Nevitt.

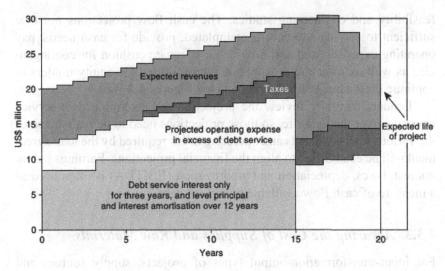

Figure 4.5: Revenues, Operating Expenses, Taxes and Debt Service Adjusted for Inflation and Escalation

Prepared by Frank J. Fabozzi and Peter K. Nevitt.

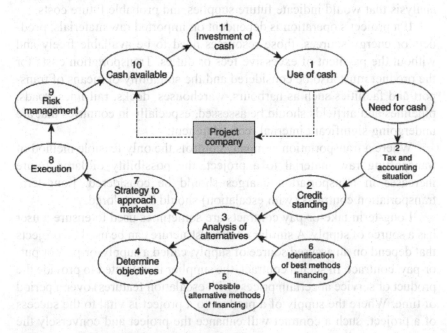

Figure 4.6: Meeting Continuing Financing Needs

Prepared by Frank J. Fabozzi and Peter K. Nevitt.

feasibility and engineering studies. The cash flow projections must be sufficient to service any debt contemplated, provide for cash needs, pay operating expenses, and still provide an adequate cushion for contingencies as well as offer the prospect of future returns for equity holders to continue their support for the project (see Figures 4.2–4.6).

Lenders carefully review the projections to determine debt service coverage over the loan life, so those projections need to be realistic since the various loan covenants and operating ratios required by the loan agreement will be established to align the financial projections. Earnings before interest, taxes, depreciation and amortization (EBITDA) is often used as a measure of cash flow available to service debt.

4.3.3. *Assuring the Cost of Supplies and Raw Materials*

For input-transformation-output types of projects, supply sources and contracts for feed stocks or raw material must be assured so that costs incurred are consistent with the financial projections. Sources and availability of those project inputs must be reviewed, possibly through market analysis that would indicate future supplies and probable future costs.

If a project's operation is dependent on imported raw materials, products or energy sources, those resources need to be available freely and without the payment of excessive fees or duties. Transportation costs for the product must also be considered and the suitability of means of transport and facilities such as harbours, warehouses, docks, rail lines, roads, pipelines and airfields should be assessed, especially in countries that are undergoing significant internal redevelopment.

Where a transportation company controls the only feasible method of transporting raw material to a project, the possibility of large future increases in transportation charges should be considered. Long-term transportation contracts (with escalation) should be explored.

Long-term take-or-pay contracts are sometimes used to ensure a user has a source of supply. A similar contract structure can be used by projects that depend on an assured source of supply, called a supply-or-pay, or put-or-pay, contract. In such a contract, the supplier is obligated to provide the product or service at certain prices (with escalation features) over a period of time. Where the supply of a product to a project is vital to the success of a project, such a contract will enhance the project and conversely the absence of such a contract may raise serious concerns as to the project's viability. If the supplier cannot furnish the product, under such a contract it must provide the product from another source, or reimburse any excess costs that the purchaser incurs in procuring the product from another supplier.

It follows that any long-term supply contract must also be enforceable. Part of the risk assessment should include the reliability of the supplier, its ability to perform, and the risk and its impact on the project if a supply contract with a foreign supplier may be subject to a force majeure interruption or an economic boycott beyond its control.

The practical value of a long-term contract with a supplier, at an attractive price and where the supplier is a sole source, must also be considered. Will the supplier use the threatened prospect of very high prices on future renewals to force renegotiation of the supply contract before its term expires?

4.3.4. *Energy Supplies Assured at a Reasonable Cost*

Long-term supply contracts for feed stocks, coal or energy (with appropriate escalation provisions) are necessary for the financial feasibility of many projects. Energy costs are especially important because of their tendency to rise and fluctuate over time. In the past, a number of project financings and their lenders have run into serious financial trouble because of their failure to anticipate cost increases in energy inputs such as electricity, natural gas, oil, coal and water. Where there are inadequate electrical energy supplies, the project may have to build its own generating plant, or provide back-up facilities especially in a power project where there may be long-term supply contracts to customers that support the project's cash flow and the possibility of the main plant going off-line for periods. Many countries have frequent power supply problems that need to be considered in the plant design process.

4.3.5. *A Market Exists for the Product, Commodity or Service*

The financial success of a project usually depends on the continued existence of a market for the product, commodity or service produced or furnished at prices that will provide the anticipated cash flows necessary to service debt, cover operating expenses and provide a return to the equity investors. Expert market surveys should provide a basis for the anticipated volume and price of the product, commodity or service to be produced and internal marketing surveys prepared by the sponsor should always be triangulated against external independent marketing studies. Competition from substitute products, suppliers closer to the markets, and less expensive sources of raw materials, feed stocks or energy should form part of any industry or market analysis.

Some projects are financed on the basis of long-term contracts to sell the product, commodity or service produced by a project to one or more users at certain time intervals, and at agreed prices with appropriate escalation. The predictable cash flow from such contracts increases the prospect that the project will be profitable, provided production costs are as anticipated, and the purchaser is financially strong and reliable. It also avoids future reliance on purchasing a key input from what may be a volatile spot market.

These contracts assume the same forms as supply contracts: take-or-pay, take-and-pay and take if tendered. In a *take-or-pay contract*, the obligation of the purchaser to pay is unconditional, even if the product, commodity, or service is not delivered. Where the project is to provide a service, such as transmission of a product through a pipeline, a long-term through-put agreement — a type of take-or-pay contract — may be used to ensure a stream of revenue to service debt. Through-put agreements take many forms, but when used as a guaranteed source of the revenue (with appropriate escalation), the purchaser of the product or service is obligated to make a payment, regardless of whether the service is used or not, provided delivery takes place. As such, stakeholders would expect to see these arrangements reported as contingent liabilities.

Conventionally, there are two component parts to such contracts: one that covers fixed costs including debt service and possibly a minimum equity return and is always paid; and a second component that represents the variable operating costs and any additional equity return and is paid if the product is required and delivered. A contract will often include so-called "hell or high water" provisions whereby the obligation to pay exists even if the project fails to generate any goods or services.

Variations of these agreements may be called tolling agreements, minimum pay contracts, all-events-tariffs, ship-or-pay contracts or may take the form of a deficiency agreement. Through-put agreements are also used where a raw material is to be furnished to a project for some value-added services, such as a refinery. A cost-of-service tariff goes a step further and provides protection against escalating costs as well as risks to the continued existence of a market. Properly drafted, take-or-pay contracts may be equivalent to guarantees of a stream of revenue but need to consider the long-term nature of the transaction.

A 65-year fixed price power purchase contract to supply Hydro-Québec (a 34% shareholder in the project) with electricity produced from the Churchill Falls Labrador Corporation hydro-electric station was signed in 1969. The contract fixed a price for electricity produced in Labrador, Newfoundland and sold to another Canadian province, Quebec. However, since 1969, end-user electricity prices have risen with the Newfoundland producer apparently contractually obliged to sell power at what is now a historically low price to Hydro-Québec and the contract has become very asymmetric. Since the power distribution lines meant all power produced had to transit through Quebec, it seemed that one Canadian province gained at the apparent expense of another, a politically sensitive situation that has received much media coverage. To illustrate the scale of the issue and its political sensitivity, reported figures suggested that Hydro-Québec reportedly received profits from the contract of approximately Can$27.5 billion up to 2017, while Newfoundland and Labrador received Can$12 billion over the same period. The latest attempt to challenge the contract in court was entered in late 2017 with one argument being that the two companies were co-venturers. A Supreme Court decision in 2018 was initially in favour of Hydro-Québec, disallowing a bid to reopen the contract before 2041. However, in 2019, the Quebec Court of Appeal ruled that Hydro-Québec's right to sell Churchill Falls Energy had a monthly cap. The case is the subject of a media lock-up.[2,3,4]

In a *take-and-pay contract*, the purchaser is obligated to take the product or service that it is provided. An alternative and more descriptive name for this style of contract would be "take-if-offered" or "take-if-tendered". Once more, the two component parts co-exist to cover fixed and activity dependent costs. A clause may be included in the agreement so that the purchaser can refuse to take delivery, provided it pays a capacity charge that covers the fixed cost elements of the project company, including debt service obligations.

---

[2]CBC Canada website segment on the Supreme Court Canada case of Churchill Falls vs Hydro Quebec.
[3]Taken from a briefing document from the Clyde Co website.
[4]"Churchill Falls Battle: Quebec Court Appeal Ruling." *Global News* Canada.

Other contractual arrangements designed to support the debt and equity service in a project would include long-term sales agreements, where pre-specified quantities and quality indicators govern a sales contract where a purchaser is obliged to take goods or services produced if they meet these specifications. In 2014, some 84% of outstanding rupee debts were related to hydropower from previous Indian-sponsored power projects with perceptions of asymmetry concerning the costs and contracts.

4.3.6. *Transportation of Product to Market*

Transportation arrangements for moving the product from the project facility to the market must be assured at a cost consistent with the financial projections. The mode and availability of suitable transportation — whether by rail or ship — should be reviewed, together with the possible need to construct any facilities needed such as roads, railroads, harbours, docks, pipelines, warehouses or airfields. The vulnerability of the project to future increases in transportation costs by companies controlling the only feasible means to move the product to market should be taken into account. Long-term transportation contracts (with appropriate escalation) may solve this problem.

4.3.7. *Adequate Communications*

Reliable telephone and other communications systems are essential to all projects today. The availability of support systems including satellite and internet links as well as telephony cannot be taken for granted. Overseas telephone calls can still take hours to complete in some parts of the world, resulting in costly delays in decision-making and thus in accomplishing objectives. Consequently, adequate and well-supported communication systems are key to successful projects, and some cost provisions may be needed in the project budget to ensure these are continually available.

4.3.8. *Availability of Building Materials*

Building materials to be used must be available at a cost consistent with the estimated construction costs, including any transportation costs.

The availability of local sources for building materials should be checked as part of contingency planning for the possible use of alternative materials. With a large project in a small country, the need for building materials and craftspeople to assist in the construction can cause ripple effects on the country's economic development as materials are pulled to the capital city or project site away from other areas also under development.

Projects have encountered difficulties because of inadequate planning for building materials; for example, reliance on the availability of local supplies of cement, that turn out to be unavailable, with the result that cement has to be imported from long distances at substantially higher cost. The delivery of just a few building, machinery or electronic components that do not meet specifications can delay an entire project until the proper replacements are found.

When imported building materials, manufactured goods or machinery are needed for the project, project managers need to secure import permits and customs clearances — sometimes a complicated and time-consuming process — and include import fees or duties at a reasonable level in the budget. The effects of any existing or potential trade embargoes that may affect imports of materials also need to be evaluated as these may delay the project or require a project re-design if the original specification cannot be met. Re-designs or re-specifications affect costs and also other features of projects, including financing arrangements.

4.3.9. *Experienced and Reliable Contractor*

The expertise and reputation of the contractor chosen to construct a project facility must be well established. The contractor must have sound technical expertise to complete the project, so that it will operate in accordance with cost and production specifications and should have previously completed similar projects successfully. The contractor should have the financial resources and experience to overcome problems in engineering, construction, start-up or operation that might arise.

Contractors need local, on-the-ground experience, as well as familiarity with the climate, culture, government infrastructure and geographic circumstances of a particular project.

Although many government contracts require acceptance of the lowest bid for a contract, or a subcontract, this can be short-sighted unless the low bidder satisfies the criteria outlined previously.

4.3.10. *Experienced and Reliable Operator*

The operator of the project, once it is up and running, must have the financial and technical expertise to operate the project in accordance with its cost and production specifications. The operator may be an independent professional operating company that specializes in providing such a service, one of the project's sponsors or co-sponsors, or another stakeholder involved with the project. Experience and expertise in operating similar projects at other locations is essential. Lenders prefer that one of the sponsors have not only a financial interest in the project but also the technical expertise to operate the facility, and experience of operating similar facilities.

Sometimes entrepreneurial companies see a chance to engage in new businesses that provide good investment opportunities, and they may proceed on the assumption that they will be able to assemble a good team to operate the new facility. However, these kinds of arrangements are fraught with problems. A number of reputable individual operating people, brought together to operate a project, will not necessarily work in harmony as a team. They will not be used to dealing with each other; each may come from a different background, and have a different way of doing things. It will take some time before such a group of people can be organized into an effective operating team. This is not an appropriate risk for lenders. Nor is diversification, as several oil companies discovered when they went into the coal mining business, believing it to be similar to the oil industry.

In some foreign operations in which a foreign joint venture partner or government agency assumes ownership and/or control of the facility over a period of time, questions may arise over who will operate the facility and the competence of such an operator. Again, this is not a risk for lenders but for equity holders. Protection may be afforded to lenders by a long-term contract with an experienced operator that the host government guarantees will survive a change in ownership control.

4.3.11. *Management Personnel*

Good management personnel as well as experienced operating personnel are needed. The general management of a project company makes the basic policy decisions, arranges the financing, provides information to lenders and investors, monitors and administers the project company and ensures the loan is repaid, primarily from the project's cash flows. So good internal systems and controls are critical, as is the ability to maintain production levels and market share. The management team must be experienced, reliable and have a good working relationship with the project lenders, so the sponsors must be able to attract and retain a good management team.

Lenders will also want to see that each of the sponsors' basic businesses as well as the project company is well managed.

The assignment of management and technical personnel to large visible projects in foreign countries leads to the risk of kidnap or extortion of personnel, shown in Table 1.1 of Chapter 1 as Risk 31 and the linked area of marine piracy. The likelihood of these events is increasing in many areas where project finance is growing — and not all kidnaps have a successful resolution. Along with appropriate insurance coverage, project sponsors should establish adequate personal security measures for staff working in areas where these are known problems and make arrangements with political intelligence providers to receive regular briefings and allow early warnings of deteriorating situations.

4.3.12. *No New Technology*

The project should not involve new technology, since again this is an equity holder's risk. The reliability of the process and the equipment to be used must be well established. If a project is to be largely self-supporting without an all-encompassing guarantee from a government agency or some other form of credit, then unless it uses existing technology, it will be difficult to find financing from conventional sources. Projects put forward by new companies to produce oil from oil shale or tar sands, gas or oil from coal, energy from garbage, gasohol from feed grains or similar promising but untried processes, may not be unsuitable for project financing in the absence of a guarantee from a very strong credit. Lenders who rely on a project's cash flows to service debt expect the project to use proven technology and engineering.

Electricity generating plants provide a good example. A 200 megawatt coal-fired plant, using standard machinery and equipment successfully used in other generating plants of similar size, and which may be purchased out of inventory from a manufacturer might easily qualify for bank financing. In contrast, in the 1990s, gas fired power plants such as Lakeland in the UK were built along the same principles, in the so-called "dash for gas" but with custom-built boilers, machinery and equipment not previously extensively used. Early projects required greater credit support from guarantors as the reliability of the cash flow they generate would be unproven because the technology was new. This new technology would cause the project be classed as a risk for equity holders, not debt providers, unless a strong financial guarantee was offered to support the project. After several years, "new" technology becomes mainstream and, continuing with our example, there are a number of gas-fired projects in existence today.

4.3.13. *Contractual Agreements Among Joint Venture Partners*

Clearly written contracts are key to successful projects. At the base of any project is a joint venture agreement and possibly an incorporated special-purpose vehicle (SPV) company or other legally separate entity. All the agreements among the joint venture partners are of importance to lenders, who want to know the identity of the companies, their ownership structure and the people who will own, operate and manage the project throughout the life of the loan. (See Chapter 11 for a more detailed discussion of entities for jointly owned or sponsored projects.)

- a good joint venture agreement will contain satisfactory provisions on these items among others;
- changes in percentages of participations by any of the partners;
- withdrawal and replacement of partners;
- addition of new partners;
- responsibility rights, and obligations of partners to each other if one partner fails to meet its financial obligations or commitments to the remaining partners;
- procedure for settlement of disputes among partners;
- voting rights of the partners on operation and management of the project; and
- assurance that the project facilities will be managed by a qualified operator for the life of the loan, particularly where the host country increases its ownership participation.

4.3.14. *Political Environment, Licenses and Permits*

The political environment for the location of the project, as well as the type of project, must be supportive of the investment and stable, with any required permits readily available, and any restrictions realistic. Good working relationships with the government officials who will be involved with the project are key to its long-term success.

The need for a stable political environment is not confined to projects located in developing countries. In recent years, a stable and friendly political environment has not always been assured even for projects located in North America and Europe.

Hundreds of licenses and permits may be required to build projects, some of which may not be available until after completion of the project, for example, certain clean air and clean water licenses. Some permits may be obtained while operating in order to continue keeping an operating license. Lenders want assurance that such permits will be granted in a fair and objective manner, based on standards and tests which are known at the outset of the project.

Severance taxes can also seriously affect the economics of a project. A severance tax is a tax imposed on the production of a particular natural resource, such as gas, oil or coal. This is a popular way to raise revenue, since the coal tax-payer/voter is subsidized. However, the uncertainty over future severance taxes can raise serious problems for a project financing, since they reduce the ability of the project to adjust prices to meet costs, make the product less competitive and adversely affect the ability of the project to service debt.

4.3.15. *No Risk of Expropriation*

Expropriation of a successful business is always a risk; it can be direct or indirect, fast or creeping. Expropriation risk can be appraised by examining the infrastructure of the country, its neighbours, its history, its power structure and its economic and political history. International lenders usually make a regular practice of keeping up to date on country, economic and political developments based on their internal expert analysis and other expert sources for the purposes of asset allocation, setting country limits and following large credits such as project loans.

Concession agreements (see Chapter 9) from central or local governments may form the basis of the project. They may be supported by separate agreements between project sponsors and the country's central bank or other government agencies responsible for natural resources or industrial development. These agreements should preserve continuity among the sponsors, the SPV company and the government when changes occur in the host country leadership, but are best characterized as letters of general understanding rather than binding commitments. Insurance against expropriation is also sometimes available but typically costly. Examples of expropriation risk include the Dabhol project in India.

Common concerns regarding the risk of expropriation by the government of a developing country can be greatly lessened if the project is owned by a number of prominent local investors from the host country or from several countries to spread risk. Another strategy is co-financing with the World Bank or one of the area development banks. This may include cross-default clauses, so that an expropriation of the mine, change of substantial ownership, or failure to pay debt will result in a concurrent default with other international loans. This would jeopardize a country's credit to an unacceptable degree.

"Creeping expropriation" through new or increased taxes, or failure to renew licenses or import or export permits, or even changes in government policy on foreign ownership is more common. Canada's one-time past policy of discouraging foreign investment in natural resources and forced divestiture of existing investments may have been well intentioned from the standpoint of Canadian policy but was a form of expropriation from the standpoint of affected investors.

The policies of some public utility commissions in the United States on assets to be included in the rate base have resulted in utilities having to sell securities at substantially under book values, in effect expropriating utility investors.

Environmental restrictions in Europe and the United States have also resulted in utilities having to sell their securities at substantially under book values, in effect expropriating utility investors. Many plants, mines and foundries have also had to be shut down for environmental reasons long before their economic lives were exhausted.

Government agencies created to market minerals from mines, while taking royalty payments may be mandated to monitor production. They may have an additional role to oversee and minimize the economic impact of transfer pricing — that is, by over- or under-invoicing between foreign and domestic units of, say, a foreign mining company — as a device to transfer capital out of the project country as another form of host government control. Such monitoring may be seen as accessing data with a view to offering a route to potential expropriation of the project if it is perceived as very successful. This is discussed in the Acacia Mining case at the end of this chapter.

4.3.16. *Country Risk*

4.3.17. *Sovereign Risk*

Country risk and sovereign risk are widely used terms, subject to many definitions in financial dictionaries, but those definitions are reasonably consistent. Country risk consists of all political, legal, regulatory, economic, exchange rate, environmental and other risks associated with investing, lending, setting up operations or trading with a foreign country. It includes, for example, the risk of a lender making a loan to a private company across a national border. Adverse country risk exists when the host country of the private company is not in an economic position to permit transfer of the amount of currency needed for the payment of interest and principal on any foreign debt (private debt has a lower priority than food payments or national debt payments to external lenders). Adverse country risk also exists if an embargo exists on certain products or repayment of debt is not permitted for domestic foreign policy reasons.

The project feasibility study should identify the nature of the country risk, appraise the significance and potential impact of the risk if realized and discuss strategies to transfer (by hedging or insuring) or mitigate such risks.

Sovereign risk is a subset of country risk that pertains to the government, including the risk that the government of a foreign country will default on its obligations; refuse to comply with a previously signed agreement; change monetary policies, tariffs or foreign exchange regulations; or impose regulations restricting the ability of borrowers, issuers securities, or other parties from meeting their obligations. This has application in project finance where the sovereign nation is not only the regulator but may also be one of the investors or joint venturers in the project. Under these circumstances, a loan to the project is in part, at least, a loan to the nation. As in expropriation, specialist advice can help sponsors to appraise and deal with this risk.

Linked to this risk is the last risk in Table 1.1 of Chapter 1 — that of a well-developed commercial legal system in place to protect property and contractual rights of host country and foreign project stakeholders.

For fast growing economies or newly industrializing economies, this can pose challenges for early project sponsors as the legal system tries to catch up with current commercial and legal practices. While it is easy to say that the well-developed US and UK legal systems offer good protection, it may be a matter of national pride to use the local legal system as the governing law for any agreements. This is also an area for expert advice.

4.3.18. *Currency and Foreign Exchange Risk*

Currency risk problems arise where revenues, expenses, capital expenditures and loans are in more than one currency and, therefore, subject the project to potential losses from currency fluctuations. Where this problem exists, strategies must be devised to match currencies of cash to be received in the future with cash required for future payments. This is because lenders will look to the sponsors to make up any foreign exchange losses by providing additional funding during construction and any future time when they are the principal obligors.

Careful analysis must be made of the expected cash flow of a project to determine which currencies will be used to finance the project, including the host country currency, and which currencies will be generated by the project. The exchange of one currency into another must be carefully managed. Artificial conversion rates can, of course, significantly affect the project. Hedging in forward currency or commodity markets should be done where possible at a reasonable cost using products such as forward currency sales and currency swaps. A multi-currency loan may help control this risk but can also create operational complications with limits placed on drawdown tranche sizes that may or may not align with the project. The bank or financial adviser to the project can provide expert advice and help in dealing with these problems.

When a project is located in a developing country, the country's currency is frequently considered a "soft" currency, tending because of domestic inflation to depreciate more rapidly than a "hard" currency such as the US dollar, euro, British pound sterling or Japanese yen. In such cases, the project sponsors incur little risk in converting hard currency into local currency for local expenses, but run significant risks if project revenues are in the local currency and debt obligations are in a hard currency. This is a serious risk for a local power project financed by foreign lenders. For projects that produce commodities traded on world markets, such as petroleum and mineral products, the solution for the project is usually to invoice in the same currency as the project loan, generally US dollars.

If the project is located in a country where there are or have been restrictions around free exchange of the currency, a pre-emptive move by project sponsors would be to ensure that the rights and obligations of the project company to deal in local or foreign currencies are spelled out in an agreement that includes the express consent of the central bank of the host country.

4.3.19. *Adequate Equity Contribution and Return*

The key project sponsors or promoters must make equity contributions consistent with their capability, interest in the project, and the risk and financial structure of the project. Lenders will require the sponsors of a project to have a sufficient financial investment, such that it will be difficult for the sponsors to abandon or ignore the project. This can give rise to the following financial management issues:

What if the sponsors say that they need funds released for corporate or personal purposes before the project has demonstrated a stable cash flow profile? Clearly the banks want the sponsors to remain engaged but also to ensure that the project is not starved of funds requiring more debt to be injected and leverage to increase. This eventuality needs to be discussed at the time of negotiation of the financial investment terms, and modelled carefully so all parties understand the risks. (Clawback clauses only have value if the money is still available for clawback!) The potential need for funds by the sponsors may also be picked up as an issue by a serious due diligence report on the sponsors and their financial health. Agencies that can provide this information exist in many countries but accurate information of this type is still difficult to access in emerging or even state-controlled economies. In the Tuna Bond case in Chapter 3, the investigation was carried out by a well-known international group. A good look at the lifestyle of sponsors can reveal some information — the government official who receives a relatively modest-state salary but has money outside the country to send his child overseas to university might cause some further questions.

Another potential pitfall can be confusion of identities where names may be common. Banks have made the wrong decision through mis-identification and not reading all of the signs properly — a multimillion-aire would not live in a poorer part of the capital.

The other danger is if the project is cash flow positive but the returns to the sponsors are less attractive than expected and the sponsors begin to lose interest. Banks are not project operators and the choice of project for a bank group is usually based as we have seen on the choice of a good contractor and a good operator. This negotiation is trickier and persuasion is always a better option than reverting to the letter of the contract. Again, modelling the returns as equity returns as well as project returns and looking carefully at the robustness of the costs and assumptions and comparing them with other industry returns can expose issues at a pre-signature phase.

4.3.20. *The Project as Collateral*

Lenders may be willing to rely to some extent on project facilities and properties as collateral and security for debt repayment. Therefore, in planning a project, it is important to try to locate and structure the project and its facilities so that they may have value to third parties. There may be local legal impediments, however, restricting the use of foreign-owned assets as collateral in the same way locally owned assets could be used. There may also be issues with remitting sales proceeds from local project asset sales.

Many projects are uniquely valuable to the parties involved but may have only limited value to third parties in a foreclosure or sale. In this case, any additional credit support for such projects must obviously then come from other sources. The term "asset lending" is used to describe circumstances in which lenders are willing to look to the collateral value of the asset securing the loan as a significant back-up source of funds to repay the debt. But this type of lending, generally does not apply to project finance. In the case of project finance, loans are repaid with cash flow, not asset sales, and banks are reluctant debtors in possession of assets on which they have foreclosed, not least as it is outside their area of expertise, and they are known to be forced sellers of these assets and thence likely to sell at lower prices.

4.3.21. *Satisfactory Appraisals of the Assets and Resources*

Independent appraisals of oil or gas or other mineral reserves and other project assets and cash flows must be available to lenders. The risk in a resource project is that the actual production and the revenue derived from it will be insufficient to pay operating costs and amortize project debt in accordance with the financial plan. For example, if a production-payment type of financing is involved, the value and amount of reserves must be of sufficient size to justify any collateral value sought by lenders and include a margin of safety. Appraisals of the value of plant and equipment to third parties are necessary if such assets are relied upon to any extent as collateral and for insurance purposes.

Consequently, lenders want to be as certain as they can be that the potential ore deposits, gas fields or oil deposits necessary to the project actually exist. The quality of such reserves, the technical feasibility of recovery, the proportion of the reserves that are economically recoverable, the ability and cost to extract such reserves must be ascertained as accurately as possible. The timing of resource recovery or production must be established. Some banks employ their own engineers to conduct such appraisals but private engineering firms are also available to perform such appraisals at a cost to the project company.

4.3.22. *Adequate Insurance Coverage*

An adequate insurance programme must be available both during construction and operation of the project because an uninsured casualty loss can be a disaster for all concerned. Therefore, as part of this process, risks should be evaluated and insurance coverage maintained at levels sufficient to provide protection.

Reviews and changes in coverage should be made as conditions change, since a dedicated project company usually has little cushion on which to fall back in the event of such a loss, except for insurance proceeds. However, insurance proceeds are assigned to lenders, so all agreements need to be clear as to the circumstances under which the proceeds from an insurance claim must be used to restore the project or to repay the debt to the lenders. Under certain circumstances, insurance proceeds during construction and/or start-up may be payable to the sponsor or a company providing a completion guarantee. This is only satisfactory so long as a responsible sponsor or other guaranteeing party is required to complete or pay back the lenders and has strong enough financial resources to be able to do so while the problems resulting from the incident requiring insurance are resolved. In the past, naïve lenders have failed to consider the period of delay between incidents and insurance payouts and the need to manage any collateral effects of the trigger incident.

Business interruption insurance will provide protection against the possibility that the project cannot be operated and interruptions to the flow of goods and/or services from a project should also be considered when structuring any offtake contracts (see Section 4.3.5).

Insurance is only as good as the financial strength of the weakest link in the chain of reinsurance — lenders may restrict where reinsurance can be written to avoid reinsurance into illiquid markets based on currencies with limited exchangeability into US dollars, or euros or those with long central bank delays in approving reinsurance transfers into strong currencies. Many groups of project finance lenders will request a specialist insurance review before and annually during the life of a financing package and want to oversee payments of premia from bank accounts that they can monitor.

4.3.23. *Force Majeure Risk*

Force majeure (which literally translated means "superior force") risks are those types of risks that result from certain events beyond the control of the parties to the project financing and thereby exempt parties from the legal consequences of non-performance. The scope of force majeure risks is specific to each project but events commonly contained in force majeure clauses include:

- war (declared or undeclared) or other military activity;
- strikes, lockouts and other labour disturbances;
- riots or public disorder;
- expropriation, requisition, confiscation or nationalization;
- changes in laws, rules or regulations;
- blockades or other closings of harbours or docks;
- severe storms and natural disasters; and
- epidemics or quarantines.

The consequences from non-performance for each event should be clearly laid out in the contract and need to be mirrored in all agreements for the project so all force majeure risks are addressed identically in every contract or agreement for a project.

Force majeure events may also occur in the project supply chain, affecting key suppliers of raw materials or services such as transportation. Parties required to take the service or product of the plant under long-term through-put or take-or-pay contracts, or take-if delivered contracts are similarly subject to such risks.

Lenders will seek to allocate risks of this sort to the sponsors, suppliers and purchasers through contractual obligation or insurance protection.

The following are practical points when negotiating certain of the more common events included in force majeure clauses.

War (declared or undeclared) or other military activity: It may not be clear when a war or other military activity should provide an excuse for non-performance. For example, does the commencement of war or other hostilities involving the project country constitute a physical impediment to performance, or should there be a requirement of hostile activity at or near the project site?

Strikes, lockouts and other labour disturbances: While these events can physically prevent performance, they also raise questions as to foreseeability and avoidability. Have these events occurred frequently in the past? Should the conduct of a party's employees excuse performance? Or should these events be restricted to those involving the employees of others? Is a settlement of the dispute possible? Are replacement employees available? Some insurance cover may be available, but may be expensive and restricted in scope.

Expropriation, requisition, confiscation or nationalization: These events are often the source of lengthy force majeure negotiations. When the non-performing party resides in the project country and is prohibited from performing by an act of the government of such country, an award of damages by a court in another country may be unenforceable. The issue becomes more difficult when the non-performing party is an agent of the host country government. Under these circumstances, there could be an argument that the entity controlling the non-performing party has caused the impediment, and thus a claim of force majeure might be difficult to support. Courts outside the project's host country may be reluctant or unable to intervene in what may be viewed as an act of state. Documentation in this area needs careful guidance from experts.

Natural disasters: Certain natural disasters such as severe storms or floods may be normal conditions during certain times of the year at the project site. Since these can be reasonably anticipated they should not excuse non-performance. To avoid ambiguity, it is worthwhile to exclude such events — as long as the risk has been addressed so that the project revenues are not compromised.

4.3.24. *Delay Risks*

A delay in completion of a project facility creates a compound problem. Interest on the construction loan continues to run, thus raising the capitalized costs of the project and resulting in a cost overrun. At the same time, the expected stream of revenue is delayed since the plant cannot operate to produce the product or service. If the delay continues for any length of time, cost of labour and materials may further increase due to inflation. The process of continually examining and tracking financing requirements is shown in Figure 4.6.

This creates serious problems in a project financing, where the ability of expected revenue to cover operating costs and amortize debt is dependent upon the assumed cost of the project. Unless the remaining construction costs are paid, the facility will not be completed, and the project will not generate funds to repay project debt. This puts the entire project in jeopardy. An overrun cost with no provision for responsibility for payment puts considerable pressure on lenders to advance additional funds.

4.3.25. *Cost Overrun Risks*

Delays cause serious problems. One is the risk of cost overruns. Cost overrun risk can be covered in a variety of ways.

Construction contract approach: The sponsors can guard against over-run risk to some extent if they can obtain some form of fixed-price or turn-key contract from contractors and subcontractors. Under those circumstances, the contract price will be higher because of the higher risk exposure for the contractor. Alternative approaches such as pain sharing/gain sharing or alliance contracting as exemplified by BP's Andrew Field development encourage contractors to evaluate and track the contract and exploit efficiencies. In this example, both cost and delivery date were negotiated between all contractors and BP. The contractors were incentivized to collaborate by the agreement that if costs were saved, all of them would share in the upside. If, however costs overran, the increase would also be shared. The project came in under budget.

Additional capital contribution from sponsor: Under this approach, the sponsors or investors must agree to come up with the additional capital, sometimes in the form of subordinated debt rather than a capital contribution, permitting return of the additional investment to the investors in some form other than as dividends or a distribution of capital, which might otherwise be in violation of loan agreements. This may be in the form of an escrow account containing sufficient funds to complete the project. An escrow account is, in effect, a blocked account established and funded by the sponsors. Funds are paid out from the escrow account for some specific purpose on the occurrence of some event. In the case of an escrow account to provide funds for completion, funds would be paid out to contractors to cover certified cost overruns. Any excess not used would be returned to the sponsor upon completion.

Standby credit facility: Another method to address a possible overrun is through a standby credit facility from the original lenders. In such a standby credit arrangement, additional borrowings may have to be covered by a lengthening of take-or-pay contracts, or price adjustment of the product or service or additional guarantees or capital contributions by sponsors may be necessary.

Completion guarantee extension to debt maturity: A completion guarantee by the project sponsor is an undertaking whereby the entire debt of the project is guaranteed until the project is complete and operating according to specifications. This type of guarantee can contain a provision that debt will be guaranteed until maturity in the event completion is not achieved by a certain date. This puts pressure on the sponsor to provide cost overrun funds needed for completion.

Take out of lenders: The loan agreement can require the sponsor to purchase the assets and take out the lenders if the project is not completed and operating according to specifications by a certain date. This may take the form of a put or call. As a practical matter, such an agreement sets the stage for lenders to renegotiate the loan on more favourable terms and conditions.

4.3.26. *Adequate Return Measures*

Lenders wish to ensure that a project has a satisfactory economic incentive as measured by projected return on equity (ROE), return on investment (ROI), and return on assets (ROA) for the sponsor investors. Lenders expect the investors in a project to be successful and to have the potential for being very successful. Lenders recognize that there is no better incentive for the success of the project and for the investors to have the potential to receive an excellent return on their investment.

4.3.27 *Realistic Inflation Rate Assumptions*

The projections and feasibility study should assume realistic inflation rates. Such rates will vary from country to country, which should be borne in mind when investors, lenders and equipment sources for a project are located throughout the world.

4.3.28 *Realistic Interest Rate Assumptions*

The feasibility study should also include projections of fixed and/or floating interest rates that will be available to the project throughout construction and operation. This is an area where the financial adviser and/or lenders to the project can provide expert help. Since a substantial part of the capitalized cost of a project will consist of interest expense, it is important that realistic interest assumptions be used for financial planning in the feasibility studies.

Finally, it should state the base exchange rate for all currencies used in the project. In the absence of any more definitive information, it should also assume that future exchange rates will vary from year to year and will be calculated with a constant purchasing power parity. By way of example, if a Japanese export credit has a low interest rate, the apparent advantage will be eroded by the fact that the debt service will increase year by year from the appreciating value of the Japanese yen resulting from the lower underlying inflation rate.

4.3.29. *Environmental Risks*

Both the sponsors and lenders to a project must be very concerned regarding harm to the environment which may result from the contemplated construction and operations. Recent examples of the damage and clean-up costs can be seen in the Macondo Well blow-out in the Gulf of Mexico and its impact on British Petroleum (BP) as the operator in 2010 and in the Exxon Valdez oil spill in Alaska in 1989. Other examples include the Aurul SA tailings dam failure in 2000 which took place in Romania but contaminated water sources in Hungary with cyanide.

A careful investigation of the history of any environmental damage to the property resulting from past usage is warranted because the new owners and lenders to the project may be held liable for any environmental clean-up required, regardless of when or how it occurred. This becomes important in the redevelopment of industrial sites, for example, for housing (brownfield sites). In the past, irate stakeholders have attempted to sue lending banks for compensation for losses caused by environmental mishaps resulting from projects they have financed.

Insurance protection may only be available for limited cover and at very high prices, and the best option may be to engage and inform key stakeholders groups as the project progresses, recognizing that this will be an additional cost. The Equator Principles, a globally recognized benchmark for managing social and environmental risks in project finance, is a voluntary code of conduct signed by many major lenders and other project finance stakeholders. Signatories pledge to follow the best practice based on the International Finance Corporation (IFC) Policy and Performance Standards on Social and Environmental Sustainability, and on the World Bank Group Environmental, Health and Safety General Guidelines.

4.3.30. *Foreign Corrupt Practices Act and Other Similar Legislation*

There are substantial opportunities for project financings in developing countries, but the legal systems in many of those countries have not yet been developed to accommodate contemporary commercial practices and the intricacies of project financing ethical norms.

In some developing countries, incentive payments are customary and even necessary to facilitate the awards of contracts, permits and even the right to bid on contracts. The challenge for project sponsors is that this is not a level playing field. There is tension between moves in Western economies towards transparent and accountable corporate practices that meet ethical standards, and more relaxed approaches elsewhere. The need to find future investment opportunities for sustainable returns for shareholders can highlight this tension for natural resource companies. This is an area where extreme caution needs to be exercised as in several jurisdictions, such as China, receiving a bribe is also an offence. In Chongqing, in China, in May 2011, the local Chinese shareholder in the Chongqing Hilton Hotel (an American chain) was jailed along with a number of other people, including government officials following a trial that found that he had paid bribes and the officials had received them in connection with certain organized crime and other activities in the hotel nightclub.

The UN and the Council of Europe have instituted codes of conduct for their employees, most notably the UN Convention against Corruption and the OECD Convention on Bribery of Foreign Public Officials in International Business Transactions. The latter was ratified by 38 countries as of March 2009. In the United States, the Foreign Corrupt Practices Act 1977 (FCPA), prevents US companies from bribing foreign officials and requires US companies' accounting practices to accurately reflect payments to foreign officials and agents.

FCPA makes it unlawful to incentivize or bribe government officials to obtain business, and it includes several types of prohibited behaviour in its antibribery provisions. Other US law includes the International Anti-corruption and Good Governance Act (2000) which regulates US assistance programmes.

The basic antibribery prohibition makes it unlawful for a company (as well as its officers, employees or agents) to offer, pay, promise to pay, or even authorize the payment of money or anything of value to a foreign official for the purpose of obtaining or retaining business or directing business to another person.

The second antibribery provision outlaws making a payment of any kind to any person, knowing that all or a part of the payment will be offered or promised to a foreign official as a bribe. A person need not witness a bribe taking place in order to know about it.

A company may not avoid liability under FCPA by closing its eyes and ignoring obvious facts that should have reasonably put the company on notice that its intermediary or agent was engaging in these payments. However, the FCPA also notes several exceptions and affirmative defences. The so-called "grease payments" to low-level employees who perform "routine governmental action" are exempt from prosecution. If the written laws of the foreign official's country permit the payment, or the payments are made as reimbursements to foreign officials for expenses associated with visits to product demonstrations or tours of company facilities it may be exempt.

Specific legislation around payments, facilitation and bribery also exists in France, Germany and the UK to name just three other countries active in overseas projects.

Additionally, all money in a project needs to be traceable and accounted for to avoid money laundering problems.

4.3.31. *Protection Systems against Kidnapping and Extortion*

Protection systems are in place against criminal activities such as kidnapping and extortion. This was addressed above under "Management Personnel".

4.3.32. *Commercial Legal System to Protect Property and Rights*

A commercial legal system is in place to protect property and contractual rights. This was addressed above under "Country and Sovereign Risk". This is an ongoing issue where there may be multiple versions of contracts with translations unable to address the subtleties of the languages involved and confusion arising involved. Confusion arises when things go wrong and the documentation is unclear.

4.4. Case Study: Acacia Mining

Acacia Mining (Acacia) was a 63.9% subsidiary of the Canadian goldminer, Barrick Gold, the largest gold mining company in the world. Acacia operated in Tanzania and its shares are listed on the London and Dar es Salaam Stock Exchanges. Mining operations began in 2000 in Tanzania, where three gold mines were active, operating through three local subsidiaries. Acacia was formerly known as African Barrick Gold but changed its name to Acacia in November 2014. The local mining companies did not change their names.

The mines produce gold, silver and copper, as gold/silver bars, known as *doré* and gold/copper concentrate — these are exported and generate foreign currency. Figures are available for mine production on the company website and the company also stresses its contribution to the local economy through various projects. The company press releases emphasize that the agreements with the Tanzanian government permit sales of fully declared gold/copper concentrate to overseas customers and permit this export and that the company has always been in compliance with its obligations and has made all royalty payments and taxes due. The exports are assessed and taxes calculated by the Tanzanian Minerals Audit Committee.

Tanzania is reported to be the fourth largest gold producer in Africa and had a relatively benevolent regime to attract Foreign Direct Investment (FDI). The 2016 Five Year Development Plan projects that the mining sector contribution to the economy is estimated at around 3% and expected to be more than 4.6% by 2025, though this includes other mining operations. In 2017, the current President of Tanzania, who was elected in 2015, announced that Acacia needed to pay $190 billion in revised taxes, interest and fines and banned all exports of the gold/copper concentrate by Acacia in March, the latest in a number of measures to increase government revenue from the sector. At the same time, the company was accused of underreporting the amount of concentrate it exports, following an exercise that sampled containers from the company. Gold bar exports continue but the effect of the concentrate export ban was thought to be around million dollars per day with a significant impact on two of its three mines, shifting one into a lossmaking state (in September, Acacia announced a reduction in activity at one of the mines). To offer an idea of scale, the penalty was estimated at around four times the GDP of the entire country.

While the Natural Wealth and Resources (Permanent Sovereignty) Law prohibits foreign courts from having jurisdiction over national resources and allows the government to renegotiate any existing contracts it deems "unconscionable", Acacia sought arbitration in London against the Tanzanian government, being joined by another major mining company anxious to protect its interests. The new rules affected incoming investment and are likely to spill over into the fledgling oil and gas extraction industry. The Tanzanian government wanted to build a smelter to keep more of the added value from its mineral resources within the country and funding this without support from mining companies could be challenging for a relatively small economy.

At the time of writing, Acacia's parent company, Barrack Gold has agreed to pay $300 million to the Tanzanian government and to give a 16% carried interest in the three Acacia mines. However, the money was to be paid by Acacia, which does not have the cash and was said not to have been part of the negotiations. There have been resignations at senior levels in Acacia. An Acacia manager was prevented from leaving Tanzania. Lawsuits were filed concerning deaths and violations of human rights. Allegations of corruption were also made.

A negotiated settlement in a case like this is clearly in all parties' interests but the signal this sends to the wider investment community may not only just be the emphasis on fairness in allocation of revenues from a national resource but also the instability of an agreed framework for the exploitation of those resources and it is the latter that can inhibit a project proceeding smoothly by adding to risks that were thought to be covered. It also stresses the importance of access to good quality local information to allow for a considered response. Finally, it highlights the need for the provision of accurate information and a degree of reasonableness on both sides.

In subsequent developments, a Western Australian company, OreCorp, announced its intention to farm-in[5] for 51% of one of the mines with the option to increase its ownership to 100% after certain payments are made. Acacia will retain the smelter contract for the ore. The dispute between Acacia and the Government of Tanzania, which was being handled by Barrick as Acacia's majority shareholder, was finally settled in October 2019 with a payment of $300 million. A 16% participation in the three mines by a new company Twiga Minerals will represent the Tanzanian government interests and the concentrate export ban has been lifted. Barrick took Acacia private through an offer for the shares completed in September 2019. Acacia's West Kenyan properties were sold in February 2019 by Barrick to Shanta Gold, an AIM listed company active in Tanzania with Acacia retaining a 2% Net Smelter Return royalty interest, meaning a percentage of gross revenue net of transportation, insurance and processing costs.

---

[5] See Chapter 15 for an explanation of this term.

Chapter 5

The Project Financing Process

Introduction

Historically, project finance activity was centred in cities with major capital markets — New York, London and Tokyo. Additional specialist centres of industry banking expertise grew up in locations that were important to certain industries such as Athens, Hong Kong and Singapore for ship lending, Houston and Dallas for oil and gas lending, and Los Angeles for film finance. Today, as the epicentre of economic growth has shifted away from the West, newer centres have grown up to provide local knowledge and local funding but successful project financing still requires good access to major capital markets and the support of large, experienced banks.

Although in theory, borrowers have a large choice of banks, not all banks are capable of structuring and arranging complex project financings. Because banks tend to specialize in particular activities, a borrower should choose carefully when selecting a bank for a major banking relationship, either for conventional financing or for project financing. In some cases, the roles of financial adviser and lead bank are separated, but not all project sponsors elect to use both, so the role of a lead bank may also encompass much of the financial adviser as well. If this is the case, then the governance issues around potential conflicts of interest need to be transparent to all parties.

5.1. Developing a Relationship With the Sponsors

The relationship with the sponsors is critical. As we saw in the Acacia case in the last chapter, the ability to intervene and get things back on

103

track using a different set of informed people can change a difficult situation into a more manageable one. Nevertheless, the sponsors are not the only stakeholders with power as the case at the end of this chapter shows. Even though stakeholders may not have political power, they can still exert significant influence.

It is a common misapprehension among younger professionals to believe that the law and the contract will fix problems and going to court is the first option and not the last. Although this may have apparent appeal in jurisdictions with well-developed commercial legal systems, for the foreigner funder, going to court in a land that is not their own and possibly in a legal system where the case lore of decisions is not clear cut, can be an expensive and potentially futile exercise.

The route of arbitration where there may be significant differences between the legal systems of the non-native sponsor and the host country, and indeed the legal systems governing the financing agreements, is attractive and can appear to offer a compromise to arguments about choice of governing law being a proxy for sovereignty over the project. However, any judgment rendered "overseas" needs to be locally enforceable to get relevant changes to take place for the project's benefit and this is not always a natural state of affairs, not least as nations do not like other legal systems or courts telling their judiciary or citizens how to act.

So as academic theory tells us, good relationships between parties can manage the difficult moments.

How does this reconcile with more frequent "cast of characters" changes within financial institutions? The answer is "not well". On the one hand, there is the danger of lack of perspective between individuals who have worked together for a long time, are too close to the project and may also have a vested friendship to be able to look dispassionately at issues. On the other hand, there is the danger from a newly arrived team member, who upsets a delicate relationship, perhaps by behaving in a culturally inappropriate manner or by an obvious lack of preparation and knowledge.

An example might be that the prevailing cultural norm in one stakeholder group in the project environment is an apparently less focused approach and an emphasis on getting to know people well before discussing business. This might include what seem to be tangential and lengthy discussions about family and social matters. We can contrast this with a different cultural norm where a direct approach is prized and the idea is to get the meeting over as quickly as possible. The first group are astonished at what they see as a lack of sophistication in not making the effort to understand the local "rules of the game", or traditions, not to mention a perceived desire not to build a longer-term relationship. The second group are bored with the idle chit chat, cannot understand why the main event is not immediately under discussion and may make the fatal mistake of underestimating the abilities of their counterparties.

Another example might be the project manager or even the lead banker who starts to refer to the project as "my project" and aligns themselves with the sponsor using "we" statements. Again, a loss of perspective.

Finally, one of the biggest changes in recent years relates to the exchange of gifts and favours between parties touched on in the previous chapter.

The Organisation for Economic Co-operation and Development (OECD) established an Anti-Bribery Convention in 1997, updating it in 2007 with further guidelines in 2011 and further expanded in and restated in 2019. This is designed to deal with inducements to foreign public officials and has been signed by all OECD member countries and 8 other countries (Brazil, Costa Rica and the Russian Federation). It operates by peer review and new laws and codes have also been enacted in a number of countries to support it or mirror it. Many public and private organizations have formal policies around gift giving and gift receiving with monetary limits placed and gifts being pooled into a draw or shared with support staff (another important and often neglected stakeholder group).

Exchanges of gifts have often been cultural norms in the past and lavish tokens can be produced, ever escalating in value. While tangible gifts can be declared, what about the case of helping someone's child get into university? Or the expectation of a "facilitation fee" or an "agency payment"? As we write this, China's leader has signalled a continued crackdown on corruption and a number of high-ranking Saudis are being detained as part of an anti-corruption measure. Non-governmental organizations (NGOs) such as Transparency International are also interested stakeholders — the latter publishes a series of country reports and publishes an annual Corruption Perceptions Index, pointing out no country is perfect. In 2019, New Zealand topped the list with no perceived corruption and Somalia was in last place. Better information flows have increased contentious issues about gifts, corruption, bribes, etc., being raised in the press or in other public meetings, but despite calls for increased transparency, much still goes on, often tacitly acknowledged or even supported by senior management, hoping not to get caught. Should this happen it is worth reflecting that the "gravity principle" applies — trouble travels downwards when looking for shoulders on which to land.

Building a sound relationship with a sponsor is the way to get the first view of a new project, but hopefully not in such a way that this includes an expectation by the sponsor that the deal is a done deal. Other tricky outcomes include that the deal envisaged is not going to work, or the deal has been obtained for a "price" or consideration (that may not be monetary) but that will come back to haunt all parties when it becomes more widely known (often when the project is in trouble)! This might include arranging the aforementioned overseas schooling for children of key project stakeholders.

5.2. The Purpose of the Call for Financing

What is required is a succinct summary of the project and what the money will be used for, broken down into its different slices or tranches by time for each project phase and by purpose and by equity and debt. What can appear is either a rambling list that is difficult to reconcile or a single sentence. Neither of these can aid in investment decision-making — in any project, the first question is always, how will any cost-overruns be managed?

A good statement of purpose shows the reader that the sponsors have thought through what is happening and any interested potential investors will be benchmarking the different cost elements against other projects. Credibility, therefore can be created or lost in this area. Footnoting the evidence to support the breakdown of funding can allow potential financial partners to see where the sums have come from and concur, guide or challenge them accordingly.

5.3. For How Long is the Loan Required?

Again, realism is needed in terms of timing and understanding the internal appetite of the bank. If a bank is only interested in five-year exposure and an opportunity is for 10 years, that bank is not the best bank. Attempting to split it into two five-year periods with a rollover to make the deal work, is very risky since if circumstances change, the finance for a project could be stopped and imminent repayment demanded before the project is established, with a resultant loss. Borrowers can ask about a bank's attitude towards tenor and a banker should also know what sort of business a bank wants to engage in at any time so that meetings are productive. Gaming behaviour around the tenor is not unknown — the 367-day loan to qualify as a long-term liability is one example, as is the 364-day loan to qualify as short-term, but all parties should remember that the type and tenor of asset will fit into different portfolio allocations and may attract different capital adequacy requirements with consequent pricing implications. Even equity is not forever, so is there an exit plan for shareholders? Asking for a slightly longer borrowing period will give some headroom in the cash flows, but prepayment options also need to be carefully examined in case of accelerated repayment. This may carry a penalty.

Balloon-type structures where partial repayment takes place over the loan period with a large amount due at final repayment defer risks and assume the probability of a successful future refinancing or a future sale. This may crystallize at a time when the market is uncertain, making it less likely to occur and giving rise to serious problems for the lenders (a potential loss) and the investors (possibility of a fire sale at a loss-generating lower value).

5.4. Additional Support or Security Offered

If guarantees or contractual support is being offered, the financial strength of the entities offering such support needs to be assessed and the nature of the support contracts examined.

A letter of comfort is not the same as a guarantee, nor is a letter of awareness, as many banks have found out to their cost.

Prior preparation of copies of any such contracts, financial information and appropriate releases or Non-Disclosure Agreements (NDAs) ready for the providers of finance means that the process is not likely to be delayed. Although letters of comfort or awareness are not enforceable, they may have a certain moral suasion, but should not be relied on.

In a number of countries, the belief exists that holding a mortgage is the best form of security because land values always rise (because they have always done so in the past). In today's social media world, pictures of banks enforcing possession of property, especially national assets to make up any shortfall are not good publicity. Taking a mortgage over a factory and "realizing" that security, or taking over a warehouse of goods, or arresting a ship or aircraft can also cause other liabilities such as unpaid wages or taxes or insurance to add to the costs and the management time to get the loan principal back. Foreign lenders cannot always take a legal security interest in domestic real estate, so assumptions need to be checked that an entity owns any security being offered and that the provider of funds understands the risks involved in taking ownership of an asset. A security interest is always a secondary source of repayment — if the cash flow is not strong then this may be a transaction to pass on! Any security should be insured by passing all insurance payments through an account that the provider of funds can monitor and choosing an insurer that has an international reputation and multiple sources of funds. Lenders have found out the hard way that the local insurance company may not be able to meet its obligations or payments by overseas reinsurers in "hard currency" are not released back to the lenders. Insurance contracts need to be assigned or the benefits pledged to the lenders as a part of the basic contract.

5.5. The Borrowing Entity

5.5.1. *The People Involved in the Business —*
The Management

It is important not make assumptions that "everyone knows" certain people, or indeed that newcomers to a market do not know how to do their homework. While it may be difficult in some countries to find out about a person's past, a hint of prior bankruptcy may cause some decision makers to think that lessons have been learned and others that another attempt with other people's money is not an acceptable risk. In other countries, almost too much information is available. Whatever the outcome — everything needs to be disclosed in order to make the best risk assessment. The curriculum vitae of key staff and a chance to meet them and assess them, preferably in a non-social situation, give a sound basis but, even so, should be double-checked.

Identities can be confusing in families where certain key names repeat across generations. Spurious claims of kinship to famous or wealthy people can also trap the unwary and have done so. Check, check and check again — if this person is a son or daughter of a wealthy family, and wants to borrow large sums of money, why are they living in a less affluent neighbourhood? Is the nature of their relationship with their family and the family assets as described by them, or is there more to the story?

5.5.2. The Group Structure

Although legal and tax considerations are important considerations for group structures, the entity receiving funds needs to be able to service debt and/or equity. Reliance on funds being channelled through from other group companies is not making a credit-worthy loan with a strong primary repayment source. In order to channel the funds, the pathway and process needs to be very clear from the outset and also speedy so that funds do not disappear in times of financial stress.

5.5.3. Historic Information for the Sponsors, Any Guarantors and Borrowing Entities

A detailed history of the organization, including any significant changes such as mergers, acquisitions, etc., is useful for a provider of funds to see as evidence of prudent management or steps being taken to change into better practice. Details of companies or businesses acquired or disposed of and details of the financial performance of the competition should link clearly to the strategic analysis.

5.5.4. Historic Financial Information for the Sponsors, Guarantors and Borrowing Entities

The last five years of detailed financial information, preferably audited by an external third party is acceptable to the provider of funds.

One challenge can be an overly close relationship with auditors where the wider audit enterprise provides other significant revenue generating services to an organization such as consulting or personal tax advice. This has triggered new legislation, as yet in progress to allow for judgment to remain impartial and unaffected by other activities.

In emerging economies, the scarcity of auditors and a less clear separation of the external audit function from the internal finance function may give rise to conflicts of interest. This has led to problems, especially where the auditor may be a related party or may be placed under pressure to produce a favourable report. Rotation of auditors to manage the potential for these challenging situations has been proposed but has also met with resistance from major firms in this area.

5.5.4.1. *Governance of Financial Decisions*

Corporate documents and policies offer evidence of good governance and also allow the provider of funds to see how and by whom such decisions are made. Companies may have boards of directors but if power resides in one individual, or an extended clique in practice, the board may have little ability to veto decisions that may change the financial structure of the entity.

5.5.5. *What is the Market for the Goods and Services and the Sustainable Competitive Advantage?*

Providers of funds want to invest in operations that generate cash flow to service their investment and to return the capital. This means that the transaction should be self-liquidating.

A good business plan needs to show appropriate stakeholders that there is a viable and sustainable market for the product or service. That may require investment in an externally produced expert market study or survey. Some banks may organize their staff into specialist industry teams, such as a real-estate group, or a natural resources group; this allows for expertise to be in-house and for proposals to be screened for risk based on accumulated expertise. For smaller banks and branches, however, this may be not be practical, but that does not remove the requirement for the funder to demonstrate to decision makers that the market is viable.

While some bankers take the view that collateral provided personally by project stakeholders is the solution to everything, as we say earlier, there can be issues about gaining ownership of the collateral and also of liquidating it. Forced asset sales by banks can offer bargains to purchasers as banks rarely run businesses and want cash to relend not assets.

When preparing the analysis of the market, it is important to be completely realistic: a product or service may be unique in its own strategic space but may well be the subject of competition by a wider market. Thus, as an example, an apparently new form of IT platform may address specific needs but the wider competition may imitate it and then spend a massive advertising budget to cause it to drop in the rankings. When looking at sustainable competitive advantage, the key question must be "how easy is it for a new competitor to set up"?

5.5.6. *Exploring Sustainable Competitive Advantage*

First, the macro environment needs to be explored; common approaches are the STEP approach and variants on it, where STEP stands for Sociological, Technological, Economic and Political. Some would add in Ethics, Environmental and Legal as separate factors.

A good STEP analysis considers the different factors that may impact on the future, sorted into the four headings. While some users of the model get excited about which list an item should inhabit, this can miss the importance of the analysis — a simple list is flat in perspective and the factors need to be expanded into weightings and impacts on the project. In this way, the analysis can be used to consider risks to cash flow.

However, the next hurdle to consider is the independence and the value of the professional judgment of those making the decisions to include items and the impact on the project. Decision-making research clarifies that in open group discussions, group members may defer to confident and powerful individuals, thus minimizing any dissenting voice. Group members may have a world view that is blinkered by filtration of information through what may be faulty cognitive lenses. Hence, a valid and well-informed external view is the best one and that is why independent reports can be valuable if time and resources are dedicated to them.

The OTSW model (more frequently known as SWOT) is another useful schema to think about firm or organization specific factors in terms of whether they are internal or external and thence consider if they may be managed to improve cash flow. Opportunities and Threats (the OT of the model) look at external factors and Strengths and Weaknesses (SW) are the internal ones. Again, an overly pedantic approach about arguments around the location of factors in the different boxes is not helpful and challenges should be raised about the basis of the origins and validity of opinions and their weighting. Some analysts may combine the two to produce a matrix that uses a template like Table 5.1 and while academic purists may object, as a thinking tool for managers, it may be helpful.

Although the famous *Five Forces of Competition* (or *Industry Attractiveness*) model set out by Michael Porter in 1980 (and widely available to view in many strategy books) is still often used for market analysis, it only reflects information *at that point in time* and *the definition of the market or industry* is critical — if too narrow, competition is

Table 5.1:   A STEP/SWOT Combination Matrix

Factors and	Opportunity			Threat			Strengths			Weaknesses		
Influences	Factor	Impact	Prob.	Factor	Impact	Prob.	Factor	Impact	Prob.	Factor	Impact	Prob.
Sociological												
Technological												
Economic												
Political												

Prepared by Carmel F. de Nahlik and Frank J. Fabozzi.

invisible; if too wide, the market is not easy to discern.[1] Porter sees the market being the line of business, so many companies will have several different Five Force models reflecting the different roles. The model is not applied to an organization as this makes it less effective as a diagnostic.

The model uses the following forces:

- bargaining power of suppliers (to the industry, not the company);
- bargaining power of buyers (from the industry — they may not be the end users);
- threat of new entrants and barriers to entry (new entrants may come in through acquisition);
- threat of substitution by new products or services (includes innovation in the industry and outside);
- competitive rivalry and its basis and intensity (includes analysis of strategic groups inside an industry).

The forces work in two directions and form the "fifth force".[2] A detailed five forces model is not easy to complete as it requires in-depth understanding of the dynamics of competition — so many are superficial and therefore less useful. Where this model can come into its own is through an analysis of the strategic groups in an industry and the basis of their membership as an indicator of types of competition and business models in use.

---

[1]Michael E. Porter, *Competitive Strategy: Techniques for Analyzing Industries and Competitors.* New York: Free Press, 1980.

[2]Readers may have already noticed that this model looks at the supply and distribution chains and the competitive landscape.

The other major approach to competitive advantage that is used in assessing projects or companies is the *Resource-Based View* (RBV) of the firm. Although Porter considers industry and market to be important — to compete in a specified market in Porter's view you need to be a low-cost producer or offer something special (differentiated) — the RBV and its proposers, attempts to look at both the industry and its factors that signal success and to look at the special characteristics of an organization that gives it sustainable competitive inside this market.

The key word here is *sustainable* competitive advantage — not just transient competitive advantage. Barney characterizes this as arising from resources, suggesting that valuable resources must be rare, inimitable and non-substitutable (VRIN) at the firm level.[3] These resources combine into capabilities that are then linked to the industry key success factors to develop a strategy that offers sustainable competitive advantage. If the resources and their capabilities are not valued by the industry, then that competitive advantage will either not exist or be unsustainable. Equally, if the industry key success factors are not recognized by firms competing in that industry, then there will be numbers of entrances and exits by firms that are unsuccessful until things change — the industry values different key success factors or firms reconfigure to meet industry expectations. Critical to this analysis is a clear understanding of the industry or more commonly industries in which the organization is competing and a pragmatic appraisal of its resources and capabilities.

Figure 5.1 may be helpful in understanding this.

The requirement for specialist industry and market knowledge explains why banks have teams or support resources that have in depth knowledge of cost structures and the basis of competition in specific industries and may specialize in lending to certain types of entities such as farmers, shipping companies or oil and gas companies.

Industries are not static, so today's success is not necessarily that of tomorrow. They are also fluid in their boundaries, especially in the new

---

[3] Jay Barney, "Firm Resources and Sustained Competitive Advantage," *Journal of Management*, 17, 1991, pp. 99–120. Note, however, this is contested space outside the US. Some think others, e.g. Birger Wernerfelt, "A Resource-Based View of the Firm," *Strategic Management Journal*, 5, 1984, pp. 171–180, have been erased from the RBV history; many Europeans favour Grant's article that was published simultaneously (1991) with Barney's. (Robert M. Grant, "The Resource-based Theory of Competitive Advantage: Implications for Strategy Formulation," *California Management Review*, 33, 1991, pp. 114–135.)

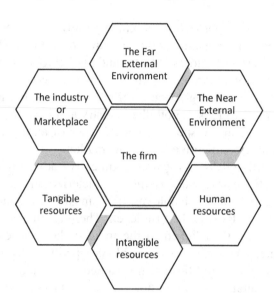

Figure 5.1:   The Layers of Influence on a Firm and its Sustainable Competitive Advantage

Prepared by CF de Nahlik, synthesized from a number of strategy approaches.

technological age, making definition tricky. Company managements will adjust resource allocation dependent in cash flow as a key enabler. The main advantage is to use this as a thinking tool to examine and test a strategy but not to rely on material given by experts.

As an example, it is easy to say that a public service may not have competition. The police service may not see a lot of different areas of competition and needs to understand the nature of the competition — competition is not from a single entity but from a series of entities that can use economies of scope or scale to make their provision of one part of the service offering of the police service or part of its "value chain" attractive — thus each service such as event security provision; personal protection; forensic crime support laboratories; in-house firearms training and certification; law enforcement will have different five forces of competition. Bundling them together may cause an overall five forces analysis to suggest there is no competition, until a privatization programme takes account of what may be cheaper when provided privately, and attractive to voters! Here the services represent different industries. The example also shows why analysis at the company level (a very common mistake) rather than the industry or market level can assist boards in making flawed decisions, believing that there is no competition.

"Bundling" products or services, while allowing for opaque pricing, can also give rise to confusion about the market served, leading to unsustainable competitive advantage.

5.5.7. Business Risks

Best practice in project management includes a risk analysis. Conventionally this includes a list of the major business risks faced by the company together with an analysis of probability, impact and mitigation steps taken or proposed by the management team, including insurance. Any pending litigation that may affect the sponsor companies should also be discussed here.

A risk register is mandatory these days and is continually updated, and there should be a risk register for both the project management and for the project financing as best practice.

5.5.8. Cash Flows

Aside from other externally audited or verified financial information on the organization, the cash flows for the venture for which the funding is required should be made available to the bank. Even if this is just working capital for the next year, it is important to understand the expectations around timing and pattern of repayment and debt service. Stock for the next year's selling season sounds fantastic, but the lender is reliant on the judgment of the creative and marketing teams and they can make an incorrect decision, especially in fast moving competitive environments. Yet again, this is why it is useful to have specialist industry teams in fund providers who may be able to spot groupthink and avoid losses.

The focus must be on cash — organizations face problems when they sell on account and do not collect, or accumulate unsold stock that may become dated and decrease in value (the classic examples of stock that may not depreciate are often named as trees for a woodland or forestry enterprise where further growth increases value and fine wines and spirits, but they must be properly stored).[4]

---

[4]It is worth checking on the format of any plan expected by potential funders to ensure all areas are covered. It is also a good idea to bring evidence of any support documentation,

The business plan lays out the skeleton of the transaction and forms the basis of other core documents. As such the directors and other important sponsors need to stand behind it legally and it therefore needs to be factually accurate and any claims made or statements made need to be supported by independent evidence. A signed copy of the business plan with a representation about the accuracy of its contents is a firm foundation for a project financing because it provides evidence that the sponsors and the team behind it are prepared to put their own reputations behind it.

5.6. Monitoring and Administering the Financing Inside a Bank

5.6.1. *Following the First Contact*

After reviewing the business plan, feasibility study or equivalent, the lender or investor will be in a position to discuss their views on the proposed financing. Presentations of this type are like job interviews or even dates. The parties are entering into a union that each hope will become a longer-term relationship with mutual benefits, so the same three areas that govern any joint venture partner selection choices apply here too — task, relationship and context drivers — all need to be compatible. Both sides need to feel they can trust each other in good times and in bad, as that trust will support the resolution of any problems that may arise without resorting to the letter of the contracts.

As the next step in building this relationship, the interested lender or investor will typically want to visit the sponsoring company to meet management, tour the facilities and pose questions resulting from the preliminary analysis. This visit presents an opportunity for the company to assess the lender and to determine whether a good working relationship can be developed between both parties. The company should determine whether the lender is familiar with the company's industry and understands its problems. The company should probe the lender to characterize its policy

---

valuations, etc., to the meeting to present it, or if by video to tell the audience that these documents are available. If they are not, or there are problems accessing this information, investors and lenders will sense that this transaction is likely to take a lot of time and may move on to easier deals.

regarding restrictive loan covenants and modifications of loan agreements. Visits can be highly informative and should not be skipped.

Project financing is a "two-way street". Because the project company's relationship with its lenders will be long-term, choosing a lender is an important decision that should not be dominated by a desire to obtain the lowest possible interest rate.

As the first step in locating sources of finance (both lenders or investors) for a proposed project financing, the project company (or its sponsor and its financial adviser which may of course be a bank) should develop a list of potentially interested lenders and investors.

Once the list is formulated and refined, the company or its adviser should contact investors and lenders in the order of their expected probable interest. These contacts can be made by telephone, email or in person. Obviously, a personal contact is most effective and is essential in most cases to engender trust.

The purpose of the initial contact with an investor or lender is to present the project to motivate the investor or lender to focus on the proposal in order to determine whether the lender or investor has an interest in the proposed financing.

In any meetings the format is usually a short presentation followed by a question and answer session. Such presentations are marketing opportunities but also need to be accurate and truthful and not oversell or mislead. An excellent presentation can get the lender or investor interested in reading and considering the plan and a poor presentation will have the opposite effect.

5.6.2. *Structuring the Transaction and Contact Points*

After the initial meeting, the lender or investor will complete its credit analysis and seek internal credit approval. If there are a number of banks involved then the lead bank will have decisions to make about underwriting a transaction (with the acceptance of the associated risks) or waiting till all participating banks have received final approvals — more on this in the next section.

If the amount is significant or the lender wishes to share the risk, an "offering memorandum" or similar will be developed. Like the business plan, the offering memorandum is a selling document and it should describe the proposed financing in sufficient detail to enable lenders or investors to determine their interest in the transaction.

The lender(s) and investor(s) interested in proceeding with the loan or investment will then be prepared to enter into final negotiations with respect to rates and terms. Several meetings are usually necessary in the case of complicated financings. When an understanding has been reached, the negotiated rate and terms are confirmed by using a commitment letter signed by both parties that indicates that a commitment is being made but final agreement is subject to approval of the project company's board of directors, the lender's (or investor's) approval committees and the execution of mutually satisfactory loan documentation. The time required for approval is a function of the complexity of the project financing but due account also needs to be taken of the possibility of delays due to holidays, absences and so on.

5.6.3. *Preparing the Documentation*

Once the lender's or investor's loan or investment committee approves the proposed financing, preparation of the loan agreement and other closing documentation begins. Usually, this involves several meetings and exchanges. Normally, the following parties are participants in these exchanges.

- The senior financial officer for the project company.
- Other key members of the company's management as may be appropriate.
- Company legal counsel and outside legal counsel, if necessary.
- Representatives of the lead lending bank and other major funding providers including those banks taking large tranches of the loan.
- Staff legal counsel of the lender or investor.
- Special outside counsel for the lender or investor.

In addition to its own legal fees, the project company usually is responsible for the fee of the lender's special counsel, appraisal fees and printing costs (if applicable). This needs to be made clear.

5.6.4. *Syndication*

Many large proposed project financings approach the lending limits of a lender, so it is in the best interests of the borrower to split the loan among a number of lenders so that they can share the risk, as well as to establish multiple banking relationships so there is no dependence on a single bank. It also allows the bank group (and indeed all the project stakeholders involved in the financing) to develop good working relationships with a view to providing additional financing for the sponsor's operations if required in the future. The inclusion of more than one set of views of the transaction can enhance the understanding of it for all parties, since each provider of funds will have a slightly different approach to the transaction.

The process of dividing up a financing package is termed "syndication" and is now used in many debt and equity contexts, though its origin was in the syndicated loan markets. An offering memorandum or its equivalent explains the deal in detail to interested parties subject to confidentiality undertakings.

Syndication can take several forms and there are a number of specialist roles.

To begin with, a bank can "bid" to underwrite the entire financial package or a given layer of it — as we shall see later, many project financings have multiple layers of debt and/or equity. This "bought deal" approach means the successful bank bidder assumes the underwriting risk and is reliant on its own capacity to absorb the transaction or its ability to find other bank participants. Bought deals will specify terms and conditions, including pricing, and there are examples of banks being unable to find takers for a specified deal at the negotiated price. In one case, the sponsors agreed to renegotiate but the failure to syndicate successfully the first time around delayed the project start-up. As a consequence, the bank concerned lost credibility in the market.

Alternatively, a bank might agree to assume a role where it agrees to put a syndicate together on a "best efforts" basis.

Managing and coordinating the syndication process (and possibly even carrying some underwriting risk, dependent on the deal), is referred to as "book running".

The bank that arranges or structures the deal is called the "arranging bank" and may or may not be the same as the advising bank.

Howsoever the process begins, once there is a need to talk to other banks, the loan is then split into "tranches" or layers with different reward packages attached to different sized pieces. So, the larger the piece or tranche, the greater is the potential reward. Voting power on syndicate matters is also linked to tranche size. Dependent on the size of tranche taken by each participant, there may be "lead managers" and other roles.

Other rewards come to banks with specialist roles such as coordinating the funding, acting as a reference for pricing purposes, and acting as a provider of specialist expertise. Clearly there can be possibilities for conflicts of interest and these should be declared as part of good governance processes.

Finding banks to participate can involve allies or even rivals of the lead bank; some sponsors use the opportunity to build closer relationships with banks that support them in other areas of their activities. Some sponsors have built the US and the UK syndicate groups that know the sponsor well and can therefore react quickly to project finance requests. Getting a new bank familiar with a sponsor takes time and can delay credit approvals. Syndicates should not be overly large as the group needs to react swiftly to events in the project.

Documentation negotiations can also take several forms — the days of the documentation coming from the sponsor's lawyers and banks being ordered to sign it are largely in the past. No sponsor wants significant delays and petty negotiations from naïve lenders that would delay the project. However, lenders will always have somewhat different views regarding the terms that make negotiating the financing package more time-consuming and subsequent changes more difficult.

Finally, communication mechanisms with the project company and/or the sponsor need to be clarified early. Costs rise if a member of staff needs to be hired just to deal with communications with syndicate members and while the ideal might appear to be that everything is channelled through the lead bank, syndicate members also like to feel they have a direct relationship with the project company and the sponsors.

The processing of the various pieces of information that are required before first drawdown of funds is usually handled by the lawyers to the various parties but once the first drawdown has taken place or any bonds needed have been issued, the transaction management switches to a different group of people who will handle the operations going forward. While some banks keep the relationship manager involved in all of the transactions relating to an organization and would expect the relationship manager to monitor the supply and conformity with transaction conditions of various pieces of evidence supplied to the lender or lending group, other banks may move the entire transaction into the hands of a post-deal management team that have the appropriate systems set-up to collect and monitor the financial health and well-being of the organization with whom there is a financial exposure.

For a client organization, it is very important that any such transition is handled carefully. The worst of all worlds is that it appears that a slick marketing operation exists up until the deal is signed after which the borrower is thrown to an uncaring and uninvolved group of people who have no apparent interest in creating any form of relationship. While we could argue that this might be appropriate for spot transactions, it does not generate any potential for goodwill on either side in the event that either the bank (bank group) or the borrower need to seek a waiver of some of the loan covenants. Force majeure can apply to banks as well as borrowers.

It is also important that members of the team that are processing ongoing financial documentation relating to a banking relationship possess the skills to go beyond inputting numbers into a spreadsheet — in other words to have the ability to study and interpret the financial statements. This is where financial scoring and the use of technology can mask issues that would otherwise be important either as a source of news about potential future business (news that a new facility is being opened in a city where the bank has a branch) or as a source of news about potential difficulties. The more notice that a bank has about such challenges — the easier it is to consider how both sides can work together to manage them and move forward.

The "workout" team (yet another group inside a bank) would almost certainly be called in if it looked as if there was the possibility that the loan would not be repaid or the contract honoured. This group normally includes highly skilled lawyers and financial analysts as well as industry specialists that may be called in for specific transactions. Its focus is not on an ongoing relationship but on minimizing any form of potential loss. Social niceties, while observed, would be taking second place to the focus on recovery of funds. Workout team membership requires a special set of skills and is not for every banker — some banks like to rotate promising staff through this group so that they can experience the consequences of bad decisions and also understand what it takes to put things right.

Finally, a post deal annual credit review process exists in most institutions, not least to monitor compliance with the expectations of various regulatory agencies so that in the event of a surprise inspection, the files are up-to-date and that there is a clear understanding of the status of the transaction. Although members of this group may not necessarily have primary contact with organizations that have a relationship with the bank, they may ask for information that will require either the post deal management team or the relationship manager to go back and request it and they often have considerable authority and influence inside a bank. Part of this group may be linked to an audit function so that there may be a regular internal inspection of the banks' operations and branches to ensure compliance with internal and external regulations and to ensure that any surprise external inspections will not reveal any nasty surprises.

5.7. The Impact of Changes to Global Regulation of Banks on Project Financing

Following the stability problems of the global banking system, a number of initiatives were put forward by central banks to ensure that banks met a minimum test of "capital adequacy" or provision of bank capital against obligations in order to show that the risk of insolvency or a run on a bank was diminished. Starting in 1991, a series of ever-tightening regulations have been imposed, introduced gradually to allow banks to change their loan and other portfolio exposure mixes and raise any capital required in an orderly manner.

The provision of capital to calculate key solvency ratios is based on grouping bank assets (loans and other exposures) into risk groupings, and the capital is considered to be either equity (Tier 1) or equity-like (Tier 2).

In practice, this has meant that bank credit committees (or lending committees) will look at asset risk classification, the existing capital allocation of the bank to its asset portfolio, the room under the model and the total yield and tenor of the transaction. By their nature, project finance transactions are riskier and generally longer term. The secondary market is not deep for all classes of transactions, so banks will either specialize in certain types of project financing deals or take the decision that maintaining the specialist staff required to be in this area versus the returns and the capital allocation required is not appropriate for the institution in that location at that time and exit the market. The result has been that the pool of banks that have the capability to structure and syndicate larger transactions has become more limited in size.

Continuing challenges as regulation develops include defining those financial institutions that are affected by these regulations, since banks are not the only providers of debt funds into the markets.

An additional effect was caused by the use of so-called "conduit structures" that did not appear on the balance sheets of banks. These Special Purpose Vehicles (SPVs) designed to insulate the main institution from any financial effects in the SPV were used for securitization of debt assets such as commercial paper or mortgages and supported by a back-up line from the parent financial institution in the event that the underlying assets could not be refinanced from the market at each 90-day maturity. No-one expected the market to fail, but as the asset quality diminished in the sub-prime mortgage boom, this was exactly what happened — the asset quality fell, as a result the conduits went in to default and the standby lines were called, backed up by the very assets the institutions had offloaded to the conduits, and thus of diminishing value. The conduit route had been attractive to move assets off the parent balance sheet and sell them to new investors, but the umbilical tether of the standby line, required to make the investment attractive, ultimately came back to haunt the parents.

A newer form of vehicle, the Special Purpose Acquisition Company (SPAC), has recently begun to attract attention. These are also known as a "blank-cheque" company. In essence, a SPAC is a shell company that raises money from investors by selling a "unit" in this IPO to investors for cash. The cash shell is then poised to complete a reverse merger with a private company, thus avoiding the time-consuming process of getting permissions, writing a prospectus and marketing the deal. The success (or failure) is based on the ability of the individuals promoting the SPAC (the sponsors) to choose target companies wisely. Venture capital or private equity firms looking to list investments that are sufficiently mature to become public companies may use SPACs as another exit route. However, not all SPACs have had a happy ending and natural resource companies, vulnerable to supply and demand risks, are considered especially risky.

Variations on the capital adequacy calculations and local stress tests of domestic banking systems have moved the capital adequacy ratios into ever more complex definitions to try and capture the essence of solvency, the latest being the liquidity coverage ratio (LCR) and the net stable funding ratio (NSFR). (The former looks at cash outflow under stress and the latter seeks to prevent a mismatch between a bank's funding and its assets in the wake of the collapse of the UK bank, Northern Rock). In essence these are short- and longer-term resilience measures.

5.8. Case Study: Blood on Their Hands

The following case study tells the story of how a seemingly great business plan can run into unexpected problems. The story of Theranos, a privately held health technology company, is well documented in the book *Bad Blood* by John Carreyrou[5] and in various documentaries, podcasts and articles. Simply stated, the CEO, Elizabeth Holmes, came up with a novel idea to look at blood testing system that would remove the need for phlebotomists to dig around looking for a vein to offer a decent size blood sample, leaving nervous patients in pain and with haematomas from failed attempts. In this pitch, the amount of blood taken would be very small, and the analysis performed on a proprietary machine with results fed back to physicians and patients very quickly. The machine would be the size of a printer. There have always been questions about the size of the blood sample obtained from this finger prick approach and the requirement for enough blood to meet a battery of tests. (We might consider the vials filled in conventional blood collection as a comparator.)

The diagnostic lab market was estimated to be worth over US$19 billion in the US and US$40–50 billion worldwide in 2011–2012 according to studies referenced in a 2016 publication[6] available on The National Centre for Biotechnology Information website, though larger numbers have also been suggested.

At age 19, Holmes dropped out of Stanford in 2003 to pursue her goal, a pathway not atypical for many disruptive start-ups on California and closely following the paths taken by her acknowledged heroes, Steve Jobs and Larry Ellison. The latter was one of her advisers early in the history of the company and an early investor in Theranos. In 2004, the company had its first round of fundraising for US$6.9 million and valued itself at US$30 million. By 2014, the company was believed to be worth US$9 billion and had raised US$400 million in equity, making Holmes the first female multibillionaire celebrated on the famous *Forbes* list.

---

[5]John Carreyrou, *Bad Blood: Secrets and Lies in a Silicon Valley Start-up*. New York, NY: Alfred A. Knopf, 2018.

[6]See "Overview of the Diagnostics Market," Chapter 3 in Chantal Morel, Lindsay McClure, Suzanne Edwards, Victoria Goodfellow, Dale Sandberg, Joseph Thomas and Elias Mossialos (eds.), *Ensuring Innovation in Diagnostics for Bacterial Infection: Implications for Policy*, Observatory Studies Series, No. 44, European Observatory on Health Systems and Policies, Denmark, 2016.

In 2013, a partnership with Walgreens commercialized the tests and opened them up to the general public by making them available at the drugstore chain in the US. In July 2015, the Federal Drug Administration approved a test for the highly infectious herpes simplex virus but by December of that year, following damning press reports, a deal with the Safeway food store group had cratered, and questions were being asked by regulators about standards compliance of a Theranos lab in Newark, California. Safeway had reportedly invested US$350 million in 800 locations to offer the instore blood tests.[7] Theranos agreed to refrain from blood testing as part of a settlement. A loan from the Fortress Group secured against the company's patents staved off bankruptcy for a short time, but after that it was all downhill. The company was charged with fraud by the SEC in 2018, with Holmes and the former company president charged with wire fraud and conspiracy, and Theranos' stock ceased trading in September 2018. The fraud trial was delayed until 2021.

How did it all go so wrong?

While the initial idea was an interesting one, the company needed to develop the test machine and the tests at a competitive price and find a market. The market strategy was a good one but while the company certainly devoted resources to the development of the testing machine and the tests themselves, this part of the plan was a failure. An initial sortie into micro fluid systems was unsuccessful and the next attempt — to repurpose a robot that had been used to dispense glue, named the "Edison" — was also unreliable. It seems much of the data provided to reassure regulators, investors and partners were based on traditional test results. Complex technical arguments about the Theranos process have been widely aired in the press, including whether the blood from a fingerprick (the Theranos proposition) is the same as blood obtained from veins and thus likely to give reliable results. Theranos also attempted to change the law in states such as Arizona to drop the requirement for a doctor's order for a blood test, making the walk in while shopping route much easier.[8]

---

[7]John Carreyrou, "Safeway, Theranos Split After $350 Million Deal Fizzles; Grocery Chain Built Clinics in More Than 800 Stores But Never Began Blood Tests; Code-Named 'T-Rex'," *The Wall Street Journal*, November 10, 2015.

[8]Ron Leuty, "Theranos: Testing Times Lie Ahead for Secretive Blood-Testing Firm," *San Francisco Business Times*, June 29, 2015.

Many board members of Theranos were high profile individuals such as George Schultz and Henry Kissinger and high profile net worth investors such as media mogul Rupert Murdoch (thought the latter sold his shares back before things went badly wrong), Betsy DeVos and Walmart's Waltons. It has been suggested that American business and government leaders lost more than US$600 million in private investments in the company.[9] Other investors included a number of well-known funds and it is hard to believe that all of these investors did not complete detailed due diligence that might have raised questions or were just blinded by a great sales pitch from a persuasive young woman, blurring over the difficult areas.

Theranos burned through a lot of money in a short time provided by funds or experienced investors — not atypical for the many start-ups in Silicon Valley. Was there an element of herd mentality in the rush to invest? We shall never know. What was different was that rather than selling devices with software that might require subsequent debugging by users, or upgrades or fixes, these tests were concerned with fundamental health issues that were nontrivial and inaccurate. Real people and their lives and loved ones were affected by these misleading or inaccurate results. All tests had to be voided with consequent financial and psychological effects on patients who did not know about their health status with any certainty. The tests and the machine delivering them just did not work and there have been suggestions of a bullying culture and worse with one apparent suicide by a Theranos key employee. This is why healthcare start-ups require closer monitoring, but realistically there is no protection against the fraud of submitting a different batch of samples (which is what it is claimed took place) so approvals would continue. The personal fallout and misery from this debacle is the stuff of which mass action lawsuits are launched against any entity involved with deep pockets and the story should serve as a warning to any venture capitalist or indeed any finance provider to check and recheck the proposition and the people again and again.

Theranos was described as a unicorn in its heyday — a privately held start-up company valued at more than US$1 billion. Sadly, this unicorn was as ephemeral as the creature of myth.

---

[9]Michael Sheetz, "Secretary DeVos, Walmart Heirs and Other Investors Reportedly Lost Over $600 Million On Theranos," *CNBC*, May 4, 2018.

Chapter 6

Project Cost Estimation

Introduction

Project cost estimation is the process of forecasting the costs of all resources related to a project. The US General Accountability Office (GAO) provides the following definition for cost estimation: "the summation of individual cost elements, using established methods and valid data, to estimate the future costs of a programme, based on what is known today".[1]

In general, costs can be categorized as the costs associated with constructing a project and the costs associated with operating a project once it is constructed. Project cost estimation is different from cost control which involves the monitoring the actual costs and comparing them to the forecasted/budgeted cost and cost validation which involves the assessment of how good the projected costs were. Cost monitoring and validation are particularly important during the portfolio construction phase.

Project cost estimation involves three key elements: scope, cost and timeframe to completion. All of these elements impact the estimation of costs for a project and as each one changes, it in turns changes cost estimates. For example, at the outset of a project, its scope may be

---

[1]*GAO Cost Estimating and Assessment Guide Best Practices for Developing and Managing Capital Program Costs.* United States Government Accounting Office, Applied Research and Methods, March 2009, GAO-09-3SP. https://www.gao.gov/assets/80/77175. pdf. One of the responsibilities of GAO is to assist the US Congress and the Office of Management and Budget in making decisions about the funding of public projects by providing information about the potential costs of such projects and project performance.

well defined. As a result, cost estimation is difficult. As the scope of the project becomes more clearly defined, it is easier to estimate cost, but it may result in a dramatically different cost estimation than when the project was less well defined. The cost can decline materially if the scope is less than originally defined and the opposite if the scope is broadened. Moreover, if the timeframe to completion increases, costs will increase because of inflation and additional financing costs. If, instead, the timeframe to completion is shortened, this may also increase costs due to the need to accelerate some tasks at a higher than expected cost and the risk of project failure. Typically, the costs of most projects are underestimated in every industry and every country as explained later in this chapter.

In this chapter, we look at four linked areas: (1) the nature of project costs; (2) estimating project costs, (3) forecasting project costs and (4) the biases in forecasting project costs. We being by looking at some facets of project costs and explain common errors in including costs or in looking at cost behaviour, as well as the idea of managing the project process to achieve goals in a tight timeframe (known as "scrum"). Scrum can be used to look at keeping costs down if the project is slipping in its budget. We discuss the need to establish a database of costs in similar projects against which new projects can be compared. We then turn to how to tackle the more complex area of technical cost estimation, followed by a review of forecasting costs and project outcomes from a more holistic perspective. In this discussion, we consider different approaches to forecasting that can be useful for project teams. Whatever the role of a project stakeholder, understanding the nature of costs in a project can assist in gaining consensus if new negotiations are required. Finally, we examine the track record of project cost forecasting and the biases that result in an underestimation of costs.

The purpose of this chapter is not to explain how to actually estimate the cost of major projects but rather to understand the issues, the challenges and the methodologies that are used to obtain cost estimates. The sponsor or the consultant will then be aware of the limitations of any proposed project cost estimates and where necessary request a revision of the estimates based on different assumptions. Nevertheless, the banker or provider of funds to a project needs to have some frame against which they can see that the project is viable and not "gold-plated". This also gives important insights into the professionalism of the project sponsor team.

6.1. The Nature of Project Costs

Although some of this section will be all too familiar to those who have studied basic managerial accounting, we provide a brief refresher.

A project's success is measured at the highest level by the excess of revenues over expenditure, a part the expenditures being related to project costs. The breakdown of those revenues to their different streams and the benchmarking with industry norms can give rise to a good handle on the expected cash inflow. It is worth remembering that cash inflows are not necessarily immediate — a good example is that of a small participant in an oilfield that is located offshore. There is no pipeline because the oilfield economics did not justify this investment and so tankers come along and lift the oil from designated locations in the oilfield. One option is to allow a bigger participant to lift its share of the oil as well, sell it and pay the proceeds. Most likely there would be a service fee for doing that. Hence, it may make sense for a smaller participant to wait until it is in a position to have a full tanker load of its own oil lifted, so that it can sell that larger quantity on the market and receive a greater share. This could take quite a long time, dependent on the daily production rate, the percentage interest and indeed weather conditions. If this course is taken, the pattern of revenues that will go into small company's bank account will not be evenly spread. Working capital will need to be produced to bridge the gap and make sure that payments of salaries, etc., take place on time.

The next two question when performing an economic evaluation of a project is (1) which costs should be allocated to the project and which costs should be allocated to the company that is making the decision to invest in the project and (2) how do these costs behave. We will look at this further in the section on sunk costs.

6.1.1. *Cost Behaviour*

To understand cost behaviour requires a knowledge of the way that those costs arise. Many simple project models will aggregate costs without breaking them down in detail. Although this can be useful for providing a "quick and dirty" insight to whether a project is likely to generate adequate returns for all its stakeholders, the danger lies in the subtleties of the behaviour of these costs over time. For example, there may be a line for labour costs and these may be projected into the future at a constant rate of escalation. The labour needed for a project may be a mixture of full-time and part-time, with the latter contracted into work when needed. Increasingly, labour is drawn from a number of countries and depending on where the contract is written, will depend on the governing laws as they pertain to labour.

As an example from shipping, the officers will probably be drawn from countries where there has been a naval tradition for a long period of time such as the US and thus these officers will be paid more, reflecting their experience and possibly unionization. In contrast, the crew may be recruited from poorer countries, where the promise of being compensated in US dollars is very attractive and wages are lower. The use of "flags of convenience" or so-called "open registries" for ships can allow for the groups to have different payment bases and bypass domestic legislation designed to protect mariners. One example is the US Jones Act (or Merchant Marine Act) of 1920. Together "with the Passenger Vessel Services Act of 1886, it reserves marine transportation of freight and passengers to US-built, maintained, documented, owned and crewed vessels".[2] There are clear rules about the numbers of US crew on a US flagged ship — 100% need to hold USCG certification and there are rules about US citizenship.[3,4] Paying all the crew on US scales would make the labour cost rise sharply and render the ship less competitive. So, ship owners use flags of convenience, registering their ships in countries where there are fewer controls. Nevertheless, it is unreasonable to assume that all of the labour costs will rise at the same rate. Instead, it might make more sense to split the labour costs into two categories — officers and crew and consider escalation based on views of those labour costs in each country.

Not all project costs "behave" in the same way. In order to de-risk the project, some costs may be hedged.[5] In these cases, insurance is taken out either as a formal insurance risk taken by insurers or by the use of derivative products (i.e. futures, forwards, swaps and options). Although it may seem that the costs are covered against defined risks and/or perhaps limited to movement within a defined band, not all risks can be addressed in these ways. Even with insurance, there may be risks as reinsurance

---

[2]US Department of Transport Maritime Administration, Cabotage laws.

[3]US Coastguard Manning Requirement Rules.

[4]US versus non US flag regulatory differences. http://onlinepubs.trb.org/onlinepubs/mb/Wells091615.pdf.

[5]For a further discussion, see Chapters 11 to 18 in the companion book.

contracts may be placed in areas of high political uncertainty. The same counterparty risk applies in derivative contracts dependent on whether they are exchange-traded products and therefore guaranteed by the exchange or directly with a counterparty. Changes to the latter's financial strength can affect the counterparty's ability to perform on the contract should it be necessary. Not all risks can be insured — political risk insurance is not universally available.

Perhaps the first way a project's costs can be managed might be by using fixed price contracts? That way all costs are "set in stone" and there can be no sudden increases. While this is a great idea in theory, there are several issues that need to be considered. This works if there is a very clearly defined project and no new technology involved or any deviation from the processes laid out in the contracts. As we will see in the case study in Chapter 10, with the example of tolling software, long-term projects involving cutting edge technology may need to adapt to new computer systems. Thus, there will be a deviation from the original plan and additional costs will be incurred. Tough negotiating of the headline price on the main contract can be offset by a careful contractor through change order costs. There may be a requirement for offset of contract expenditures against local projects or goods and services. Here there may be quality or suitability difference issues making it necessary to spend more than budgeted on bridging the gap. Finally, a local content specification in the contract specified for bidding cannot always be satisfied because the resources are not locally available, and the contractor must invest to ensure that the contract terms can be met, and local resources used. These costs will not be absorbed without questions being raised.

Alternatively, the cost-plus contract form could be used and costs would be covered with a defined margin. However, the contracting entity or project sponsor would not be happy as there might be unnecessary "gold-plating" — using the very highest specification materials when there would be little difference in performance from using cheaper ones and there is no cap on the contract so expenditure could run out of control causing issues for the sponsor and other stakeholders. In Section 4.3.25, we mention the idea of gain sharing as a cost management strategy.

6.1.2. *Sunk Costs*

In this section, we look at "sunk costs" — those costs already incurred that are not retrievable. Sunk costs are important in decision-making because of a phenomenon known as the "sunk cost fallacy". This occurs when a decision maker looks at the sunk costs and believes (often mistakenly) that by spending even more money, a situation can be retrieved. An example can be seen in the Theranos case at the end of the last chapter. The machine did not work, but more money was thrown at the problem to come up with a less than perfect fix rather than accepting that there had been an error and starting again from scratch.

The feasibility study costs are sunk costs, and essentially the cost of an option on the project and as such are an equity matter and should not be attributed to the project directly. The feasibility study is the basis for the sponsor company to decide to invest in the project and as such is outside the main project envelope. If the project does not go ahead, the cost is written off but the practice of including it, often as an asset, if the project does go ahead is to be discouraged. The project boundaries relate to the project after the decision to go ahead has been made, but for smaller sponsors, the possibility of recovery of this cost is very attractive. Even less palatable is borrowing the money for the feasibility study. If this is not a "dead cert" or "sure thing" then it may not be paid back. It is an equity risk and should be paid for by equity funding, not debt!

Historic problems have occurred when research and development costs (and these need to be separated into the two categories) were lumped together and capitalized on the balance sheet pending a successful outcome. In extreme cases, companies went into bankruptcy because they ran out of cash. The same approach has been used with natural resource companies where potential gold mines of the future have been captured on the balance sheet as valuable assets even though they might never happen. The result of this has been a tightening of the accounting rules and stock listing rules after disappointed investors complained. There are strict conventions relating to the amount of a resource that can be capitalized and declared as an asset that relate to an independent expert assessment of the probability (P) of its realization. Reserve reports will use the newer nomenclature of P90, P60 or even 1P, 2P rather than the older terms such as "proven", "probable" and "possible" to give decision makers and other interested stakeholders a figure for the expert estimated probability of this reserve number being met or exceeded. These terms only apply to technical reserves and are strictly defined by various professional bodies. Care needs to be taken that the engineering definitions that are technically based are not confused with the economics and surplus cash flow or profitability.

6.1.3. *Project Cost Structures*

All costs have their own pattern of behaviour. They do not universally increase on a linear basis. Capacity constraints mean that some costs will be "stepped" whereby a larger facility is built to cope with the new increased volumes and this may mean that for a time, economies of scale and scope are not optimized until enough volume builds up at the new plant. There may also be requirements to put additional infrastructure in if volume increases and that together with construction can lead to timing delays for the new increase to go on stream.

For example, an airport is running at capacity. It needs a new runway to deal with projected traffic increases. The new enlargement will require planning permission before any work can start. Expansion of an airport will inconvenience those living nearby and they may object and delay the process. There will also be a significant financing requirement. Once the approval has been granted, roads may need to be re-routed or even new roads built to move people and goods to the expanded airport. Construction contracts will be let or awarded and manpower and materials sourced to build the new runway. Jet fuel storage tanks may need to be built to support the increased number of planes. Other facilities such as shops, may need to be approached to ensure all space is producing the most revenue possible. Skilled support people will need to be hired and a training programme put in place to ensure succession planning. Airline staff to staff the new terminals (so a need for functioning electronics to link into various systems seamlessly, not least air traffic control and booking systems) and possibly more immigration and customs staff will also need to be found. However, provision of these additional resources and services may be outside the direct control of the project even though they are "mission critical" to its success.

Understanding the pattern of cost increases especially when they are non-linear is key to cost control and project optimization.

6.2. Forecasting Project Costs

The art of good forecasting of costs is closely linked to and an extension of the project cost estimation. While the simplest way is to use some form of extrapolation, the granularity of the costs may make this a much more complex exercise than simply plugging in a percentage increase number to the project model. The use of expert systems such as rule-based forecasting relies on the expertise of managers because of their experience to weight different factors in an extrapolation. The limitation is that the series being forecast is statistically "well-behaved" and follows a known pattern. Other forecasting methods rely on judgement and behavioural factors more and more but are reliant on methods to structure and ascertain the nature of the expert knowledge and how to apply it.

More recently we have seen artificial intelligence used to create expert forecasting systems and replicate skill judgement such as in the area of playing chess or medical diagnostics. The cost of the systems is beyond a smaller project sponsor's budget. However, to manage an asymmetry where contractors may have access to such a system in-house and a local sponsor host may not, professional cost estimating firms have attempted to fill the gap.

Scott Armstrong[6] in his excellent edited collection of papers on forecasting, talks about the need for simplicity, consideration of all of the important variables (based on theory and practice), the requirement to collect the longest series of data possible, consideration of all previous work and going from the general to the specific (not the other way around) when looking at statistical models. While this may seem like common sense advice, all too often these ideal processes get overtaken by lack of preparation, surrender to external pressures or overconfidence. Getting a forecaster to specify why a model may contain errors or just be wrong — something that may be considered a natural pairing with a future estimate of a project — can be perceived as criticism and result in defensive behaviour that is not helpful to the economic evaluation of a project. Using feedback should improve the forecast, but that is dependent on a supportive and constructive corporate culture, a topic that is beyond the scope of this book.

6.2.1. *The Forecasting Team*

The use of workshops to assess risks overlaps with the forecasting activity. Such workshops are well developed in many large companies that regularly execute megaprojects. Manuals setting out how the workshop

---

[6] J. Scott Armstrong (ed.), *Principles of Forecasting: A Handbook for Researchers and Practitioners*. New York, NY: Springer, 2001.

should run may be available, and perhaps a process for exposing the risks perceived to be associated with a particular project, since there is no single list and risks are perceived differently by different stakeholders.

Related to this will be scenarios derived from specialist teams that are short-term in nature (maybe up to 3-year assignments) in order to stay fresh. These teams will develop two or three complex and detailed scenarios against which all projects will be measured and evaluated. The scenario team may be isolated from day-to-day project life. However, once they leave the team, former scenario developers can be useful members of risk and other workshop groups. The danger lies in the same team evaluating all projects. On the one hand, this can give rise to development of a detailed database of projects improving expert judgement by team members. On the other hand, there is a real danger of "group think" or convergence. In a stable environment, this is less important than in the more politically unstable areas where many large natural resource projects take place. There needs to be careful questioning based on different backgrounds and perceptions and different access to sources of information to elicit the widest most possible views on risks. There are challenges within a group where more junior members may get overruled by senior individuals or feel unable to contribute for cultural reasons. Finally, the use of external team members may appear attractive but can give rise to information leakages. There are also additional costs associated with the use of external team members.

For the smaller sponsor or provider of goods and services to a project, risk workshops may just not be an available option. The temptation is to look at data provided by official sources on economic outlooks, price forecasts, and the like. This may appear to be a safe option but all forecasts are coloured by the objectives of the provider of the forecast. No government will be happy to say that its economy is not in good shape and indeed will be trying to suppress such information because of the potentially negative impact. Here again, risk consultants, political risk consultants and industry consultants will all be happy to sell a report or their services.

6.2.2. *Behavioural Economics and Decision-Making*

One of the most interesting developments in economics since the 1970s has been the rise to prominence of the recognition that rationality is bounded (to use the term of Herbert Simon, the 1978 recipient of the Nobel Prize in Economic Sciences) and that the individuals who trade in markets or make complex financial decisions are not completely rational. The acknowledgement of behavioural influences and the move away from purely statistical modelling affects projects and their financing in a number of ways.

First, project champions can fall in love with their projects — Who has not seen a "pet project" that makes no economic sense go ahead? When the project champion is a senior member of an organization this can be a serious problem. In fact, studies have shown that once a project begins, it is rarely terminated even if the performance indicates that there is underperformance.[7] The reasons are psychological, conflicts of interest and erroneous decision-making based on sunk costs.

Second, members of project teams can also become isolated from reality leading to behaviours that are not acceptable to wider stakeholders. British Petroleum and its partners did not handle the Gulf of Mexico oil spill in a way that was satisfactory to their stakeholders in the immediate aftermath of the accident. However, there are many other examples. Placing pressures on operational staff that can cause problems is not something that is visible to the providers of finance until things go wrong. So, knowledge of the customer should also include knowledge of their internal culture, admittedly very difficult to achieve in a competitive banking market without investing in the time to look at members of the organization in other contexts.

In the preceding paragraph, we discussed about groupthink, another manifestation of a behavioural problem within a team.

When a project has derailed, commitment may escalate rather than terminate the project, on the grounds that a "bit more might fix it", similar to the sunk cost fallacy already mentioned. This is a common trading error in financial markets but is also seen in mega projects that for whatever reason cannot be stopped.

In the case at the end of this chapter, a flagship project conceived for all the right reasons has gone badly wrong! Some are to do with costs and others to do with the "softer" criteria mentioned in this chapter.

---

[7] See Isabelle Royer, "Why Bad Projects Are So Hard to Kill," *Harvard Business Review*, 81, 2003, pp. 48–45 and by Duncan Simester and Juanjuan Zhang, "Why Are Bad Products So Hard To Kill?" *Management Science*, 56, 2010, pp. 1161–1179.

6.3. Methodologies for Estimating Project Costs

Different estimation methods are used at different stages of the project.
We briefly review the more popular ones here.

6.3.1. *Historical Cost Data Analysis*

This methodology, also referred to as analogous estimate analysis, uses
the realized costs on different segments of similar projects as the foundation for estimating the corresponding costs for the project whose
costs are being sought. Of course, the analysis involves adjusting
costs to account for differences in a project's size, location and market
conditions. For example, in the construction industry, even for two
construction projects that are similar, the likelihood that construction
process will be exactly replicated is very low because projects are often
site-specific.[8]

Reference costing is one example of analogous estimate analysis and
has some similarities with expert and parametric cost estimating. Used in
the UK National Health Service, it allows the cost elements of new projects to be compared against a database of costs collected on all projects
providing secondary healthcare from 2008 to 2017. The data are collected
using guidelines specified by the Department of Health and collected by
the Service Evaluation body, Monitor. Reference costing is also linked to
reference class forecasting, a technique used by some consultants and
academics to blend better cost estimation and the psychology of decision-
making to improve outcomes in major projects. More recently, its use has
been extended to other large projects.

The key risk with any analogous cost estimation system is maintaining an accurate reference cost base and not relying on mechanical inputs
to update it without some judgement being applied to look at the reliability and validity of the numbers. The activities that produce costs can
change in nature and process re-engineering or innovation can cause costs
to be reduced, but the application of that innovation to each project needs
to be scrutinized.

---

[8]Abdulelah Aljohani, Dominic Ahiaga-Dagbui and David Moore, "Construction Projects
Cost Overrun: What Does the Literature Tell Us?" *International Journal of Innovation,
Management and Technology*, 8 (2), 2017, pp. 137–143.

6.3.2. *Parametric Cost Modelling*

The parametric model uses statistical analysis of historical cost data to obtain an estimated cost. Typically, the statistical tool used is multiple regression analysis where the dependent variable is the project cost for the projects in the sample and the independent (explanatory variables) are what have been determined to be the drivers of project cost. For example, in projecting the cost of facility, cost data of recent projects (adjusted for inflation) would be the dependent variable and project physical data such as square footage, floor plan layout, electrical and plumbing requirements and location would be independent variables.

6.3.3. *Bottom-Up Analysis*

Each activity has different component costs (individual work packages). The analysis begins with these activities and rolls up the estimated costs for all of the individual work pages to obtain an estimate for total cost of a project. This approach is also referred to as detailed estimating or engineering build-up because it begins with identifying the tasks that are to be estimated and based on the lowest task level create a range of estimates. It works best for projects that have a well-defined scope so that the tasks can be defined but not for projects whose scope is not well defined.

6.3.4. *Top-Down Analysis*

With top-down analysis, it is assumed that the project's total budget is determined when the project begins. Given the total budget, the forecasting team proceeds to identify the costs of each activity. An activity is a task or job. Following this approach, the forecasting team determines the number of required activities to complete the project and then determines the quantity of each activity that can be realized within a fixed budget. The forecasting team may then decide to either add or eliminate certain activities in order to stay within the fixed budget.

Once the general scope of a project is defined, this top-down approach is used at the early stage of a project and the major activities of the project are identified. The result of a top-down analysis is a rough estimate (a ballpark estimate) of the project. However, the level of detail at this stage is typically unavailable or is very limited. An estimate of the activities is done one by one. The principal benefit of this approach is the likelihood of being able to utilize more holistic data from similar completed projects. In doing so, unforeseen risks for which contingencies must be taken into account are identified. Moreover, this approach reduces the risk of failing to identify certain costs or activities.

6.3.5. *Three-Point Estimate Analysis*

For each activity cost, three cost estimates are made: pessimistic cost, most likely cost and optimistic cost. The weighting scheme is selected by the forecasting team. Two popular weighting schemes are the triangular distribution and the beta distribution.

For the triangular distribution, the cost estimate is obtained as follows:

Cost estimate = (pessimistic cost + most likely cost + optimistic cost)/3

As can be seen, the triangular distribution gives equal weight to all the pessimistic and optimistic costs as it does to the most likely cost.

The most commonly used weighting is the beta distribution given by

$$\text{Cost estimate} = (1/6) \text{ pessimistic cost} + (2/3) \text{ most likely cost} + (1/6) \text{ optimistic cost}$$

Greater weight is assigned to the most likely cost using this weighting scheme. This weighting scheme is based on the Program Evaluation and Review Technique (PERT), a technique that is used in planning and scheduling large and complex project to analyze a project's tasks.[9]

A measure of risk of provided by the beta distribution is the variance which is computed as follows:

$$\text{Variance of the cost estimate} = \frac{(\text{optimistic cost} - \text{pessimistic cost})^2}{36}$$

---

[9]PERT was developed in the late 1950s by the US Navy's Special Projects Office in managing the Polaris nuclear submarine project.

Since the variance is in squared units, taking the square root of the variance of cost the cost estimate gives the standard deviation which is easier measure to understand since it is in terms of cost, not cost squared.

6.4. US GAO Guidance for Estimating Project Costs

Organizations sponsoring or funding infrastructure projects typically provide manuals to provide guidance in estimating costs. For example, in its 440-page cost estimating manual, the US Government Accounting Office (GAO) provides cost guide principles that should be used to assess how credible a programme's cost estimate for budget and decision-making purposes and the status of a programme using earned value management (EVM). EVM compares the budgeted cost of work with the outcome at that point with the earned value and is used to determine the progress of a project against baseline assumptions, making it part of the cost and scheduling activity. The Earned Value is the percentage of completed work at that point multiplied by the budget at completion, so it does not reflect any added synergistic value from a completed project. EVM is reliant on three sets of information: earned value, actual cost and planned value. By comparing actual value created or added at a given point in the project schedule with anticipated value created or added at that point, progress can be assessed and interventions planned for.

In a 1972 report, *Theory and Practice of Cost Estimating for Major Acquisitions*,[10] the GAO identified the basic characteristics of effective cost estimation that it studied and that are still valid today. These basic characteristics are shown in Table 6.1.

The GAO has described the best practices that should be followed in order to develop accurate and credible cost estimates for a project. The cost estimating process is shown in Table 6.2. Moreover, the GAO identified 12 steps that should be followed to generate reliable and estimates. Table 6.3 shows the 12 steps of a high-quality cost estimating process and the risks associated with each step. These risks represent

---

[10]Comptroller General of the United States, *Theory and Practice of Cost Estimating for Major Acquisitions*, pp. 31–32.

Table 6.1: GAO's Basic Characteristics of Credible Cost Estimates

Characteristic	Description
Clear identification of task	Estimator must be provided with the system description, ground rules and assumptions, and technical and performance characteristics.
	Estimate's constraints and conditions must be clearly identified to ensure the preparation of a well-documented estimate.
Broad participation in preparing estimates	All stakeholders should be involved in deciding mission need and requirements and in defining system parameters and other characteristics.
	Data should be independently verified for accuracy, completeness, and reliability.
Availability of valid data	Numerous sources of suitable, relevant, and available data should be used.
	Relevant, historical data should be used from similar systems to project costs of new systems; these data should be directly related to the system's performance characteristics.
Standardized structure for the estimate	A standard work breakdown structure, as detailed as possible, should be used, refining it as the cost estimate matures and the system becomes more defined.
	The work breakdown structure ensures that no portions of the estimate are omitted and makes it easier to make comparisons to similar systems and programs.
Provision for program uncertainties	Uncertainties should be identified and allowance developed to cover the cost effect.
	Known costs should be included and unknown costs should be allowed for.
Recognition of inflation	The estimator should ensure that economic changes, such as inflation, are properly and realistically reflected in the life-cycle cost estimate.
Recognition of excluded costs	All costs associated with a system should be included; any excluded costs should be disclosed and given a rationale.
Independent review of estimates	Conducting an independent review of an estimate is crucial to establishing confidence in the estimate; the independent reviewer should verify, modify, and correct an estimate to ensure realism, completeness, and consistency.
Revision of estimates for significant program changes	Estimates should be updated to reflect changes in a system's design requirements. Large changes that affect costs can significantly influence program decisions.

Prepared by Prepared by Comptroller General of the United States, *Theory and Practice of Cost Estimating for Major Acquisitions.*

Table 6.2:   The Cost Estimating Process

Initiation and research	Assessment	Analysis	Presentation
Your audience, what you are estimating, and why you are estimating it are of the utmost importance	Cost assessment steps are iterative and can be accomplished in varying order or concurrently	The confidence in the point or range of the estimate is crucial to the decision maker	Documentation and presentation make or break a cost estimating decision outcome

Prepared by Figure 1 (p. 7). *GAO Cost Estimating and Assessment Guide Best Practices for Developing and Managing Capital Program Costs.* United States Government Accounting Office, Applied Research and Methods, March 2009, GAO-09-3SP.

the challenges faced in estimating project costs which can result in poor estimates.

6.5. How Good Have Project Cost Forecasts Been?

Now that we have provided guidance on project cost estimation, the interesting question is how good practitioners have been in estimating costs. The literature on estimating costs for mega projects, however, has shown that the track record with respect to coming close to a project's completion cost being close to the budgeted cost is dismal. The following is a summary of these studies:

- A 1995 study by The Standish Group of more than 8,000 projects reported that only 16% of the projects could satisfy the three performance criteria: completing projects on time, within budgeted cost and quality standard.[11]
- Sebastian Morris estimated that delays and cost overruns were common for public projects in India.[12]

---

[11] The Standish Group Report, *Chaos Report*, 1995.
[12] Sebastian Morris, "Cost and Time Overruns in Public Sector Projects," *Economic and Political Weekly*, 25 (47), 1990, pp. M154–M168.

Table 6.3:   **The 12 Steps of a High-Quality Cost Estimating Process**

Step	Description	Associated Task
1	Define estimate's purpose	■ Determine estimate's purpose, required level of detail, and overall scope ■ Determine who will receive the estimate
2	Develop estimating plan	■ Determine the cost estimating team and develop its master schedule ■ Determine who will do the independent cost estimate ■ Outline the cost estimating approach ■ Develop the estimate timeline
3	Define programme characteristics	■ In a technical baseline description document, identify the programme's purpose and its system and performance characteristics and all system configurations ■ Any technology implications ■ Its programme acquisition schedule and acquisition strategy ■ Its relationship to other existing systems, including predecessor or similar legacy systems ■ Support (manpower, training, etc.) and security needs and risk items ■ System quantities for development, test, and production ■ Deployment and maintenance plans
4	Determine estimating structure	■ Define a work breakdown structure (WBS) and describe each element in a WBS dictionary (a major automated information system may have only a cost element structure) ■ Choose the best estimating method for each WBS element ■ Identify potential cross-checks for likely cost and schedule drivers ■ Develop a cost estimating checklist

(Continued)

Table 6.3:   (Continued)

Step	Description	Associated Task
5	Identify ground rules and assumptions	▪ Clearly define what the estimate includes and excludes ▪ Identify global and programme-specific assumptions, such as the estimate's base year, including time-phasing and life cycle ▪ Identify programme schedule information by phase and programme acquisition strategy ▪ Identify any schedule or budget constraints, inflation assumptions, and travel costs ▪ Specify equipment the government is to furnish as well as the use of existing facilities or new modification or development ▪ Identify prime contractor and major subcontractors ▪ Determine technology refresh cycles, technology assumptions, and new technology to be developed ▪ Define commonality with legacy systems and assumed heritage savings ▪ Describe effects of new ways of doing business
6	Obtain data	▪ Create a data collection plan with emphasis on collecting current and relevant technical, programmatic, cost, and risk data ▪ Investigate possible data sources ▪ Collect data and normalize them for cost accounting, inflation, learning, and quantity adjustments ▪ Analyze the data for cost drivers, trends, and outliers and compare results against rules of thumb and standard factors derived from historical data ▪ Interview data sources and document all pertinent information, including an assessment of data reliability and accuracy ▪ Store data for future estimates

7	Develop point estimate and compare it to an independent cost estimate	■ Develop the cost model, estimating each WBS element, using the best methodology from the data collected, and including all estimating assumptions
		■ Express costs in constant year dollars
		■ Time-phase the results by spreading costs in the years they are expected to occur, based on the programme schedule
		■ Sum the WBS elements to develop the overall point estimate
		■ Validate the estimate by looking for errors like double counting and omitted costs
		■ Compare estimate against the independent cost estimate and examine where and why there are differences
		■ Perform cross-checks on cost drivers to see if results are similar
		■ Update the model as more data become available or as changes occur and compare results against previous estimates
8	Conduct sensitivity analysis	■ Test the sensitivity of cost elements to changes in estimating input values and key assumptions
		■ Identify effects on the overall estimate of changing the programme schedule or quantities
		■ Determine which assumptions are key cost drivers and which cost elements are affected most by changes
9	Conduct risk and uncertainty analysis	■ Determine and discuss with technical experts the level of cost, schedule, and technical risk associated with each WBS element
		■ Analyze each risk for its severity and probability
		■ Develop minimum, most likely, and maximum ranges for each risk element
		■ Determine type of risk distributions and reason for their use
		■ Ensure that risks are correlated

(Continued)

Table 6.3: *(Continued)*

Step	Description	Associated Task
		■ Use an acceptable statistical analysis method (e.g. Monte Carlo simulation) to develop a confidence interval around the point estimate
		■ Identify the confidence level of the point estimate
		■ Identify the amount of contingency funding and add this to the point estimate to determine the risk-adjusted cost estimate
		■ Recommend that the project or programme office develop a risk management plan to track and mitigate risks
10	Document the estimate	■ Document all steps used to develop the estimate so that a cost analyst unfamiliar with the programme can recreate it quickly and produce the same result
		■ Document the purpose of the estimate, the team that prepared it, and who approved the estimate and on what date
		■ Describe the programme, its schedule, and the technical baseline used to create the estimate
		■ Present the programme's time-phased life-cycle cost
		■ Discuss all ground rules and assumptions
		■ Include auditable and traceable data sources for each cost element and document for all data sources how the data were normalized
		■ Describe in detail the estimating methodology and rationale used to derive each WBS element's cost (prefer more detail over less)
		■ Describe the results of the risk, uncertainty, and sensitivity analyses and whether any contingency funds were identified
		■ Document how the estimate compares to the funding profile
		■ Track how this estimate compares to any previous estimates

| 11 | Present estimate to management for approval | ■ Develop a briefing that presents the documented life-cycle cost estimate
■ Include an explanation of the technical and programmatic baseline and any uncertainties
■ Compare the estimate to an independent cost estimate (ICE) and explain any differences
■ Compare the estimate (life-cycle cost estimate (LCCE)) or independent cost estimate to the budget with enough detail to easily defend it by showing how it is accurate, complete, and high in quality
■ Focus in a logical manner on the largest cost elements and cost drivers
■ Make the content clear and complete so that those who are unfamiliar with it can easily comprehend the competence that underlies the estimate results
■ Make backup slides available for more probing questions
■ Act on and document feedback from management
■ Request acceptance of the estimate |
| 12 | Update the estimate to reflect actual costs and changes | ■ Update the estimate to reflect changes in technical or programme assumptions or keep it current as the programme passes through new phases or milestones
■ Replace estimates with EVM EAC and independent estimate at completion (EAC) from the integrated EVM system
■ Report progress on meeting cost and schedule estimates
■ Perform a post mortem and document lessons learned for elements whose actual costs or schedules differ from the estimate
■ Document all changes to the programme and how they affect the cost estimate |

Prepared by Table 2 (pp. 8–10), *GAO Cost Estimating and Assessment Guide Best Practices for Developing and Managing Capital Program Costs*. United States Government Accounting Office, Applied Research and Methods, March 2009, GAO-09-3SP.

- For construction costs in Saudi Arabia from 2005 to 2015, Abdulelah Aljohani found that 70% of the projects could be labelled as failures and it cost the country more than SAR1 trillion (£202 billion).[13]
- For 16 US rail projects, Nasiru Dantata, Ali Touran and Donald C. Schneck found that the cost overrun was about 30%[14] and two earlier studies by Don Pickrell found rail projects has a 61% cost overrun.[15]
- For 161 transport projects in Korea, Jin-Kyung Lee found cost overruns of about 52%.[16]
- Cost overruns ran at 122% for seven mega projects and 29 medium-sized projects in Korea.[17]
- Himansu found that in India 90% of the projects experienced cost overruns.[18]

However, several researchers have found far fewer overruns in some cases. For example,

- The average overrun for mega worldwide offshore projects was 10% according to a study by Booz Allen Hamilton.[19]

---

[13] Abdulelah Aljohani, "Cost Overrun Causality Model in Saudi Arabian Public Sector Construction Projects," Doctoral Dissertation, Robert Gordon University, November 2019.

[14] Nasiru A. Dantata, Ali Touran and Donald C. Schneck, "Trends in US Rail Transit Project Cost Overrun," Transportation Research Board 2006 Annual Meeting.

[15] See Don H. Pickrell, *Urban Rail Transit Projects: Forecast Versus Actual Ridership and Cost*. Washington, D.C.: Department of Transportation, 1990 and "A Desire Named Streetcar Fantasy and Fact in Rail Transit Planning," *Journal of the American Planning Association*, 58, 1992, pp. 158–176.

[16] Jin-Kyung Lee, "Cost Overrun and Cause in Korean Social Overhead Capital Projects: Roads, Rails, Airports, and Ports," *Journal of Urban Planning and Development*, 134, 2008, pp. 59–62.

[17] Seung L Sand Hyun, Sungmin Yun, Hyoungkwan Kim, Young Hoon Kwak, Hyung Keun Park and Sang Hyun Lee, "Analyzing Schedule Delay of Mega Project: Lessons Learned From Korea Train Express," *Engineering Management, EEE Transactions*, 56, 2009, pp. 243–256.

[18] B. Himansu, *Avoid Cost Overrun for Megaprojects*. Project and Technology Management Foundation News Letter: DLF City, India, 2011.

[19] M. G. McKenna, H. Wilczynski and D. Vanderschee, *Capital Project Execution in the Oil and Gas Industry*. Booz Allen Hamilton: Houston, 2006.

- A study for the Florida Department of Transportation found that for 3,120 road projects in the US, the overrun averaged 9%.[20]
- For construction projects in Portugal,[21] Pakistan[22] and Nigeria,[23] the average cost overrun was 12%, 10% and 14%, respectively.
- Ram Singh reported that for 925 infrastructure projects in India, the average cost overrun was about 14%.[24]
- The average cost overrun for 620 road projects in Norway was about 8% according to James Odeck.[25]

In the UK, the National Audit Office examined construction performance in the case of public finance initiatives (PFI).[26] For a 1999 government survey, 73% of the construction projects resulted in costs to the public sector exceeding the contract's agreed upon amount and that 70% of the projects were delivered late. In contrast, in 2002 the percentages were 22% and 24%, respectively. By 2009 65% of contracts were delivered to budget price and 69% to timetable.[26]

There have been several studies that suggest reasons for cost overruns. Himansu provides 173 causes for cost overruns in mega projects.[27] From his and other studies, the main causes are as follows:

[20]R. D. Ellis, J.-H. Pyeon, Z. J. Herbsman, E. Minchin and K. Molenaar, *Evaluation of Alternative Contracting Techniques on FDOT Construction Projects*. Tallahassee: Florida Department of Transportation, 2007.

[21]N. Azhar, R. U. Farooqui and S.M. Ahmed, "Cost Overrun Factors in Construction Industry of Pakistan," First International Conference on Construction in Developing Countries, Karachi, 2008, pp. 499–508.

[22]D. Moura, C. Veiga-Pires, L. Albardeiro, T. Boski, A. L. Rodrigues and H. Tareco, "Holocene Sea Level Fluctuations and Coastal Evolution in the Central Algarve (Southern Portugal)," *Marine Geology*, 237, 2007, pp. 127–142.

[23]A. Omoregie and D. Radford, "Infrastructure Delays and Cost Escalation: Causes and Effects in Nigeria," The 6th International Postgraduate Research Conference in the Built and Human Environment, 3–4 April 2006, Delft University of Technology, International Council for Research and Innovation in Building and Construction.

[24]Ram Singh, "Delays and Cost Overruns in Infrastructure Projects: An Enquiry into Extent, Causes and Remedies," *Working Papers* 181. Centre for Development Economics, Delhi School of Economics, 2009.

[25]James Odeck, "Cost Overruns in Road Construction — What Are Their Sizes and Determinants?" *Transport Policy*, 11, 2004, pp. 43–53.

[26]Private Finance Practice. *Performance of PFI Construction*. 2009. National Audit Office, London.

[27]B. Himansu, *Avoid Cost Overrun for Megaprojects*. Project and Technology Management Foundation News Letter: DLF City, India, 2011.

Errors in initial design:

- Frequent design change
- Increased financing costs
- Poor scheduling of time
- Poor project supervision.

It should be acknowledged that a project that may be viewed as a failure due to a substantial cost overrun may still be a successful project from the perspective of each stakeholder who will have their own view of whether a project is successful.[28]

6.5.1. *Changes and Variations*

The effects of change orders and variation orders on project costs link several of Himansu's criteria in the preceding paragraph. Errors in initial design can arise from several causes: genuine errors and mistakes, lack of familiarity with the up-to-date and anticipated specifications required from the project, leading to suboptimal choices and unanticipated changes in technology.

All three of these challenges point to a need to have good quality up-to-date information about competitors and about future expectations for that industry from end users. Many of us will have seen domestic building projects around us where the specification has constantly changed because of the whims of the end users and the effect on the schedule in terms of local disruption continuing for longer as well as listening to the effects on the costs as we are told of the builders' inefficiencies but never of the inefficiencies of the homeowner/contracting party. Sadly, similar events can happen, especially in public sector projects, where the public sector representative is unprepared and inexperienced compared with the contractor. Over-specification can be a nightmare for a contractor because it may be difficult to get hold of the goods or services in the specification and/or there may have been an upgrade, in which case the specification will need

---

[28]For example, Lim and Mohamed provide a framework for analyzing the success of a project during its different phases: C. S. Lim and M. Zain Mohamed, "Criteria of Project Success: An Exploratory Re-Examination," *International Journal of Project Management*, 17, 1999, pp. 243–248.

to be changed. Under-specification can lead to misunderstandings and confusion and less than optimal solutions. Good practice project management requires the codification of each change by a change order and it is naïve to consider the change orders are generated without cost.

Consider then the extreme case of communications procurement as a country upgrades its mobile communication system to the latest model. Some of this technology to support the infrastructure may well be emergent, meaning it is untested. Some of it may come from another country, and the home country may be reluctant to allow another foreign power access to its mobile communication system. A concrete example of this would be the case of Huawei in the UK. In 2018, British Telecom announced that it would be removing Huawei equipment from key areas of its mobile communications network because of discomfort about Huawei's connection to the Chinese government and potential espionage. In 2019, Vodafone followed suit and numerous other countries have also either banned or limited the use of this equipment. However, there is then a need to find a solution and that may involve a complex and expensive workaround. If there are a limited number of suppliers of some very specialist equipment, then this becomes very difficult. Undoubtedly costs will rise in this case.

There can also be problems where public money is involved. Many defence projects go over budget because of the large sums of money involved, the long lead times for the project, and the lack of availability of a prototype for testing studies can lead to overreliance on the contractor and thence an instant asymmetry of power and information in the contract. There can also be an understatement of budgets through a reluctance to disclose the full cost in case the project is declined as too expensive and adjustments to the project schedule, especially with a public service budget which is calculated year by year, to have lower expenditure in the earlier years.[29] Finally, the remoteness of the project from the everyday lives of the decision makers can mean that the attitude to risk and risk management is limited to the "here and now" rather than to the project's operation. This myopia can cause a significant cost to arise to fix problems at a later stage, when it is more expensive to do so.

In Chapter 9, the case study will show what happens when under-specification occurs, costs are kept down but end-user safety is threatened. Did those involved in the school's project think through the implications

[29]UK Parliament Defence Select Committee report, Section 2, 5 February 2013.

of the decisions to cut costs. Their lives were not affected, but the lives of thousands of other people were, with attendant costs to businesses as well as social and emotional costs to the stakeholders.

As a provider of finance, either equity or debt, changes can affect the financial dynamics of the project and thus its financial health. While nobody wants to have to deal with change orders about the type of pencils being used in the office, it makes sense to have covenants and agreements so that the cumulative amount of change orders triggers upward reporting and that individual amounts of change orders are also set as a cap.

6.6. Case Study: Brandenburg Gateway — The New Berlin Airport

As Berlin reassumed its position as the capital of a united Germany, it became clear that the three airports (Tempelhof, Schönefeld and Tegel) were insufficient to manage traffic to such a prestigious city. They were largely ex-military airports in nature, not easy to access and ageing, with associations of the unhappy regime of World War II in the case of the Tempelhof airport. What was clearly needed to bring the national carrier to Berlin from its Frankfurt base and demonstrate the new confidence of the country was a new airport.

Tempelhof airport, the most central of the original three airports was no longer fit for today's planes and closed in 2008, after many protests and a referendum. It is now a skatepark and home to many refugees. Schönefeld airport, a souvenir of the former Soviet zone pre-unification, lacked modern facilities and though originally scheduled to close, now looks as if it will receive some modernization and remain open. Tegel airport, built in just 9 days to help with the airbridge for supplies at the end of the Second World War, remains the major airport for the city and as air traffic has grown, is stretched to its limits. Tegel airport is scheduled for closure once the new airport (Brandenburg airport) opens, though this decision is being contested by the local residents.

And what of the new airport, Brandenburg? Announced in 2006, it was expected to be large enough to handle the traffic forecasts of 27 million passengers each year and to cost €2 billion. The building was completed in 2011 but the airport finally opened in late 2020. There have been problems with fire safety equipment, automatic doors that failed to open, insufficient numbers of check-in desks and some believe the airport will be overcapacity when the doors finally open, with passenger estimates at 34 million and rising to 58 million by 2040. In all, over 550,000 faults have been identified ranging from cabling to the wrong lightbulbs.[30] Meanwhile, costs have also risen to around triple the original estimate. In 2018, the maintenance costs were estimated at €10 million per month.[31]

This unfortunate state of affairs has been attributed variously to a number of factors[32]:

- A reported bias in the specification favouring one of the two bidding entities. The bid was annulled but the two rival bidders joined together to work on the contract.
- A series of complaints from nearby residents restricting flights and causing the scheduled closure of Tegel and Schönefeld airports to concentrate all traffic on one airport. There were also claims for soundproofing from local residents.
- Claims from various stakeholders for damages arising from the impact of the delay on businesses. These include Deutsche Bahn, builder of a station under the new airport and from several outlet stores. Additionally, the revenue forecast has been affected by the reluctance of airport shops in other Berlin airports to relocate.
- The lack of a coherent project management team.
- The inability of the project to continue financing — by 2016, an EU facility was requested in order to keep the project viable and this was eventually granted after being guaranteed by two local states and the Federal German Government. A refinancing signed in February 2017 allows an additional €2.2 billion as equity contributions and to refinance part of the existing debt. Further debt requests occurred in 2018 (€2.8 billion of which some €500 million was approved, threatening the project with bankruptcy). Just two months

---

[30]"Berlin Brandenburg: The airport with half a million faults", Chris Bowlby for BBC News, 29 June 2019.
[31]"Berlin's New Airport is finally set to open — its future is up in the air", Deutsche Welle website, 3 June 2020.
[32]For a more detailed discussion of the delays in the opening of the airport, see Ben James, "The Sad Tale of Berlin Brandenburg Airport," April 27, 2018. Onemileatatime website.

before the latest opening, there has been a request for further funding of €300 million ($354 million) to be made up of loans of €201 million and a grant of €99 million.[33]Allegations of financial irregularities have also been made at the time of writing following the Wirecard audit scandal.[34]

Capital costs have risen from €2.83 billion in 2009 to €7.3 billion ($8.1 billion) in 2020[35] with operating costs and further work still to be funded.

An OECD report produced as part of the procurement toolbox project lists the following key failures[36]:

- Inexperienced and non-specialist management and supervision
- Inaccuracy of budget estimation
- Poor planning and procurement
- Changes and variations
- Lack of internal communication.

Brandenburg airport was conceived with the best of intentions. However, the delivery of the project was flawed and costs went out of control as technology and other demographic issues moved on, short cuts appeared to have been taken to save money and managers have faced allegations of salaries that are over generous, leaking money from the project. It has opened but in the middle of the coronavirus pandemic when air travel was restricted.[37]

---

[33]Pilar Wolfsteller "Berlin's new airport needs €300m in additional funding," *FlightGlobal*, 9 September 2020.

[34]Dominik Bath, "Flughaven im Visier der Strafverfolger," *Berliner Morgenpost*, 14 July 2020.

[35]"Berlin Brandenburg Airport Might Finally Open," *Fortune Magazine*, 26 Jan 2020.

[36]OECD Public Procurement Tool Box (2016) Country case: "Governance failures in the management of the Berlin Brandenburg International Airport."

[37]Simon Calder, "New Berlin Airport Welcomes its first passengers — Nine years late," Independent newspaper, 31 October 2020.

Chapter 7

Financial Models[*]

Introduction

Most loan, franchise and concession agreements will require that project sponsors provide the information generated from a financial model so that the investment properties of a project can be understood. It is needed to ensure that the future cash flows are sufficient to repay the debt obligations under the anticipated conditions, as well as other possible scenarios including pessimistic ones. A well-constructed model will provide the user with the ability to undertake a wide variety of "what-if" analyses. The information generated from a model is not only needed at the inception of a project but throughout the project's life. It must continue to demonstrate the viability of the project to its stakeholders.

Models are usually developed by suitably qualified specialists using a spreadsheet. In the early phases of a project, a model is normally developed by the sponsor as part of the project proposal taken to providers of finance. During loan negotiations, the bank may take over responsibility for the model or create its own model. This responsibility will typically remain with the bank but will sometimes revert to the sponsor after the financial close-out.

This chapter provides an overview of the key elements of a spreadsheet model. It is important for the modeller to understand the theory behind the model. An experienced modeller will know when certain factors can be safely ignored. For instance, a model for a project with only one currency

---

[*]This chapter is contributed by John Macgillivray, Managing Director of Project Planning and Management Ltd.

155

may safely ignore any currency adjustments. However, if a second currency is introduced and the exchange rate of the two currencies is expected to change over the project's life, the modeller must understand how to add the necessary currency adjustments. It provides a simple overview of the main considerations which a modeller must address when building a model. It is effectively a check list. It is not a means of learning how to model. That exercise requires more than a chapter, it needs an entire book.

7.1. Project Finance versus Public–Private Partnership (PPP) Financing Models

PPPs are a subset of project financing. As such, from a modelling perspective, there are very few differences between financial models for a project financing and a PPP financing. The main difference is that PPPs usually have a revenue stream based on the project's availability whereas conventional project financings usually have a revenue stream dependent on the product (or service) availability with price and demand critical to both. In addition, a project financing will often produce a product whereas a PPP often provides a service. However, these are not hard and fast rules and there are project financings with capacity and operating and maintenance payments and PPPs in which the investor takes a market risk.

7.1.1. *Characteristics of a Project Finance/PPP Model*

A project finance/PPP financial model will typically have:

- A functional currency
- Usually two bank accounts (operating and escrow)
- A waterfall of accounts
- Cash traps (restrictions on dividend policy)
- Cash sweeps (sinking funds and loan prepayments)
- Loans.

7.2. Models in Different Phases of a Project

Models are used in different phases of a project: planning, negotiating, and constructing and operating phases.

In the early planning phase, models are used to optimize the design configuration. It is not necessary to include the financial components such as funding, taxation and accounting in this phase of model formulation.

In the planning phase, the model needs to contain the project finance components such as the accounting, the funding and the taxation calculations. The model should be developed in such a way that the user sets the ratio of local to foreign costs and the model calculates the periodic construction cost drawdowns in the different currencies. The user also sets the initial debt to equity ratio and the model calculates the funding drawdowns (loans and equity).

During the negotiating phase, the model should be developed in such a way that the user sets the construction drawdowns and the software calculates the ratio of local to foreign currencies. The user also sets the funding (loan and equity) drawdowns and the model calculates the initial debt to equity ratios in each currency. During this phase the model will be used to compare quotes from competing contractors. These may not have been submitted on the same basis. For instance, one may have better operating costs, another a shorter schedule and a third one a lower price. It may also be used as a Public Sector Comparator (PSC) for use by government bodies when deciding whether to use a PPP with the private sector or invest in the project using traditional methods in the public sector (see Chapter 9).

During the construction and operating phases, the model should be similar to the one aforementioned, but the user introduces the actual accounting figures for past periods. The actual figures are used for the following two purposes:

- to calculate more accurate loan coverage ratios over the remaining periods starting with an audited not an estimated position;
- to calculate more accurate key criteria such as the internal rate of return (IRR) and net present value (NPV) with actual figures for the former periods and not estimated figures.

7.3. Model Best Practice

There are no internationally recognized standards for the development, layout and formulae for use with project finance or PPP models. In the absence of such standards, the following guidelines are often adopted:

- separate inputs from calculations and results;
- use only one unique formula in each row or column;
- make it read like a book, from front to back, top to bottom and left to right;

- use multiple worksheets so you can insert rows and columns into the model;
- use each column for the same purpose throughout the model;
- calculate in nominal terms and convert to real terms where necessary;
- include basic charts of the cash flows so that you can see what effect your changes are having ... "a picture is worth a thousand words";
- no external links to other spreadsheets;
- keep formulae simple;
- use range names (but not excessively);
- use stylesheets;
- include a documentation sheet to explain assumptions made;
- no hard-coded inputs in formulae;
- make all calculations visible, do not hide any;
- use the data validation routine to ensure that the user inserts figures between predetermined limits;
- make the model flexible;
- make the model accurate;
- avoid circular references;
- minimize Visual Basic for Applications (VBA) code;
- include cross-checks and a test module; and
- include a single summary page with all key input and results.

7.4. Model Flexibility

A well-designed model will contain the following basic input parameters which the user can change by simply inserting a different input number or series of numbers:

- start-date;
- construction schedule;
- revenues;
- production/availability;
- operating costs;
- project life;
- accounting date;
- exchange rates;
- inflation rates; and
- interest rates (in real terms).

A model designed for use in the planning phase will also have the following input parameters:

- capacity;
- capital cost;
- ratio of foreign to local currency costs; and
- initial debt to equity in the local and foreign currencies.

7.4.1. *Modules within a Model*

Figure 7.1 illustrates a suggested layout for a model. The layout presented in the figure has the advantage of separating the construction phase costs in the first module from the operating phase costs in the second module. The second and third modules clearly separate the project from the equity cash flows.

It is a good idea to separate out the project from the equity cash flows. The latter includes the funding, taxation and accounting calculations. As a general rule, if the project does not meet the investor's hurdle rates calculated on the project cash flows, there is no creative financing structure which will make it more attractive for the equity cash flows. The only

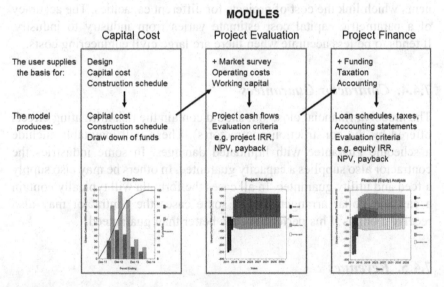

Figure 7.1: Suggested Layout for a Model

Prepared by John Macgillivray/Project Planning and Management Ltd.

exception to this rule is the rare occasion when the government makes concessions (as, for instance, significant grants in the field of renewable energy).

7.4.2. *Inflation and Exchange Rates*

When inflation rates in the country where the project is located are different from those found in the countries of the various entities providing finance for the project, this can have a significant effect on the future exchange rates of the various currencies. In such cases it is necessary to predict and apply varying exchange rates over the life of the project. This can be done by assuming a constant purchasing power parity between the currencies.

7.4.3. *Parametric Capital Cost Estimate*

As discussed in Chapter 6, models developed in the early planning phases may contain a parametric capital cost estimate. This feature is useful for carrying out sensitivity analyses on the project capacity. It may even reveal an optimum plant capacity. The estimate will typically contain Lang exponents which link the cost of projects for different capacities. The accuracy of a parametric capital cost estimate varies from industry to industry. It tends to be less accurate when there are large civil engineering costs.

7.4.4. *Contractor Guarantees*

The model at financial close-out should contain the risk mitigating effects offered by the construction contractor(s). These will inevitably include a schedule guarantee with liquidated damages. In some industries the contractor also supplies a capacity guarantee. In others he may also supply a feed and utility guarantee. In all cases the formula will typically contain a cap and collar arrangement. In some cases the contractor may also receive a bonus if his performance is better than guaranteed.

7.4.5. *Revenues*

Revenues for a product sold on the open market will depend on the effective price for the product and the size of the market. The effective price, more popularly referred to as the "netback price", is the amount received after deducting all the costs associated with delivering one unit of a product to the marketplace. Such costs would include, for example, production costs, transportation costs, importing costs and royalty fees.

In other cases, the revenue may be based on the sum of a capacity payment and an operations and maintenance payment. The capacity payment is designed to recover the project's fixed cost plus a return to the investor. It may be payable over the life of the project or concession or over a shorter defined period. The operations and maintenance payments are designed to cover the periodic operating and maintenance costs including fuel price in the case of a power plant. The capacity payment may or may not be index linked; the operation and maintenance will inevitably be index linked.

7.4.6. *Operating Costs*

Operating costs can conveniently be de-composed into fixed and variable costs. Fixed costs are wholly or substantially constant regardless of the production rate or availability of the project. Such costs include wages, maintenance, insurance and local taxes. Variable costs are substantially and directly dependent on the production of the project and include items such as feed, fuel, catalyst and chemical consumptions.

7.4.7. *Seasonal Variations*

Models for projects in some industries should take into account seasonal variations in production. This occurs in renewable energy projects such as wind farms, insolation (solar) projects and run-of-river hydropower projects. This is particularly important for the calculation of the periodic loan cover ratios which will vary from season to season.

Long-term variations should be considered such as those produced by, say, the north Atlantic oscillations on these renewable energy projects in western Europe.

7.4.8. *Operator Guarantees*

In some projects, particularly PPPs with a capacity element, the special purpose vehicle (SPV) offers an availability guarantee to the user of the facilities (usually a government agency). This guarantee is similar to the contractor guarantee but is calculated on a periodic, typically annual, basis.

7.4.9. *Columns Per Year*

How many columns should the model contain for each year? The figure varies depending on the modeller and the nature of the project. It varies from 1 to 12. It has even been done on a four-week period. Some models retain the same number of columns during the construction and operating periods. Others use, say 12 columns in the construction phase and 2 in the operating phase.

7.4.10. *Working Capital*

Working capital is the capital needed on a day-to-day basis for the operation of a business. It is defined as the difference between current assets and current liabilities.

Current assets are the entity's most liquid assets and defined as assets that can be turned into cash in one operating cycle or one year, whichever is longer. Current assets include:

- inventories including feed and/or fuel, product and spare parts;
- operating cash usually expressed as a percentage of annual operating costs;
- goods in process; and
- accounts receivable for each of the products/markets.

Current liabilities are obligations due within one year or one operating cycle (whichever is longer) and include:

- accounts payable for each of the operating costs;
- current portion of long-term indebtedness; and
- short-term bank loans.

It is important in modelling that the periodic calculations of the working capital and the calculation for the initial working capital be included. These are the funds the project company will need to bridge from start-up to receipt of a strong cash flow stream to meet its obligations and grow. The periodic figures are used in the calculation of the project's IRR, discussed in the following section, and in the balance sheets. The initial working capital is used in the calculation of the project funding and may be required in several currencies.

7.5. Discount Rate

The calculation of a project's NPVs requires the use of an appropriate discount rate. Sometimes a single rate is used in all phases of the project. At other times there may be more than one, for instance, one in the construction phase and another lower rate in the operating phase. There are various financial models that project how the appropriate discount rate for the equity component should be calculated. The well-known capital asset pricing model (CAPM) asserts that the discount rate for equity should be as follows:

Equity discount rate = risk-free rate + beta × equity risk premium

The risk-free rate is usually the yield on government debt for an equivalent period. A project's beta is its systematic risk relative to the market and is typically estimated using regression analysis. A beta of one means that, on average, the project has the same risk as the market.

Although the CAPM has come under attack since its introduction in the 1960s, it is still typically used in the analysis of capital projects. Holding aside the criticism of the CAPM on theoretical grounds and the lack of empirical evidence, the implementation of the model is not straightforward. Assumptions have to be made about the inputs: the risk-free rate, the equity risk premium and beta. The CAPM provides little guidance as to what the risk-free rate means. Typically, it is a government bond rate but there is still the issue of the maturity that should be used for the debt. Should it be a short-, intermediate- or long-term rate? The equity risk premium is the subject of considerable debate in the finance literature. Empirical evidence of the historical risk premium in the United States and the United Kingdom show considerable variation. Many practitioners today tend to use between 3% and 4%, although structural changes in financial markets since 2008 are likely to alter this view.

Beta is another controversial input that must be estimated. Although it sounds simple to estimate a company's beta using historical price data, the application to projects of the type discussed in this book or even corporate capital projects is not simple. It involves identifying a publicly traded company that is substantially in the same industry and using the beta of that company as a starting point. The beta must be adjusted for differences in financial structures, more specifically differences in leverage.[1] To adjust for this, some companies calculate project betas for their internal investment portfolios rather than using market betas which, as we have said, may belong to diversified companies with a different product mix and thereby reflect betas that might not be good analogies. An example might be a large integrated oil company looking at a new exploration project. Market betas may be available for other integrated companies or for smaller exploration companies. The former may have a different business mix while the latter may have a share price driven by considerations other than oil exploration. In this instance, an examination of the company's own portfolio might be considered to generate a "better beta" for evaluating future investments.

7.5.1. *Weighted Average Cost of Debt*

The weighted average cost of debt (WACD) is used in the calculation of the loan and project life coverage ratios and as a component in the calculation of the weighted average cost of capital (WACC). The loan documentation will usually define the method of calculating the WACD. In the absence of a definition, sum the weighted interest for each loan to produce the WACD.

7.5.2. *Weighted Average Cost of Capital*

The discount rate for the calculation of the equity NPV with a mix of equity and loans is calculated as the WACC. The formula for the WACC is as follows:

$$\text{WACC} = d \times \text{WACD} \times (1 - \text{corporate tax rate})$$
$$+ (1 - d) \times \text{equity discount rate}$$

---

[1] For a more detailed explanation of how this is done, see Chapter 16 in Frank J. Fabozzi, Pamela P. Peterson and Ralph Polimeni, *The Complete CFO Handbook: From Accounting to Accountability*. Hoboken, NJ: John Wiley & Sons, 2008.

where d is the percentage of debt at the start of the operating phase. The corporate tax rate is the marginal tax rate faced by the sponsor. The calculation assumes that the sponsor is in a tax regime where interest payments are tax deductible.

7.6. Key Project Selection Criteria

The key approaches typically used for project evaluation and selection and their advantages and disadvantages are summarized in Table 7.1.[2]

7.7. Currency Adjustments

When an account (such as a loan, a bank account and a sinking fund) is held in a currency that is not the same as the functional currency, the opening balance for any period is not the same as the closing balance for the previous period because it has been converted at a different exchange rate. It is therefore necessary to include a currency adjustment to account for this.

The balance sheet should contain the accumulated currency adjustments during the construction phase. Either the balance sheet or the profit and loss statements should account for the currency adjustments during the operating phase.

7.7.1. *Interest Rates*

Interest rates can be found in many areas of a project finance model. The project pays out interest on all loans and any preferred equity. It receives interest on the balance held in bank accounts and sinking funds. Interest rates may be fixed or variable meaning that they will increase as inflation increases. The model should contain a proper linkage between interest rates and inflation and it should use the Fisher equation to determine the nominal from the real interest rate:

$$i = (1+r) \times (1+\pi) - 1$$

---

[2] For a more detailed discussion of each of these criterion and their advantage and disadvantages, see Chapter 13 in Frank J. Fabozzi and Pamela P. Peterson, *Financial Management and Analysis*. Hoboken, NJ: John Wiley & Sons, 2003.

Table 7.1:   Key Project Selection Criteria

Criterion	Advantages	Disadvantages
Net present value (NPV)	Takes into account the time value of money.	Can produce different results and thence different selection decisions dependent on discount rate used.
Internal rate of return (IRR)	Takes into account the time value of money.	1. Can lead to incorrect decisions with mutually exclusive investments. 2. More than one IRR can result when a project has cash flows when there is more than one change in sign, such as a project with projected negative cash flows at the end of a project's life. 3. Assumes cash flows can be reinvested at the computed IRR.
Modified internal rate of return (MIRR)	1. Takes into account the time value of money. 2. Allows for the incorporation of reinvestment rates for interim positive cash flows.	Can lead to incorrect decisions with mutually exclusive investments.
Payback	Simple concept easy to calculate.	1. Does not take into account the time value of money. 2. Ignores cash flows beyond the payback date.
Profitability index (PI) also called the value to investment ratio (VIR) and benefit cost ratio (BCR)	Takes into account the time value of money.	1. Can lead to incorrect decisions with mutually exclusive investments. 2. Can produce different results and thence different selection decisions dependent on discount rate used.

Prepared by John Macgillivray/Project Planning and Management Ltd.

where

    i = nominal interest rate

    r = real interest rate

    π = inflation rate

Interest rates are usually quoted on an annual basis but applied half yearly or more frequently. They should be converted to a semi-annual rate (or other) with the following formula:

$$i_e = [(1 + i_a)^{1/n} - 1] \times n$$

where the subscripts e and i denote the semi-annual and annual interest rates, respectively, and n is the number of times the interest is paid per year.

In any particular period, the interest rates should be calculated on the basis of the opening balance for loans and for sinking funds. The reason for this is that the changes to the funds are made at the end of the period (usually, six months) period when the loan coverage ratios are calculated. In the case of the bank accounts, the interest earned is calculated on the basis of the average of the opening and closing balance. This may pose problems with any escrow accounts and generate circular references on a spreadsheet, which may require algebraic solutions to overcome them.

7.7.2. *Controlling the Project During its Life Span*

The aforementioned key criteria are applied to the debt and the equity cash flows at the initial decision phase. As the project progresses, however, the various stakeholders use ratios to ensure it remains in a healthy state. Lending institutions usually measure the ability of borrowers to satisfy the contractual payments by calculating coverage ratios for a given period (usually calculated annually or semi-annually) each one defined as:

$$\text{Coverage ratio} = \frac{\text{Net operating revenue}}{\text{Value associated with the loan}}$$

In a debt service coverage ratio, the denominator is the loan amount outstanding at the end of the period. In an interest cover ratio, the denominator is the interest paid during the period. A coverage ratio may be expressed for the prior period, the last two (or more) periods, the next period or the next two (or more) periods. The model may also need to calculate the average debt service coverage ratio (ADSCR) and the minimum for all future periods.

A life coverage ratio is calculated similarly for each period. In this case, the numerator is the NPV for the future net operating revenues over either the remaining life of the loans (the loan life coverage ratio) or over the remaining life of the project (the project life coverage ratio). The loan agreement may allow the balances in the escrow account and the debt service reserve account to be added to the numerator.

The loan agreement will have one or more financial covenants which refer to the coverage ratios. Some of these covenants will impose restrictions on the payment of dividends (cash traps). Other covenants will divert funds into reserve accounts and sometimes trigger the mandatory payment of senior loans (cash sweeps). The wording for these covenants is critical and must be modelled accordingly. Some can be readily modelled in a spreadsheet, others are difficult and can produce circular references.

7.7.3. *Functional Currency*

The functional currency is the currency in which the local legal and fiscal authorities will accept the company accounts. It is usually the local currency but not necessarily the currency in which the model displays the projections. The following entries on the balance sheet should be carried forward from one year to the next in the functional currency:

- assets;
- un-depreciated assets;
- equity and reserves;
- tax credits.

Some countries have a high local inflation rate resulting in a low recovery of the capital cost over the life of the project (i.e. the depreciation). This effect can produce higher taxation levels than would otherwise be the case. In order to compensate for this, governments will sometimes allow a foreign currency to be used as the functional currency. This happens occasionally in the oil and gas industry.

If the model displays the projections in a currency other than the functional currency it must contain appropriate adjustments to the depreciation calculations. Otherwise the corporate tax calculations will be incorrect.

7.7.4. *Funding*

The model should take account of the anticipated loan drawdown and repayment schedules for the project loans or other financing mechanism.

7.7.5. *Taxation*

There are numerous levels of tax which local, state and federal authorities can impose on a project company. Some are based on property values, others on income (profit) and others on interest and dividends.

For the determination of profit-based taxes regimes, capital allowances can vary from one tax authority to another. Each tax authority will have its own basis for calculating profits and some may allow inflation for the un-depreciated portion of the capital cost. Some tax authorities may allow the company to carry forward tax losses for a limited number of years; others may allow a similar carry back.

Project finance and PPP projects can be subject to one or more of the following bases:

- bonuses (oil and gas);
- royalties (mineral extraction, oil and gas);
- production sharing or concession agreement tax such as a Petroleum Revenue Tax PRT (oil and gas);
- local taxes;
- import duties;
- sales tax (e.g. value-added tax, VAT);
- interest withholding;
- corporate tax;
- dividend withholding;
- carbon taxes.

Sales taxes are usually recoverable from the government but there may be a delay, in some countries this may take more than six months. This delay can cause a funding problem in the construction phase and needs to be taken into account in the model.

7.7.6. *Sinking Funds*

The project may contain one or more of the following sinking fund requirements in its financing arrangement which should be included in the model:

- *Debt service reserve account*: Used to pay the debt service on certain specified loans when the cash flow is too low.
- *Major maintenance account*: Used, for example, in the dry docking of ships and the resurfacing of a toll road.
- *Abandonment account*: Used at the end of the project life, for example, in the decommissioning of offshore platforms.
- *Additional investment account*: Used to add an additional lane on a toll road when the level of service falls below a specified amount.
- *Preference shares*: Used to pay dividends to preference shareholders when there are insufficient funds to do so.

Note that the target for the debt service reserve account is usually based on the debt service for the next one or more operating periods. It should take account of the shortened debt service resulting from loan prepayments and extended debt service resulting from cash shortfalls.

7.8. Bank Accounts

There are usually two types of bank accounts:

- *Operating Accounts*: An account for making payments for day-to-day operating costs. It is usually located onshore and denominated in the local currency.
- *Escrow Accounts*: An account for disbursing loan repayments, payments to and from sinking funds, dividends. The order is set in the waterfall of accounts. Sometimes escrow accounts may be located offshore to the project and may be denominated in a foreign currency, i.e. one different from the local currency of the country in which the project is located.

7.8.1. *Waterfall of Accounts*

The waterfall of accounts is also known as the cash waterfall or the cash cascade. Examples are shown in Figures 7.2–7.4.

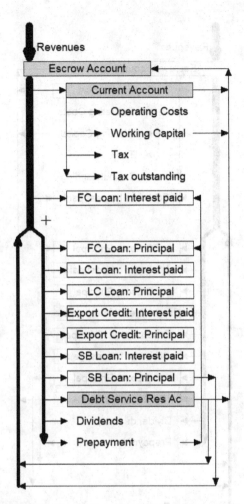

Figure 7.2: **Waterfall of Accounts for a Typical Non-Recourse Loan**
Prepared by Promoter Software Ltd.

The project cash flows are paid into an escrow account from which they are distributed to a current account for day-to-day operations of the project, including the working capital and for tax payments. Surplus funds are distributed to make payments on senior commercial loans, mezzanine loans, standby loans, sinking funds and dividends, usually in that order. There may be a loan prepayment provision which can occur before or after any dividends are paid to the shareholders. If the prepayment occurs

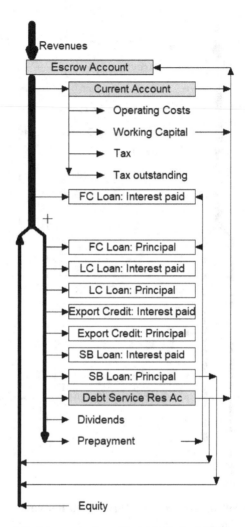

Figure 7.3:   Waterfall of Accounts for a Typical Limited-Recourse Loan
Prepared by Promoter Software Ltd.

after the dividends, the loans will only be prepaid when cash traps limit the dividend payment and allow funds to reach this last item in the waterfall. Loan interest is paid before loan principal.

A shortfall of funds may be made good initially by the funds in any debt service reserve account. Any further funds may come from one or more of the following sources:

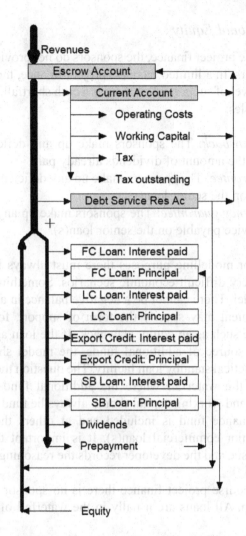

Revenues
Escrow Account
Current Account
Operating Costs
Working Capital
Tax
Tax outstanding
Debt Service Res Ac
FC Loan: Interest paid
FC Loan: Principal
LC Loan: Interest paid
LC Loan: Principal
Export Credit: Interest paid
Export Credit: Principal
SB Loan: Interest paid
SB Loan: Principal
Dividends
Prepayment
Equity

Figure 7.4: Waterfall of Accounts Where the Reserve Account is above the Main Waterfall

Prepared by Promoter Software Ltd.

- Additional equity
- Additional loans say from a standby loan
- Credit from a feed/fuel supplier.

7.8.1.1. *Additional Equity*

In a non-recourse project finance, the sponsors do not provide any guarantees to the lenders. In a limited recourse project finance, the sponsors will provide some level of support when there is a cash shortfall. The following are some examples:

- *Dividend clawback*: The sponsors make up any deficiency up to a limit set by the amount of dividends already paid.
- *Interest guarantee*: The sponsors make up any deficiency in the interest payable on the senior loan(s).
- *Cash deficiency guarantee*: The sponsors make up any deficiency in the debt service payable on the senior loan(s).

Note that for modelling purposes there must always be a source of funds even in very difficult economic scenarios. Something has to "give way" in the model. There cannot be a negative balance in a bank account. The loan agreement may specify the form of support, for instance, an equity guarantee such as an equity clawback. If the loan agreement does not specify the source of additional funds, the model should typically contain a hypothetical standby loan facility. The question then arises about the position in the waterfall where the additional funds are injected. Operating costs and working capital should always be funded. Sometimes a major maintenance fund is included and at others the interest and principal on senior commercial loan(s). It is important that the model addresses this issue and the developer records the reasoning for the choice made.

In a non-recourse project finance there is no sponsor guarantee and no equity top up. All loans are usually in the waterfall of accounts (see Figure 7.2).

In a limited-recourse project finance, there will be some sponsor support and additional equity injection if there is a shortage of funds during the operating phase. If the sponsors provide an interest guarantee, for instance, one or more of the loans will have an assured source for its interest payment and it will appear above the waterfall of accounts (see Figure 7.3).

Debt service reserve accounts are usually located in the waterfall, but some sinking funds such as a major maintenance fund may be located with the operating costs and has to reach its target regardless of the available funds (see Figure 7.4).

There are many variations on the cash flow diagrams presented in Figures 7.2–7.4. It is important to understand the intended flow of cash in any project financing and the modeller should have a clear idea of the diagram as applied to the project being studied.

When modelling a project, it is often said that the key calculation is the one for the cash flow available for debt service (CFADS). This is usually true for non-recourse project financings. But some projects have one or more loans and/or sinking funds above the waterfall of accounts and always payable as for the operating costs. This would be the case with a limited recourse project. A more accurate statement would define the key calculation as the cash flow available for the waterfall of accounts (CFAWAC). In Figure 7.2, the CFADS and CFAWAC are the same and coincide. In Figures 7.3 and 7.4, they differ and diverge.

7.9. Dividend Cash Trap

There are usually covenants in the loan documentation which restrict the payment of dividends dependent upon certain criteria. The criteria are typically calculated based on the accounting statements or loan projections. They effectively dictate the dividend policy.

In a given project there may be one or more cash traps set up so that dividends (which are outflows of funds from the project) may only be payable once these targets are met. The following are examples:

- The debt to equity ratio (no payment of dividends when the debt to equity ratio is above a certain figure).
- The loan coverage ratio (either a periodic or a life coverage ratio, for instance no payment of dividends when the DSCR projected for the next two periods is below a certain level and the historical DSCR for the previous two periods is below another level).
- The proportion or amount of cash available for dividend payment (for instance, only 50% of payments in the first two years of commercial operation).
- The legal requirement in some jurisdictions that the dividends may only be paid out of profits.

7.10. Loan Prepayment

Loan prepayment is a cash sweep account for senior loans. However, not all loans permit prepayments or there may be a specified period of time during which prepayments may not be permitted (i.e. a lockout period). These conditions allow the debt finance providers to receive some certainty about their returns rather take all the upfront risk, but be refinanced out at the earliest available opportunity.

A prepayment may be specified as follows:

- At the end of the waterfall when a cash trap prevents payment of dividends.
- In the waterfall before the dividend payment if a coverage ratio is either below a low level (in which case all cash available is diverted to prepayment) or above a high level (in which case the excess cash is shared with the dividends).
- At the start of the waterfall when the project is in default (say a coverage ratio is below a certain level) and all available cash flows are diverted to prepayment.

Prepayment of part of a loan will have an effect on the remaining payments. The calculations are done using one of the following methods:

- *Order of maturity*: The loan repayments for the next period(s) are affected.
- *Inverse order of maturity*: The loan repayments for the last period(s) are affected.
- *Pro rata*: The reduction is spread through the remaining periods.

7.11. Loan Repayments

If the repayment of the loan interest and principal are above the waterfall of accounts, then the model would normally make provision for the following line entries:

- interest rate;
- opening balance;
- loan drawdown;
- repayment;

- closing balance;
- currency adjustment (if there are loans in currencies other than the functional currency);
- interest paid;
- fees.

If there is a prepayment, there will be an entry for it. The balances, repayments, interest paid and currency adjustments must be calculated taking into account the effect of the prepayment.

If the repayment of the loan principal is within the waterfall of accounts, then the model would normally make provision for the following additional line entries to cover the case where there is a shortfall of funds: principal brought forward, repayment due, repayment made and principal carried forward to next period.

If the interest on the loan is within the waterfall of accounts, then the model would normally make provision for the following additional line entries to cover the case where there is a shortfall of funds: interest brought forward, interest due, interest paid, interest carried forward to next period.

7.12. The Accounting Statements

The International Financial Reporting Standards (IFRS) allows companies to present their main accounting statements in more than one format. For instance, the balance sheet may be presented by classification, by order of assets or by net assets. Similarly, the funds statements may use the direct method or indirect method for determining the cash flows and may just show the sources and uses of funds or break them down into funds generated from operations, from investing and from financing.

It is considered good practice to include the balance sheet in a model because it acts as a check on the model and because some balance sheet ratios may be used in the calculation of the cash traps.

7.12.1. *Break-Even Analysis*

The model may be used for carrying out a variety of breakeven calculations predicted for each period over the operating life of the project.

These can be carried out on the price and capacity (the latter needs a VBA routine in Excel). The following two break-even values are usually calculated:

- Profit = operating costs + depreciation + interest paid
- Cash = operating costs + debt service

7.12.1.1. *Foreign Exchange Savings*

Despite the fact that a project may sometimes prove to have marginal economics, the host government may be interested in encouraging it because it produces a significant net inflow of foreign exchange. The model should calculate this inflow on a periodic basis through the life of the project by adding the following components:

(i) *Inflows into and/or savings in outflows out of the country*:
   Construction phase:
   - foreign loan drawdown;
   - foreign equity inflow;
   Operating phase:
   - earnings from exporting the product.
(ii) *Subtracting the following outflows*:
   Construction phase:
   - import of equipment and materials;
   Operating phase:
   - import of catalysts, chemicals, feedstock materials;
   - foreign loan debt service;
   - dividends paid to foreign shareholders.

In practice, there are other indirect effects. Consider, for example, the case where the project uses equipment and materials purchased locally from dealers who themselves import the items.

7.12.2. *Scenario Analysis*

There are many occasions when the user wants to carry out a "what if" analysis by varying several inputs at a time and preserving the input and results as a separate "case" or "scenario". Typical examples are:

- *Planning phase*: different project capacities and configurations.
- *Negotiating phase*: different bids from competing contractors and financiers.
- *Construction phase*: a budget case set at the start of construction.
- *Operating phase*: a high and a low case for different product prices, demands and utilization factors.

In a spreadsheet this can be accomplished by

- Inserting a "hook" into each important variable in the main input sheets so that the model uses the figure for the selected scenario rather than the figure for the base case.
- Inserting a scenario worksheet in which the user can set the various scenarios and choose the case from a drop-down box.

7.12.3. *Sensitivity Analysis*

In a sensitivity analysis, a simple automated routine can be used to change one input at a time. It then recalculates the model and records the results. At the end of the routine it produces a spider diagram, an example of which is shown in Figure 7.5.

Although sensitivity analysis is easy to perform, it has the following shortcomings:

- It fails to take into account the probability of the occurrence of the event. For example, sensitivity analysis may indicate that the project's NPV will drop below zero if the capital cost increases by 25%; however, it offers no insight into the probability that this event will occur.
- It ignores the correlations or interactions among the variables in the analysis. For example, the effect of a longer construction schedule on the viability of the project can be assessed in isolation but a longer construction schedule is also likely to adversely impact the construction costs which, in turn, will have a separate effect on the viability.
- The practice of varying the values of sensitive variables by standard percentages does not necessarily bear any relation to the observed or likely variability of the underlying variables. For example, although using plus or minus 30% as the extreme limits for the production rate may be realistic it does not necessarily make sense to do so for the

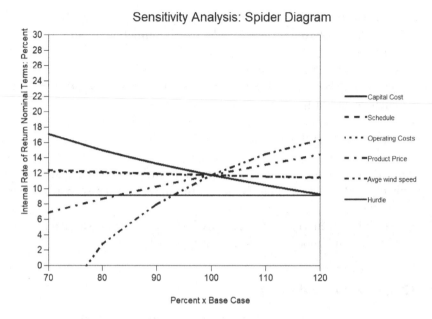

Figure 7.5:   Sensitivity Analysis: Sample Spider Diagram

price of the product if the product is, for instance, crude oil in the last year of the analysis.

7.12.4. *Risk Analysis*

Developers of major projects regularly carry out a risk analysis of the estimated project costs and schedule. The exercise follows an onerous procedure in which experts in different fields assess the risks. The results of this exercise are recorded in a series of risk registers and are used as input to a Monte Carlo simulation analysis in a schedule package.[3] The Monte Carlo analysis produces a histogram showing the number of occurrences on the vertical axis against the schedule range on the horizontal axis.

Similar analyses can be done with a financial model. The deterministic model as described in this chapter is converted to a stochastic model

---

[3] For a discussion of Monte Carlo simulation and software available, see Dessislava A. Pachamanova and Frank J. Fabozzi, *Simulation and Optimization Modeling in Finance*. Hoboken, NJ: John Wiley & Sons, 2010.

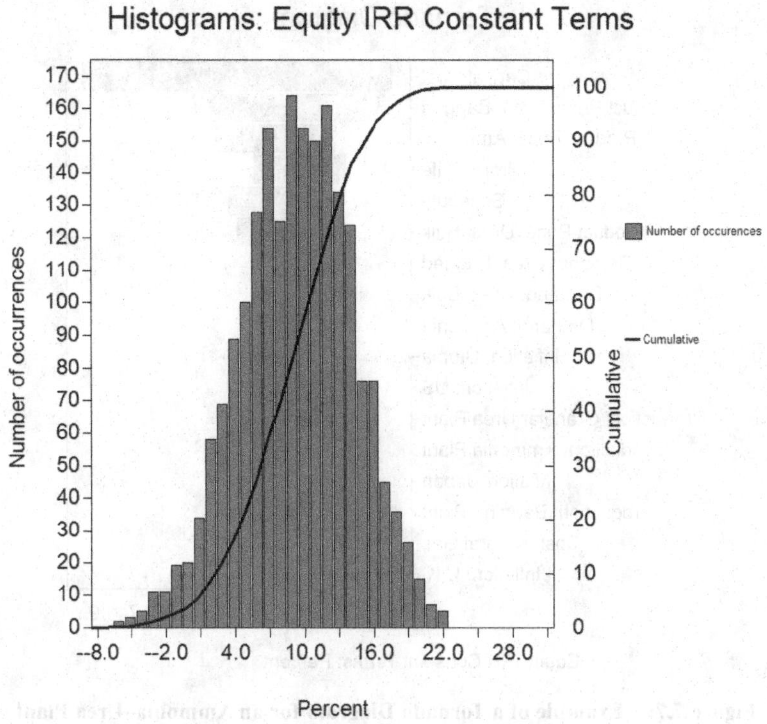

Figure 7.6:   **Sample Histograms for Equity IRR in Constant Terms**

after a review of the upper and lower limits on all inputs. Once they have been selected, a routine inserts random numbers chosen to lie between these limits and the model is recalculated. This is repeated several thousand times. The model keeps a record of the results for each calculation. At the conclusion it prepares a series of histograms for all results including the equity NPV, IRR and the maximum additional funds needed during the operating phase and calculates selected confidence limits as shown in the example in Figure 7.6.

7.13. Tornado Diagrams

A tornado diagram displays the impact on a selected result when changing a single key parameter — first with a low limit and then with a high limit. These limits are typically the same as those figures contained in the inputs for the Monte Carlo analyses.

Tornado Diagram

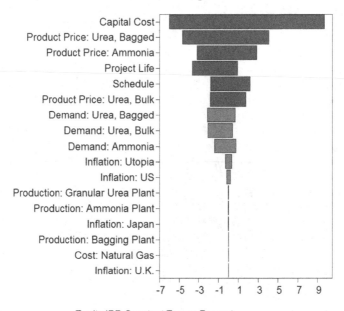

Equity IRR Constant Terms: Percent

Figure 7.7:　Example of a Tornado Diagram for an Ammonia–Urea Plant

The tornado diagram displays the results in a sequential order, with the variable having the largest impact shown at the top of the diagram, as shown in Figure 7.7. The order of the variables may also change depending on which of the project selection approaches shown in Table 7.1 is used. So, for instance, the variable order shown for the IRRs may be different from the variable order for the NPVs.

While a tornado diagram can be more informative than a spider diagram generated by employing sensitivity analysis, it is more time consuming to develop properly.

7.14. Goal Seeking

The model should make use of the built-in goal-seeking facility to allow the user to change a variable (say capital cost or project price) and obtain a desired outcome (an equity IRR, loan cover ratio and the like).

7.15. Cross-Checks

The model should have a worksheet devoted to a series of cross-checks which help to ensure the model's integrity. For instance, it should contain a function to check that the balance sheets balance and a function to verify that the ending cash on the cash flows statement equals the sum of the balances for the escrow account and the sinking funds. Moreover, there should be functions to check that table subtotals throughout the model add up both horizontally and vertically to the same total number.

7.16. Testing the Model

The model should contain a VBA procedure for carrying out a series of automatic tests if written in Excel, or the equivalent procedure for other packages. The tests insert a series of numbers into the following main input parameters, calculate the model and check to see whether the cross-check results described previously are correct.

- construction period;
- project life;
- accounting period;
- factors such as the capital cost, operating costs, capacity payments and availability.

There are third-party tools to audit models. As a first step, however, the modeller should use the automatic tests aforementioned. In addition to these tests, banks may require a third party to audit the model.

7.17. Modeller's Review of the Legal Documentation

The loan agreement will contain important information for modelling the project, so it is vital that the modeller review the lenders' documentation before it is finalized. The modeller (and legal consultants) should look out for:

- the functional currency or currencies if there is more than one currency;

- the waterfall of accounts and how any major shortfall in cash will be made good (standby loan, equity support). If there is a standby loan or equity support, at what point in the waterfall does it support the shortfall?
- if there is an interest guarantee from the shareholders (or debt service guarantee), to which loan(s) does it apply?
- how is the target for the debt service reserve account adjusted for pre-payments? (A lender may feel that the original targets should remain, but the borrower may feel that as the project progresses successfully, the reduction in loan balance warrants a reduction in the target figure.)
- how are currency adjustments to be handled during the operating phase, through the profit and loss account or through the balance sheet?

7.18. Version Control

Model files are typically used by a variety of different people all of whom may be interested in making changes to the input. Files change hand and may be modified by different people. It is important to keep track of the changes and to ensure that there is a single master model and that this file is readily identifiable.

7.19. Audit Trails

Comprehensive models for large and complex projects need to take their input data from a variety of sources in different fields. They may need information from technical specialists, market analysts, cost estimators, financiers and taxation specialists. Some of the inputs may come from in-house sources, while others from reports produced by outside consultants.

It is invariably necessary to keep track of who entered or updated the basis for the model and when that individual made the change. In addition, it may be appropriate for the user to record some explanatory notes, perhaps on the source of the information.

7.20. Complex Models

Some projects will contain more than one party for whom the model should calculate a set of cash flows.

7.20.1. *Multiple Countries*

Some projects will contain elements which are located in more than one country. This is the case with for instance:

- A liquefied natural gas project consisting of the gas development, the liquefied natural gas plant, the shipping and one or more unloading terminals.
- An international cable telecommunication company with one or more landing stations in different countries. The company owning the cable in international waters may be registered in a third country with a favourable tax regime.
- An international pipeline project.
- A rail or road bridge or tunnel linking two countries.

In these cases, there will usually be an SPV in each of the countries, each with its own revenues, costs and accounting statements. Typically, a single model which incorporates the accounts for each company in separate worksheets is produced, but of course, this adds complexity to the model.

7.20.2. *Multiple Points of View*

Projects have multiple stakeholders. For example, consider a lease agreement. The lessor and lessee are stakeholders wherein the former invests in leased asset and the latter operates the project.

In these cases, the revenues for the investing party may be the operating costs for the other party. The model should illustrate the cash flow for both parties and determine the NPV and other key criteria for each.

7.21. Using VBAs

It is common for users and auditors of project finance and PPP models to specify that the model should not contain any VBA code. The reason for this requirement is that the code is more difficult to audit than the formulae within the spreadsheet cells. However, there are occasions when some code is necessary as outlined in the following subsections.

7.21.1. *User Defined Functions*

Microsoft Excel contains an IRR function in which the formula assumes that all cash flows are received on an annual basis. It also contains a function named "xIRR" that calculates the IRR whenever the intervals between cash flows are not yearly. Excel contains an MIRR function for the modified IRR in which the user specifies a reinvestment rate. This function assumes that all cash flows are on a yearly basis. However, Excel does not contain an equivalent "xMIRR" function for cash flows received more than one time per year. The user can overcome this limitation by creating the function as a User Defined Function with VBA.

7.21.2. *Test Code*

As explained earlier in this chapter, the modeller will find it useful to develop a simple VBA procedure to test the model. This test procedure should be used whenever the modeller makes any significant changes to the model.

7.21.3. *Analyses*

Sensitivity, capacity break even, Monte Carlo analyses and tornado diagrams can all be generated readily with relatively simple VBA code.

7.21.4. *Iterative Calculations*

There are a number of occasions when the formulae in a spreadsheet produce circular reference. These may be overcome by VBA code or by setting the iteration option in the calculation settings to overcome the circular reference. The latter solution is not recommended because it obscures additional circular references which the developer could inadvertently introduce. The following formulae frequently produce circular references:

- Setting a desired ratio of local to foreign currency costs (in a planning phase model).
- Setting a desired initial debt to equity ratio when there is more than one country and the inflation rates in each differ (in a planning phase model).
- Calculating dividend payments when these are restricted by debt service cover ratios to be calculated for future periods.

7.22. Alternatives to Spreadsheets

Modellers that do not want to develop a model using a spreadsheet in the manner described in this chapter can use specific software that is available to produce models in a wide variety of industries.

We close this chapter with a case study that has endured over many years and illustrates the difficulty of valuing an asset, asymmetries in negotiating and desired outcomes, and how lengthy court cases can result in the destruction of lives.

7.23. Case Study: Valuing Bula Mines

When Patrick Wright's cattle died unexpectedly, little did anyone expect that this would be the start of a very controversial project that would keep litigants busy for almost 50 years, be debated in the press and the Irish Government, and become a famous teaching case study in business schools.

Mr. Wright was a dairy farmer in County Meath in the Republic of Ireland. His land included a lead-zinc orebody (the reason for the cattle's demise) some of which was close to the surface and the rest of which lay underground. As is often the case in minerals projects, Mr. Wright owned the land but it was believed that the Irish State owned the minerals rights. In the late 1960 and in 1970, an exploration company, Tara Exploration and Development Company Ltd. (Tara, hereafter) was set up to explore for minerals and found rich deposits under Mr. Wright's lands and this news was made public in official journals as required by both law and Stock Exchange regulations. Tara then attempted to negotiate with the Irish Government for development rights, at which point it was discovered that Mr. Wright also owned the mineral rights, not the Irish State, thus requiring Tara to negotiate with Mr. Wright to acquire the land and the mineral rights. At this point, another bidding group appeared and bought the land, conveying it to a new company, Bula Mines (Bula hereafter). The consideration was £0.5 million cash, £0.3 million[4] when mining commenced and a 20% share interest in Bula. (At the time, the Republic of Ireland's currency was the Irish pound.)

---

[4] In this case study, £ means Irish pounds or punt. The Irish pound separated from the UK pound in 1979 leading to the establishment of a formal exchange rate. In 2002, this was replaced by the euro.

The orebody extended to an area outside of Mr. Wright's property — for this part, the mining rights were owned by the state — but optimal commercial exploitation required the unification of the two pieces of land and rights. A Compulsory Purchase Order for the land and rights now owned by Bula was quashed by the Courts and the compromise that was reached was for the Minister to acquire 49% of Bula's shares with a power of attorney over 21% of the voting rights granted to one of the Bula principals. Around 25% was in the form of a gift and the remaining 24% would be purchased. However, the two parts of the orebody were being developed separately.

In order to work out a price for the shares, cash flows needed to be prepared so that the Bula project could be valued. In 1974, Rio Tinto Zinc (RTZ) a large multinational mining company was commissioned by Bula to carry out a feasibility study. To give a sense of scale, the Tara orebody was estimated at 63 million tonnes and Bula's at 19.6 million tonnes in an article published in the *Irish Times* after the RTZ report became public.

Meanwhile, Bula commissioned a second report from Bechtel in 1976 to evaluate the project. Bechtel accepted the RTZ estimates of reserves and the capital costs. The river diversion and preparation for underground mining were expected to cost £5 million in 1977 costs. However, there were two areas of debate. The first was the operating cost estimates that were significantly lower than those of other Irish mining companies (with track records). The second was the metal price estimates. Two well-known and regarded journalists took opposing views on this with articles published in the press. The final decision on valuation went to the London Institute of Arbitration.

The experts disagreed in some other key areas, notably the extraction rate, the ore quality, the timing of the project and future tax and inflation rates, all of which form part of the expert personal judgment of those making the appraisal and of course the discount rate used. The latter reflects project risk and Bula was a new company that was unlikely to support debt without some form of external guarantee. Using the CAPM, the following assumptions were made: (1) a beta of one, (2) a risk premium of around 8.8% by comparison with the UK market, and (3) an inflation rate of 10% which was reasonable at the time, suggesting a nominal discount rate of 18.8%. Once the total NPV was calculated, the amount due to Mr. Wright had to be subtracted. Sensitivity analysis also needed to be performed and this showed that a higher recovery rate and a 10% error in operating cost estimation had a relatively small impact on the computed

NPV. The NPV was more severely impacted by delays, especially if significant capital had already been spent or by any delays or problems with the initial open cast mining planning application. This was compounded because the capital had already been spent, but no revenue was received. Tax benefits were also affected because the trigger point could have been the date of expenditure and therefore their value, if revenue is deferred, decreases. Project cash flows were also very sensitive to the discount rate used.

In addition to the two journalists, no fewer than four other experts looked at valuing Bula, including Bechtel. The range of numbers for the valuation of Bula was from over £100 million to less than £10 million. The numbers were discussed in the press and in the *Oireachtas*, the Irish State legislative body because a special bill had to be passed in order to approve the government payment to Bula.

There have been various suggestions that the wide range of numbers arose because of one or more of the following: nominal cash flows were discounted by real discount rates, the tax was not correctly calculated, the mineral prices were optimistic, or the valuation team did not have sufficient access to the data. In the end the government paid £9.54 million for its stake, but the problems did not end there.

During this time, Tara and Bula were also involved in a plan to divert an underground part of Blackwater River (also known as the Kells Blackwater) to access some 12 million tonnes of ore at a cost of £2 million. The Kells Blackwater is a well-known river for fly fishers and especially for wild brown trout (and salmon at this time). Environmental uproar ensued, not least as fishing-related tourism was important to the local economy. Another unacknowledged issue was the need to build a smelter to transform the ore concentrates into metal for both projects.

Bula struggled to obtain planning permission for its open cast mine and further governmental financial support was granted. The company finally received planning permission for wholly underground mining in 1983 (open cast had been refused) but by then the company had borrowed substantially, securing this debt against mortgages on the orebody. There were also complications arising from a lack of clarity inside the Bula corporate structure whereby payments were made to individuals rather than the company. Bula went into liquidation in 1985. Ultimately, the Bula assets were sold by the Official Receiver to Tara Mines (by then a subsidiary of the Finnish company Outukumpu) in 2001 for £27.5 million (€34.9 million), making the 24% share worth £6.6 million. The first claim on this money was from the creditor banks believed to be owed in excess of £20 million. This did not stop further litigation and costs in 2003, resulting from various court cases, were estimated at €4.8 million including interest. The government attempted to reclaim those costs and by 2010 had issued bankruptcy proceedings against two of the original Bula shareholders. In March 2018, almost 50 years later, the Bula saga was eventually put to rest with the two individuals declared bankrupt.

The lessons that can be learned from this saga are many and the lengthy court transcripts provide interesting insights into the various individuals involved, the intersection between politics and self-interest, and the wide variation in approaches to what may appear be a simple cash flow calculation. The variation in the numbers also offers food for thought in terms of approaches made by different experts. It becomes easy to see how different parties in a project may have very conflicting views as to what it is worth and what its profile looks like and why a single agreed model can make a lot of sense. However, any model is only as good as the assumptions that are used and those assumptions need to be the best available at the time. There was a lot of press commentary about the agreement on some of the basic figures for Bula but the divergent views on some of the key aspects of the valuation analysis. Certainly, the use of proxies contributed to the confusion and therefore the temptation to use beta values from established markets in risky projects without adjusting for that risk can lead to poor decision-making. This case also illustrates another point — legal costs can be very substantial and the process of going through the legal process can delay a project and consume funding. Inexperienced stakeholders can very often believe that litigation should be the first action rather than the last, because "the contract says so". Even though the contract may indeed confirm a position and say that legal costs should be borne by the other side, collecting the money is a very different matter and getting the judgment enforced can be yet another challenge!

Chapter 8

Financial Modelling for Different Industries[*]

Introduction

Projects in some industries provide a service, others produce one or more products. Projects in some industries can be readily expanded to meet increasing demand. Others have a fixed capacity which can only be expanded in size by installing a new plant in parallel with the existing one. Some need regular annual maintenance, others need major maintenance at longer intervals. It is useful to examine the characteristics of projects in different industries and to highlight the key features which affect the cash flows and the financial model in each.

In this chapter, we describe a number of industries which are often the subject of project financings and public–private partnerships (PPPs). The description includes:

- a list of characteristics which sets the industry apart from other industries. This list will include items which the modeller *may need* to take into account;
- where appropriate, some reminders of other key factors which the modeller *ought* to take into account;
- typical cash flows for projects in that industry.

---

[*]This chapter is contributed by John Macgillivray, Managing Director of Project Planning and Management Ltd. Further information on modelling may be obtained from https://www.promoter.com.

The main purpose of a financial model is to determine the base case cash flows and key results and to carry out "what-if" analyses. In theory, any rigorous model should handle changes to all key parameters which could affect the cash flows such as price, demand, capital cost, construction schedule, country macroeconomic data, etc.

In practice this does happen effectively for many projects in industries where the modelling is relatively simple. However, for projects in other industries the modelling is more complicated. The technical formulae are complex and a spreadsheet is not always the ideal tool. In such cases the modeller often ignores how these key parameters affect the cash flows and the result is not always satisfactory.

The cash flow figures illustrated in this chapter are all figurative and in real (as opposed to nominal) terms. There will be many variations from one project to another.

8.1.   Extractive Industries

8.1.1.   *Oil and Gas Development Projects*

Oil and gas development (as opposed to exploration) projects consist of wells and equipment plus one or more of the following: platform, pipeline and terminal. Such projects:

- are technically complex, particularly if the project is offshore;
- contain significant amounts of equipment and material which may need to be imported;
- produce oil and gas products which are sold on the open market;
- have a production profile which usually increases rapidly and then declines gradually as the reservoir is depleted;
- earn foreign exchange generated from the sale of the product in international markets;
- usually benefit from economies of scale;
- are subject to complex taxation calculations (bonuses, royalties and production sharing in a concession);
- have a high level of risk;
- have a high level of regulation;
- have a long time span before a return on investment is received;
- have higher rates of return than projects in other industries. Each development project has to cover the cost of unsuccessful exploration

projects which might outnumber them by 10 to 1. The costs of these exploration programmes are "sunk" and are not included in the investment decision (though they may be included in taxation calculations).

There is some further discussion on specific oil and gas project financing in Chapter 15.

Modelling considerations for oil and gas development projects: In the early planning phases, the model should include a simple method for calculating the production from the decline rate and plateau. In later phases, the production should be based on detailed evaluations produced by specialists.

Typical oil and gas development project cash flows: Typical project cash flows are illustrated in Figure 8.1. The revenues will typically be held at a plateau level for several years as determined by the capacity of the processing equipment and pipelines. It may increase in the early years if the project is commissioned before all the wells are drilled. This is often a decision favoured by financiers because the cost of many of the wells can be funded from the early cash flows. The operating costs will typically be much smaller than the revenues. The installation must typically be decommissioned at the end of the field's economic life.

8.1.2. *Mining Projects*

Mining projects can be categorized by the way that the ore is recovered.

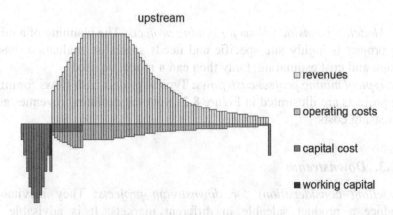

Figure 8.1: Typical Cash Flows for Oil and Gas Development Projects

- *Surface*: Mining such as open-pit mining and strip mining;
- *Sub-surface*: Mining conducted underground classified by the characteristic of the rock being mined: There are three directions by which an underground mine may be conducted: drift mining, mining horizontally, shaft mining, mining vertically and slope mining, mining at an inclined angle;
- *Others*: Such as borehole mining, box cut, deep sea mining.

Such projects:

- produce extracted mineral which may consist a single product or it may be an ore with a variety of different products all worth extracting. For instance, bauxite is used solely for the production of aluminium but orthomagmatic sulphide deposits may contain platinum, palladium, rhodium, iridium, ruthenium and osmium;
- produce minerals which typically goes through a concentration (beneficiation) process at the mine to produce a more valuable concentrate and tailings. The concentrate will be used as feedstock to a metallurgical plant located on site or remotely (and therefore not part of the project);
- are subject to royalties payable to the host government;
- produce revenues which may decline with time as the richest seams are exhausted;
- incur costs which increase with time as the distance for transporting the mineral increases;
- require clean-up costs to be accrued to restore sites once mining is over.

Modelling considerations for mining projects: The planning of a mining project is highly site specific and needs specialist evaluation, basic design and cost estimating. Only then can a model be used.

Typical mining project cash flows: Typical project cash flows for mining projects are illustrated in Figure 8.2. Note the declining revenues and increasing costs.

8.1.3. Downstream

Modelling considerations for downstream projects: They inevitably produce a product saleable in different markets. It is advisable to

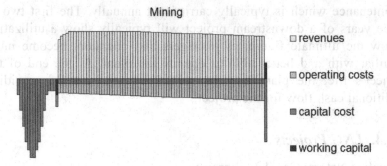

Figure 8.2: Typical Cash Flows for Mining Projects

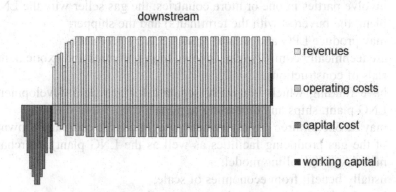

Figure 8.3: Typical Cash Flows for Downstream Projects

include routines for calculating the shipping costs to each market and a netback price. The local market is usually the most profitable but once it is saturated in any period the balance must be diverted to more distant and less profitable markets.

Typical downstream project cash flows: Typical project cash flows are illustrated in Figure 8.3. The revenues are essentially constant in real terms over the project's life. However, two competing effects will result in a pattern that differs from that shown. If the local and more profitable market is expanding in size, then the revenues will increase over time. However, if the commodity price is declining, then the revenues will decrease. In practice, both effects play a part in altering the pattern. The revenues and operating costs are affected by regular maintenance which is typically carried out annually. The first two or three years of a downstream project will typically show a utilization below the ultimate figure, as managers and operators become more familiar with and better able to operate the plant. At the end of the project's life, the plant may be sold for scrap, thereby providing additional cash flow for the project.

8.1.4. *LNG Projects*

Liquefied Natural Gas (LNG) projects:

- involve very large investments;
- involve parties in one or more countries: the gas seller with the LNG plant, the buyer(s) with the terminal(s) and the shipper;
- may produce LPG and natural gasoline as by products;
- are technically complex (can involve high pressures and exotic materials of construction);
- have funding which is usually separate for gas field development, LNG plant, ships and unloading terminal;
- may be one of three project models: integrated (the company is owner of the gas producing facilities as well as the LNG plant), merchant model and the tolling model;
- usually benefit from economies of scale;
- earn foreign exchange for the gas producing country.

Modelling considerations for LNG projects: The nature of the model must reflect the legal basis for the project. In an integrated project, the company is the owner of the gas producing facilities as well as the LNG plant. The model will contain both the upstream gas production facilities and the LNG plant, usually both located in the same country. It may also include:

- the LNG ships, usually registered with a flag of convenience; and
- the LNG terminal, almost always in a third country.

The functional currency will usually be different in each country.

In a merchant project, the company buys the gas, produces and sells the LNG and typically takes the market risk. In a tolling project, the company charges a tolling fee which may contain a fixed and variable price.

Typical LNG project cash flows: For the LNG plant itself, see the section on downstream projects. For the gas production facilities and the LNG tankers, see the sections on the relevant industries.

8.1.5. *Oil Refineries*

This category includes both crude oil and condensate refineries. Such projects:

- are technically complex (can involve high pressures and exotic materials of construction);
- contain significant equipment and material which may need to be imported;
- produce large volumes of the product;
- produce products which are sold on the open market (crude oil is sometimes processed on a toll basis);
- generate small profit margins;
- earn foreign exchange generated from the sale of the product in international markets;
- have annual maintenance shutdown which will reduce revenues and variable operating costs for about a month;
- usually benefit from economies of scale;
- are subject to straightforward taxation calculations.

Modelling considerations for oil refineries: In view of the small margins and technical complexity of a refinery, it is important that the design basis for the model is determined by specialists who set the optimum cut points, yields, feed and product densities, capital and operating costs. They will usually use proprietary software to optimize the design. These results are then used as inputs for the financial model. (See also the comments on downstream projects.)

Typical oil refinery project cash flows: Typical project cash flows are illustrated in Figure 8.4. The cash flows are similar to a downstream project but the costs and revenues dwarf the amount of the capital investment. The working capital is a significant part of the initial investment, particularly at times when the price of oil is high.

Refinery

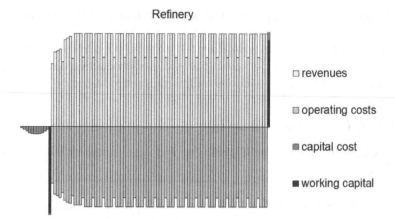

Figure 8.4:   **Typical Cash Flows for Oil Refinery Projects**

It is often more instructive to view the marginal rather than the full cash flows. The marginal cash flows are the full cash flows reduced by the cost of the crude oil feedstock.

8.1.6. *Petrochemical*

Downstream petrochemical applies to ethylene and benzene, toluene, xylene (BTX) based petrochemicals, nitrogen-based petrochemicals (methanol, ammonia, and urea), other fertilizers (e.g. phosphates), pulp and paper, gas processing (e.g. liquefied natural gas plants and liquefied petroleum gas plants), metallurgical and a broad range of industrial plant. The following characterize such projects:

- are technically complex but the designs are usually well proven;
- may contain a sequence of plants each one producing a product which is used as a feedstock for the next project on the same site. Some of the product may also be sold. This design complexity can complicate the model;
- contain significant equipment and material which may need to be imported;
- produce products usually sold on the open market;
- have products with prices which may follow a cyclical pattern, for instance, in the pulp and paper industry;

- earn foreign exchange generated from the sale of the product in international markets;
- have a production profile which usually increases rapidly to the design capacity where it stays for the duration of the project;
- have an annual maintenance shutdown which will reduce revenues and variable operating costs for about a month;
- are subject to straightforward taxation calculations.

8.1.7. *Fertilizers*

Fertilizers usually consist of one or more of the following components: N (nitrogen) from sources such as ammonia, urea, ammonium nitrate, P (phosphates) from reacting sulphuric acid with mined phosphates and K (potash expressed as K20) also usually mined.

Fertilizer projects:

- involve very large investments;
- are technically complex (can involve high pressures and exotic materials of construction) but a mature industry;
- may contain a sequence of plants each one producing a product which is used as a feedstock for the next project on the same site. Some of the product may also be sold. This design complexity can complicate the model;
- have a feedstock in the case of an ammonia plant (the source of nitrogen) is usually natural gas; other feedstocks such as naphtha and fuel oil tend to have higher capital and operating costs. The location of ammonia and urea plants is therefore located near cheap sources of natural gas;
- products which are sold on the open market;
- production which usually increases rapidly to the design capacity where it stays for the duration of the project following the pattern in Figure 8.4;
- annual maintenance shutdown which will reduce revenues and variable operating costs for about a month;
- usually benefit from economies of scale;
- earn foreign exchange generated from the sale of the product in international markets.

8.1.8. *Water Treatment*

Water treatment plants produce drinking or other water from springs, rivers or other freshwater projects such as dams. Waste water is more complex than one producing water from a spring or river. It usually has a large waste water treatment section which increases the capital and operating costs. Sea water (desalination) can be achieved by the use of reverse osmosis or by waste heat typically from a steam generating power station.

Such plants:

- are technically simple;
- produce products usually sold to a captive market;
- do not earn foreign exchange;
- usually benefit from economies of scale;
- contain significant equipment and material which may need to be imported;
- are sometimes subject to a joint venture between the public and private sector.

8.1.9. *Metallurgy*

Applies to: steel, aluminium (electrometallurgy), copper, titanium, nickel, zinc and precious metals such as gold and silver. Such projects:

- have very large investments;
- rare technically complex but in a mature industry;
- involve the processing of an ore to produce a metal;
- usually extract the metal from their ore by one or more processes of mineral processing, hydrometallurgy, pyrometallurgy and electrometallurgy. (Hydrometallurgy involves leaching, solution concentration and purification and metal recovery. Pyrometallurgy typically involves calcining, roasting, smelting and refining);
- may involve the consumption of quite large quantities of power (as in aluminium production);
- have products which are sold on the open market;
- usually benefit from economies of scale;
- can earn foreign exchange generated from the sale of the product in international markets.

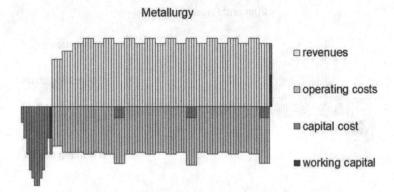

Figure 8.5: Typical Cash Flows for Metallurgy Projects

Modelling considerations for metallurgy projects: See the comments on downstream projects.

Typical metallurgy project cash flows: Typical project cash flows for an aluminium project are illustrated in Figure 8.5. Note the replacement costs for electrolytic cells. See also the comments on cash flows for downstream projects.

8.1.10. *Pulp and Paper*

These large projects may consist of a pulp plant, paper plant or a combination of both. They are characterized by:

- a need for large cheap power sources and proximity to large areas of suitable forest;
- technical complexity especially as environmental issues continue to grow in importance;
- significant equipment and material which may need to be imported;
- products usually sold on the open market;
- earns foreign exchange for the product which is sold on international markets;
- pulp and paper prices tend to be cyclical over several years;
- usually benefit from economies of scale;
- production which usually increases rapidly to the design capacity where it stays for the duration of the project.

Pulp and Paper

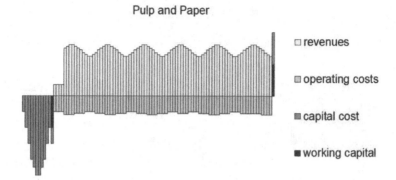

Figure 8.6:   **Typical Cash Flows for Pulp and Paper Projects**

Modelling considerations in pulp and paper projects: See the comments on downstream projects.

Typical pulp and paper project cash flows: Typical project cash flows for pulp and paper projects are illustrated in Figure 8.6. The revenues will usually show a cyclical trend. See also the comments on typical cash flows for downstream projects.

8.1.11. *Power*

8.1.11.1. *Electric Power or Electricity Generating Projects*

Included in the power industry are any power projects producing electric power as the main product. Possible fuel sources include natural gas, fuel oil and coal on conventional power and uranium on a nuclear power plant. (Power plants based on renewable energy such as wind, solar, tidal and hydroelectricity have renewable fuel sources and are discussed separately.) Classic electricity generating projects:

- are technically complex when large, but simple if small;
- contain significant equipment and material which may need to be imported;
- may be base load or swing producers;
- produce power sold in a closed market;
- produce power that cannot usually be exported so as to generate foreign exchange (but subsea distribution cables may exist as part of the project);

- generate revenues which are either (a) governed by negotiated tariffs with escalation and indexation clauses and tariffs split into capacity (fixed) and fuel (variable) elements or (b) from a power supply which the operator bids for on an hourly or other basis in the case of a merchant power plant;
- have a large variation in fuel price;
- are subject to an annual maintenance shutdown on conventional power plants which will reduce revenues and variable operating costs for about a month per year;
- produce byproducts such as low-pressure steam and desalinated water for which there may be a suitable local market;
- may have to pay (and accrue) for a large decommissioning cost as in the case of a nuclear power plant;
- are generally subject to straightforward taxation calculations but may have to pay environmental taxes (e.g. carbon tax and cap-and-trade) or receive subsidies (in the case of renewable energy).

Modelling considerations for electricity generating projects: There are no special considerations for electricity generating projects other than payments if the project is offline as a result of the power utility decision and any costs associated with the need to keep standby fuel on site.

Typical electricity generating project cash flows: The revenues for a base load power plant with a power purchase agreement (as shown in Figure 8.7) will typically have a capital cost recovery element and an operating and maintenance component. The capital cost component may be repaid over the project's life or over a shorter period.

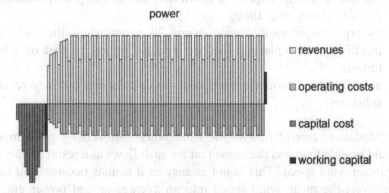

Figure 8.7:   Typical Cash Flows for Conventional Power Plant Projects

The cash flow for a renewable energy projects will have a larger capital cost (per MWh) but much smaller operating costs since they use no fuel.

8.1.11.2. *Wind Power*

Modern wind farms consist of an array of wind turbines each with a typical capacity of 1–8 MW. Each turbine consists of foundations, tower, nacelle, hub and rotor, drive train (gearbox and generator), electronics and controls. Such wind farms:

- are dependent on the wind which may not be blowing. Under these circumstances the load must be taken up by other power plants;
- may be located onshore or offshore. Offshore locations involve expensive platforms and undersea cables but usually benefit from higher average wind speeds;
- need to be located at sites where the average wind speed is high. Generally speaking, wind speeds are highest on hills and ridges and lowest in sheltered terrain. The order is typically as follows: hills and ridges > open sea > sea coast > open terrain > sheltered terrain;
- are technically simple but offshore installations are more challenging;
- produce low capacity factors;
- have no input fuel cost and low operations and maintenance costs;
- experience seasonal fluctuations in wind which affects the cash flows;
- are maintained twice a year. Condition Monitoring Systems (CMS) can help pre-empt expensive down time due to component failure;
- degrade slowly over time;
- undergo major maintenance every 20 years when the sails and machinery are replaced. The performance returns to that of a new turbine.
- are subject to straightforward taxation calculations but may receive subsidies.

Modelling considerations for wind power projects: A good model should be able to assess the impact on the cash flows as a result of varying the mean wind speed. This is not as easy as it sounds because you have to convert the mean wind speed into an average annual power output. This can be complicated. It is a function of the wind speed, air density, the rotor area and efficiency factor. The efficiency factor is a product of the mechanical, electrical and aerodynamic efficiencies. This latter efficiency is subject to a theoretical maximum of 16/27 (Betz' law).

The mean annual power production is calculated as follows:

- adjust the average wind speed for wind shear and the wind farm height and temperature.
- calculate the capacity factor from the turbine manufacturer's figures and the wind speed distribution (see Figures 8.8–8.10) from actual measurements or from a suitable Weibull distribution. This is done as follows: For each element of the wind histogram, multiply the percent occurrence by the corresponding element on the turbine power curve. Add these figures together for the mean annual power production and divide by the peak output for the capacity factor.
- consider repeating this process for each month of the year. Monthly variations in the average wind speed have a direct effect on the cash flows and can be significant.

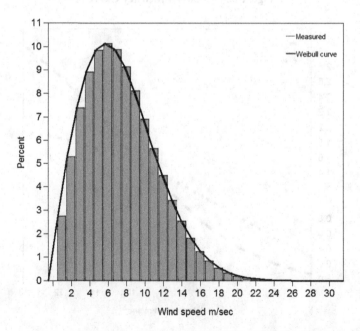

Figure 8.8:   Monthly Average Wind Speed

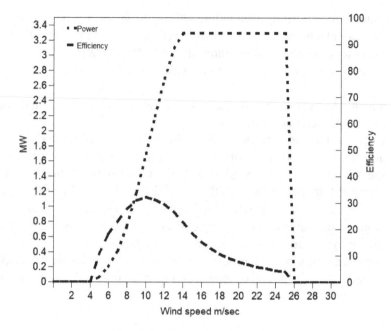

Figure 8.9:   Power Efficiency Curve

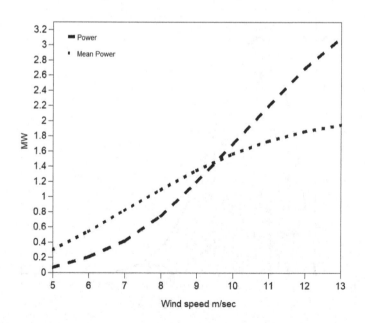

Figure 8.10:   Mean Power from Mean Wind Speed

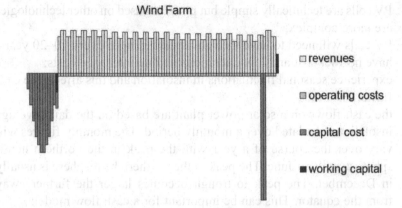

Figure 8.11:   Typical Cash Flows for Wind Farm Projects

Typical wind power project cash flows: Figure 8.11 illustrates the cash flows on a wind farm project. The project has a high capital cost but very low operating costs. The chart also illustrates the gradual decline in efficiency and the need for additional investment in inverters. Notice how the revenues vary seasonally.

8.1.11.3. *Solar Power*

The sun is a renewable source of energy which can be used to generate solar power. Such power plants:

- may be based on photo-voltaic cells which are cheap (and becoming cheaper) but relatively inefficient. Their operating costs are very low. They are also limited to generating electricity during daylight hours. However, they may be supplemented by the use of storage batteries which can hold the output for a few hours to deliver power during the peak consumption period;
- or may be based on mirrors heating a medium such as hot salt which are more expensive but also convert more of the sunshine into power. Such plants are also able to store the hot medium to generate power via a steam turbine for a few hours after sunset. These plants may be based on fixed or moveable mirrors. The moveable mirrors are more expensive but are more efficient. Their operating costs are low but significantly higher than for PV cells;

- PV cells are technically simple but projects based on other technologies are more complex;
- PV cells will need to have their inverters replaced every 10–20 years;
- have no fuel cost and low operations and maintenance costs;
- experience seasonal fluctuations in insolation and this affects the cash flows;
- the cash flows on a solar power plant are based on the daily average insolation calculated over a monthly period. The monthly figures will vary over the course of a year with the peak in the northern hemisphere usually in June. The peak in the southern hemisphere is usually in December. The peak to trough becomes larger the further away from the equator. This can be important for a cash flow model;
- are subject to straightforward taxation calculations but may receive subsidies.

Modelling considerations in solar power projects: Monthly variations in solar insolation have a direct effect on the cash flows and can be significant. They must be included in the model. Long-term degradation in the cells/mirrors should also be taken into account.

Typical solar power project cash flows: Figure 8.12 illustrates the cash flows on PV cell project. The project has a high capital cost but very low operating costs. The chart also illustrates the gradual decline in efficiency and the need for additional investment in inverters. Notice how the revenues vary seasonally.

In the case of a project with a CSP system, the capital and operating costs will be higher. The revenues may also be higher if the project is selling power at peak demand times.

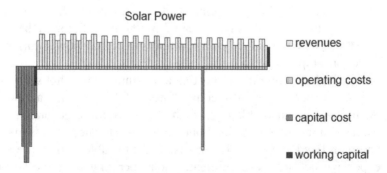

Figure 8.12:   Typical Cash Flows for Solar Project

8.1.11.4. *Hydro Power*

There are four main types of hydropower projects:

Run-of-river hydropower projects have no, or very little, storage capacity behind the dam and generation is dependent on the timing and size of river flows. Such projects fall naturally into two categories:

- Upland projects that use the natural fall of the river to create the necessary head, which is then commanded by tunnel, canal or surface conduit. These are typically high-head, low-flow schemes.
- Lowland projects that are sited at barrages on the more mature, lower reaches of rivers, where they rely solely upon the head created by the barrage. These are typically low-head, high-flow schemes.

Reservoir (storage) hydropower schemes have the ability to store water behind the dam in a reservoir in order to de-couple generation from hydro inflows. Reservoir capacities can be small or very large, depending on the characteristics of the site and the economics of dam construction.

Pumped storage hydropower schemes use off-peak electricity to pump water from a reservoir located after the tailrace to the top of the reservoir, so that the pumped storage plant can generate at peak times and provide grid stability and flexibility services. Typical cycle times are 4–8 hours but some have cycle times of more than one day.

Marine/offshore technologies are a less established, but growing group of technologies that use power of currents or waves to generate electricity from seawater. These include hydrokinetic (river, ocean and wave), tidal barrage and tidal stream, osmotic and ocean thermal technologies.

Such projects:

- are technically simple;
- contain some equipment and material which may need to be imported;
- have a long construction period when the project is large and there is a large civil engineering component;
- have a long project life, typically 40–100 years or more;
- have no fuel cost and low operations and maintenance costs (2%–4% of capital cost);
- experience seasonal fluctuations in water flow which affects the cash flows;

- have a wide range of capacity factors typically in the range of 25%–90% but some outside this range, depending on the design basis;
- offer other benefits including flood protection, drought management, drinking water supply, irrigation, navigation and tourism, all which typically do not offer clear and direct revenue streams to reservoir developers;
- have potential impacts on the local environments and the possible displacement of communities from project sites;
- need major maintenance every 10 years for runner replacement, every 20 years for SCADA, control systems, etc., every 30 years for switch-gear and utility equipment;
- reservoir projects may take up to two years or more to fill before they can start producing power;
- allow more renewable power projects, especially wind and solar, to be added to the system by providing rapid-response power when inter-mittent sources are off-line; and pump water to energy storage when such sources are generating excess power;
- may affect more than one country and may need international agree-ments. Typically, the upstream parts of the river are exploited for hydropower and the downstream parts for irrigation. The planned developments by one country to dam parts of a river may have nega-tive implications for countries further downstream of the river, such as flooding and irregular water availability;
- impact the rate of sediment transport in a river, in many cases leading to sediments becoming trapped behind the dam rather than flowing downstream. This can have a direct effect on the operating life and the electricity output of hydropower plants, and the distribution of sedi-ments and nutrients downstream. Effects of sedimentation include reduced reservoir and flood management capacity due to the loss of storage, a shortened power generation cycle, and higher maintenance costs;
- the civil costs of reservoir schemes are very site specific and difficult to estimate without a detailed design.

Modelling considerations in hydro power projects: Monthly varia-tions in river flow have a direct effect on the cash flows and can be significant in run-of-river projects. They should be included in the model and can be generated from the flow duration curve.

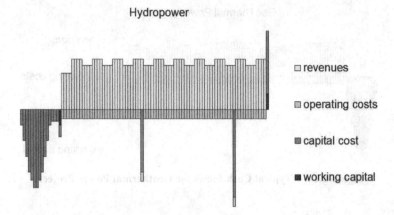

Figure 8.13:   Typical Cash Flows for Hydro Power Projects

Typical hydro power project cash flows: Figure 8.13 illustrates the cash flows on a hydropower project. The project has a high capital cost but very low operating costs. The figure also illustrates the need for additional investment in runners at 10-year intervals. Notice how the revenues vary seasonally.

8.1.11.5. *Geothermal Power*

Electricity production using geothermal energy is based on conventional steam turbine and generator equipment, in which expanding steam powers the turbine/generator to produce electricity. Geothermal energy is tapped by drilling wells into the reservoirs and piping the hot water or steam into a power plant for electricity production. The type of power plant depends on a reservoir's temperature, pressure and fluid content. There are four main types of geothermal power plants: dry-steam, flashed-steam, binary-cycle and combined cycle (hybrid). Figure 8.14 shows a typical geothermal model. Such projects:

- are technically simple;
- contain significant equipment and material which may need to be imported;
- usually base load;
- may produce a very small amount of CO_2 greenhouse gas;

GeoThermal Power

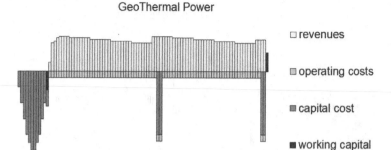

Figure 8.14:   Typical Cash Flows for Geothermal Power Projects

- need a relatively shallow source of hot steam/water. Often located in areas of volcanic activity evidenced by hot springs and/or geysers;
- have high capital costs and low running costs;
- have capital costs which are highly site specific and the location of the site needs to be reasonably close to consumers;
- may be risky due to unpredictable geology;
- may require enhanced steam production by using fracking techniques;
- will typically replace wells and pipework every 15 years or so;
- need a larger number of operating and maintenance personnel than some other renewable energy projects such as solar (PV cells) and wind farms.

Modelling considerations in geothermal power projects: The planning of a geothermal power project is highly site specific and needs specialist evaluation, basic design, cost estimating and a market survey for the power price and demand. The evaluation entails the sinking of a test bore hole to determine the subsurface conditions. This is a time consuming and expensive process. Only then can a financial model be developed.

8.1.12. *Transport*

8.1.12.1. *Toll Roads*

Highway toll roads, bridges and tunnels are included in the industry category referred to as toll roads. A toll road may include service areas which will generate additional revenues. Such projects, often operating under concession structures:

- are technically simple but may become a little more complex if the terrain is difficult (e.g. bridges and tunnels);
- have a capital cost that is very dependent on terrain and rights of way, and can be difficult to predict;
- contain little equipment and material which may need to be imported;
- need a reasonably high volume of traffic to make them economically viable;
- have traffic forecasts which are difficult to predict;
- have revenues usually collected directly from motorists through toll gates. These usually go to the operator but sometimes they are transferred to the government who reimburses the operator with an availability concession. If there are no toll gates the government authority pays the operator with either (a) shadow tolls or (b) an availability concession;
- tolls may be collected at toll booths, via electronic toll collection or a combination of the two;
- serve a market which is price elastic. The usage will depend on the toll rate and the model should include a formula for the usage which contains an elasticity factor;
- are subject to road resurfacing and/or additional lanes which may be required during the life of the project/concession;
- contain revenues which usually come from tolls paid by road users but can be from the government based on availability or a combination of the two;
- have varying degrees of government support. Sometimes the government will pay the concessionaire capacity and operations and maintenance costs. At other times the concessionaire will pay the government;
- may be partially funded by a section of the highway which is opened to the public before the entire project is completed (see the case in Chapter 10);
- contain straightforward taxation calculations.

Modelling considerations for toll road projects: The basic design of the highway is usually carried out by a state entity. The market survey is an essential component of this design. The capital cost estimate is based

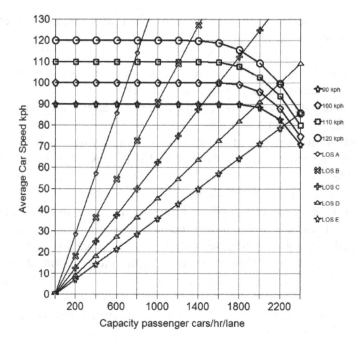

Figure 8.15:   Speed-Flow Curves with LOS Criteria in a Toll Road Project

on a bill of materials and is heavily dependent on the terrain in which the highway is located. The model can only be developed and used after this design and cost estimate have been completed.

The design is for a specified level of service (LOS). If the demand is expected to increase with time, the model should estimate the date when an additional lane is needed to ensure that the specified LOS is maintained. In order to do this, the model needs to contain the formulae to generate the speed flow curve with LOS criteria (see Figure 8.15). The model should use this information to produce a chart illustrating the vehicle density over time as shown in Figure 8.16 and the predicted dates when the operator must invest in additional lanes. The information will also be used to calculate the required target for the sinking fund to handle this major additional investment.

Typical toll road project cash flows: Typical project cash flows for toll road projects are illustrated in Figure 8.17. The revenues increase over the life of the project. They may reach a plateau if the demand exceeds the

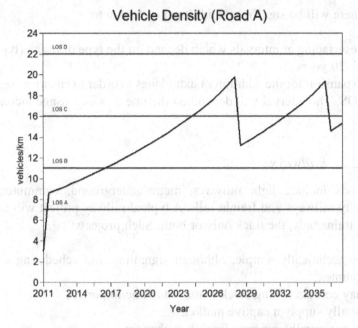

Figure 8.16:   Vehicle Density Over Time in a Toll Road Project

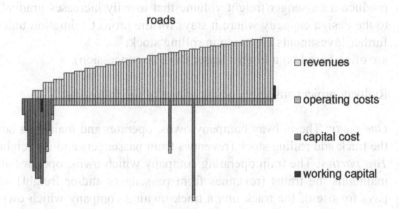

Figure 8.17:   Typical Cash Flows for Toll Road Projects

design capacity. There may be a stepwise increase in the revenues as the project's operator increases the tolls. The operating and maintenance costs are usually a small fraction of the revenues.

There will be significant additional costs due to:

- Resurfacing at intervals which depend on the type of usage (typically 15–30 years).
- Expansion for the addition of extra lanes in order to ensure a specified LOS. The interval will depend on the rate at which usage increases.

8.1.12.2. *Railways*

Railroads include light railways, metro/underground, commuter, fast inter-city railways and freight rails. A typical railway project will consist of the trains only, the track only or both. Such projects:

- are technically simple, although signalling and scheduling can be complex;
- may contain rolling stock that needs to be imported;
- usually supply a captive market;
- do not usually generate foreign exchange;
- are subject to straightforward tax calculations;
- produce a passenger/freight volume that usually increases gradually to the design capacity where it stays for the project's duration unless further investments are made in rolling stock;
- are often based on a PPP (a lease, BOT or concession).

Railway projects usually consist of one of the following:

- *One party*: The railway company owns, operates and maintains both the track and rolling stock (revenues from passengers and/or freight).
- *Two parties*: The train operating company which owns, operates and maintains the trains (revenues from passengers and/or freight) and pays for use of the track *and* a track owning company which owns, operates and maintains the track (revenues from the train operating company's usage of the track).
- *Three parties*: A train operating company which leases and operates the trains (revenues from passengers and/or freight) and pays for use of the track *and* the rolling stock company which owns the trains (revenues from leasing the trains to the train operating company) *and* a track owning company which owns, operates and maintains the

track (revenues from the train operating company's usage of the track).

Modelling considerations for railway projects: As passenger demand increases, there comes a time when the operator needs to invest in additional rolling stock. It is not acceptable for the model to assume that revenues can go on increasing without such investment. To do this the model needs to contain a calculation of the required number of trains for each period over the operating life of the project. These calculations will include a headway calculation which forms the basis for a timetable. The model should also assume that a sinking fund will be used to fund the additional investment when it is needed.

Typical railway project cash flows: Figure 8.18 illustrates the cash flows for a railway project. Note the gradual increase in revenues from increasing demand and the corresponding increase in capital costs as additional trains are added.

8.1.12.3. *Airports*

Airport projects consist of one or more of the following elements: airside facilities (such as the runway(s) and hangers) and the landside facilities (such as terminal buildings and car parks). Such airports:

- Are technically simple, although some items such as instrument landing systems and radars are complex.

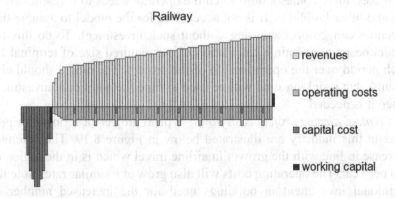

Figure 8.18: Typical Cash Flows for Railway Projects

- Contain relatively small amount of equipment which may need to be imported.
- Generate revenues from a wide variety of sources such as (a) airside: landing fees, aircraft parking fees, fuel fees and utilities, and (b) landside: passenger fees, car parking fees and shop leases.
- Serve the airline market which has shown a steady increase in size each year (but the Covid-19 pandemic in 2020 may change this). This increasing demand needs continuing investment (e.g. larger terminals, car parks, sometimes additional runways).
- Generate revenues from one of two methods: compensatory or residual cost. There can also be a hybrid of these two. In the compensatory method, the airport operator sets the fees and takes the risks. In the residual cost method, the airlines share the costs after taking credit for passenger side revenues.
- May be set up as a PPP project with the airport owner paying the state for the concession.
- Are usually subject to International Civil Aviation Organization (ICAO) rules. These rules contain provisions for fair pricing and transparency.
- Wide range of contractual arrangements. No two airports are the same. "Seen one airport and you have seen one airport".
- Are subject to straightforward taxation calculations if the airport is in the private sector. Public sector owners usually do not pay corporate taxes.

Modelling considerations in airport projects: As passenger demand increases, there comes a time when the operator needs to invest in terminal and other buildings. It is not acceptable for the model to assume that revenues can go on increasing without such investment. To do this the model needs to contain a calculation of the required size of terminal for each period over the operating life of the project. The model should also assume that a sinking fund will be used to fund the additional investment when it is needed.

Typical airport project cash flows: Typical project cash flows for projects in this industry are illustrated below in Figure 8.19. The revenues increase in line with the growth in airline travel which is in the region of 5% per year. The operating costs will also grow at a similar rate. Note the additional investment in buildings need for the increased number of passengers.

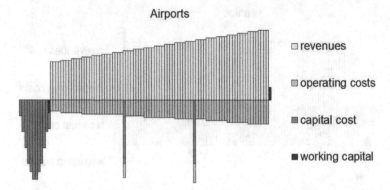

Figure 8.19: Typical Cash Flows for an Airport

8.1.12.4. *Shipping*

This category includes all forms of shipping, particularly larger ships such as oil and combined form tankers such as Oil-Bulk-Ore carriers, bulk and chemical carriers, reefers and cryogenic ships. It also includes ferries as well as drill ships and exploration rigs (including those used on land). Such ships or rigs:

- Are technically simple, although liquid natural gas (LNG) tankers require specialist metallurgy and refrigeration systems.
- Contain significant equipment and material which may need to be imported.
- May be financed as a bare boat charter, essentially a lease usually from the shipbuilder to the operator.
- Generate revenues from voyage charters or time charters. On a voyage charter all costs are paid for by the owner. On a time charter the charterer pays for voyage costs such as port costs, bunker fuels and canal transit dues.
- Are relatively easy to finance if the ships are dedicated to a project on a long-term charter, not otherwise (unless the ship is very specialized or the market is tight, this is rarer).
- Are subject to operating costs mainly consisting of the fuel (usually marine diesel).
- Are dry docked at regular intervals, usually every two to three years during which time the ships incur the costs of dry docking and do not

ships

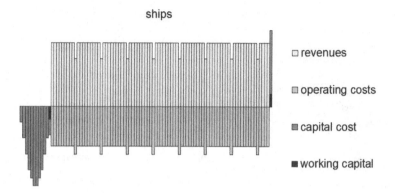

□ revenues

▨ operating costs

▪ capital cost

▪ working capital

Figure 8.20:   Typical Cash Flows for Shipping Projects

generate any revenues. The length and cost of the dry docking may increase over the life of the ship.

• Are registered in a country where taxes are low or non-existent and where regulations allow ships to be manned by foreign and usually cheaper labour (flags of convenience such as Panama or Liberia).

• Are often subject to little or no taxation calculations.

• Incur insurance costs composed of hull and machinery, war and cargo.

• May carry load in one direction only (oil and product tankers, LNG/LPG tankers, bulk carriers) or in both directions (cruise ships, container ships, general cargo, ferries).

Modelling considerations in shipping projects: Dry docking, insurance and maintenance must be considered.

It is helpful to use this shipping model to determine the fixed and variable (distance related) shipping costs for each ship category and size. These figures can then be used in models for projects which produce a product (as opposed to a service). They determine shipping costs to different markets and hence the net back price for each market at the factory gate.

Typical shipping project cash flows: Typical project cash flows for shipping projects are illustrated in Figure 8.20. Note the dry docking incurs a regular cost and a loss of revenues.

8.1.12.5. *Pipelines*

Pipelines include any project in which gases or liquids are transported by pipeline. The term usually applies to oil and gas pipelines, both onshore and offshore and to multi-product pipelines onshore, but also to water or sewage projects. The project typically consists of the pipeline (usually buried underground if onshore), the pumping (or compressing) facilities, any storage facilities and the supervisory control and data acquisition system. Such projects:

- are technically simple (unless in deep water or in high mountains or a multi-product pipeline with multiple product tanks);
- contain some equipment and material which may need to be imported;
- earn their revenues from a throughput agreement with a take-or-pay clause;
- have their tariffs negotiated with escalation and indexation clauses and split into capacity (fixed) and operating (variable) elements;
- sometimes take title to the product and sells it at the other end;
- do not usually earn foreign exchange unless it is a cross border pipeline;
- are subject to straightforward taxation calculations.

Modelling considerations in pipeline projects: There are no special modelling considerations.

Typical pipeline project cash flows: Typical project cash flows are illustrated in Figure 8.21. The revenues are typically constant over the project's life unless the pipeline is transporting the products from an oil or gas field in which case the profile will be the same as the profile for the field. The operating costs are minimal with variable costs mainly composed of the pumping (or compressing) costs.

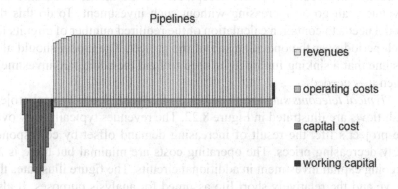

Figure 8.21:   Typical Cash Flows for a Pipeline

8.1.13. *Telecommunications*

8.1.13.1. *Submarine Cables*

This category includes domestic and international telecommunication cables and one or more landing stations. The telecommunication cable industry is a rapidly evolving industry with many technical changes. Such projects:

- are technically complex;
- contain significant equipment and material which may need to be imported;
- have revenues come from a combination of leases, indefeasible rights of use (IRUs) and other sources;
- have revenues which are difficult to forecast because demand increases rapidly and prices fall equally rapidly. The expected lives of such projects may be short to account for this uncertainty in the market;
- are subject to ongoing investment for additional circuits at the landing/termination station(s);
- have an ever-present risk of sea damage to cables;
- include a deep-water cable which if located in international waters will be owned by a company incorporated in a tax haven;
- are subject to straightforward taxation calculations.

Modelling considerations in telecoms submarine cable projects: As demand increases, there comes a time when the operator needs to invest in additional circuits. It is not acceptable for the model to assume that revenues can go on increasing without such investment. To do this the model needs to contain a calculation of the required number of circuits for each period over the operating life of the project. The model should also assume that a sinking fund will be used to fund the additional investment when it is needed.

Typical telecoms submarine cables project cash flows: Typical project cash flows are illustrated in Figure 8.22. The revenues typically vary over the project's life, the result of increasing demand offset by correspondingly decreasing prices. The operating costs are minimal but there is an ongoing capital investment in additional circuits. The figure illustrates the above and the relatively short life assumed for analysis purposes. It also

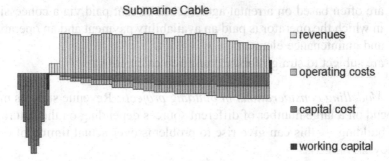

Figure 8.22: Typical Cash Flows for Submarine Cables Project

illustrates the capacity limit reached before the end of the project's life, with a consequent reduction in the subsequent annual revenues.

8.1.14. *Buildings*

Building and real-estate projects cover a wide range of industries including those schools, hospitals and prisons all typically found in PPPs which we discuss in Chapters 9 and 10. Such projects:

- are technically simple but may become a little more complex if it is a hospital with major diagnostic equipment;
- contain little equipment and material which may need to be imported;
- do not usually generate foreign exchange;

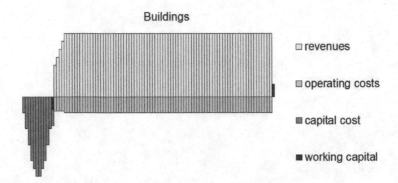

Figure 8.23: Typical Cash Flows for a Building Project

- are often based on a rental agreement/s or rent paid via a concession in which the operator is paid an availability payment and an operating and maintenance element;
- are subject to straightforward taxation calculations.

Modelling considerations in building projects: Revenue streams may depend on a large number of different sources depending on the nature of the building — this can give rise to problems over actual timing of cash inflows.

Typical building project cash flows: Typical project cash flows for building projects are illustrated in Figure 8.23. The revenues will typically be constant over the life of the project. The operating and maintenance costs will vary considerably from one project to another.

Chapter 9

What's Different About Public–Private Partnership Projects?

Introduction

An increasing number of project finance transactions are part of an initiative used by governments to look at improving major project contracting, delivery and operation through the use of a partnership process between the government and private contractors and a special purpose vehicle (SPV) company, similar to many other forms of project financing described in this book.

One of the attractions of this procurement initiative has been its treatment on government balance sheets — in many cases it has been "off-balance sheet" and therefore politically expedient because it has permitted the development of large projects without impacting on perceptions of the government's overall borrowing requirement or indeed financial liabilities. Although these arrangements have been used extensively in the UK where the concept originated, the idea has been employed in other countries where tightening government revenues encouraged the public procurement process to consider private finance and private sector approaches to large projects. However, whether these projects will remain off-balance sheet is a moot question in the light of the accounting profession's moves towards more accurate reporting of financial obligations, post Enron, Carillion and other financial scandals. (Carillion is discussed in a case study in Chapter 12.)

In this chapter, we examine a number of forms of these projects and consider the advantages and disadvantages of each. Before doing so, we provide some definitions.

9.1. What is a Public–Private Partnership?

A Public–Private Partnership or PPP (PFI in the UK or P3 in the US) is generally considered to be a type of procurement characterized by a form of agreement between a public agency or government department and a private sector organization (or group of organizations) that exists to procure, build or develop a facility or service and that shares risks and rewards between the public and private sector partners.

A PPP describes the overarching approach used to assist in more efficient procurement or management of projects that may be only partly privatized. Consequently, some or all of the asset ownership remains in public hands, and the project is set up to operate the facilities through a concession, but it may include fundraising for the project and a shift in ownership — even if only during the life time of the finance — to the private sector.

Recent joint efforts by MLAs such as the World Bank and EBRD to come up with a Book of Knowledge (BoK) about PPPs have culminated in a long treatise that begins with a series of definitions by different stakeholders and then produces another one. What is certain is that it is necessary to ensure all parties to any discussion are clear about their mutually agreed understanding of the term in the specific context.

So, for a PPP, the national government or one of its agencies:

- supplies the project cash flow via project service contracts; or
- underpins project revenues and thus could be seen as a lender of last resort inasmuch as politically it would not be expedient for the project to fail; or
- provides tax incentives or amnesties.

PPP can thus be solely a procurement process for government using private sector techniques, or a mixture of any combination of the aforementioned three approaches.

We have mentioned the concept in law of being able to separate ownership and control of a group of cash flow generating assets — a theme that recurs throughout many of the previous chapters and underpins project financing. In order to do this, there needs to be an appropriate and robust legal system that permits recognition of this difference between ownership and management rights, and that supports financial structures underpinning the project. In some jurisdictions the issue of ownership rights is far from clear and so difficult changes need negotiation before any political effort can be dedicated to supporting project finance.

This clarification is vital in the area of PPPs, where the assets or services being financed are state-owned and/or politically sensitive. Political influence can delay projects, require the involvement of stakeholder representatives who are unfamiliar with contractual and financial structures and the longer-term implications but have claims relating to ownership rights and cause difficulties during the project life, making such projects less attractive than had been assessed at the start of the project.

An example of these rights might be those of farmers who farm land on which a road is to be built, but whose rights are not enshrined in law, despite their establishment over multigenerational farming of that area. Though legally, it may appear that the farmers have no rights that need to be considered, in practice their needs (if they are to be displaced or their livelihood affected) should be a part of any plan. Leaving this to the host government may not always have a satisfactory outcome: farmers newly re-housed in apartments in badly constructed high-rise blocks, where any compensation payment made to move them from a project site has been forcibly used to pay for this new abode is not a good solution as has been seen in the some hydropower dam projects and was the reason why in the Dagachhu hydropower case discussed in Chapter 2, so much effort was put in to making sure the local people were treated fairly.

9.2. Background and Rationale for Public–Private Partnership

The origins of public–private partnering go back to the early 1990s and a desire by the then government of the United Kingdom to continue to outsource and privatize business areas. With a major privatization programme largely over, attention focused on large government capital projects where it was perceived that commissioning and procurement could be improved by a transfer of knowledge from the private sector. In certain areas, particularly defence programmes, significant overspends attracted negative press comment.

Initially, PPPs focused on the design, construction, finance and operation of real-estate projects for the public sector — one such project that was among the first was a new Treasury (Ministry of Finance) building. Subsequent UK governments — especially under the Labour administration — expanded the initiative, with one driver being the accounting treatment discussed earlier whereby these projects were not included in the government's balance sheet. During this time, a range of projects were completed including military housing, schools, hospitals and highway tolling projects.

The results, which were analyzed by the UK's National Audit Office (NAO), suggest that the benefits have not always accrued to the public purse, but maturity in this sector has also generated standardized contract terms and a body of internal knowledge within the public sector, so improvements were expected. The long-time frames of PPPs mean that those projects finishing and thus evaluated at end of life or close to end of life will have been initiated under different frameworks and a less well developed and shared knowledge base.

More recently, the emphasis has shifted to energy and communication infrastructure projects (including satellites) and PPP concepts have been adopted by countries outside the UK.

For example, three contrasting sewage projects in Hungary have included different approaches.

(1) In Budapest, a minority interest is held by the municipality and it also holds a "golden share" that allows it to outvote managerial decisions made by the project company. The majority partner was Suez-Lyonnaise and the project included the physical assets of the water company. Nevertheless, incremental projects were expected to be 100% owned by the municipality.

(2) In Debrecen, the municipality decided to incorporate a separate company and use public funding and local suppliers which, the project claims, have kept costs down. The European Investment Bank refinanced long-term commercial debt provided by two local banks and the project also included UK PHARE funding, European Bank for Reconstruction and Development (EBRD) funding and some other government money.

(3) The third project at about the same time period was for Szeged. In this case, the municipality formed a majority-owned partnership with a foreign contractor (now known as Veolia) and the facility was operated by a company with a 70% foreign ownership. This arrangement has been problematic and was only resolved after eight years of renegotiation. Under the new arrangement, the 51%/49% company makes a rental payment for the infrastructure assets, and operates and maintains the water and sewerage system, paying monies into a construction fund which belongs to the municipality. Since the municipality is liable for a shortfall in the revenues, the construction fund could be used to cover this — a matter of concern for some foreign observers in the early days.[1]

---

[1] UK Parliamentary Research Paper 01/117, published 18 December 2001.

Ownership	PPP process
Public Sector keeps it all in house as an agency/ permanent concession	• May use existing public sector procurement processes. • May raise commercial debt supported by cash flows or uses public sector debt. • Public Sector ultimate owner.
Owner/private sector finance provider/ Reverting concession to public sector	• May use private techniques such as Design-Build-Operate-Transfer (DBOT); Build-Own-Operate-Transfer(BOOT) or Build Operate-Transfer (BOT) but ownership reverts to public sector. • May include commercial debt during development and operational stage.
Public Sector owns/ controls via a renewable concession/private sector finance	• May use Design-Build-Finance-Operate (DBFO) concession. • BOOT concession. • Maintenance concession.
Private Sector Owner/ Private sector finance	• May use Asset Capitalisation model. • Divestiture of public sector assets. • Build-Own-Operate (BOO). • Most likely to include increased private equity.

Figure 9.1: Different Forms of Project Ownership in a PPP Context

Prepared by CF de Nahlik from various publicly available sources.

PPPs are especially interesting in an economic development context and, as such, many PPPs may include funding from regional development banks — the aforementioned examples included EBRD and the European Investment Bank. This funding support may be contingent upon public ownership or public control and so financings of this type tread a delicate line regarding structure and ownership (and, of course, now control under the new IFRS regulations) to ensure eligibility for a mix of differing funding sources.

We can consider PPPs to lie along the spectrum from public to private ownership as shown in Figure 9.1.

9.3. Different Stakeholder Groups, Their Various Needs and How These May Change Over the Lifetime of a Project

Graeme Hodge set out a list of 15 objectives of PPPs as part of a review, considering the objective/promise made by government thus[2]:

1. "Enables provision of infrastructure without increased public sector borrowing
2. Reduces pressure on public sector budgets
3. Provides better value for money (VfM) for taxpayers
4. Reduces risks to government from infrastructure projects
5. Improves accountability
6. Provides better on-time delivery
7. Allows better on-budget delivery
8. Allows greater infrastructure (project) innovation
9. Encourages a more innovative public sector
10. Improves business confidence
11. Improves political feasibility to impose user fees
12. Enables the full life-cycle costs of infrastructure to be provided
13. Boosts sales of professional PPP services abroad
14. Supports businesses in difficult global market conditions (business assistance/subsidy)
15. Provides a crucial tool to underpin the broad societal objective of economic development".

Many of these could be applied to other projects, but those focusing on the public sector and the political aspects of PPPs offer insights into points of greatest contention with the various stakeholder groups. As we discussed in other chapters, the stakeholder landscape is not flat and with projects of such long duration, the power and influence of different groups will vary during the life of project. The challenge for both public and private sector sponsors are the personal perceptions of stakeholder groups, especially users, relating to the project delivery. When this involves healthcare, reactions can be very emotional.

---

[2]See Chapter 5, p. 87 in Graeme A. Hodge, Carsten Greve and Anthony E. Boardman (eds.), *International Handbook on Public–Private Partnerships*. Edward Elgar: Cheltenham, UK, 2010.

Some of the criticism of PPPs has arisen because of the blurring of high-level political agendas with local needs. An example might be that funds do not exist to prioritize the upgrade of a hospital, but a PPP solution could make this happen. The short-term nature of much government planning conflicts with the longer-term nature of PPP projects. Continuing the hospital example, closing a local hospital could manage concerns about the fabric of an elderly building and the health risks posed by it and allow for concentration of specialist facilities in a major hospital perhaps some 20–30 miles away. However, patients have to be able to access the new hospital and that requires infrastructure planning such as transport services and parking arrangements. PPPs can often charge for car parking in hospital projects and this has been unpopular. Since the various stakeholder interests may be represented by different departments and thus different budgets, there can be friction and the end user can lose out.

One of the other challenges that can arise is that governments and government structures are very likely to change over the period of a PPP. Aside from the challenges this can introduce in terms of contract parties and a possible need to novate agreements, it can also affect the decision-making process and this will impact on the change management process.

Relationships inside any stakeholder group are a blend of the personal and the inter-organizational, with strong personal relationships working to resolve potentially intransigent inter-organizational differences. Proactive management can be assisted by a good understanding of all of the interested stakeholder groups and their varying interests at any point in time during the project's development. Clearly this suggests that stakeholder management needs to be proactive and indeed interactive. In today's age of almost instant communication and social media, small groups can accrue enormous power and influence. The communication works both ways — letting stakeholders know what is happening and engaging with them on a regular basis can manage fears and concerns and enable problem areas to be nuanced to address them, if necessary, rather than allowing them to escalate and cause conflict.

An example might be a case of a child turned away from an emergency department in a hospital because it was closed. Instead the family had to embark on a long journey to a hospital that was open and during that time further damage occurred because an injury that could have been managed had help been prompt, escalated into a more serious issue. The family would be angry and upset that their child was not promptly treated. The hospital may have been closed because of funding issues, possibly related to a poorly negotiated PPP structure, but this is of little direct interest to anxious parents. Certain forms of the media would take this story and turn it into headline news. However, even though every life is precious, this was a single case, and may not have been representative. All the lives and injuries that were treated successfully become invisible as a single stakeholder group dominates the media. The root cause lies with the poor negotiation, something back in history for the current stakeholders, who are living with the consequences of a decision to not ensure that all parties to the negotiation, stakeholders during that time, were fully equipped to negotiate and also to think through the long-term consequences of the decisions that they made. All too often, the public sector parties are inadequately briefed and prepared to negotiate long-term contracts for user groups with whom they have little direct contact.

Good stakeholder management requires investment of time and resources and good communication with all the stakeholder groups, both present and emergent. All too often, this task is delegated, poorly resourced and reliant on static information that may be historic. Good dynamic stakeholder management that is well resourced and communicates regularly and interacts proactively can be a powerful contributor to a successful PPP.

9.4. Key Requirements for a PPP Transaction

Each PPP transaction has unique characteristics that co-evolve in importance from the moment of inception to the point where the project has ended. In this section, we group the key requirements for these partnerships into high-level headings. The long-term nature of these projects means that capturing and collating key drivers over time produces the following five key headings.

- Value for money
- Reallocation of risk and risk management
- Innovation
- Enhanced performance and more transparent performance management
- Lower cost than an equivalent public sector comparator (PSC)

Each of the above could be broken down further.

9.4.1. *Value for Money*

The most important requirement for any of the public–private partnership projects is that the project has to exhibit "value for money" for the government or public sector.

The definition of value for money can be problematic and needs to be clarified and contextualized for each project to ensure transparency around the measurement of the project success. Cost savings are clearly an indicator of value for money, but a number of projects may also have requirements to include a certain specified "local content", either to ensure that the project funding is spent in the local economy, through local resourcing of component materials, procured services or labour, or to look towards technology and skills transfer to the local population. This can conflict with a need for cost saving.

Value for money begins at the phase where the project model is constructed and needs to be demonstrated to make a case for a PPP route. There are many cases where the cheaper option might have been to use existing public sector resources and a PPP route has proved to be costlier.

Once the tendering process starts, then a claim of value for money is supported by evidence of a strong competitive field. From the contractor's point of view, PPP tendering may be less attractive because there may be a poor understanding of project design by the public sector commissioning body, possibly because this is not a route that has been used before. So, there may be a drain on contractor resources in order to educate the public sector partner in order to scope a viable project. The tendering process may also be lengthy and require the preparation and submission of many documents, exposing the contractor to significant upfront costs with a lack of certainty around the final award of the project.

Even when the project is awarded, reporting requirements may be more onerous than for many private sector projects and require a higher level of disclosure — project administration costs may therefore be quite considerable. Project specifications can change prior to the award, or even in some cases after the award where technological innovation may have a significant impact on the project's success. This is more likely when the project has an extended construction time and uses technology that is fast-changing. Examples of this might be some of the problematic information technology projects providing support for government services, especially

IT driven projects. These challenges have resulted in a comparatively small number of contractors that have become highly specialized in PPP/PFI[3] tendering and project execution, though this in turn leads to risk concentration problems in contractors and possible challenges to the value for money criterion if all bids are close in price and specification.

9.4.2. *Reallocation of Risk and Risk Management*

The second requirement for choosing a PPP structure is the belief that the private sector understands certain types of risk rather better than the public sector, and therefore allocation of those risks to private sector organizations that possess this superior knowledge, together with the extensive due diligence that accompanies PPPs, can bring costs down. For this to work, the risks need to be thoroughly documented, understood and appropriately weighted and allocated. In an award of a project to a private sector partner, both sides need to ensure that an appropriate structure for managing those risks, including penalties if appropriate, is laid out within the documentation.

The risk adjustments can either be made to the individual cash flows or in some cases they have been included in the discount rate, though this is a much blunter instrument.

So, for example, if construction of an incremental project looks as if it is likely to overrun, this would be identified through the reporting mechanisms and the agreements would spell out the clear mechanisms for discussing and resolving the problem with payment penalties as the ultimate sanction. Very often PPP contracts are fixed price in nature and may include the construction element and the operation element in a single sum if a "whole-life cost" approach is used. "Gain sharing" in the construction contract phase has not been widely reported, though many public sector organizations have insisted on gain sharing if the project is refinanced.

The introduction of standard contract models into PPPs in countries where this financial approach is quite widely used has also led to better governance. Many publicly available reports written by the UK NAO

---

[3]PFI or Private Finance Initiative is the name given to an early version of PPPs in a UK government initiative.

have also led to a better understanding of the risks, how to allocate them and mitigate them for different categories of projects.

9.4.3. *Innovation*

A third factor in choosing a PPP is when best practice in innovation in design derived from the private sector can be applied to public sector projects. Evidence suggests that this transfer is not always a happy one — inexperience, leading to lack of attention to design specifications by public sector bodies has often meant that the project has ended up following the form of previous projects. Innovation is often not ranked especially highly when bids are scored in the tendering process and innovative aspects of one bid will form part of the intellectual property of that bidder rather than being transferred to the government. So prior planning and negotiation about the ownership of existing and derived intellectual property are key in a case where innovation is a critical ingredient.

Some stakeholders may have a perception that innovation may drive costs up, causing less experienced public sector bodies to choose existing designs structures and delivery models, which while they might minimize the risk, may not ultimately give rise to optimized value for money in the realized service delivery.

9.4.4. *Enhanced Performance and More Transparent Performance Management*

Expectations from PPPs may be that improved service delivery will result from a transfer and absorption of lessons learned from the private sector into the partnership and thus on into the public sector.

Efficiency gains can be difficult to quantify, not least over long-term projects. Indeed, being locked into a long-term contract may inhibit the introduction of new best practice to enhance efficiency and act as a drag on the project's ability to deliver stakeholder benefits.

Service level agreements (SLAs) are now becoming widespread in the public sector, outlining the service to be provided, costs, availability and the schedule of payments for the service and so on, and supported by the inclusion in the agreement of penalties should the service provider fail to deliver. The concept of SLAs may be novel in countries undergoing rapid economic transition and the cultural change associated with the introduction of this type of formalized delivery can require sensitive handling in all cases.

Transfer of staff previously working in the public sector to the new operating company with private sector employment practices may include a change in terms and conditions of employment. Negotiating these transfers of professional or clinical staff, especially when trade unions may be involved, cannot be rushed and further highlights the requirement to have realistic timetables set at the beginning of a project.

9.4.5. *Lower Cost Than an Equivalent PSC*

The last factor (and often the most contentious) considers whether a public/private sector partnership will save money for the "public purse". To demonstrate this, the proposed PPP route needs to be compared with the same project financed through the public sector. This takes place through the value for money route discussed previously and by comparing the PPP with a totally public sector version of the same project, using what is called a PSC.

Cruz and Marquez offer a literature review comparing a number of different definitions of PSC from around the world.[4] While the definitions in various countries show some convergence, they use different approaches to the costs included in the calculation. To understand this better, we need to look at two different approaches to costs in cash flow projections.

The life cycle cost analysis (LCCA) approach[5] considers all costs of owning and operating a facility including its ultimate disposal. The PSC calculation is a more typical cash flow analysis and looks at revenues as well as costs, both direct and indirect, but the inclusion of different cost elements, especially in non-standard projects, arises from the expertise of the

---

[4]Carlos Oliveira Cruz and Rui Cunha Marques, *Infrastructure Public–Private Partnerships: Decision, Management and Development.* Springer-Verlag: Berlin, Heidelberg, 2013.

[5]X. Meng and F. Harshaw, *The Application of Whole Life Costing in PFI/PPP Projects.* In: *Proceedings 29th Annual ARCOM Conference*, S. D. Smith and D. D. Ahiaga-Dagbui (eds.). 2–4 September 2013, Reading, UK, Association of Researchers in Construction Management, pp. 769–778.

model builder. With long-term forecasts, for which there may be no support-ing data, there is substantial room for error. At the point of comparison, the calculations are reduced to two numbers arising from the PSC and the PPP.

"The system is open to manipulation for two reasons:

- In most cases, there has been no serious choice between the PFI project and the PSC so that that optimum bias has often been used to make the PFI a winner. An example of this was the optimism bias assumed in the Full Business Case (FBC) of the NNUH. A cost overrun of 34.22% was assumed for the PSC. Note the precision. Not 35%. Nor 34%. But 34.22%. Unsurprisingly, in 1999, the Select Committee on Health com-plained many times about the FBC of the NNUH. As the Chair of the Committee put it; *In other words, the full business case does not tell us the full business case* (see Edwards, June 2009, p. 86).

- It is fairly easy to manipulate the comparison since the PFI contract approval goes through a number of stages. Thus the PFI price may be shown to be lower than the PSC at the Outline Business Case stage (when initial approval is given) but once approval has been given the PFI price is free to rise and has done so. As Hellowell and Pollock 2007 (page 18) have pointed out, the average cost increases for 43 'prioritised' schemes between the Outline Business Case stage and the stage at which contract were signed was 74%. The same point is made in the evidence of the National Audit Office when it says 'VFM [Value for Money] is most at risk during the final stage of negotiations, when negotiation is with a single preferred (or final bidder) and competitive tension is at its weakest'".[6]

The economic argument for the PPP route suggests that the private company can benefit from economies of scale and scope because it has considerable experience in delivering these types of services or indeed these types of projects. However, PPP projects usually borrow at a higher cost of funds than the public sector. To balance these factors the service provision in the PPP should be cheaper than a PSC because inefficiencies inside the public sector would suggest that these economies are not cap-tured in this approach.

---

[6]Chris Edwards, "Private Gain and Public Loss; The Private Finance Initiative (PFI) and the Norfolk and Norwich University Hospital (NNUH): Case Study." University of East Anglia, 2009.

This argument applies to many projects where non-financial drivers may be pointing to a course of action that requires justification with numbers. In other words, the incorporation of qualitative factors into what is in essence a quantitative calculation.

Many public and private sector alternative financial cases may not be directly comparable, posing difficulties for project selection. Here are four examples:

- Where the PPP has included various improvements adding to the cost (innovation).
- Where the normal public sector process of funding the project as it is constructed is compared with the PPP deferring payments for the project until construction was completed (evidencing value for money).
- Expectations that the public sector sponsor should pay a premium to transfer certain risks to the private sector, further loading the costs (risk transfer).
- PPPs may be discounted at a higher rate, reflecting its higher cost of capital.

Related to this is a further area of concern by stakeholders — the perception that contractors have been able to reap extraordinary benefits from the projects and that government officials have not always been able to demonstrate that they have considered both the short- and long-term implications of the contracts and that as agents for the taxpayer, they may not have chosen projects that have always demonstrated the best value for money. Often what may seem like an attractively (low priced) construction phase is then followed by an operating phase where benefits and profits are clawed back over many years. This becomes unpopular with stakeholders when (say) hospital beds are unavailable because funds are diverted to meeting operating and maintenance phase contractual obligations.

Finally, making a direct comparison with a PSC can be further complicated if there is a single contract for both construction and operation (becoming less likely). In such a situation, if costs overrun, they may be deferred into the operating phase in order to meet completion targets and avoid heavy penalties. Thus, the comparability between the public and PPP alternative may not be clear cut, further underpinning the need to build and test models under several realistic but complex risk scenarios as suggested in Chapter 7.

9.5. Key Components for a PPP

Just as with other project financing models, public–private partnering projects have the same requirements which include:

- the main SPV project company, often including public sector shareholders, known as a TOPCO;
- the project's assets should be contained in a SPV (known as a CAPCO);
- an off-take style contract for the service provision to the end user, or other contract that records the service to be provided, any performance measures, the payment mechanism and procedures for the management of any adverse circumstances needs to be clearly defined;
- conventionally the operation of the project is carried out by another SPV called an OPCO; and
- there needs to be a mutually agreed upon definition of and allocation of risks among all partners, usually in the form of a risk matrix.

9.5.1. *Classic Form of a PPP*

While each project has unique characteristics, it is possible to generalize the form of one of these projects as shown in Figure 9.2 and in this section, we examine the types of PPP structures currently in use. Many projects use a concession structure to structure the cash flow generation process. In common with other structures in this book, these contract forms have existed for a long time. In the Roman Empire, tax collection was "farmed out" and the right to collect taxes in a given area, or concession, was assigned to groups of individuals known as tax farmers, who were obliged to collect a specified amount of tax on behalf of the Roman Empire. The tax farmers were required to pay over the amount agreed at the time of bidding, but any surplus was theirs to keep, explaining the negative image of tax collectors in older literature. The concessions to collect taxes were often auctioned and over time, legislation was enacted to protect the taxed from over-enthusiastic over-collection in the name of the Emperor. This practice also existed in Ancient Egypt and the Ottoman Empire and a bureaucracy existed to monitor the payments. The tax farmer was liable for any under collection of tax revenues.

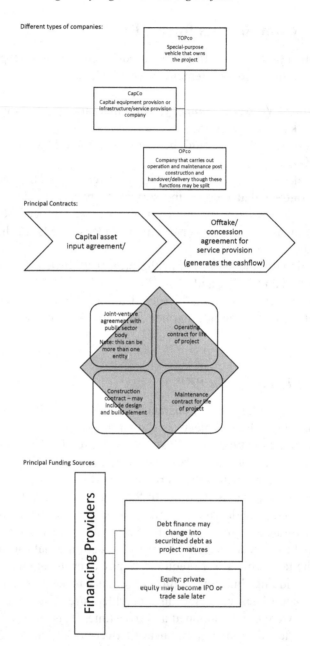

Figure 9.2:   PPP at a Glance

Prepared by CF de Nahlik from various publicly available sources.

More recently, concession agreement structures have appeared in governmental partnerships to exploit and develop natural resources, whereby resource owning governments will grant or award the rights to explore and develop minerals for a fee (concessions), with a revenue-sharing arrangement with the concession holder if the exploration is successful. The concession agreement structure has a long case law, and as such became a useful mechanism for allowing public sector activities to be conducted by private sector companies.[7]

In a classic concession agreement structure, the first stage is to develop a robust business case for the transfer of the assets and/or service involved, and to specify any incremental investments. This is very often when the project may encounter problems later because the business case is over-optimistic or fails to take into account all of the risk factors. Concessions are long-term agreements, often with limited possibilities for renegotiation of the terms. As noted in Chapters 7 and 8 where we discussed project modelling, we saw that one of the challenges in the area of project finance has always been the justification of high sunk costs when developing a sound project model.

After the business case has been examined and approved, one of the next stages is to make sure that the service can be transferred to the private sector under existing legislation. This may require specific legislation to be enacted, which will take time. Then the tender for the concession has to be written. Most public sector procurement now requires external tendering for which there may be both local rules and possibly other external rules that need to be followed in order to attract certain financing — an example of this would be following the EU directives on public procurement.

Once the concession is awarded, several SPVs are set up to act as a holding company, to hold the assets and to provide operating services as shown in Figure 9.3.

---

[7]Concession agreement structures are outside of the scope of this book. A useful reference text for lessons learned is J. Luis Guasch, *Granting and Renegotiating Infrastructure Concessions: Doing It Right*. World Bank Institute Development Studies: Paris, 2004.

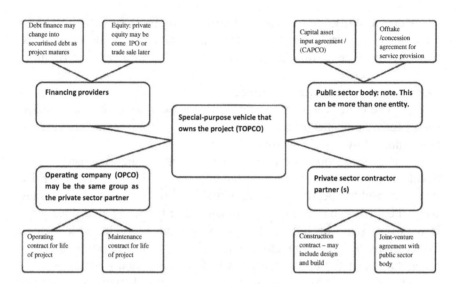

Figure 9.3:   Typical Generic Structure for a PPP/PFI Project

Prepared by CF de Nahlik from various publicly available sources.

The concession agreement will normally:

- Specify the terms of the concession including any incremental work to be done to upgrade the assets to produce the service.
- Clarify the responsibility for obtaining the finance for maintenance and upgrading (including any responsibilities of the public sector partner such as providing guarantees for any finance).
- Set out the terms under which the concessionaire will offer the service to service users including escalation for inflation.
- Address risks such as bankruptcy of the concessionaire, cost overruns, problems in obtaining planning permission, audit provision for the concession while it is operating, any assignment of the concession arrangements that are permitted and hand over on termination or expiry of the concession agreement.

This particular model has been especially popular for road and rail projects but also for schools, jails, some IT projects, etc.

The challenges that early projects have faced have often come from over-optimistic modelling, especially when tolling revenues are collected in a currency other than the host country currency (a situation likely to pertain where the construction costs may be in a foreign currency that may be stronger than the local currency, or where there may be exchange control restrictions). Traffic estimates which relate to projections of economic development and projected demand have also been over-optimistic in some cases. Existing assets have required unplanned additional expenditure by the concessionaire in order to bring them up to levels required for service provision — this may only have become clear after handover. Yet another challenge has arisen where commitments have been made by public sector partners to the private sector partners, possibly in the form of keep well or comfort letters.[8] When the project has run into financial problems, the keep well letter has assumed the form of a guarantee, thus crystallizing liabilities that may have been overlooked.

Nevertheless, despite these challenges, the concession model has worked very well in many cases, and continues to be an attractive option, especially when the public sector partner and the private sector partner truly work together to deliver the project.

9.6. Lessons Learned from PPP Projects to Date

The long-term nature of PPP projects (25–30 years is not unusual) together with the public sector expectations around cost control mean that these projects are largely financed on a fixed term basis using interest rate swaps to lock in the costs of debt for the project for the public sector borrower. One point of negotiation is likely to be when the swap takes place and the length of the contract — it was only 20 years ago that a number of UK public sector municipalities required rescuing when swap contracts they had entered into had moved against them. Since then Italian municipalities appear to have similar problems, suggesting an understanding of the risks associated with swap contracts is not widespread in many public sector organizations.[9]

The basic leverage structure has often been of the order of 90% debt to 10% equity, reflecting the attractiveness of this higher spread quasi-government backed debt and the relatively thin capitalization of the

---

[8] See Chapter 12 in the companion book.
[9] Rachel Sanderson, Guy Dinmore and Gillian Tett, "Finance: An Exposed Position," *Financial Times*, March 8, 2010.

companies has meant that returns to equity holders have been very attractive in many cases. This apparent contradiction with the "value for money" criterion that public sector contractors should uphold (mentioned earlier in this chapter) has been the cause of charges that the private sector parties in PPP contracts have received excessive returns. As credit has tightened, margins have increased with estimates of margins of 250 and 300 basis points over the cost of funds for the senior debt component.[10] In addition to healthy loan spreads, transaction fees and other financing costs such as commitment fees are starting to make the PPP a relatively less attractive proposal not only in the UK but also in countries where there may be large government borrowing problems. Initiatives to stimulate investor interest in longer-term bonds associated with PPPs have not been warmly embraced because of the risks of service contract renegotiations.

Historically, US monoline insurers with triple-A credit had offered support to bond issues as a senior debt component of PPPs. However, following the subprime mortgage problems in the US, this "wrapping" to support the debt in order to decrease its cost as a result of the triple-A backup has all but disappeared, leaving projects dependent on senior debt provided by banks and other long-term lenders.

Some commentators have discussed the use of "mini-perms" — a form of short-term three to five-year finance that bridges the gap between the construction finance and a longer-term "permanent financing" in PPPs. Mini-perms are usually structured with a balloon repayment; a "hard" mini-perm will have an ultimate maturity date before which refinancing must take place, and a "soft" mini-perm will incentivize refinancing before the final maturity date. Thus, far they have been used in large road and defence contracts.

Once the project is up and running, PPPs are just like other projects in that much of the risk is front-end loaded. However, the long-term nature of the finance means that the public sector purchaser may be locked into very expensive financing costs priced to reflect the high risk at the beginning of the project and has been unable to exit through refinancing without payments to the lenders to break the agreements. As the sector has matured, the new contract forms include the ability to refinance, often with a gain-sharing arrangement where the gains from refinancing are

---

[10]National Audit Office Report, *Financing PFI Projects in the Credit Crisis and the Treasury's Response*, HC 287. London: The Stationery Office, 2010–2011.

split between the private and public sector parties to the contract. Current debates in this area include those around the right of the government or a public sector agency to demand refinancing once a project is in the operational stage.

In general, governments are able to borrow at a lower cost than most private companies and so, for those governments that may be able to consider direct capital market funding for large infrastructure projects as opposed to private sector funding through a PPP, there may be a shift in the types of project identified inside the four boxes shown in Figure 9.1.

Equity exits may take the form of a bundled portfolio of PPPs held by a private sector service provider and offering an investor a range of risks in a number of different projects through the use of routes that are analogous to securitization and other vehicles discussed in Chapter 7 of the companion book.

Two recent developments in the UK have raised some alarm bells about the PPP approach that may resonate elsewhere.

The first is the demise of Carillion, a major PPP contractor and operator. Carillion filed for bankruptcy in late 2017, leaving a number of PPP projects unfinished. It has been suggested that the company bid for work at prices that were too low to ensure profits. This event caused some concern and a re-examination of the PPP model and dependence on a small number of contractors.

The second was the publication of an NAO report in January 2018 looking at a revised PPP policy framework (to be known as PF2). It remains UK policy to keep PPP deals off the government balance sheet. This report reignited comments in the Press and social media about previous PPP transactions and their problems.

Each PPP transaction has its own unique characteristics, and a short chapter cannot cover the many forms that are available. Yet, the key messages common for all projects can be identified. They are:

- clarity around the definition, scope and nature of the transaction;
- meeting the value for money test;
- reallocation and acceptance of risk;
- adoption of innovation and best practice; and
- introduction of performance management systems and benchmarking of any private sector project against a PSC.

However, the balance and mix of large numbers of stakeholders can extend the negotiating phase on projects of this type.

The political nature of a transfer from the public sector to the private sector is very emotive in many national contexts — letting *foreigners* own core national assets can be negatively perceived by the electorate.

Finally, the long-term nature of the projects and their political embeddedness will inevitably mean that the negotiation will take place and the financial structures that support these projects need to be able to have the flexibility to cope with change of political matters.

9.7. Case Study: School's Out![11]

In 1998, Edinburgh Council began the process of getting approval for a PPP entity, to realize its mission of "Investing in Education". It was hoped this would receive funding to overhaul its education provision by creating new schools, refurbishing existing schools and amalgamating some to create economies of scale and to provide schools that were equipped for the future in areas of demand. The project met the first "affordability criterion" and the sale of sites arising from the rationalization of school sites that this project anticipated would deliver a capital contribution towards the project of some UK £15.4 million. Eight initial bidders were reduced to four, two asked to produce "best and final offers" and a preferred bidder appeared, with the loser designated as a "reserve bidder". A PSC was used to examine the project and the final assessed construction risk of £5.043 million and operational phase risk of £8,381 million brought the total adjusted PSC to £7.602 million more than the net present value of the PPP bid. The full business case was published in 2006 and was subject to scrutiny by Audit Scotland and the Scottish Executive, recognizing the separate identity of Scotland in the government structure of the United Kingdom. The initial project was for a design build finance and operate and maintenance agreement for 13 new or refurbished schools and related projects with four further projects added in 2003 and 2004. The contracts required the PPP company to undertake maintenance, cleaning, catering and other facility management of the school accommodation for a 30-year period.

---

[11]National Audit Office Report, *Report of the Independent Inquiry into the Construction of Edinburgh Schools*, 2017.

In January 2016, just prior to the opening hours of the school, a wall collapsed at Oxgangs school, releasing nine tonnes of masonry in an area where children congregated. Fortunately, no one was hurt, but the effects of this resulted in significant disruption to the education of many children in Edinburgh (and of course, their parents or carers) for an extended period. Putting this into numbers, 17 schools were closed requiring the relocation of 3,198 primary school children, 4,327 secondary school pupils, 107 children with additional support requirements 655 teachers and 738 nursery children. What was originally expected to require a quick resolution became a critical issue when the same causal factors (failure to embed structural ties into walls properly) were identified in a number of other schools in the PPP project. This deficiency was also discovered at other schools in Scotland. As the investigation continued, fire hazard issues were identified. The PPP contractor was responsible for the costs of the repairs (so risk was transferred) and the Audit Scotland (AS) report suggests that this was done as quickly as was possible and to a good standard. Schools reopened between the end of May and the end of August.

There were no collateral warranties in favour of the Council from any subcontractors or professional teams appointed by the building contractor. Independent certification of the construction project, during the initial construction phase was inconsistent. Drawings and other documentation were found to be missing when the remedial works called for them — a deficit in an area that would be the contractor's responsibility.

Because all local authorities are under major pressure to save money, the opportunity to take on a project which saved scarce resources would have been very attractive. What appears to have happened is that the public sector client relied on the contractor for quality assurance. More usually a Clerk of Works would be appointed by the Council as an independent scrutineer employed by and working for the public sector commissioning body and this person would have identified any deficiencies that arose. The Audit Scotland investigation report also suggests that the public sector entity had failed to recognize that the PPP option requires significant internal resources and external support for them. These findings are also borne out by anecdotal evidence on other PPP projects. Self-management of building projects and the absence of completion certificates for some projects also point to a naïve approach to these projects and have implications for other support services such as insurance.

This brief case offers a thought-provoking insight into the effects on stakeholders if clear responsibilities are not set out in a PPP, it is not monitored, and subsequent major problems arise. Lessons could be learned from it by public sector and contracting entities. However, while the PPP financing package drew no criticism (other than indirectly when comments suggested changes were costly and bureaucratic — something most likely a result of the original contract between public sector entity and contractor), it is easy to see that reputational issues for finance providers could come under scrutiny if further disaster had struck. The finance is not isolated from the project, no matter what the contracts say, in today's world of social media!

Chapter 10

Public–Private Partnerships in Practice

10.1. Different Forms of Public–Private Partnerships (PPPs)

We begin with a summary of the different types of public–private partnerships (PPPs) which include:

- "Pure" concession agreements.
- Design-build-operate-transfer (DBOT) and build-operate-transfer (BOT) projects.
- Design-build-finance-operate (DBFO) projects.
- Build-own-operate (BOO) projects.

Each of these types of PPP can be looked at from three dimensions with respect to the allocation of responsibility between the private and public sectors: ultimate asset ownership, funding and operation and maintenance. Of these, ultimate asset ownership is the public entity's responsibility while funding and operation and maintenance are the responsibility of the private entity.

10.1.1. *"Pure" Concession Agreements*

In the first type of structure, the public sector sets up an agency to handle an activity such as providing mental health services or managing

road networks. The agency is a route to introduce private sector performance metrics into an activity and to look at investment and operating
cost management through a service agreement or a longer-term concession to provide services. At this point, the ownership remains inside the
public sector, though in the special case discussed next, partnering with
private sector bodies can occur. This is a form of joint venturing (discussed in Chapter 11) with risk taking by all parties. It is not procurement.
Private sector money, grants or other funding sources may be used.

LIFT as a special case: One way to try and manage the inflexibility,
especially in healthcare projects where a commitment to a building for
25 years may not be consonant with changes in clinical care over that
time, is to use a local improvement finance trust (LIFT). In this model, a
LIFT company is construed as rather more of a true joint venture than the
client/contractor mode commonly seen in PPPs. The local National Health
Service trust is a 20% shareholder of the company as well as the community health partnership and the private sector. This approach has placed a
number of burdens on health administrators who did not always have the
appropriate expertise to make private sector financial decisions, manage
the commissioning process to develop and include private sector innovation and optimize the opportunities offered through participation in the
governance structures associated with this mechanism. The result has
been that a lot of early LIFT companies had expectations of improvements
through the involvement of the private sector, especially around innovation in design that were not always met because of poor public sector
preparedness.

One of the other challenges facing any public sector initiative of this
type was that of a major change and a reorganization as a constant
dynamic inside the commissioning organizations. This led to delays in
bringing projects to fruition and also led to uncertainty about future supplies of pump-priming funding for projects, impacting the ability to seek
private funding because of the uncertainties. Not all of these projects were
privately funded: in the Rossendale £10 million LIFT scheme, the primary
care trust contributed the capital costs and ownership of the project reverts
to it when the partnership terminates.

Other quasi PPP schemes include nominations agreements for
residential accommodation schemes and third-party developer lease
schemes. These schemes would probably fall into the first category shown
in Table 10.1.

Table 10.1:   Contract Types and Ownership, Control and Funding Issues

Contract type	Ownership of Assets During Contract	Control for Contract Period	Funding
Pure Concession Agreement	Public	Private	Private
DBOT and BOT	Private	Private	Private
DBFO	Private	Private	Private
BOO	Private	Private	Public/Private

Note: This table is based on research at the University of Melbourne.
Prepared by CF de Nahlik from material on the former website of The University of Melbourne Public Private Partnerships group.

10.1.2. *DBOT and BOT Projects*

The second project grouping includes DBOT and BOT projects.

Once more, during the project's life it is controlled by the private partner and owned by the joint-venture company, although at the end of the project the ownership reverts to the public sector. Consequently, the private sector input comes from the design, construction and operation.

In the case of DBOT, the project specification may be made by the public sector partner but, as suggested earlier in this chapter, this may stifle innovation that may be valuable in terms of delivering an enhanced service or looking at process re-engineering to bring costs down. DBOT offers a public sector partner a route to a project without incurring all of the costs upfront, as would be the case in a normal public sector transaction. It also offers deferred ownership, possibly making it easier to manage within tight budgetary constraints.

The challenges are to ensure that the public sector partner scopes the project very carefully, especially around the service contract and that the risk assessment and agreement regarding risk allocation are sophisticated. Some early projects completed under the schemes have been less successful because start-up has been delayed as a result of changes to the specification, or risks have been poorly understood at the outset and emerge later as serious problems for the project's viability.

Transfer at the end of the project's life also needs to be carefully documented so that there are no surprises. The public sector partner may be considering that revenues raised by the project will be in the local currency as a part of planning for the transition and, unless they are prepared to take the foreign exchange risk, this places constraints on contractors who will need to raise finance locally rather than from larger overseas markets. Given the long life of projects, and the movement of personnel, unless the documentation and the agreement are really clear at the outset, end of project transfer can be a source of future dispute.

Another potential area of discord is any revision to the revenue model during the project's life such as a change to tolling charges. These changes are likely to arise from political decisions and thus may be in conflict with the expected returns by debt and equity holders. In a worst-case scenario where the debt in a project of this type fails to be serviced, lenders may need to take over the project. Therefore, at the outset, provisions for this contingency need to be agreed upon with the public sector entities — not always something that is very palatable politically when lenders may be non-nationals.

10.1.3. *Design-Build-Finance-Operate*

In DBFO projects, ownership remains vested in the public sector entity during the project's life, so this has similar elements to a lease. The Highways Agency in the UK has used DBFO structures to build several river crossings (bridges and tunnels) and a toll road, and the projects have been positively reviewed. The DBFO company finances and builds the road as well as operating and maintaining it for the period of what is essentially a concession. The Highways Agency pays the DBFO company a "shadow toll" on roads that are not subject to commercial tolling arrangements, based on usage patterns, maintenance history — and the like. This payment is used to service the debt.

In order to manage construction standards, a penalty arrangement exists for lane closures, so the incentive is not to cut costs in construction. DBFO has also been used to construct car parks at hospitals, where patients and visitors are charged for parking. This has been politically very sensitive — when these projects began, stakeholders had not thought through the major financial impact of parking charges on patients with long-term illnesses who require frequent visits to the hospital, and who may not be working as a result of their illness. Press coverage of incidents like this has often focused on the PPP structure as the cause of the problem, especially the negotiation of variation in the contracts as we saw in the previous chapter in the various UK public inquiry documents.

In the US, the DBFO approach has been slightly different inasmuch as the more extensive debt market available to public sector entities has led to debt being raised by the public sector partner rather than by the private sector partner (see Table 10.1).[1]

10.1.4. *Build-Own-Operate*

The final category of projects, BOO projects, has been the one most widely developed in the private power sector. Here the public sector benefits from facilities such as power supply or desalination works, which are built, owned and operated by a private sector contractor, usually under a concession agreement. A potential attraction for the private sector might be the long-term possibility of privatization of this particular service or asset bundle. The attraction to private sector investors, analogous to the case of BOTs, is the possibility of long-term growth in the sector and a technology basis that is not thought to be likely to radically change over the period of the project.

In the specific cases of power and water, projects have been problematic because much of the facility is difficult and expensive to inspect in order to develop a clear view of the existing condition of the assets. These are projects where the currency risk from local currency payments and external currency funding may be most acute. Very often, equity is hard to come by for projects of this type in newer environments, making the project's success reliant on enhanced contributions from local government or grants and other funding from regional development banks, and the public sector support may not end there. In one early Malaysia water project, for example, additional government support was required because of the difficulties in collecting the tariffs. These projects are asset intensive and as such may look at relatively high levels of debt to equity, such as 60%–70% debt and additional government support. One notable exception to this is the English and Welsh water companies that have elected to fund projects like this through bond issues, possibly as a result of their longer track records.

A BOO project, often a power project, will usually have a long-term contract in place before financial close to provide the cash flow to service the debt.

---

[1] See, for example, the US Department of Transportation Federal Highway Authority site https://www.fhwa.dot.gov/ipd/p3/default.aspx?ref_site=kl.

10.2. Different Types of PPP Projects

Next, we look at the common types of PPP projects.

10.2.1. *The Freestanding or Commercial Partnership*

In a freestanding or commercial partnership, the private contractor designs, builds and operates the facility but sells the services to third parties or the general public. An example of this would be a toll road. The debt is serviced by the revenues from the facility and there is no governmental support in the form of financial top-ups or contributions to the cash flows. The government contribution to the facility may be in the form of an existing road, or through support in terms of legislation or planning permissions, the latter including the choice of route for roads and rail links.

10.2.2. *Joint Ventures*

In the joint venture project, both public and private partners contribute but the private sector has overall control of the delivery of the project. The public sector contribution can take a number of forms, similar to those seen in concessions discussed earlier. However, responsibilities need to be very clearly delineated and there also needs to be a very clear allocation and acceptance of risks. There may be assistance from the public sector partner with any requests for planning permission. The private sector entity raises the funding and cash flow is derived from end users or customers to service the debt.

10.2.3. *Services Sold to the Public Sector*

When public sector activities are constrained by tight budgets, big-ticket items may be viewed by end-users and the general public as essential, but may not be affordable. Such examples might include new hospital or school buildings and clinical equipment, such as scanners, with or without expert technicians, or even staffed units, such as drug dependency support services. In this context, leasing might be one possible solution, but another might be the provision of services by an external contractor to the public sector. An example might be mobile cancer screening units.

The costs to the public sector entity that are passed through by the private sector contractor need to be assessed for "Value For Money" against alternatives, or Public Sector Comparators as discussed in the previous chapter. One cause of concern has been that public sector payments have been cross-subsidizing the use of high capital cost medical equipment by other private third-party users, so the contracting arrangements need extensive scrutiny and reassurance that this is not the case. The third-party provider of the service will probably seek to raise finance against the public sector contract, so this is a form of true project financing, but as in other cases, the risks relating to ownership — either directly as a lessor or indirectly as a potential debtor in possession — need to be thoroughly assessed. There also needs to be strong safeguards around maintenance of items of equipment and a careful review of insurance cover relating to the service provision.

As an example, let us consider a simple toll road example. A private sector company offers to build and operate a toll road in a country that is adapting to a more open economy. It will be a time-bound concession (i.e. for a specified number of years) and use the toll monies collected to repay the external finance costs and generate a return for the private sector company appointed as the concessionaire. The concessionaire's financial statements and management costs are in US dollars and the on-the ground costs in a mixture of local currency and US dollars (to pay for the bought-in tolling equipment such as automatic card readers, money collection, tolling booths, signage, etc.). The concessionaire requires revenue from the project in US dollars.

Very often the new toll road is built to replace an existing elderly key highway, possibly going through town centres and subject to congestion, constricting the flow of goods and services that would enhance economic growth. The slower road continues to exist, toll-free. Something that was free for use in the past may now require payment for faster transit times, with the free option continuing for the more congested traditional route. Although there may be arguments that the only way for a new road to be built is under these conditions, cynical voters and other political stakeholders might consider who is undertaking key risks.

Now let us consider our example splitting it into two alternative scenarios. In the first alternative, the revenues are collected in local currency so there is an exchange risk when remitting back to the concessionaire. Who should take on this risk? Who has signed the concession agreement? Is it the local government that may not have a steady source of US dollars? Is it the central government that may have other priorities for scarce hard currency and have agreed to the road project for political reasons? Will this mean diverting dollars that might be used for important imports such as fuel or medicine to pay foreign contractors their profit? A PPP can become a political football as rival political parties may want change or even sequestration and internal conflicts can overrule foreign concerns in such a political debate.

In the second alternative scenario, the toll payment is made by the motorist or the freight company in US dollars. The exchange risk is now transferred to the user. Do individuals have easy access to this currency? What are the hidden charges for a dollar toll payment? What about the exchange rate that is used by the processing banks: official (favourable to the government) or unofficial (true reflection)?

An early example from Mexico (a peso economy but where dollars were in limited use) illustrates what can happen. In the early 1990s, a large local Mexican construction company, Empresas ICA, went public, listing in the US and raising money via a US dollar bond issue to fund its plans to build a number of toll roads in Mexico under 20-year concessions. However, initially, the toll roads, while faster, were ignored in favour of the free traditional routes. As a result, predicted revenue targets were not met. The company, the subject of a series of Harvard Business School case studies, embraced the political move to construct a number of tolled highways to the point where they accounted for around a quarter of its 1991 revenues. This decision was to prove disastrous as the peso devalued and government spending was cut, forcing a move to foreign projects to generate non-peso revenue that stretched the company's core competencies. The financial problems came to a head and a fire-sale of assets together with government support ensured the company survived. Toll roads became the norm and revenues are now collected in US dollars or pesos depending on location. However, in late 2016, the company again filed for a pre-packaged bankruptcy for several units and the causes seem to include a currency mismatch — peso income and dollar debt.

Closer to home (of one of the authors) is one of the UK's toll road projects, the Birmingham North Relief Road, designed to relieve the congestion around Birmingham at peak times. The 27-mile road was built and is operated under a 53-year concession as a PPP by Midland Expressway Ltd., originally owned by Macquarie Infrastructure Group but sold in 2017 to IFM (owned by several Australian pension funds) following an effective transfer of control to the bank group that had funded the project.

A three-year construction period after several delays meant work finally started in 2000 and the road opened in 2003. Tolls are charged in UK pounds, so no exchange exposure, but the project has historically been realizing losses. Usage has been low because the local road users and freight companies are reluctant to pay what were seen as high toll charges (£6.90 one way for a car during the week and £12.00 one way for an HGV during the week recently) so they continue to use the free but congested M1 motorway around Birmingham. This project has now been restructured and write-down of the debt is expected to make the project a success for its new owners, though 2019 figures continue to show losses.

These two examples illustrate the challenges of PPP projects:

- they are long-term in nature;
- many things are bundled into a single contract or aggregated into a series of contracts;
- they may require a mindset change to pay for something that has hitherto been free (so the decision by the user is that of time saved versus cost);
- the pricing decision is very sensitive;
- they are vulnerable to exchange risk if there is a currency mismatch at the payment, debt or corporate treasury level;
- they are often burdened with high debt costs; and
- there is an issue about implicit government guarantees for strategic projects.

10.3. Accounting Issues for PPPs and PFIs

An anomaly exists in that, at the time of this writing, many government accounting mechanisms do not recognize PPPs as part of the overall government borrowing figures under the European System of National and Regional Accounts (ESA) and especially the ESA 95 standard. In contrast, many projects are coming back on to public sector financial statements as International Financial Reporting Standards and especially International Financial Reporting Interpretations Committee 12 (IFRIC 12) which relates to concessions, a popular structure in PPPs and PFIs, are adopted. International Public Sector Accounting Standards (IPSAS), IPSAS-32 specifies the recognition of PPP assets and liabilities as part of a standard on service concession agreements. There are also requirements to report PPPs as part of government obligations, so the 2016 EPEC/Eurostat joint guide to the statistical treatment of PPPs sets out a basic premise of allocating the PPP to the balance sheet of the entity that bears most of the risks and benefits from most of the rewards. As a secondary consideration, control of the specification, service delivery and control of the asset after the PPP agreement has ended can determine where the asset is reported. Eurostat requires governments to report PPP projects where the construction demand or availability risk is retained by the government, and this is further developed in the European Manual on Government Deficit and Debt and the European System of Accounts (ESA2010). The rationale to ensure governments are not overextended via "invisible" contingencies is a logical one and speaks to a transparency agenda.

The treatment of PPP projects from an accounting standpoint will continue to be clarified over the next few years. As governments seek to deliver state-of-the-art facilities to those communities that they serve, these mechanisms for financing large public sector projects are unlikely to diminish in importance, but the form they may take will be influenced by accounting issues as well as by costs. A detailed technical discussion of these developments is outside of the scope of this book. However, we note the following two key lessons that should be drawn.

(1) It is unlikely that, given the long life and size of many of these projects, and their residual claims on government finances, they will continue to remain off-balance sheet in public accounts, considering an increased expectation around transparency and accountability for spending to the electorate.
(2) The anomaly that appears to exist between the different ways that these projects are reported in different sets of accounts is also likely to disappear.

Therefore, the future emphasis in these projects is more likely to be more on value for money and less on financial engineering.

10.4. PPP in Different Country Contexts

Despite the best efforts of multilateral funders, and their support and development of the professionalisation of PPP participants, the concept is not universal. Variations appear as a result of political approaches and different legal systems, requiring a different approach to the contract structure.

Earlier in the book, we discussed the important difference between ownership and control and how this drives some of the structures that we see in project financings. However, not all legal systems recognize this difference and this automatically limits the volume of project financings and PPPs in those countries. Some countries have a set of clearly stated PPP programme objectives, policy statements or even laws. Examples would include Brazil, Bulgaria, India, Indonesia, India and Australia. In the US, PPP frameworks are developed at state level. There may also be minimum size criterion for PPPs, reflecting the higher costs of negotiation and finance provision. Frameworks can be very useful for managing disputes by including mechanisms such as mediation and recognizing the importance of escrow accounts and performance bonds.

Another challenge is that the contracts are often between 20 and 30 years — or even longer as in our case study at the end of this chapter — a time span during which many political changes can take place and thus influence the environment of the PPP. Consequently, countries that may be in the process of redefining their legal and political systems, and possibly most in need of some sort of infrastructure investment that can be financed through PPPs, may offer uncertain environments to providers of capital. The ability of a project to raise money through a long-term bond issue in order to take out the term providers of capital may be affected by political risk and an absence of personal or financial product-led savings that might find these attractive investment assets.

Finally, different forms of legal system may of necessity give rise to "incomplete contracts" and thus the relationship between stakeholders can be critical in terms of making the contracts a success.

If we consider the difference between civil law and common law, it is possible to generalize that civil law countries tend to use concession contracts and common law countries tend to use fully private "special purpose vehicle" or SPV type companies to provide product or service under government regulation. Countries that were formerly part of larger groups including empires, may draw their legal system from that of the former dominant player in the group. As an example, many former Commonwealth countries follow traditions from UK law, some African countries follow French legal traditions.

Earlier in this chapter we discussed potential difficulties in transferring ownership control of assets to the private sector and even to external stakeholders from outside the country so this limits security for lenders. There is also a need to have a legal structure that allows for the creation of the special-purpose vehicle and its segregation and link to the cash flow that ultimately will service the debt. The PPP payment mechanism will also affect the delivery: if the user is paying, such as in a toll road, these payments may be supplemented or underwritten by a host government in the light of certain service benchmarks. Land and real estate values around the site of such a PPP can rise, allowing others to benefit from the project investment. There is an inevitable desire to capture some of this incremental value by the project stakeholders, leading to potential scope creep; however, because the government is paying, such as in the case of hospitals or prisons, the project then becomes directly exposed to political risk and to any such risks that may arise should payments be made in an external currency.

A discussion of the specifics of different PPP programmes is beyond the scope of this chapter. Readers are referred to works such as Chapter 2 of the APMG PPP certification guide that deals with different regimes in further detail and a discussion of the complexities of a PPP from the political insider viewpoint.[2]

10.5. PPPs in China

One of the countries where PPPs have been widely used to develop infrastructure projects is China. PPPs in China at the time of writing are very different from the PPPs that we have seen in other countries. In China, private companies have competed directly with state-owned enterprises (SOEs) to participate in PPP projects. PPPs have developed in a number of stages. Initially promoted and adopted as a mechanism in the 1980s, early projects were supported by limited institutional guarantees and limited legislation. Fiscal deficiencies in local governments led to a growth in the market and some enhancement of institutional protection. The financial crisis in 2008 led to a replacement of the private companies in

---

[2]*APMG Public-Private Partnership (PPP) Certification Guide.*

PPPs by SOEs and public tendering was partly withdrawn. The sector then went through a revival as demands increased and state governments began to initiate specialized legislation. At the time of writing, a number of foreign providers of funds have become less active in the market. Chinese PPPs are subject to a number of layers of approval and operate in a sensitive political environment. Expert advice should be sought and retained throughout the project.

There are a number of laws enacted in China to govern PPPs. Although the framework is clear, local project data that is required to model a project successfully often remains incomplete or unavailable. Conclusions from research in this area suggests that there is a need for a focus on clear negotiations of task and risk allocation between all parties at the start of the project.

In general, approval procedures have been very cumbersome requiring signoff by large numbers of government and local bodies in China. This means that changes to projects are also cumbersome and may require lengthy public hearings to take account of the views of all stakeholders. One problem has been that China's State Council has considered the fixed returns for foreign investors to be incompatible with the benefit sharing between Chinese and foreign investors. This is believed to have led to early foreign participants in the market such as Thames Water and Anglian Water withdrawing.

There are still challenges about asymmetry of experience such as in the case of the Lianjiang Sino-French Water Supply Project, where the contract was signed prior to a detailed investigation of the water consumption and estimated cost by the local joint-venture partner. When it became clear that users would be paying a higher price for the services and this would affect the local water supply, a renegotiation was required and the different stakeholders were unable to agree. The water plant said to have been unoccupied for a decade. What is presently described as PPP in China is quite different to that seen in other countries and tends to favour local banks with the State or local state entities as key stakeholders making such projects have a more political emphasis.

Comparisons of PPPs are inevitably out of date once they are published and the projects themselves need a long time in operation in order to assess them. We close with a case study from Canada that has undergone a number of cycles of change and offers thought-provoking lessons (see footnote 3).

10.6. Case Study: Highway 407 in Canada[3]

Highway 407 has been a controversial project in Canada since its inception. In the 1950s, the government of the Province of Ontario began a series of projects to plan and construct a series of multi-laned controlled access highways to facilitate traffic flows in the Toronto region. The first of these, Highway 401, soon reached high congestion levels and the two major stakeholder groups — the truckers, bringing materiel across Ontario to support industry and commerce and the private users, getting to work, taking children to school and so on — were united in their lobbying for a new highway to solve this problem.

In the short-term, Highway 401 was enlarged to include new lanes, but the booming economy of the late 1980s led to ever-increasing congestion and to what was known as the "401 parking lot" problem. The decision to proceed with the development of Highway 407 was taken in 1986, following a helicopter flight by the Deputy Minister of Transportation to survey the problem. The plan was to construct a 69 kilometer section and to build it as a toll highway, using the first all-electronic tolling system with no toll booths on the highway itself.

The Ministry of Transportation of Ontario (MTO) had established processes in place for highway construction along with roads and bridges. The budget also had to support maintenance. In common with many public service departments, budget allocation was an annual exercise, with project funding only committed one year at a time and fierce competition for funds. Political considerations also were very important. Defined projects were put out to sealed bid from pre-qualified contractors with limits placed on exposure to any single contractor. The detail of the project scope allowed competition only on price and technical supervision by the MTO was close. Performance guarantees were not sought and innovation was handled by the MTO and factored into the project scope. Though the projects could be small, there was enough work to go around for small and large companies and the system was viewed as free of taint even though it was believed that road builders tended to support one political party.

However, in 1990, a change of government occurred in Ontario and there was a move to increase the size of the work packages for construction

---

[3]This case draws extensively on Chandran Mylvaganam and Sanford Borins, *If You Build It: Business, Government and Ontario's Electronic Toll Highway*, Toronto: University of Toronto Press, 2004.

contracts and to use the contractors' expertise in the design and build function. A deep recession required significant re-planning and there was concern about provinces debt, ratings and the consequences of a downgrading on the cost of borrowing for new projects. At this time Highway 407 was not scheduled to be completed until 2020 though work had already taken place on interchanges such as that between Highways 407 and 400, completed in 1989 at a cost of Can$50 million. Investments like this being carried by the province pending completion of the larger project.

The concept of a toll road, though becoming popular in Western Europe, was alien to Canadian road users and indeed the Burlington Skyway Bridge had tolls removed in 1973 because the cost of collection was greater than the receipts — rumoured to be a function of low toll rates and "leakage". However, with the financial challenges facing the government, there was concern that tolls raised would need to be ring fenced so that those revenues would not be dissipated on other projects.

In 1993, it was decided that the project would go ahead and that safeguards would be put in place to ensure that the bidding process would be free from lobbying. Meetings with key stakeholders including trucking groups, automobile associations and organized labour as well as environmental groups were held to ensure that the project would be acceptable to the key stakeholders. The request for qualifications (RFQs) stage produced two major Canadian bidding groups, closely followed by an American firm. Though the latter group was supported by a major Canadian bank, it was not taken forward because of issues with the previous contract and a plan to toll Highway 400 to pay for Highway 407, which was deemed politically unacceptable.

The emphasis for the two surviving consortia was on value engineering. This stage was expected to take two to three months, required a review of standards and procedures and the generation of sufficiently detailed design such that a guaranteed maximum price could be set and the consortia were paid a fixed sum for their work on this phase.

This was followed by a request for proposals (RFPs) and negotiations were expected to be concluded by 1 November 1993, with an agreement with the winning consortium by the end of 1993. In the meantime, construction of Highway 407 was set to continue to guarantee employment. The Ontario provincial government was looking for innovative approaches and a partner that would design, build, finance and operate the highway with a reversion to the government after a given period time. Only one proposal was permitted per group and lobbying was expressly prohibited.

The proposals remained confidential as did the evaluation process for several reasons: the need to safeguard proprietary information and to discourage any attempts to game the system or to affect the trading value of the companies in each consortium.

The tolling partners were added after the group began work. The government department controlling the process had vetoed exclusive arrangements thus allowing it to choose a civil consortium from one team and a tolling partner from another. The tolling system would be almost unique and include transponders as well as plate recognition and billing software competences.

Though the process ran late, in January 1994 the objectives of the province became clear: these included thoughts around the issue of the additional cost if the borrowing was carried out by a private consortium (as compared with borrowing by the province) and the need for guarantees (previous experience suggested that the private sector was shielded from risk but was able to gain all the upside). There were also finer points around the setting of toll levels including the inflation basis for any increases and the implications for the province of any shortfall in toll revenues. It was decided that two options should be considered for further development: a single project composed of the best of both DBFOs and a DBO project with the financing provided by the province. While these were under consideration, work continued on Highway 407 for 1994, and further contracts were awarded with the view that these would be taken over by the winning bidder.

The final decision considered the public financing option on the grounds that if the private financing route was chosen and it was guaranteed by the province, there would be an additional borrowing cost of 0.25% which would add Can$30 million to the project's net present value. If the financing was on a non-recourse basis then the additional cost would be in the range of Can$35 to Can$100 million. Private sector equity would also expect a minimum return of 12% and that would increase project costs further, making the likelihood of government subsidies greater.

The award was not without controversy and there were calls in the Press for details of the bids to be made public. There were claims that fundraisers for one particular political party had swung the decision. The losing bidder did not get an expected in-depth post-award debriefing because it had threatened a lawsuit, and it was believed the debriefing would be counterproductive and this atmosphere of rancour continued into the next phase of the project.

The total contract award was Can$929.8 million and negotiations began in earnest. The choice of the tolling system required a new consortium to work together and this caused delays with this part of the project.

10.6.1. *The Start of the Project*

Meanwhile, the MTO began to discuss eastern extension of Highway 407 as a separate unsolicited project with the losing bidder. Though formal RFQs were issued for this and for a western extension, a provincial election and change of government stopped the process.

The main Highway 407 project continued during 1995 and 1996, with a bonus signed for early completion of the civil work. The Provincial Auditor released a report suggesting that there would have been more bids if the project had been unbundled further. It also noted that the length of merging lanes had been decreased from 500 m to 466 m (the latter was the standard when imperial, as opposed to metric, measures were used) and this was seized on by the Press with the headline "Police fear toll highway will be a killer: head-on crashes certain, they say" and a banner headline "Highway 407 safety rules lowered: report".

An independent enquiry found that the value engineering process lacked explicit consideration of safety, with the primary focus being on cost-cutting. The installation of crash cushions around lighting poles, bridge supports, *et cetera* were also raised and these were added to the project specification and completed.

10.6.2. *The New Tolling Technology*

Highway 407 was now ready for traffic as of June 1997, but the tolling technology was not.

The toll system supply agreement, a contract worth Can$53.4 million was signed in September 1995 and weekly reports were sent to that part of the provincial government managing the project. Their deadline was for tolling to be operational for transponders by December 1996 and full tolling by March 1997.

By the fall of 1996 it was clear that these deadlines would be missed. As of January 1997, the consortium began paying monthly penalties.

The highway opened in June 1997 for free use but this led to a traffic loading of over 300,000 vehicles per day rather than that anticipated by tolling of 100,000 vehicles per day. The tolling system kept crashing as a result of computer capacity problems to do with processing data — heavy transponder and video imaging records' and eventually full electronic tolling commenced on 14 October 1997 at which point the traffic levels fell. By February 1999, traffic levels were back at just over 200,000 vehicles per day. At this point, the government began to look at privatization.

10.6.3. *The Next Phase of the Project*

With an election looming in early 1999, the incumbent Ontario government wanted to produce evidence that the budget was moving towards balance, and also to cut taxes and boost spending. One route to do this would be through privatization of various assets and in February 1998, Highway 407 was considered for a potential IPO. However, it soon became clear that this would take time and that a privatization was more likely to bring in more money so appropriate consultants were hired to begin work by preparing an expression of interest document for prospective bidders.

The group that had designed and built Highway 407 was one of the bidders and generally considered to hold an advantage. The losing bidder had also teamed up with Spanish and Australian partners and a company partly owned by the local government employees pension fund in Ontario. The third bidder was a Spanish and Quebecois group alongside another Canadian pension fund with the final bidding team including the original unsuccessful third bidder for the DBO contract. All bidders had strong financial partners.

In 1998, RFPs were issued to the four consortia requesting the price they would pay for the existing highway and the right to construct additional sections of which one was mandatory. There were four options in the Eastern extension. The RFP also included a draft management contract demonstrating consistency with the public interest. A detailed DBO proposal for the Western and Eastern construction sections under one of the options could be submitted as a separate package with a guaranteed maximum price, allowing the government to have a fall back if the privatization price was not considered acceptable, but not all bidders were allowed to produce this.

The timetable (based on a document that was still incomplete) was extended to March and again there were statements that explicitly prohibited contact between those making the decision in government and the consortia. There were suggestions that such contacts did take place.

There were differences inside the government concerning whether it should be an outright sale of the highway or a lease/concession of 35 years, the most common practice at that time. The consortia were asked to submit non-binding indicative bids in early February for lease periods of 55, 99 and 199 years. It was decided that, on the basis of the consultants' views, their best value for government was a 99-year lease. (Consultants were rumoured to be being paid over Can$20 million.)

The consortium that had designed and built Highway 407 withdrew, following a token bid of one dollar. The other three bids consisted of two close together and one offering the government a significantly larger sum. Two bidders were asked to rebid and the third bidding group mentioned above (the Spanish/Quebecois group) was selected on the basis of a bid of Can$3.107 billion and a 99-year lease. The new owner was able to toll all sections of the highway and the setting of tolls, penalties and interest rates was left up to them. The deal closed on May 5, the day before the election was called. The government claimed that it had sold a highway that had cost Can$1.5 billion to build for Can$3.1 billion and thus had made a "profit".

10.6.4. *Objections to Increases in the Level of the Toll after Privatization*

By September 1999, off-peak tolls had risen by 12% and in less than four years toll rates had increased by 29.5% in peak hours and 73% in a diminished number of off-peak hours.

The enforcement of the collection of tolling revenues was carried out by the new concessionaire but the sanction for non-payment, a "denial of registration", was enacted by the Ontario Government through the MTO. Not all vehicles had transponders, so the plate recognition scheme picked up tolls due. The process of advising Highway 407 users of their tolling dues payable was not carried out in accordance with the agreed process outlined in the documentation. This led to unhappiness by road users (and thus voters) and became an issue for the provincial government and the concessionaire, not least when a class-action suit was launched on behalf of approximately 840,000 drivers who had been subject to an administrative fee for late payment that had been raised from Can$15 to Can$30.

Thus, the incoming provincial government in 2003 made it an election pledge to force a rollback of toll levels. The bond rating agencies advised them that the contract was ironclad. Not disconcerted by the stakeholder unrest, the concessionaire increased tolls. The government, staggering under a Can$5 billion deficit that it had inherited, dug its heels in and claimed breach of contract on the grounds that the agreement cited that the concessionaire must obtain the government's permission before making material changes to the highway. The Ontario Superior Court recommended arbitration and the arbitrator ruled that this was not a material change to the highway.

While road users were on the side of the government, the concessionaire was backed by bond rating agencies, etc. The concessionaire company was required to provide the province with annual audited traffic reports. The government disputed the numbers. The dispute escalated further when the Spanish government supported the concessionaire by reportedly threatening to block a proposed Trade and Investment Enhancement Agreement between Canada and the European Union unless the provincial government of Ontario backed down over the tolls.

By 2006, an agreement was reached with the appointment of an Ombudsman, discounts were promoted for certain groups of users and road widening and other projects were brought forward.

A rare interview with one of the investors in the concessionaire in 2017 suggested the project might be worth as much as Can$45.3 billion by 2026 in a "best case scenario", describing it as a "cash cow" with an analyst using the term "value-generating monster".[4]

10.6.4.1. *Lessons Learned*

What this case illustrates (using its detailed description of some of the processes around contract bidding, etc.), are several factors that are important for all PPPs. These may be self-evident but bear repeating:

1. The need for detail in the project that is being financed — the contrast between the DBO contract and the concession contract and the problems that then ensued from incomplete information says it all.
2. In the first negotiation, the steps to ensure that there was no hint of influence or discussion between the government and the bidders were

---

[4]Geoff Zochodne, "Highway 407 Could be Worth up to $45B in a Decade, and That's Good News for SNC Lavalin," *Financial Post*, September 27, 2017.

painstaking and confidentiality and the importance of proprietary information were respected.

3. Political change can have major repercussions for long-term projects, especially around service charging.

4. Forced membership of consortium is never easy.

5. New technology can, as in this case, be the subject of risk estimates, probabilities, impact, *et cetera*, but the effect on a project when it does not work properly can be devastating.

Chapter 11

Structures for Jointly Owned
or Sponsored Projects

Introduction

Most projects have multiple core stakeholders and may have multiple owners. While many companies prefer absolute ownership and control of vital supply and distribution projects, as technology and services move around the world, jointly owned or controlled projects comprising partners with mutual goals, talents and resources are the norm. They may take place because:

- The undertaking is beyond a single company's financial and/or management resources.
- The partners have complementary skills or, in the case of projects in some foreign countries, political expertise or presence (this would include requirements for local ownership of a project).
- Economies of a large project lower the cost of the project or service substantially over the possible cost of a smaller project if the partners proceeded individually.
- The risks of the project are shared.
- One or more partners can use tax benefits arising from the project.
- Off-balance sheet financing can be arranged by sponsors, using the project company as the borrowing entity, though changing reporting regulations make off-balance sheet reporting increasingly more difficult.
- Requirements of financial covenants and indenture restrictions can be met.

- An increased debt leverage can be obtained, though again, bank regulatory frameworks make historic high leverage levels no longer possible.
- To obtain or maintain control over a resource or market position, but attention needs to be paid to increasing regulation of market dominance.
- If one or more of the parties proceeds alone, it may not have access to funds from lenders due to political or financial reasons.
- A special purpose entity (SPE) or special purpose vehicle (SPV) is required, possibly to isolate the project from stakeholder financials.

There are a number of key basic forms for jointly owned projects:

- Corporations
- Partnerships
- Limited partnerships
- Limited liability companies
- Contractual joint ventures (including undivided interests)
- Unincorporated joint ventures
- Franchises (including concession agreements)
- Trusts

Not all of these structures are available in all jurisdictions, or if they are, they may not carry the same benefits that of the US-based structures on which much of today's project financing is based. For example, in the UK, it is not easy for tax benefits that may accrue to a corporation, to pass through to individuals as exist in US limited partnerships. Each of these organizational forms in the list needs to be structured in a variety of ways to meet local legal and tax objectives. The variations, and some of the advantages and disadvantages of each, need to be carefully considered at the outset, taking account of local laws as well as the governing law of the agreement (any judgements will need to be enforced locally). As we said at the outset, not all jurisdictions recognize the separation of ownership and control at an organizational and at personal level. We begin with a short discussion of the research driving the choices of form of partnership before proceeding to a discussion of the accounting considerations.

11.1. What We Now Know About Partnering

Recent recipients of the Nobel Memorial Prize in Economic Sciences have focused on areas associated with the costs of transactions (Oliver Williamson — jointly awarded with Elinor Ostrom in 2009); contract theory including bargaining costs and incomplete contracts (Oliver Hart — jointly awarded with Bengt Holmstrom in 2016) and 2014 for work in market power and regulation, though he is also known for his work in game theory (Jean Tirole — 2014). That these three economists all won the prestigious award within a relatively short time frame shows the importance now attributed to contracts and especially in the area of co-operation, because "getting it wrong" is a very expensive exercise. Most projects require cooperative activity to be successful and projects that use resources from one country to develop assets in another one will often take the form of a joint venture or other partnership route.

Looking at each set of ideas and paraphrasing, Williamson promoted the idea of markets versus hierarchies and the challenges presented if an organization has very few sources for a particular requirement, especially if it has specialist characteristics. Under such circumstances, it might make sense to control supply through vertical integration. He also developed the taxonomy of different forms of co-operation on which Figure 11.1 is based. We can see how this taxonomy works in project organizations and in project financing throughout the two books. One example is the area of concessions, the subject of the previous chapter. Lin Ostrom's work on Commons is not so directly relevant to projects but is

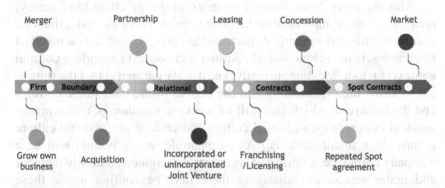

Figure 11.1: Decisions About the Forms of Co-operation

Based on Oliver E. Williamson, *The Economic Institutions of Capitalism*, New York, NY: Free Press, 1985.

likely to become more so as projects based around commonly owned areas such as water become more controversial in terms of stakeholder management.

Hart's work looks at contract theory when information is asymmetric (it is rarely symmetric!) and specifically defines the idea of incompletion in contracts. Most contracts are incomplete because not all events can be foreseen (especially with long contracts) and when a situation that is not explicitly addressed in the contract arises, it is usually managed by the legal system governing the contract. The theory was developed using the US and UK legal systems found in many commercial agreements. However, as the geographic spread of projects has increased, and sovereign considerations have come to the fore, legal systems face difficult tests if such issues are not known and there is no established legal precedent. The use of arbitration in a neutral country to attempt to resolve the issue; arbitration has become more common and much faster route in recent years. Holmstrom, who shared the prize, looks at corporate governance and incentives, and particularly the area of "moral hazard". We can observe moral hazard in projects when assumptions are made about state sponsorship or implicit guarantees and more risk is taken because there is a belief about a "bailout" often from a financially stronger parent (the "implied guarantee" or a host government). Jean Tirole looks not only at regulation and banking but has also published on the subject of game theory. The latter area is of interest when considering partnering, especially when adverse events occur.

Moving away from Nobel Laureates to the practical (and messy) area of research into real partnerships, joint ventures and alliances, several themes have emerged: partnerships are successful as a result of three key sets of factors — task, partner and context (including cultural context) factors. Most importantly, know your partner(s) — take time to get to know the organization and the people inside their home cultures and the culture in which you will be working together. (Culture means national culture, organizational culture and craft or professional culture as just three manifestations.) As an example, an individual will be a company employee, a citizen of wherever, an engineer, a family member and under certain circumstances there may be conflict inside these cultures!

A simple partner diagnostic is shown in Table 11.1.

Table 11.1: What to Look for in a Project Partner

Examples of Task-Related Criteria	Examples of Partner-Related Criteria	Examples of Context Management-Related Criteria
Process and other specialist know-how	Developing personal relationships at multiple levels	Establishing robust government relations, including local government
Equipment and other asset ownership or access	Location and support of JV personnel, families and other needs	Knowledge of local law and local expertise
Knowledge management and the ability to deliver it to the project	Respecting local customs and traditions	Knowledge of current NGO and other norms regarding the proposed activity
Relevant complementary experience, e.g. mining	Trust at individual level	Regulatory permits and knowing how to finalize them
Power plant maintenance experience	Stakeholder management	Stability of a regime and good information
Financial strength	Congruence of attitude to risk and risk management	Process management to minimize pollution and local disruption
Supply chain links	Decision-making capacity	Import and other taxes
Technology access	Ability to "sell the project" locally	Managing corruption and other difficult issues

Note: This is a very short sample list of some examples from what should be a very thorough process.
Prepared by Carmel F. de Nahlik and Frank J. Fabozzi, based on multiple academic sources.

11.2. Accounting for Joint Ventures

Joint ventures are attractive to some sponsors because of the potential off-balance sheet accounting treatment of the debt of the project company, where not more than 50% of the project company is owned.

If a parent owns more than 50% of a corporation, contractual joint venture or partnership, general tradition or practice in many countries require line-by-line consolidation of assets and liabilities for financial accounting purposes.

This is based on the premise that more than 50% ownership results in control over the venture,[1] and that control requires consolidation. Such consolidation on a line-by-line basis can adversely affect the financial statements and ratios of the parent.

On the other hand, ownership of 50% or less of a joint venture company is generally insufficient to achieve control, and in such case the parent can use the equity method of accounting which requires only a one-line entry on the balance sheet disclosing the amount of investment in the joint venture company. Likewise, only a one-line entry is required on the profit and loss statement. Less than around 20% ownership generally requires no disclosure.

However, in the revised US rules, the main change (in line with other regulators) is that the emphasis is now on control — and this may not be as simple as just determined by voting rights or ownership, so there are two key tests for accounting purposes that separate ownership and control, recognizing one may not automatically lead to the other. New terms in use include "variable interest entity", designating an entity under common control (VIE) and "voting interest entity" (VOE). If an entity is not a VIE, then the VOE test should be applied to determine consolidation, with a "related party tie-breaker test" to determine if consolidation is required, even if the VIE is small. In US GAAP, the term "joint venture" has a very specific meaning, and confusion can arise when entities that come together to (say) explore for oil and gas may be termed a joint venture without meeting this formal definition. For the US, a new standard, ASU 2015-02, Consolidation (Topic 810): was released in 2015 and amendments to this were issued as Accounting Standards Update 2016–2017, Consolidation (Topic 810). This anticipates all joint relationships being examined and accounted for.

In the EU and UK, FRS 102 in the UK and Ireland covers entities not using the EU standards of FRS 101 and FRS 105. IFRS 10 (includes some aspects of IAS 27), IFRS 11 and 12 replace IAS 31 with some changes of meaning, so care needs to be taken.

This is an emerging and changing area, so expert advice should be sought and careful thought given to the structure at as early a stage as possible. There are often separate regulations relating to specific types

---

[1] Note this is not necessarily the case because it is possible to have some shares that have multiple votes, some shares that may carry no votes and some special classes of shares that can outvote any other decisions.

of investments, e.g. qualified affordable housing programmes in the US (FASC Update 2014-01, topic 323).

11.3. Corporations

A corporation may not be a satisfactory way in which to structure a joint project financing because a sponsor cannot file a consolidated federal income tax return for the project. Although it may be possible for tax benefits from investment tax credit, energy tax credit, depreciation, and interest expense to be claimed by the project corporation, these tax benefits will be delayed for a considerable period or lost forever if the project corporation has limited taxable income. Corporations can be used as entities for jointly owned projects without a loss of tax benefits if the project equipment is financed through a "true lease" from a third-party leasing company able to claim the tax benefits and pass through most of those tax benefits to the lessee in the form of low cost lease payments. For countries wanting to stimulate investment in activities with high capital asset investment or to stimulate local manufacturing of such assets, a programme like this would be supported by tax offsets from companies with lower fixed costs, such as retailers. This was what fuelled the UK programme in the 1980s where companies such as Marks and Spencer (retailing) leased high price assets to other companies, because they could offset the first year 100% capital allowances for tax purposes against their profits. If the project sponsors can use tax benefits, a corporation can be used as an entity for a project without wasting tax benefits using a tax-oriented lease from the sponsors to the entity in which the sponsors claim the tax benefits of ownership under the lease.[2]

Today, leasing is a declining activity and is now either limited to specialist programmes or to high capital cost equipment such as aircraft. Some forms of pseudo-leasing, essentially deferred purchases, are used for items like cars.

11.3.1. *Example of a Corporation Jointly Owned by Sponsors Which Borrows to Finance a Project*

A jointly owned corporation borrows on the basis of its own credit to finance a project. Typical projects include electricity generating, refining

---

[2]See Chapters 13 and 14 in the companion book for coverage of leasing.

or processing plants. Investment and operating expenses are segregated for purposes of the project company. Rates necessary to meet costs and to provide a return on equity can be easily identified.

Income tax: The project company files its own income tax return and may not be consolidated on any sponsor tax return, dependent on sponsor ownership and local regulations.

Debt rate: The debt rate will usually be higher than the debt rate of the individual participants or sponsors.

Sponsor's balance sheet and loan covenants: The investment in the project company may be shown as a one-line equity investment entry for a sponsor that owns less than 50% of the controlling stock, and the debt of the project company may be off-balance sheet for the sponsor. If the sponsor owns more than 50% of the controlling stock, a line-by-line consolidation is required. If less than 50% owned, project company liabilities will probably not constitute debt for debt-equity ratios, or a loan for loan or mortgage restrictions.

Variances:
- same as above, with credit backed by long-term take-or-pay contracts in proportion to ownership (take-or-pay contracts were discussed earlier in this book);
- same as above, with credit backed by obligations of the owners to make up deficits; and
- same as above, with true lease from one or more sponsoring parties able to claim tax benefits.

Advantages for the sponsor:
- debt of the project company may be off-balance sheet for the sponsor if less than 50% owned and not controlled (but take care with new regulations!);
- outside loan covenants restricting debt of leases;
- capital preserved for other uses;
- economics of a large-scale project achieved by combining and concentrating financial resources and technical skills;
- an essential facility built without the sponsor-participant being required to pay the entire cost of the project;
- cost segregated for rate-making purposes;
- risks of the project are shared;
- loan is non-recourse to sponsor; and

- insulated from tort and contractual liabilities of the project company, subject to piercing the corporate veil or proof of an agency relationship.

Disadvantages for the sponsor:
- higher borrowing cost;
- lack of absolute control over the facility; and
- possible loss or delay in claiming tax benefits by the jointly held company.

This structure can be problematic to negotiate if the different sponsors are of quite different size and creditworthiness, as the larger company may perceive that it is supporting the smaller ones and sacrificing lower borrowing costs to do so. This was the rationale for the absence of field financings in the North Sea and other natural resource project areas. Some of the consequences can be seen in the case study at the end of this chapter.

11.3.2. *Example of a Joint Venture Corporation with Tax Benefits Claimed by One Party*

One advantage of a corporate joint venture may be the opportunity which exists for one party to claim the entire tax shelter attributable to the project company. (Again, this is an area for care!) This is shown in Figure 11.2.

The following is assumed in the illustration shown in Figure 11.2. Corporation A needs coal but has no operating experience. Corporation B is an operator. Corporation B can use tax benefits from modified accelerated cost recovery system (MACRS) depreciation, but Corporation A cannot use tax benefits. They decide to enter into a corporate joint venture on the following basis:

1. The project company is formed. Corporation B provides capital and loans to the project company and is issued 100 shares of its common stock, which is 100% of the original issue.
2. Corporation A loans or purchases non-voting preferred stock of the project company which is convertible into 100 shares of its common stock after 10 years, with anti-dilution protection. This loan (or purchase) provides the bulk of the capital for the project.

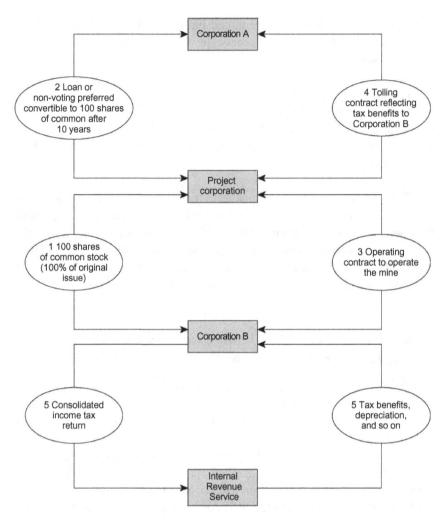

Figure 11.2:   Joint Venture with Tax Benefits Claimed by One Party

Prepared by Frank J. Fabozzi and Peter K. Nevitt.

3.   The project company enters into a 10-year operating agreement with Corporation B whereby Corporation B will operate the mine.

4.   Corporation A enters into a 10-year tolling agreement for the purchase of coal from the project company. The tolling agreement reflects most of the tax benefits which can be claimed by Corporation B.

5.   Corporation B files a consolidated income tax return with the project corporation and claims the tax benefits of depreciation on qualified equipment of the project company.

6. (not shown) Corporation A converts its debt (or stock) to 100 shares of common stock of the project company after 10 years. Corporation A and Corporation B are then equal owners of the project company.

Advantages for the sponsor:

- debt of the project company is off-balance sheet for the sponsor if less than 50% owned;
- outside loan covenants restricting debt or leases;
- capital preserved for other uses;
- economies of a large-scale project achieved by combining and concentrating financial resources and technical skills;
- an essential facility built without the sponsor–participant being required to pay the entire cost of the project;
- cost segregated for rate-making purposes;
- risks of the project are shared;
- loan is non-recourse to sponsor; and
- loan is insulated from tort and contractual liabilities of the project company, subject to piercing the corporate veil or proof of an agency relationship.

Disadvantages

- higher borrowing cost;
- lack of absolute control over the facility; and
- possible loss or delay in claiming tax benefits by the jointly held company.

11.4. Partnerships

Dependent on the jurisdiction and the recognition of legal definition of a partnership, a partnership can operate a project, hold property, hold property in its own name and enter into a financing arrangement in its own name. Partnerships, as entities for joint legal ownership of a business or a project, may have numerous advantages from an income tax standpoint.

Often, a partnership is not a separate taxable entity, does not pay income tax and files a partnership income tax return which reports the revenues, deductions and credits attributable to the partnership. The partners report their distributive shares of these items plus their distributive shares of partnership income and loss, thus permitting immediate benefit by the partners for tax purposes of available depreciation deductions, operating expenses, investment tax credit and interest deductions.

A corporation, on the other hand, pays tax as a taxable entity and claims available tax deductions for depreciation and operating expenses, on its own returns. In start-ups, these deductions must be carried forward for many years until the corporation is taxable. When dividends are paid, stockholders must pay tax on such distributions of profits.

The US concept of a general partnership presents problems from a legal standpoint because general partners generally are jointly and severally responsible for all partnership liabilities which cannot be satisfied from partnership assets. These include liabilities for contracts, debt and tort liabilities. In the case of a corporation, stockholders are not generally responsible for such liabilities. Limited partnerships avoid this problem.

However, partners can protect themselves to some extent by forming subsidiaries to enter into a partnership agreement to operate a joint venture. If the subsidiary is nominally capitalized and has limited operations, the parents may possibly still be held to be the true partners by piercing the corporate veil. (Special purpose subsidiaries to act as partners may be preferable in any event, to avoid the parent unnecessarily having to qualify to do business in a state, or unnecessarily subjecting itself to a regulatory agency.) This is shown in Figure 11.3.

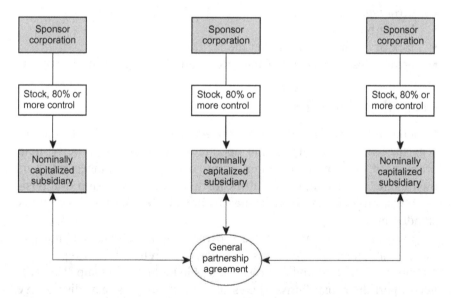

Figure 11.3:   General Partnership with Nominally Capitalized Subsidiaries

Prepared by Frank J. Fabozzi and Peter K. Nevitt.

Further steps can be taken to protect joint venturers who wish to operate as a partnership. One such step is to require lenders to limit their recourse for loans against the assets of the partnership and waive rights against the assets of the partners. Lenders will go along with such limitation if the assets of the joint venture are strong enough to support the transaction. In such circumstances, these assets may include an unconditional take-or-pay or through-put contract from a responsible creditworthy stakeholder.

Another step is an agreement among the partners not to enter into loan agreements or material contracts without the consent of all or some specified percentage of the partners, in order to protect the joint assets from financial threat. This type of agreement is typically buttressed by cross indemnities of the partners or their parents.

Potential tort liabilities, in excess of partnership assets, can usually be covered by insurance.

Care must be taken that, in limiting the functions of the partnership, the resulting entity does not constitute an association which will be taxable as a corporation. Normally, it is possible to form a partnership which will not be deemed to be an association even though protective steps are taken to limit the exposure of the partners to debt and contractual liability by agreements with creditors and among themselves.

Financial accounting for partners in reporting liabilities of partnerships usually follows the same rules as for corporations. More than 50% control generally requires line-by-line consolidation. Less than 50% control but more than 20% control generally requires only a one-line entry of the partners' investment. However, when the lenders to the partnership agree that they will seek recourse against only the partnership assets and not the assets of the partners, the partnership debt is not included in the balance sheets of the partners, but in the footnotes. To qualify for such treatment, the partnership must have entity status to own property and borrow funds in its own name (not a contractual joint venture, discussed later).

A disadvantage of a partnership as compared with a corporation is the inability of the partnership to issue securities which qualify as legal investments for insurance companies. However, this problem can be solved by establishing a corporation known as a corporate financing vehicle. The partnership issues debt certificates to the corporate financing vehicle, which in turn issues debt securities with identical terms which are secured by a pledge of the partnership securities and partnership obligations. The debt certificates issued by the corporate financing vehicle then can qualify as a legal investment for insurance companies. This was shown in Figure 11.2.

11.4.1. *General Partnership to Operate a Project*

Two or more parties decide to jointly own and/or operate a business through a general partnership. This is shown in Figure 11.3.

Limited recourse secured debt supported by a take-or-pay from the sponsor partners. Two or more companies desire to enter into a partnership for the purpose of owning or operating a joint project or business and wish to limit their partnership contractual liability.

The partnership enters into loan agreements for financing major assets which are secured by those assets, other partnership assets and the assignment of a take-or-pay contract from the partners for product produced by the partnership. However, the loan agreement limits the lenders' recourse to the partnership assets and to the proceeds from the take-or-pay contract. It can be used for almost any processing or production project.

This is illustrated in Figure 11.4. In the figure it is assumed that:

1. Three partners enter into a general partnership agreement to operate a project as a partnership. Each partner also enters into a take-or-pay contract with the project.
2. The partnership enters into a security agreement with an indenture trustee, which includes a mortgage on certain property to be acquired by the partnership and an assignment of proceeds from the take-or-pay contracts.
3. The partnership enters into a loan agreement with a group of lenders under an arrangement whereby the lenders agree to limit their recourse against the partners to the partnership assets only. Loan proceeds are paid to the indenture trustee, which in turn pays the manufacturer the purchase price of the property to be acquired by the project. The manufacturer than conveys title to the partnership in the partnership name, subject to the mortgage.
4. The partners make payments under the take-or-pay contract directly to the indenture trustee. The partnership makes any additional payments to the indenture trustee required to meet current debt payments.
5. The indenture trustee pays the debt service.
6. Funds not needed to service the debt are paid to the partnership as set out in the loan agreement.

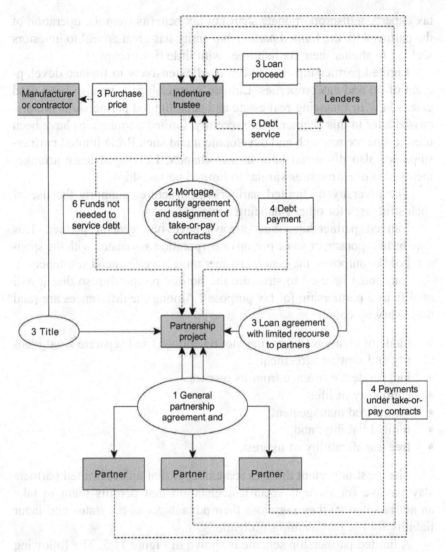

Figure 11.4: Partnership with Limited Recourse Debt Using Take or Pay Contract
Prepared by Frank J. Fabozzi and Peter K. Nevitt.

11.4.2. *Limited Partnerships as a Specialist Form*

Limited partnerships are entities which expressly limit the liability of limited partners to the amount of their capital investment. Since limited partners can, nevertheless, claim a proportionate share (and, according to some tax experts, a disproportionate share) of tax benefits from the operation of the partnership, the limited partnership entity has great appeal to investors seeking to shelter their tax liabilities with little risk to capital.

Limited partnerships have been used extensively to finance development of oil and gas properties. Limited partnerships have also been used extensively in financing real estate and such limited partnerships are discussed later in this chapter. More recently, limited partnerships have been used to finance research and development and such R&D limited partnerships are also discussed later in this chapter. Leveraged lease arrangements also use structures similar to limited partnerships.

The diversity of limited partnership structures supports the use of such structures for other financing contexts.

Limited partnerships must always have one general partner. This may be the sponsor, or some person or corporation associated with the sponsor. For tax purposes, the general partner must have financial substance.

Care must be used to structure the limited partnership so that it will qualify as a partnership for tax purposes. Among the differences are (and these vary by country):

- mode of creation (intent may not be enough) and separate legal identity and written agreement;
- independent existence from its owners;
- continuity of life;
- centralized management;
- limited liability; and
- free transferability of interest.

The most important thing to remember is that unless limited partners stay passive (or there is specific legislation that permits them to take an active interest) they may lose their advantageous tax status and incur liability for the partnership's obligations.

A limited partnership scheme is shown in Figure 11.5. The following is assumed:

1. A limited partnership is formed upon the general partner agreeing to act as general partner and the completion of a sale of a unit to the general partner.
2. The partnership enters into an agreement for management services with a designated manager (usually a separate entity). These services might include sales of units, organization of the partnership, the investment of partnership funds and management of partnership assets.

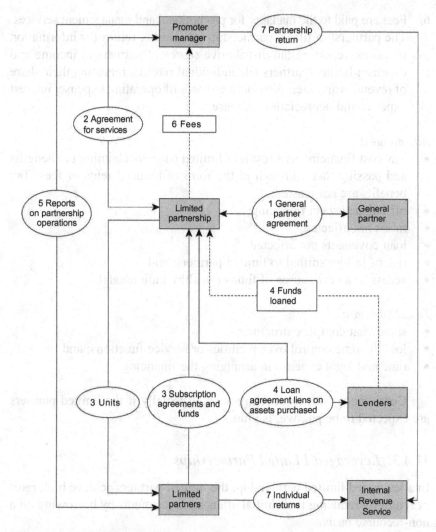

Figure 11.5: Limited Partnership

Prepared by Frank J. Fabozzi and Peter K. Nevitt.

3. Subscriptions for limited partnership interests are sold, funds advanced and units issued.

4. A loan agreement is negotiated, funds are advanced and liens are recorded on purchased assets. These funds are invested in the assets or activities of the partnership.

5. The activities of the partnership begin. Reports on partnership activities are distributed by the manager.

6.   Fees are paid to the manager for promotional and management services.
7.   The partnership files a partnership income tax return for information purposes, reporting the distributive shares of partners in income and expense; limited partners file individual returns, reporting their share of revenues and their distributive shares of operating expense, interest expense and depreciation expense.

Advantages:
•   low cost financing as a result of limited partners claiming tax benefits and passing them through in the form of reduced rents or fees. Tax benefits are not wasted;
•   off-balance sheet financing;
•   ratios not affected;
•   loan covenants not affected;
•   risk of failure shifted to limited partners; and
•   access to a new source of funds (wealthy individuals).

Disadvantages:
•   somewhat complex structure;
•   loss of some control over facilities or service functions; and
•   time and legal expense in arranging the financing.

Compliance with local regulations, especially if the limited partners are expected to be passive, is vital.

11.4.3. *Leveraged Limited Partnerships*

In a leveraged limited partnership, the limited partners achieve high rates of return by reducing their initial after-tax investments by borrowing on a non-recourse basis.

One form of leveraged partnership provides that a portion of the original investment of a limited partner is in the form of a recourse note. This type of investment is called staged equity, meaning that the equity is paid in over time. In some circumstances, the limited partners may be permitted, under this arrangement, to take tax deductions equal to, or in excess of, their initial cash investments. The limited partner pays the note over a period of time as the partnership needs the funds. If the partnership is generating payments due to the limited partners, the note may be paid by offsetting such payments against the obligations under the note.

11.4.4. *R&D Limited Partnerships*

R&D limited partnerships have been used successfully in a number of countries to accomplish off-balance sheet project financing of research and development expense. Many of these R&D limited partnerships have been formed in the United States. Although, and most have been privately placed, there have been large public placements of units made. Unfortunately, in the past, some very large and visible publicly placed R&D partnerships have failed. In some cases, partnerships have moved towards pooled investments in the asset base in order to spread risk. Different countries have different tax advantages to support R&D and so expert advice must be obtained.

The R&D partnership model is also popular between firms and universities, not least in the pharmaceutical and healthcare areas. So-called "technology transfer" agreements can use expertise to assist organizations, or organizations can assist universities to develop or capitalize on research. It can be extended to patient groups and other stakeholders. The pace of innovation, the demand for new drugs and the pricing challenges resulting from different national regimes encourage partnering to exploit particular skills. A number of acquisitions in this sector have resulted from larger companies "buying" rather than "making or developing" potential drugs. These collaborations can take place all along the spectrum that is shown in Figure 11.1.

The same rules apply to R&D partnerships as apply to all attempts to join forces with a different entity, notably "know your partner" at the different levels from those working together to those managing and administering the partnership. Investing in the time to really understand the nature of the issues and the temperaments of the individuals at the so-called "sharp edge" of the partnership is time well spent as that relationship can overcome difficulties without a need to resort to the agreement and the law. Nevertheless, the structures may be worth considering in the right circumstances, subject to meeting the regulatory requirements for optimal tax treatment.

If the project is successful, the partnership (and limited partners) may be compensated in a variety of ways, which are set forth in the terms of the contracts between it and the corporation. Some of the methods used are:

- the sponsor may have an option to purchase the exclusive rights to the products developed. Purchase price may be paid in stock or cash;

- the sponsor and the limited partnership may enter into a joint venture to manufacture and/or market the products developed; and
- the sponsor may have an option to obtain an exclusive license to manufacture and/or sell the new products in return for payments to the partnership in the form of royalties.

The royalties may be based on:

- sales (either a fixed amount per unit sold or a percentage of the selling price);
- profits from sales of the new products; or
- a certain percentage of sales until the limited partners have received a specified return on their investment or recovered costs, after which the percentage may decrease.

The sponsor can protect itself by making royalty payments subject to a ceiling and payable only if the corporation has a positive cash flow from manufacturing and selling the new products.

The sponsor may also have the right to purchase the exclusive rights to the basic technology and to the products developed after it has begun to pay royalties to the partnership and it may have the right to offset some or all of the royalties against the purchase price.

However, the rights and compensation paid to the limited partnerships obviously have a significant effect on the attractiveness of the investment to investors.

Accounting: Accounting is treated differently in different jurisdictions and local expertise should be sought. Not all jurisdictions recognize limited partnership structures for R&D development but may offer incentives to joint venture partnerships involved in innovation.

Advantages for a sponsor:
- large amounts of capital for R&D can be obtained with a good track record;
- expense of R&D may be moved off the income statement;
- better financing costs can be obtained because investors may be able to claim all or part of their investment as a tax loss until the project becomes profitable;
- no adverse effect upon the financial statements of the sponsor;

- risk of failure of research and development activities shifted to limited partners;
- tax benefits are used currently for a good purpose and not wasted;
- the sponsor can retain control over the R&D project as well as control over other operations;
- issuing equity to raise funds for R&D would result in expanding the ownership of the enterprise, may impact the earnings per share and might result in loss of control;
- avoids debt service requirements for future cash flow, avoids impact on debt to equity ratios and strengthens financial ratios for rating services;
- the sponsor retains greater flexibility in dealing with the limited partnership than in a group of stockholders;
- access to a new source of funds;
- lower initial costs using debt to finance R&D; and
- qualified research and development personnel can be hired who otherwise might be concerned about the funding and dedication of resources to research and development.

Disadvantages for a sponsor:
- although limited partners have no legal management rights, it is not realistic to expect that investors in a limited partnership project will always agree with the general partner's actions. If the limited partners sense that development is being poorly handled, or that better opportunities are available for exploiting a developed product, they may attempt to impose their views through lawsuits, effectively throwing management into the hands of the courts. This is where issues may potentially arise about limited partners, their roles and the tax regulations;
- the sponsor may be particularly vulnerable to attack at the point where a commercially profitable product has at last been developed. Although the corporation that formed the partnership will have an option to acquire exclusive rights to the development, the limited partners may object that the option was not negotiated at arm's length, or should for other reasons be revised. Since contracts between corporations and affiliated limited partnerships are rarely negotiated at arm's length, such arguments may receive a sympathetic judicial hearing;

- the eventual costs of a successful R&D development will probably be higher than if the R&D had been developed with conventional financing. This is because the potential rewards offered to investors must usually be substantial to attract risk capital; and
- a lot of time and expense is required to establish an R&D limited partnership.

11.5. Contractual Joint Ventures

The term "joint venture" is used in connection with project financing to describe all kinds of contractual relationships between investors in projects. Jointly owned corporations or limited liability companies are referred to as joint ventures, and general partnerships and limited partnerships may also be termed joint ventures.

Although, the use of the term to describe corporation and partnership structures is not incorrect, there are contractual relationships called joint ventures which are neither partnerships nor corporations. Such joint venture-type agreements are used in project financing where the participants desire to minimize the duties and obligations among themselves and for each other's actions.

A joint venture closely resembles a partnership. However, the parties contract among themselves, rather than enter into a partnership agreement. One of the joint venture parties, with extensive experience in the type of project to be constructed and operated, is typically designated to the manager, with delegated authority to act for the joint venture. In the alternative, the participants may, by agreement, appoint a corporation to act as an agent for purposes of operating the project. The best way to describe a joint venture is to note the difference between a joint venture and a partnership:

- Partners have general agency for one another. Joint venturers do not.
- Partners may be jointly and severally liable beyond their investment. Joint ventures are liable only to the extent of their investments and advances to the project.
- Property of a partnership may be held in partnership name. In certain cases, the property of a joint venture may be held as tenants in common, where each party holds an undivided interest. Joint ventures may also incorporate and own shares according to their ownership in

- the activity in order to have a distinct legal entity for governance and management purposes.
- Generally, partners may sue each other about matters relevant to the partnership agreement only by bringing suit for an accounting (equity) action. Joint venturers may sue each other for breach of contract.
- The joint venture often has a fairly limited purpose and life, which may be determined by the nature of the project.

The Alaskan pipeline project was one of the most famous joint venture arrangements. There, the participants organized a new corporation to serve as operating agent, the Alyeska Pipeline Company. The facilities are held in proportion to expected use and each of the joint venturers is responsible for financing costs of the project in proportion to its interest in the project facility.

A joint contractual venture resembles a limited partnership more than a general partnership. But there are differences in that a limited partnership must have at least one general partner. Although the party designated as the operator of a joint venture has some characteristics of a general partner, the operator does not have the broad management control or the general liability characteristics of a general partner.

A major motivation for creation of a joint venture which is neither a partnership nor corporation is its status for income tax purposes, including such things as taking advantage of the method of depreciation or interest capitalization. It is very important that each party to the joint venture is permitted to make independent elections with respect to income and expense items in its own tax return.

A ruling on the tax status of a contractual joint venture is advisable, since a joint venture resembles an association taxable as a corporation as well as taxable as a partnership. Where members retain the right to take a share of the project produced in kind, or where any agency to sell the product is revocable, the tax authority (for example, the Internal Revenue Service) may take the position that the association is not taxable as a corporation because of lack of joint purpose and centralized management.

Contractual joint ventures by their nature do not constitute legal entities which can easily borrow for their own account (except in the case of some production payment loans). Leases offer a financing vehicle well suited for joint ventures, since each joint venturer can be a co-lessee of an undivided interest in the leased asset, if this is the model in use. Joint venturers can arrange separate financing of their undivided interests in the joint venture and the joint agreement can be drawn with this type of financing in mind so as to provide collateral to lenders to the joint venture members.

Financial accounting for ownership of joint ventures usually follows the same rules as for ownership of corporations. More than 50% control generally requires line-by-line consolidation. About 50% or less than 50% control but more than 20% control generally requires only a one-line entry of the investment in the project.

Joint ventures have been used in recent years by electric and gas utilities seeking energy sources. They have also been used extensively in developing and operating mines. Joint ventures are used in the development of oil and gas production, but other forms of ownership may be favoured primarily for tax reasons. As noted earlier, the term joint venture is used to describe partnership and jointly owned corporations. There are "joint ventures" and "joint ventures". It is important to keep the distinction in mind when discussing project financing.

11.5.1. *Joint Venture Supplier Financed by Advances of Each Joint Venturer*

A contractual joint venture (not a formal partnership or a corporation) constructs and operates a facility to provide a product or service to members of the joint venture. The project is financed by capital advances and operating advances from each joint venturer. The project is owned as tenants in common. Capital expenditures and operating expenses are shared in proportion to ownership. Liability of each joint venturer is limited to the investment.

The obligations of the parties to the joint venture are set forth in an operating agreement. If one does not pay its share of expenses, its share is forfeited to other parties or may be sold to a new venturer. Other venturers are often required to assume obligations of a defaulted venturer in proportion to their investment. Voting may be done on the basis of majority in interest and majority in number. Changes in the operating agreement may require more than a majority vote. Typical projects include liquefied natural gas (LNG) plants and facilities, coal gasification plants, pipelines, and some natural resource projects and electrical generating plants. An example is shown in Figure 11.6. More commonly nowadays, is the existence of a power purchase agreement (PPA) from a utility that enjoys a good

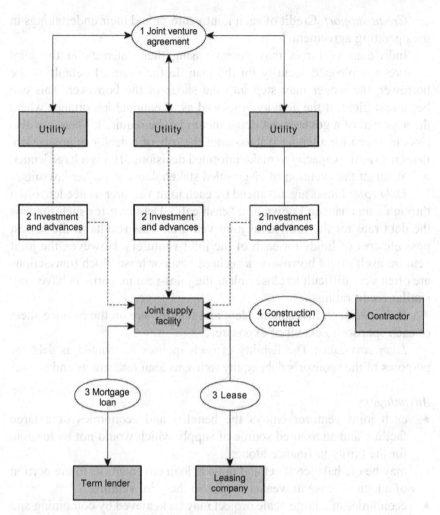

Figure 11.6: Joint Venture Electricity Generator
Prepared by Frank J. Fabozzi and Peter K. Nevitt.

credit rating. The focus of the financing switches under these circumstances to an assessment of the quality of the revenue stream from that contract and its format — take or pay, take and pay, take if tendered, etc.

Rate base: Where a sponsor is a public utility and the project is to assure a source of supply, its direct investment may usually be included in the sponsor's rate base.

Income tax: Expense and income flow back to sponsors.

Credit support: Credit of each joint venturer and their undertakings in the operating agreement.

Individual venturers may borrow using their interests in the joint venture as a pledged security for the loan. In the event of default by the borrower, the lender may step into the shoes of the borrower. This can become difficult if the activity is viewed as of national importance where the approval of a government department may be required. There are also risks involved for a lender if it assumes the role of a debtor in possession. Does it have the capacity to make informed decisions? If it is a large lender, will it attract the attention of disgruntled stakeholders and other lawsuits?

Debt rate: Funds are advanced by each joint venturer as needed, often through a mechanism known as a "cash call". Debt cost for such funds is the debt rate for the individual joint venturer. This results in the lowest possible cost of funds for each of the joint venturers. However, the joint venture itself might borrow on a secured basis or lease. Such transactions are often very difficult to close unless the joint-venture partners have very similar credit ratings.

Balance sheet: Investment, debt and liability are on the balance sheet of each sponsor to extent of exposure.

Loan covenants: The liability of each sponsor is counted as debt for purposes of the sponsor's debt equity ratios, as loan restrictions and so on.

Advantages:
- each joint venturer enjoys the benefits and economies of a large facility, and an assured source of supply which would not be feasible for the utility to finance alone;
- may be off-balance sheet and outside loan covenants as to the portion of a loan or lease to weaker credits in the joint venture;
- economies of a large-scale project may be achieved by combining and concentrating financial resources and technical skills of several venturers;
- an essential facility is built without the sponsor participant being required to pay the entire cost of the project; and
- the borrowing cost may be lower.

Disadvantage:
- lack of absolute control over the facility.
- A lack of control over the timing of capital expenditure and consequent tax offsets as discussed in the case study that follows.

11.5.2. *Exploration, Development and/or Operation of a Mine under a Joint Venture Operating Agreement*

Several parties who can use the production of a mine enter into a joint venture to develop and operate a mining property. They construct and operate the mine under a joint operating agreement which typically contains the following provisions.

The joint operating agreement (JOA) defines a particular scope of activity to be carried out by the joint venturers and limits the activity to a particular area.

Title to the property is generally held by the parties as tenants in common. Each of the parties has an undivided interest in the project and in all mineral interests subject to the JOA. Each party makes capital advances and operating advances to the project as needed to carry on the activity of the project in proportion to its respective interest.

One party is designated the operator of the project. The operator has day-to-day management responsibility for the project and work plans approved by the parties. Major policy decisions are made by a joint operating committee (JOC) composed of representatives of all the parties. The committee approves work plans for proposed new undertakings of the joint venture. The committee approves all major expenditures. The approval of a new work plan or major expenditure may require a majority in number as well as majority in interest of members of the committee. Such work plans may also be subject to government approval and indeed may be set by a host government.

Each party to the agreement shares in the production of the project in kind in proportion to its interest in the project. Generally, each party uses the production. However, arrangements may be made for other disposition. Where some parties may have small interests, this may require scheduling until they are in a position to "lift" enough output to allow it to be traded on the appropriate market or sold to another user. An example would be the offtake from an oilfield using a floating production system that offloads into tankers, a smaller participant may wish to wait until it accrues a full tanker load as discussed earlier in this book.

In the event a party fails to provide its allocable contribution, the agreement may provide various remedies, including complete forfeiture, forfeiture of project until sufficient produce is sold to cover the deficiency and sale or assignment of the interest of the defaulting party to a third party. An example is shown in Figure 11.7.

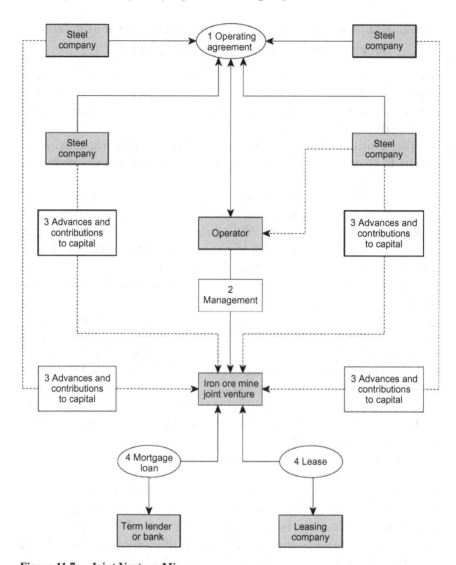

Figure 11.7:   Joint Venture Mine

Prepared by Frank J. Fabozzi and Peter K. Nevitt.

Income tax: Parties need to ensure they can make an election not to report income from the joint venture as a partnership. This permits each joint venturer to make independent income tax elections with respect to its respective share of income and expense items in its own tax return. A ruling on the tax status of the joint venture is advisable since a joint venture resembles an association taxable as a corporation as well as a partnership.

Credit support: The credit support comes from the creditworthiness of each joint venturer and its undertakings under the operating agreement. A party to the joint venture may borrow using its interest in the joint venture as pledged security for the loan and so, in the event of default by that specific joint venture partner, the lender may assume the borrower's interest. There can be problems, however, with natural resource investments where the host government may not want bankers, as opposed to resource development professionals, in the partnership, and so the host government may reserve the right to give prior approval. It may also affect the dynamics of the partnership if the bank has limited expertise in this area. Finally, the bank is likely to want to seek an exit to its involvement and thus that may also impact on the plans of other members of the joint venture.

Debt rate: Funds are advanced by each joint venturer as needed. Debt cost for such funds is the debt rate for each joint venturer. This results in the lowest possible cost of funds for each of the joint venturers. However, the joint venture itself might borrow on a secured basis or a lease. In such instances, the lender or leasing company will lend or lease on the basis of the collateral, the obligations of the joint venturers and the importance of the project to the joint venturers.

Balance sheet: Investment, debt and liability are on the balance sheet of each sponsor to the extent of exposure. If a party owns and controls over 50% of a joint venture, a line-by-line consolidation may be appropriate. If voting is on the basis of both a majority of parties and a majority of investment, mere ownership of more than 50% may not require consolidation.

Loan covenants: The liability of each venturer is counted as debt for debt-equity ratios and as loans for loan restrictions. Borrowings of a joint venture less than 50% owned by a party are probably not included.

Advantages:
- Availability of the right either to file a partnership return or to elect not to file a partnership return, thus preserving for each joint venturer the right to make income tax elections.
- May be off-balance sheet and outside loan covenants as to the portion of the loan or lease to other credits in the joint venture.

- Economies of a large-scale project are achieved by combining and concentrating financial resources and technical skills.
- An essential facility is built without the sponsor-participant being required to pay the entire cost of the project.

Disadvantages:
- Lack of absolute control over the facility.
- A lack of control over the timing of capital expenditure and consequent tax offsets as discussed in the case study that follows.

11.6. Case Study: Bits and Pieces

An example of this, illustrating the additional dangers of tax-driven deals and overoptimistic projections in joint ventures, occurred when the North Sea became a mature oil province and many large companies that were leading groups developing or producing oil fields realized that they were starting to pay significant tax, making the UK a comparatively less attractive investment area. British Petroleum (BP) and Occidental (Oxy) decided to reduce their shares of two of the first oil producing fields — Forties and Claymore — by running tender offers to sell small participations in units of 0.25% interest in the fields to other oil and gas companies in the North Sea. The attraction for the two larger companies was that the well-established production was generating income on which a high marginal rate of tax was being paid and BP and Oxy had limited tax offset in terms of anticipated exploration costs. They also saw the production about to enter a steep fall as the field entered its final phase of productivity (the decline phase), so that the recapturing of tax losses across years would be difficult.

In contrast, smaller companies involved in exploration and development activities, had tax absorptive capacity as a result of the tax losses from their other existing exploration commitments, but no income against which they could offset the losses. Many were optimistic that they could match tax losses against shares in the Forties or Claymore oilfield income and follow the field decline curves closely, since to miss a year or loss/income matching would have a significant impact on the project net present value.

The UK government also saw this as a way to boost smaller companies and grow the domestic oil and gas corporate sector. Thus far, this sounds like a "win–win" situation.

In order to borrow money to fund the tenders for the "Forties units" or "Claymore units", the smaller companies needed to persuade banks to lend as much as possible, and preferably on a non-recourse basis. Non-recourse financing was needed because the smaller companies typically had few other producing assets to generate cash flow and the Forties and Claymore fields had a production history that was mature and stable. Some banks provided loans based on high loan-to-asset ratios assuming that the debt would be repaid from assigned cash flows that would be enhanced by an offset of all of the tax payable as a result of the current and future exploration activity of the smaller companies.

However, the smaller companies had small stakes in their other investments and as such had limited influence on decisions about the timing of when wells were drilled and thus when the absorptive tax capacity was incurred. All of the larger companies were pulling back their investment in the North Sea, and thus were reluctant to agree to commit to exploration expenditure just to help out the smaller companies, when the larger companies paid most of the drilling costs. The tax offset was confined to North Sea income and costs only, so not offsettable against any other oil and gas activity in other areas. Thus, some of the more bullish smaller companies that had been successful in the tender offer began to see that they would be unable to optimize their income from the tax offsets and the cash flow to repay the loan was unlikely to be sufficient. The result was consolidation, resale and exit among the smaller companies and some pain to bankers.

So, while the income of the project entity can be controlled to some extent by the sponsors, unrealistic assumptions can cause problems as illustrated earlier or tax adjustments may be subject to attack by the authorities if not evidentially at arm's length and may give rise to loss of deductions. Timing problems in a tax-driven structure tax may also result in insufficiently enriched cash flow to meet the higher debt service requirements. The message from this example is to be extremely careful when the amount and timing of the generation of the tax enrichment is in the hands of powerful stakeholders with very different agendas.

Chapter 12

Construction Financing

Introduction

The objectives and considerations of project sponsors or a project company in connection with any construction financing, independent of the type of permanent financing to be used, are generally:

- to obtain financing at the lowest effective interest cost;
- to make the best use of any and all construction period tax deductions or credits;
- to optimize the allowed revenue effects resulting from the regulatory treatment of the transaction;
- to achieve the targeted balance sheet and financial reporting treatment;
- to obtain financing with minimum adverse impact *vis-à-vis* covenants contained in debt agreements;
- to maintain flexibility regarding the type of permanent financing ultimately employed; and
- to accommodate the amount and timing of differing types of construction period borrowing instruments (for example, tax exempt, commercial paper, early take-down of long-term funds, bank lines).

Each construction financing is different and involves establishing priorities for these objectives. This discussion has particular application to the United States where typically construction financing is often provided by one set of lenders and long-term financing is provided by another set of lenders. However, the same principles apply in other countries.

A key factor in construction financing is the type of guarantees and bonds used to guarantee completion and performance under construction contracts. These include bid bonds, performance bonds, advance payment guarantees or bonds, retention money guarantees or bonds and maintenance bonds.

12.1. Estimation of Funding Needs

Construction financing begins with an estimation of the costs associated with the initial establishment of the project and then the procurement of the funds of the estimated amount at the lowest funding cost that does not jeopardize the project's completion and satisfies the other sponsor objectives enumerated at the outset of this chapter.

The non-financing costs that must be considered in estimating financing needs are those associated with:

- land acquisition;
- improvement/preparation of the site;
- building permits;
- architectural design;
- engineering design;
- construction costs;
- feasibility studies;
- insurance during the construction phase;
- taxes during the construction phase; and
- inspection tests.

In infrastructure projects, the major non-financing cost is typically the construction cost. Consequently, cost estimation for this component is critical. Of course, the decision to proceed with a project will have been based on cost estimates for aspects of the project design. These estimates are either provided by the project sponsor's engineering team or by a firm specializing in cost estimation that is retained by the sponsor. The degree of accuracy of these cost estimates will vary based on the stage of construction and are expected to be more accurate than in the initial planning stage. Moreover, typically there is a cost estimator who specializes in each design phase.

In estimating each of the aforementioned cost components, an estimate must be made for unexpected costs that might arise during the construction phase. For example, when site preparation begins, it may be determined that the conditions were not as expected, resulting in additional costs. The project's design may have to be altered for some reasons. If a project is undertaken in an economic environment where employment is high, this may result in higher construction costs because of the need to pay a more competitive wage rate to attract workers. When costs are to be incurred in a foreign currency, if exchange-rate risks are not hedged, estimates of the impact of adverse currency movements must be incorporated into the estimated costs.

In the United States, for example, the recommended practice for estimating costs has been codified by AACE International, Inc, a professional association for cost and management professionals that offers several specialized certification programmes such as cost estimation, planning and scheduling and project controls.[1] (Cost estimation is covered in Chapter 6.) In addition to base estimates provided, estimates are provided for specific project risks classified as contingencies, allowances and reserves. As described in the primer for the CCT, one of the certifications awarded by AACE International, these are defined as follows.[2]

A *contingency* is defined as:

> "An amount added to an estimate to allow for items, conditions, or events for which the state, occurrence, or effect is uncertain and that experience shows will likely result, in aggregate, in adding costs. Typically estimated using statistical analysis or judgment based on past asset or project experience...
>
> To an estimator, contingency is an amount used in the estimate to deal with the uncertainties inherent in the estimating process. The estimator regards contingency as the funds added to the originally derived point estimate to achieve a given probability of not overrunning the estimate (given relative stability of the project scope and the assumptions upon which the estimate is based)".

---

[1] Examples of the certifications awarded by AACE International are the certified cost consultant (CCC), the certified cost technician (CCT), the certified cost engineer (CCE) and the certified schedule engineer (CSE).

[2] These definitions are taken from *AACE® International's Certified Scheduling Technician (CST) Primer*. *AACE* International, Inc, pp. 21–23.

An *allowance* is defined as:

> "Resources included in estimates to cover the cost of known but undefined requirements for an individual activity, work item, account or sub-account...
>
> Allowances are often included in an estimate to account for the predictable but indefinable costs associated with project scope. Allowances are most often used when preparing deterministic or detailed estimates. Even for this class of estimate, the level of project definition may not enable certain costs to be estimated definitively".

Finally, a *reserve* is defined as:

> "An amount added to an estimate to allow for discretionary management purposes outside of the defined scope of the project, as otherwise estimated. Use of management reserve requires a change to the project scope and the cost baseline, while the use of contingency reserve funds is within the project's approved budget and schedule baseline...".

12.2. Construction Financing General Categories

Construction financing falls into two general categories:

- Special purpose entity (SPE) project financing, in which construction projects are domiciled in SPEs established by the project sponsor(s) — referred to as *construction intermediaries* — whose borrowing is based upon direct or indirect credit support provided by the project sponsor.
- Direct financing by the sponsor using corporate funds available from the various direct borrowing facilities that the project sponsor has arranged, including new facilities that may be specifically related to (and drawdowns or take-downs thereunder timed with) construction expenditures. Conventionally, such disbursements are made against certification by an independent expert to stop potential fraud.

12.3. SPE Project Financing

SPE financing, or project financing of construction intermediaries, may include both corporate and trust vehicles with degrees of ownership and/

or control on the part of the sponsor ranging from none to full control. Typically, the sponsor will assign its interest in the project and other contract rights to the construction intermediary. The construction intermediary then has the right to obtain the necessary funding. With the project economically isolated in the construction intermediary, a wide variety of borrowing alternatives are available to the project entity, including bank lines (which include revolving and term credits), commercial paper and early take-down or drawdown of permanent financing monies.

Although in part credit support for debt financing obtained by the construction intermediary is supported by the work in progress for the project, there is typically sponsor credit support in the form of an obligation that under certain circumstances requires that the sponsor purchase the project or the notes representing the project's debt at completion. Sponsor credit support in the form of an unconditional take-or-pay contract may, in turn, support a take out by long-term lenders or a lessor. The necessity of an equity investment by the sponsor in the project entity is a function of the collateral and the nature of credit support. Absence of an equity investment from a sponsor means the lenders are taking an equity risk but receiving a lender's (lower) return. Interest rates should approximate those available to the sponsor directly, unless the sponsor's credit support is conditional or ambiguously indirect.

As explained earlier, funding needs based on estimated construction costs are based just that: estimates, or best guesses at the time. During the construction process, there can be shortfalls due to an underestimate of the construction costs or other contingencies that increase construction costs. In such cases, the sponsor may be required to supply the shortfall.

Using a construction intermediary approach to construction financing in the case of the United States may facilitate efficient use of construction period tax benefits from interest deductions, either through transfer to a third party or through capitalization of expenses, with depreciation tax deductions ultimately available on such capitalized expenses as a component of plant cost. The use of asset-oriented tax benefits is of primary concern to project companies considering a leveraged lease[3] as the form of permanent financing, and particularly to those sponsors and/ or project companies experiencing a very low declining federal income tax liability as a result of new plant acquisition and the absorption or early years accelerated tax depreciation.

---

[3]Leveraged leases are discussed in Chapter 13 of the companion book.

Accounting and tax treatment from the sponsor's standpoint varies according to the nature of its ownership, control and contingent obligation to support the credit (see the previous chapter). Interest during construction may be capitalized, and off-balance sheet financing may be possible in some instances but parties should always check the latest consolidation requirements and pre-qualification requirements for any assets involved. Figures 12.1 and 12.2 show two examples of construction intermediary trusts, covered by SEC Codification of Staff Accounting Bulletins, Topic 10: Utility Companies and in particular, the part headed Financing by Electric Utility Companies Through Use of Construction Intermediaries.[4]

The illustration provided by Figure 12.1 is based on the following:

1. A utility assigns its interest in the construction site and other construction rights to a construction financing intermediary trust.
2. The utility contracts with the intermediary to purchase the facility upon completion and agrees to assume or settle construction loans that the intermediary is authorized to borrow during construction, and to pay interest on the construction loan.
3. The construction intermediary borrows from banks on the basis of a lien on the work in process and the agreements of the utility to assume or settle construction loans on completion.
4. The facility is completed, the utility purchases the facility, and settles or assumes liability for the construction loans.

In Figure 12.1, the arrangement clearly falls within the scope of the topic because the lenders rely primarily upon the credit of utility for take-out.

The example in Figure 12.2 attempts to shift the obligation off the balance sheet, or at most to a footnote, by casting the transaction as equivalent to a purchase of equipment that does not become an obligation until delivery of the facility built to specifications, though this is also covered in the questions. During construction, the lenders look primarily to the credit of the contractor and to the bonding company for assurance that a facility will be built to specification.

---

[4]SEC Codification of Staff Accounting Bulletins, Topic 10: Utility Companies.

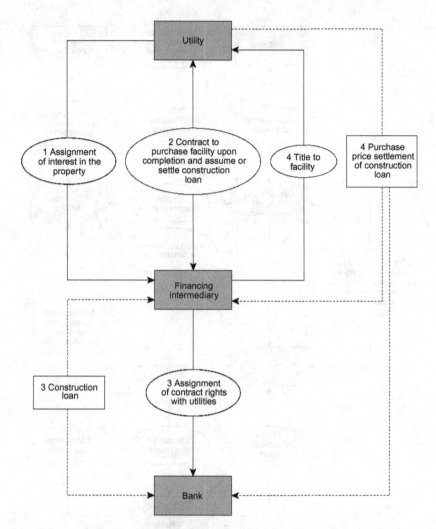

Figure 12.1:   Financing of Construction of a Utility by a Construction Intermediary in which Creditors Rely Primarily upon the Credit of the Utility

Prepared by Frank J. Fabozzi and Peter K. Nevitt.

Figure 12.2 is based on the following:

1. The sponsor agrees with the construction intermediary trust to purchase a facility built to certain specifications. The purchase price and time frame for delivery are established.

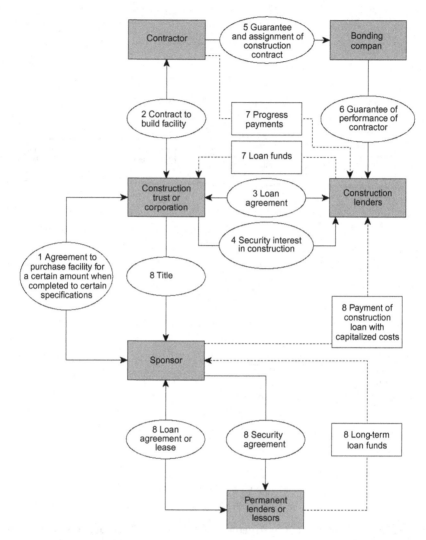

Figure 12.2:   Construction Financed through Construction Trust which Relies on the Credit of the Contractor

Prepared by Frank J. Fabozzi and Peter K. Nevitt.

2.   The contractor agrees to build the facility at a price and on terms consistent with the contract between the sponsor and the construction trust.

3.   A loan agreement is entered into between the construction intermediary trust and the construction lenders.

4. The construction trust assigns a security interest in its assets to the construction lenders.

5. The contractor enters into an agreement with a bonding company to provide a bond sufficient to guarantee performance and provides the bonding company with a guarantee and an assignment of its rights under the construction contract as security.

6. The bonding company provides a guarantee. (A bonding company guarantee may not be available at a reasonable price, in which case the lender must look to the financial resources and reputation of the contractor.)

7. Construction loan funds are advanced as needed and progress payments are made to the contractor.

8. The facility is completed to the specifications called for in the contract, the permanent financing is arranged by the sponsor, the construction loan is repaid, title passes to the sponsor, and a security interest passes to the permanent lenders or lessors.

12.4. Direct Construction Financing

When arranging construction financing without the use of a construction intermediary or double A rated project company, all borrowing avenues usually available to the sponsor can be used to fund the construction.

However, a primary concern when considering permanent financing alternatives is the security interest which under such circumstances may automatically be attached or claimed for the benefit of existing secured lenders under open-ended indentures. Such a situation may ultimately require substitute collateral, such as cash or other property, to release the property being financed to the permanent financing providers secured under a leveraged lease or secured debt. If a lease is contemplated as the permanent financing, this problem may be solved by having the lessor take title to the facility during the early stages of construction. Under such circumstances, the leasing company can either claim tax benefits from deductions for interest paid during construction or capitalize interest and claim tax depreciation deductions on such expense as part of the component plant cost, with most of such tax benefits passed through to the project company in the form of reduced rentals.

12.5. Construction Financing Using Leveraged Leasing

As explained in Chapter 13 of the companion book, while it is possible to arrange a facility lease in a fairly short time, the financial planning for a large facility is complex and may involve a typical lead time extending over many months.

A leveraged lease financing structure may be used in construction financing. The participation agreement and the lease agreement may contemplate that the title to the property to be leased will be transferred to the owner trustee (lessor) while the facility is still in the early stages of construction. In this situation, the construction contract is assigned by the lessee to the owner trustee and construction financing is arranged.

Although the facility will usually be constructed by a third-party contractor, the sponsor may wish to supervise the performance of the construction contract with the third-party contractor. In this situation, a construction supervision agreement is entered into between the lessee and the owner trustee. The purpose of this agreement is to arrange for and require the owner trustee to use the services of the project in the capacity of construction supervisor to oversee the construction testing, delivery and acceptance of the facility.

To the extent that a project financing is to be accomplished through a leveraged lease, the mechanics include a sale by the sponsor of the project to the owner trustee for leaseback. The sale price to the lessor may include capitalized costs that are related to the utility's overhead and financing costs during construction. However, where the construction period extends over a considerable time, the contractor may require progress payments during construction. In such a situation, the parties may agree that the owner trustee will take title to the facility during construction, so that the lease involves an interim lease term during construction that precedes the base lease term. Where this type of arrangement is made, a separate interim loan (construction loan) agreement is entered into by the lessee, the owner trustee (the entity named to hold title to the equipment and represent the owners or equity participants), and the construction lenders (who are usually not loan participants during the base term lease). The lessor's equity investment and short-term construction loan financing is used until the completion of construction, acceptance by the lessee, drawdown of the long-term financing (leveraged debt), and commencement of the base lease term. The lessee pays interim rents to the owner trustee in an amount sufficient to cover both the interest cost of the construction loan and provide an adequate return to the equity participants. In the alternative, construction loan interest may be capitalized into the cost of the facility and included in the total cost of the facility which is to be financed by the lease.

Construction financing is usually provided by commercial banks. Such financing is secured by an assignment of interim rents and by the lessee's obligation to pay off the principal of the loan if the long-term lenders fail to provide the financing or if the facility is not constructed or completed by a certain date. In such a situation, the equity participants will also look to the lessee's guarantee to recover their investments plus an adequate return. All of the lessee's guarantees of construction loans are eliminated on or before completion and acceptance of the leased equipment and commencement of the base term of the lease. Eliminating lessee guarantees of the owner trust debt obligations may also be necessary in order to comply with the local tax rules.

Construction supervision agreement: The construction supervision agreement is between the utility lessee and the partnership. The participation agreement contemplates that the title to the property to be leased will be transferred to the owner agent (lessor) while the plant is still in early stages of construction. Although the facility is being constructed by a third-party contractor, the utility lessee has been supervising and wishes to continue to supervise the performance of a construction contract with the third-party contractor. Therefore, the purpose of this agreement is for the partnership to use services of the utility in its capacity as construction supervisor to oversee the construction testing, delivery and acceptance of the facility. The importance of a construction supervision agreement is also shown in the case study in Chapter 10.

Construction contract assignment: The participation agreement and the lease agreement contemplate that the partnership (lessor) will take possession of the facility during the early stages of construction. The construction contract must be assigned by the utility lessee to the partnership.

12.6. Stage Payments in Practice

These will vary dependent on the type of project. Many projects over a certain size are now required by law to be submitted to a formal bid/tender process. (We saw mention of this in the Bhutan case.) This requires careful construction of the specification and a clear set of bid/tenders and award criteria — the cheapest is not always the best value for money as if it runs into financial problems as a result of mispricing, then the project sponsor may be in a no-win situation — pay more money and keep this contractor or pay a premium to get someone else in to finish the job. Rather than disburse all payments in one lump sum, payments are usually released on the basis of completion certificates provided by the independent professionals taking in to account that there may need to be some aggregation to make bank or other funding payments efficient as mentioned previously.

The case study at the end of Chapter 10 looked at the PPP in Edinburgh and the challenges that resulted from poor governance and supervision issues during construction. Using an independent surveyor or architect allows for accurate representation of progress by a trained professional with insurance cover, should the need arise to take action. The fees are direct costs, and thus part of the project, but whether there is a single person in this role or the providers of finance insist on their own professional being involved (need to ensure good working relationships) this external check and validation is an important part of the quality control process. Personal experience has shown one of us that it is not enough to entrust this to a lending officer if this skill is not part of his or her armoury. If the project is politically sensitive (and overrunning, as is often the case) then this may compound difficulties for local staff reporting on it.

Most projects, though, rely on subcontractors that are often paid late and may be forced to accept renegotiated terms of trade if the main contractor is under financial pressure. An evaluation of subcontractors and their subcontractors builds strong foundations for a successful project outcome but it is not always conducted.

Suppliers to a contractor are often designated by their position in the contract hierarchy (as discussed earlier in Chapter 2), so Tier 1 (will have direct contract with contractor or possibly project sponsor or owner); Tier 2 (will have direct contract with Tier 1 supplier) Tier 3 (will have direct contract with Tier 2 supplier), etc. Descending the supplier hierarchy moves away from the source of cash flow, and any delay in Tier 1 payment will have knock-on effects further down the hierarchy. Subcontractors may also have had to invest in specialist tools and have expectations about economic order quantities to recoup that cost. They may find they are required to hold stock for use further up the supply chain. All of this can contribute to fragility lower down the supply chain and that can be catastrophic if there is a problem at the top. The Covid-19 global pandemic has revealed the fragility (but also the robustness) of many supply chains.

The "easy" answer is that suppliers can use a form of invoice discounting to generate early cash flow, but of course that will depend on the name on the invoice. With the development of electronic procurement systems, computer runs to generate invoices may not be made daily, or even weekly and the production of complex documentation to be uploaded and passed as acceptable on a procurement system is not always easy for smaller craft-focused entities. The margin of discount can be significant and only applied to a cherry-picked list of better credits (i.e. the ones that would pay in full anyway, albeit possibly late). At the time of writing, reverse factoring is one such technique in supply chain finance, designed to help lower-tier suppliers. In reverse factoring, a bank steps in between a company and its suppliers and offers discounted funds for working capital to the suppliers. In the case study at the end of this chapter, we consider how this change in procurement, described as beneficial for suppliers, ended up causing further problems.

Government attempts to set expectations about payment by large firms within a certain number of days can be "managed" by procuring though subsidiaries or even subcontracted entities. Many subcontractors to major companies are paid late, or paid late and not paid the face value of the invoice but have little choice but to put up with this.

12.7. Pre-Financing

For domestic and leisure developments, we have seen the use of off-plan sales where the apartment may be sold off-plan (i.e. before construction begins with a number of staged payments up to completion). This allows the sponsor to generate cash as construction proceeds and the purchaser to own an asset that could be sold on for a profit if the market improves, i.e. a hedge against future property rises.

A variation on this is the "time share". Time shares in several countries have been the subject of pressurized selling claims. As a result, there is now legislation in place to protect naïve purchasers (in this context, naive means inexperienced) and to ensure there is a cooling off period.

There are also limits to the duration of a timeshare contract — at the time of writing these are less likely to be "in perpetuity" with a 50-year cap becoming the norm.

A "timeshare" is the right to use a specified apartment or house usually in a holiday development and its associated facilities for a specified period, usually sold in one-week increments. These usually offer a "right to use"[5] but it may be in the form of a deed of ownership. Thus, the week chosen will be priced accordingly — high summer might attract premium pricing and late November a lower price, depending on the weather, school holidays, etc. In the past, the purchasers have been able to trade their weeks for other weeks in other projects owned by the same group but the liquidity of the market is not uniform and some owners have been locked in. These trades may or may not attract an additional fee. Problems have also arisen concerning the liquidity of the investment, especially as owners have aged and been less able to travel. For better projects these internal markets are buoyant but for problematic resorts this can result in illiquid investments. The situation concerning inheritance is also not always clear. Buildings operating under high loading require more maintenance and this is often an ongoing cost overlooked in the heat of the moment at the time of purchase.

More recently rather than buying a specified week, a flex-time or even floating week where there is not a specified apartment or time have been sold but the right to a period of time and these are now outlawed under Spanish law. Problems have been experienced around gaining access to the resort during peak times, or lack of availability of a suitable resort apartment. This illustrates the need for care and good legal advice. There is also a structure known as a "long-term holiday product" that offers the purchaser discounts or benefits at participating resorts.

As well as the upfront payment to purchase the right to occupy, there will be annual service charge payments to maintain the estate and the size and rises in this charge have been the subject of disputes. Service charges can not only be a source of additional revenue to an unscrupulous developer but can also be a surprise to a purchaser.

The financing structure starts with an initial investor who undertakes to build the resort and market the timeshares. A professional

---

[5]Though in Spain, it may be possible to register the rights on presentation of an escritura or deed. The UK government investigated timeshares in 2014 and the laws are changing in many countries!

trustee entity holds the real estate occupancy rights in trust for the owners and is tasked with protecting their rights. It does not necessarily own the real estate which may stay with the developer. An owner/occupier committee is formed from representatives of these two stakeholder groups and runs the resort, sets management fees, further sales and re-sales and future developments. The management company represented on the committee, may be a related company to the developer and is employed by the owner occupier committee. Ownership is subject to set of rules.

This approach is also seen in retirement villages where those over a certain specified age can move into a development on a full-time basis. These developments will have communal facilities, such as a spa or a leisure or sports facility, sometimes including a golf course. A leasehold in an apartment or house is purchased and a service fee is paid depending on services required as well as care charges. The "exit fee" that is payable when the resident is no longer in occupation can be sizeable — 10% is the norm but cases have been reported of as much as 30%. The sale is normally back to the operator and many operators say that this premium is used for maintenance and to keep service charges down for other residents. Newer legislation is focusing on capping the exit fee and declaring it in the purchase documentation.

Yet another variation is seen with a novel approach to care home and hotel financing. In this model, the investor buys a lease on a room in the hotel or care home and this is registered with the appropriate authority. The owner may have the right to occupy for a specified number of days each year and for the rest of the time, the room is rented out and the owner receives the rent (net of a fee). The income may be guaranteed. There is a right of resale at the end of the investment period. In this model, the investor may take on the financial risk through a mortgage to finance the investment. Since this is still a new form of investment and may not be universally regulated, there is uncertainty about the resale values if the hotel business goes through a down turn.

We have heard of a novel form of PPP being used for these projects in China.[6]

---

[6]Shijing Liu, Hongyu Jin, Benzheng Xie, Chunlu Liu and Anthony Mills, "Concession Period Determination for PPP Retirement Village," *International Journal of Strategic Property Management*, 22, 2018, pp. 424–435.

12.8. Film Finance: A Special Case of Construction

Film finance and its related creative industry activities, such as computer games, videos, etc., uses some of the older ideas from project finance and construction finance such as the idea of royalties. The film is usually owned by a special purpose vehicle (SPV) and the cash flow generated by the sale of its distribution rights (including video or other streaming services) repays the lenders. Film financing may also attract certain tax benefits and so finance may be structured using the limited partnerships we have seen in the previous chapters. The asset bundle being financed is the intellectual property (IP) and the physical generation of the master negative copy together with associated property rights in various channels.

Considerations may include:

- The first stage is to produce the negative copy when the filming is completed — but costs can still rise at the post production stage and before distribution. Filming on location can be delayed or affected by issues such as weather or adverse health issues and insurance is usually carried for key personnel.
- A completion guarantee issued in favour of the funder is provided by a specialist insurer and budgets are now very strictly monitored. Gap financing, a form of mezzanine finance to bridge any shortfalls can be high risk in a film context.
- Film funding can come from government or local grants, tax enhanced investments, hedge funds or other pooled private sources, banks, and equity investors, including peer to peer lending and specialist crowd-funding platforms, such as Kickstarter (though the latter is used for smaller creative projects).
- Preselling a part of a series or film franchise based on the original author, script, cast and director can raise money and shift risk.
- Other forms of finance include a negative pick-up, a form of deferred purchase where a studio buys the completed negative from the producer for a specified price at a specified future time, leaving the producer to fund the project in the interim.
- Product placement fees can contribute to the overall cash flow.

Many computer games or app developers fail to make money and the product is developed through individual or small number employee enterprises. What every developer hopes is that it will be picked up by a larger group, such as Harpan LLC being bought by Zynga for US$42.5 million or go public through an IPO such as that proposed by Rovio, the designer of Angry Birds, valued at just short of $1 billion and planned to raise $30 million in 2017.

The completion bond idea from film finance is used in some video game projects and insiders estimate that US$200 million of video games used this technique. In this context, the game developer is contracted by a publisher with a budget and a schedule agreed. The project is funded by a loan, supported by the completion bond that covers the lender if the project breaks the terms of the agreement with respect to time and cost. Once the product is completed, the equivalent of the negative is handed over and the publisher's payment is used to pay off the loan.

For smaller game developers, options include "bootstrapping", a "lean and mean" approach where the game is usually self-funded and staged. While this is the slowest form of development, it allows the developer to maintain control of the process and the intellectual content. Crowdfunding and business incubators may offer facilities while grouping developers together to allow peer to peer exchanges.

Although many outsiders see a clear gap between content generation and content distribution, for gaming insiders this is becoming more blurred. Publishers may also look to pick up new ideas and thence reach out to smaller game developers but may want to control the IP.

Tax treatment of video games is complex. In the UK, designing, producing and testing the game are the core activities attracting relief and the original concept design, debugging and post release maintenance are non-core for tax relief calculations.[7]

Several high profile, high net worth individuals were "outed" in the UK press as members of syndicates using capital allowances for film production as offsets against taxes payable. The cases, the first of which were heard in June 2017, hinged on the definition of "capital". The court ruled that the scheme was a form of "tax avoidance". The ruling is being appealed and a number of investors are also suing advisors. Subsequent cases continue.

---

[7]HMRC "Internal manual Video Games Development Company Manual" Published:12 April 2016, updated:1 December 2020.

12.9. Case Study: Carillion

Carillion, at one time the UK's second largest construction company, held a number of PPP contracts with the UK and other governments and employed some 43,000 people around the world. It is currently in compulsory liquidation (as of January 2018). An alarm was raised in May 2017 about "sloppy accounting", and a planned rights issue of shares was dropped in the summer of 2017 when the company's advisers refused to underwrite it. Governance issues were identified in August 2017 and cash flow reports prepared on a weekly basis in October for internal use by a well-known external consultant suggested that the company would be insolvent by March 2018. Carillion's small and medium-sized entities (SME) that were suppliers have been caught up in the fall-out from its demise.

The company had switched its maximum payment terms of trade from 65 days to 120 days and announced the "Early Payment Facility" in 2013. This followed on from a UK government concern responding to SME lobbying pressure concerning late payment to suppliers as a result of the 2008 financial crash. In 2012, the government launched the "Supply Chain Finance Scheme" whereby the bank operating the scheme for a large company would advance 100% of the face value of an invoice approved for payment "at lower interest terms"; in other words, the supplier would be advanced the money priced at the large purchasing company's credit rating cost of funds and the bank would rely on the invoice being paid to liquidate the debt. While Carillion was not "charging" for the facility, the suppliers were *de facto* taking on loans to receive monies they were owed. All payments defaulted to the 120-day system, thus aiding Carillion's cash flow. When Carillion went in to liquidation, the obligations crystallized as belonging to the SMEs and had no liquidation possibilities from Carillion.

A survey suggested debts to suppliers are estimated at around £75 million for engineering services alone with some other companies with less than 10 employees owed as much as £250,000. Any private sector work undertaken by suppliers before 15 January 2018 would be treated as unsecured debt.[8]

---

[8]The following article summarizes the shock of the collapse: Herpreet Kaur Grewal, "'Seismic Fallout' from Carillion Collapse," *Facilitate Magazine*, January 31, 2018.

The construction activity in a project may be the responsibility of one company, but underneath it often sits a larger number of smaller entities. To support these may require skill enhancement training to bring the quality up to that expected in international projects, the provision of local financial facilities to support them so they do not fail and scrutiny of the main contractor's practices around payment. All of these can ultimately contribute to reputational damage for key stakeholders including the providers of finance.

Chapter 13

An Overview of Trade Financing[*]

Introduction

Trade financing is a specialist area of banking that requires specialist knowledge of:

- countries;
- commodities;
- associated risks and risk management products;
- local and international law;
- documentation conventions; and
- cash flow-based financing.

In this chapter, we can only offer a very general overview. We shall look at the development of trade financing in terms of the instruments used including those used for pre-export finance, specific issues around supply chain financing, financing commodities, forfaiting and factoring, and countertrade and conclude with a case study.

Modern trade finance will include a number of different and more complex configurations including supply chain finance (SCF). Just as with any treasury department, the focus is on working capital and liquidity

---

[*] Some of the content in this chapter previously appeared in Carmel de Nahlik, *The Successful Banker's Handbook*. London: Euromoney, 2015. The rights to this book were reverted to Carmel de Nahlik and she has granted permission to reproduce the material here.

management. We already defined this in Chapter 2 as the management of the gaps in the "cash to cash cycle", where:

$$\text{Working Capital} = (\text{Accounts Receivable} + \text{Inventory})$$
$$- (\text{Accounts Payable} + \text{Cash})$$

Trade financing is both domestic and export oriented and in difficult export situations, there may not be 100% collection of the accounts receivable category, inventory may be illiquid and may have an associated holding cost to maintain appropriate levels to meet demand. Cash must be freely exchangeable, not blocked funds or requiring complex remittance approval.

13.1. How Trade Finance Developed

Current estimates suggest that over 80% of global trade is accounted for through open account trading. This bilateral trade approach sells without the intervention of third parties and is dependent on high levels of mutual trust and knowledge. However, though many large transactions by value are bilateral, a greater volume of smaller transactions require additional support and safeguard.

In a project finance context, a provider of export finance, often an export credit agency (ECA), provides a guarantee to the bank for the loan. There may also be pre-export financing. The ECA may lend directly or offer a guarantee based on the amount of local "content" in the goods being exported. The two key interlocking ingredients are the title or ownership of the goods and the payment.

The key risk for an exporter is that the buyer refuses to pay for the goods, and for an importer the risk is that they may pay but not receive anything. Distances combined with different jurisdictions and cultural practices mean dispute resolution can be costly and protracted. Historically, the way this was managed was through the use of "letters of credit" or documentary credits that offer a route to ensure that the seller receives the money provided they have shipped the goods that were specified and the buyer makes the payment provided the goods they have received were as specified.

A bank stands in the middle of the transaction, "negotiating" the documents, thus ensuring that the seller receives a specified amount of money within a specified point in time. In return for this support the bank will insist on strict terms being observed; those terms being laid out in the documentation. Banks deal in documents and not in goods and so are only interested in consistencies or inconsistencies within the documentation.

Letters of credit come in a number of forms:

- *irrevocable*, meaning once issued they cannot be changed or cancelled by the bank for any reason and at any time;
- *revocable*, meaning that they can be changed or cancelled;
- *unconfirmed*, meaning that when a buyer arranges the letter of credit, the issuing bank is responsible for making the payment;
- *confirmed*, meaning a bank known to the buyer agrees to guarantee payment even if the issuing bank fails to do so;
- *transferable*, meaning a letter of credit may be passed from one beneficiary to another, common in transactions where there may be a number of intermediary parties;
- *standby*, meaning a contingent commitment from a bank supporting a buyer's payment to the seller — these are not expected to be drawn;
- *revolving*, meaning a single letter of credit that may roll over to cover a series of shipments in a transaction;
- *back to back*, meaning that two identical letters of credit reflecting the two sides of a transaction are in place if there is an intermediate party in the transaction and a transferable letter of credit is not suitable;
- *red clause*, meaning an advance payment in an agreed amount from the bank is paid to the seller to finance the manufacturer or purchase of the goods to be delivered. The monies are repaid against receipt and a written undertaking from the seller to deliver the transportation documents before the credit expires. Originally the clause was written in red ink; and
- *green clause*, meaning that as well as the red clause provisions, an additional document is required providing proof that the goods to be shipped have been warehoused.

Letters of credit are the subject of a set of international rules developed by the International Chamber of Commerce (ICC) known as the Uniform Customs and Practice (UCP) for documentary credits. The current UCP standard, UCP 600 came into effect in 2007 and sits alongside some guidance for banks, the International Standard Banking Practice for the Examination of Documents under Documentary Credits (ISBP) and eUCP designed to cover e-commerce. Letters of credit must specify that they are subject to UCP 600 — it is no longer an automatic default. URR 725 covers bank-to-bank reimbursements as a complement to UCP 600, with ISBP 745 linking the UCP rules and offering guidance on the practical task of handling and negotiating the documents.

The letter of credit is accompanied by additional documentation to make the transaction work. As a minimum there needs to be a commercial invoice and an export packing list. Transportation documents will include *airway bills* if the goods are going by air and which are specific to the carrier company (DHL, UPS and so on) or a *bill of lading* if the goods are going by sea. The latter can take two forms: a *straight* bill of lading that cannot be altered or a *negotiable* bill of lading (or shipper's order bill of lading) that can be traded while the goods are in transit.

There is usually additional customs documentation. Compliance with export regulations is represented through export licenses if needed and in the case of the US, destination control statements. In some cases, there may be a requirement for a certificate of origin and there may be shipment-specific certification surrounding biohazards, analyses, ingredients (especially if going to countries where dietary laws are observed), inspection and so on. The documentation is required to satisfy customs in the importing country and any problems with the documentation or inconsistencies can cause delays or a failure of the transaction. Much of this documentation is now completed online.

Rather than the use a documentary letter of credit, some exporters may decide to use a documentary collection route. In this approach, the exporter passes responsibility for collecting the payments to their bank (the remitting bank) that sends the documents to the importer's bank (collecting bank) with the instructions for payment (the collection cover letter) and an appropriate bill of exchange or draft for immediate payment or payment on a future specified date. The banks exchange the documents for money.

The key difference between letters of credit and documentary collections lies in the absence of a verification process and thus limited recourse for the collection route if the payment is not made. As a result, it is a less expensive route. Another advantage is that the importer does not pay before shipment of the goods, and that control over the goods remains with the exporter until the draft is accepted. Complications can occur when transactions use air or overland delivery routes as agents may be required to ensure that the goods are not received by the importer without payment.

In the UK, one of the older trading nations, the financial record of the transaction that forms part of the documentation is known as a *bill of exchange* also sometimes known as a *draft*. However, it is worth noting that drafts are normally *negotiable instruments* meaning that they can be transferred, whereas only bills of exchange that are specifically termed *to order* may be negotiated.

The bill of exchange represents an unconditional order by one party (the *drawer*) to another party (the *drawee*) to pay an amount, or "*certain sum*" at a specified time. As such, once it has been accepted by the drawer, in the form of a signature, it becomes a post-dated obligation, similar to a post-dated cheque. (In fact, cheques used in current accounts owe their origins to bills of exchange.) The word *draft* is often used interchangeably with *bill* in the context of sight drafts and term drafts.

Many jurisdictions have passed laws to govern the format and usage of bills of exchange of which the Bill of Exchange Act (1882) in the UK (adopted by many ex-Commonwealth countries and other trading partners of the UK) and the Geneva Convention of 1930 offer strict definitions of what constitutes a bill. The Geneva Convention has been adopted by many countries and an updated UNCITRAL Convention on International Bills of Exchange and International Promissory Notes was published in 1988.[1]

Article 2.1 defines an international bill of exchange as one that specifies two of the following places and indicates that any two specified are in different states:

- the place where the bill is drawn;
- the place indicated next to the signature of the drawer;
- the place indicated next to the name of the drawee;
- the place indicated next to the name of the payee; and
- the place of payment.[2]

Article 3.1 of this document defines a bill of exchange as a written instrument that:

- Contains an unconditional order whereby the drawer directs the drawee to pay a definite sum of money to the payee or to his/her order;

---

[1] This legislation specifically excludes international cheques.

[2] United Nations Convention on International Bills of Exchange and International Promissory Notes.

- is payable on demand or at a definite time;
- is dated; and
- is signed by the drawer.

The bill of exchange can form part of the documentation required to provide credit for the supplier or recipient of goods during the period between the contract signature and an agreed future date through the process of *acceptance* of the bill, and then *endorsement* and transfer to a third party (the bank or other provider of finance). It also offers evidence of the terms for payment within the legal system.

If the buyer and/or a bank accepts the bill of exchange, it is committing to pay the amount under the terms specified. Thus, a banker's acceptance of a bill places the credit of the bank behind the transaction and makes that bill liquid in a secondary market. At this point it can separate from the underlying transaction.

The process of *negotiation* is the transfer of the monetary claim represented by the bill to a third party in exchange for a payment, based on the face value of the bill and subject to the documentation provisions. Sometimes a bank will purchase a bill at face value, more usually a discount is offered to take account of the risk. Bills may be discounted *with recourse* provided that they have a defined maturity date and the buyer has accepted the bill. Recourse in this context means that the bank has recourse to the seller of the goods. Bills can also be discounted *without recourse*, more commonly when the buyer is very well known and thus their commercial abilities trusted or if the bill has already been accepted or guaranteed by another bank with a good credit rating. If a bill is refused, or "protested" then the legal process to establish the claim requires a subsequent presentation by a legal official and a statement of the reason for the refusal to pay or *dishonour the bill*.

13.2. Hawala and Hundi

The techniques of *hawala* and *hundi*[3] represent an informal and very important way of moving funds around outside the banking network.

---

[3]Marina Martin, *An Economic History of Hundi,* 1858–1978, PhD dissertation. Department of Economic History, London School of Economics and Political Science: London.

Hawala is a longstanding payment system originating from India that uses a network of trusted agents to move money across countries. It is largely used to make payments outside a country of residence where there may be delays or other problems in gaining access to convertible external currency. The *hawala* system is neither regulated nor the subject of any legal system and, therefore, relies entirely on the trustworthiness of the agents and a password system to move the obligations around. As such, although its primary use is to enable *hawala* users to meet legitimate obligations, it has also been of interest to those bodies concerned with the funding of counterterrorism since the absence of written records may make it an attractive conduit.

A *hundi*, developed in the Middle Ages in India, is a form of remittance instrument or IOU and can also be used as a bill of exchange. Whereas *hawala* transfers money by transferring an obligation and is entirely driven by trust and honour, the *hundi* system uses forms and is covered by the Negotiable Instruments Act of 1881 with the instruments recognized by the Reserve Bank of India. *Hundis* can be related to underlying trade.

13.3. Specific Issues Around Supply Chain Financing as a Form of Trade Financing

As we saw in Chapters 2 and 12, larger companies will often rely on a supply chain for components that may lie outside their own corporate boundaries. A good example is the automotive industry where suppliers are designated as Tier 1, Tier 2 or Tier 3. A lower tier supplier may need to invest in very specific tools in order to produce the components required — Does the top-level car company have an obligation to finance the production of the tools? What happens if car sales fall, or a model flops and the supplier is left with an investment, attendant debt and no sales?

Another issue in supply chains is that of delays in payment and we looked at the working capital gap in Chapter 2. The smaller supplier has much less financial clout to make sure that they receive prompt payment so they may be "carrying" the larger company for significant periods.

Finally, more recently we have seen instances in the UK where supermarket suppliers have been asked to make payments in order to be allowed to sell their goods through supermarkets.

The concept of specific SCF is relatively new. One challenge faced by all stakeholders is that there is a lack of clarity in terms of what is meant by the different products and also in the vocabulary used.[4] The European Banking Association (EBA) review of SCF divides SCF into three groups of instruments:

- Receivables purchasing including receivables discounting, forfaiting, factoring and payables financing.
- Loan or advance-based techniques including distributor fiancé, loans against inventory and pre-shipment finance.
- Bank Payment Obligations discussed briefly in Chapter 2 and linked to the SWIFT payment system discussed next.

In the second quarter of 2013, the interbank payment system, SWIFT, published the results of their initiative to try and improve management within the supply chain from the start of the transaction, by looking at pre-shipment services (similar to red clause letters of credit) with the particular objective of supporting small and medium-sized enterprises (SMEs) through the use of technology.[5] One of the challenges for banks and clients in today's world of electronic platforms is that interoperability remains a problem. We can think of this as being like mobile phones. Not so long ago, travellers were unable to use mobile phones in different countries because of different standards. The SWIFT initiative brings back into prominence the role of the correspondent bank as a potential source of access to a larger base of suppliers. The latter can be assessed for creditworthiness through the use of the local correspondent bank but this presupposes that the local bank has the information to make such credit decisions and it also ignores some of the cultural problems that have been outlined earlier in this text such as closeness to certain politically or economically important groups. The promise of paper-free BPOs is potentially less attractive to smaller SMEs though, not least as there is a cost to bringing suppliers onto an electronic platform.

In all instances, the best credit decision for the bank is that the owner of the supply chain, the buyer, will approve the invoice for payment and will pay on time. While various governments have tried to introduce

---

[4]For a list of the latest EBA definitions, see the European Banking Association website.
[5]The latest information can be found on the SWIFT website.

initiatives to ensure that this happens, in that smaller suppliers are not disadvantaged, the reality appears to be that this does not always work very well. Another problem is that once the suppliers drop below Tier 1, the order and invoice are possibly not from the supply chain owner and, therefore, may not have the same creditworthiness support. This may occur when components are made into sub-assemblies that are then uploaded into the supply chain for final assembly into the product.

An example of supply chain problems and the effect they can have on the various suppliers may be seen in the supermarket business. Suppliers to major supermarkets are often required to make a payment to the supermarket in order to qualify for listing, meaning that their goods will be sold. They also make other financial arrangements to occupy the best points on the shelves or at the end of aisles. Delisting can be ruthless, and pressure on suppliers to offer promotions including "buy one get one free" (BOGOF) has also been reported. While there are supply codes of practice in many industries, including supermarkets, the enforceability of any findings may not always be retrospective and many industry groups have significant commercial and political power.

13.4. Financing Commodities

Estimates suggest that the commodity trade finance business is worth around US$1.5 trillion a year and is seen as both low return and low risk.

Commodities are primary products rather than undergoing any further processing and are usually split into two categories: soft commodities that include agricultural products, such as coffee, cocoa, sugar, wheat and milk, and hard commodities that include gold and oil. There are about 50 major commodity markets worldwide that have evolved from physical trading, where the material is delivered to the buyer, both spot and forward in nature through to derivative transactions, which are largely financial in nature.

Figures 13.1 and 13.2 show the trade flows for typical hard and soft commodity transactions.

The Chicago Board of Trade (CBOT), now part of the Chicago Mercantile Exchange (CME) group of exchanges, is a designated contract market (DCM) and one of the major commodities and derivative exchanges. Electronic trading has largely taken over from the old open outcry or pit trading, but the latter still remains important. Contracts are

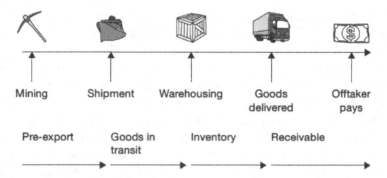

Figure 13.1:   Trade Cycle for Hard Commodities

Prepared by Carmel F. de Nahlik, *The Successful Banker's Handbook. London*: Euromoney, 2015.

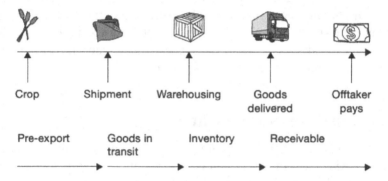

Figure 13.2:   Trade Cycle for Soft Commodities

Prepared by Mariya Bezhena for Carmel F. de Nahlik, *The Successful Banker's Handbook. London*: Euromoney, 2015.

offered in designated volumes and product grades, and for delivery on predetermined dates. Each contract has very detailed specifications including the location of delivery and approval of warehousing. The market is heavily regulated with membership held by individuals and firms, and limits on trading positions including margins.

In contrast, the London Metal Exchange (LME) is the world's largest market in futures and options on base and other metals and also includes warehousing through approved warehouses. It is one of the last exchanges in Europe where open outcry trading still takes place though this may change as a result of ongoing consultation as of January 2021. The LME also acts as a market of "last resort" for metals.

Not all those trading on exchanges are buying or selling with end use in mind. Large food and other commodity processing companies require commodity finance, but fortunes have been made and lost by individuals and financial institutions through speculative commodity trading. Banks have also recently returned to commodity finance. Commodity financing might be required for the purchase and sale of physical commodity, risk management costs, storage costs, transportation and related costs, as well as the financing made available to traders, including banks own proprietary traders.

Another way to look at this is to group it into different product areas.

- *Pre-export finance*: Providing finance for input costs that is secured against physical production and that may or may not be combined with off-take agreement and risk management, especially around price risk.
- *Borrowing base or collateral pooling facilities*: Providing finance for working capital or asset investments, where the security is provided by title over a portfolio of cash generating assets, such as accounts receivable, forward oil sales, and in a less liquid form dependent on the commodity, against inventory or equity.
- *Inventory finance*: Providing finance secured by title over physical inventory and/or delivery certificates. Closely linked to this may be finance related to warehousing or other storage facilities and the financing of goods in transit.

Additionally, the area of commodity finance within a financing institution may cover the financing of equity interests in production and/ or tolling, or even forfait/barter arrangements. The latter are discussed later in the section on "Forfaiting and factoring".

Some banks have begun testing market appetite from long-term providers of finance, such as pension funds and insurance companies, for securitization to provide liquidity and thus credit to smaller commodity houses, as compared with the giants such as Glencore, Vitol and Cargill that are often able to borrow at relatively low rates.

The key risks in commodity financing relate to the flow of goods from their origins and the realization of cash flow from the export and sale of commodities in countries with convertible currency. Commodity finance focuses on individual transactions and the overall corporate performance capability as compared with more conventional balance sheet lending. In this instance it is very similar to project financing, and indeed there are many overlaps in the techniques and approaches. Both approaches rely very heavily on cash flow and risk management with the commodity acting as security.

Willem Klaassens from Citibank[6] suggests that performance risk can be broken down into three critical areas — themes that recur elsewhere in this book:

- *Technical ability*: The production and distribution capabilities, capacity and process management.
- *Financial ability*: The capability of a company to control its working capital such that it can sustain corporate existence, maintain fixed assets and acquire any precursors necessary for production.
- *Legal ability*: The strength of enforceability of the contract in a timely manner and in the appropriate currency.

While there are major global players such as those mentioned, technological changes have also given rise to a growing but influential group of players based outside major centres but using subscription data sources and live feed such as Bloomberg to provide information to support proprietary (or own account) trading. Rather than the technology intensive "high frequency" trading (HFT), dependent on shaving nanoseconds off the response time to the market, these firms, termed "point and click", use bright recruits from emerging countries to sift through data and trade. Western competitors argue that the offshore entities receive advantages from exchanges in the form of lower fees and other incentives, and may benefit from specialist tax treatment if they are classed as service companies, rather than trading entities.

There are regional and international trading companies but at the production end, especially in agriculture, the industry may be very fragmented. Where commodities are grown by poor farmers and sold to major multinationals, safeguards are now considered important to ensure that fair prices are paid. The Fairtrade initiative is just one of these, and traceability as well as conforming to ethical standards is now the new norm.

---

[6]Willem Klaassens, "Structured Commodity Finance: A Proven Tool with a Pragmatic Take on Risk," Citibank Asian Trade Finance Yearbook, 2005.

This can apply to gemstones and jewellery metal as much as to chocolate in a chocolate bar.

Risk management in commodity financing can be conducted through the use of derivatives such as futures, options, swaps, forwards and other hybrid products. While many commodity derivative contracts are traded on exchanges such as the CBOT, not all commodities have a market in associated derivatives, so risk management of price or delivery using these products may not always be straightforward. In some cases, it may be that it is difficult to convert a commodity into cash inside a country and this is where countertrade can become important.

13.5. Forfaiting and Factoring

Both forfaiting and factoring are financial products that are designed to manage the risk of non-payment, or to bring forward payment and may also be used if the seller is expected to give credit terms to the buyer and wishes to manage their working capital.

Forfaiting is the process whereby exporters can obtain cash by selling what are usually medium-term foreign currency-based account receivables at a discount on a "without recourse basis". In forfaiting, the invoices are normally (but not always) guaranteed by the importer's bank which can allow the exporter to take the transaction off balance sheet. Clearly there is a minimum transaction size, estimated to be around US$100,000 to make the transaction worthwhile and there needs to be legally robust documentation of the obligation.

Factoring is the domestic form of forfaiting, whereby a company passes title to a group of invoices to a bank or specialist factoring company that offers a discount on their face value. Factoring can be with or without recourse and be for domestic or international invoices.

While factoring as a product was promoted by banks during times of credit restriction, organizations considering the factoring route need to remember that the bank or factoring company can cherry-pick the invoices, and may be offering to discount the very invoices that are most likely to get paid. This was discussed in the previous chapter in the Carillion case study. However, factoring and forfaiting can be beneficial to bridge timing gaps especially when invoices are not paid on time and a factor credit is extended, or if credit is formally extended as part of the transaction or for smaller companies, using a bigger bank that will pressure the buyer for payment.

The discount rate in both cases will reflect the risk, the repayment structure and any history of the buyer. There is an International Forfaiting Association (IFA)[7] and an International Factoring Association[8] that provide more information. There are also indigenous entities such as the Asset-based Finance Association in the UK and the American Factoring Association as well as many domestic factoring companies and a European Federation for Factoring and Commercial Finance (EUF).[9]

13.6. Countertrade

What happens if a sale is made but the buyer is unable to pay in a convertible currency, or wishes to offer goods in exchange? The major expertise developed out of Eastern Bloc trading and so banks in Germany, Austria, Hungary and Switzerland have long histories in this area. Countertrade transactions are presently under scrutiny as conduits for money laundering.

There are a number of different forms of countertrade.

- *Barter* is when goods and/or services are exchanged against other goods and/or services of equivalent value without any balancing payment being made between the buyer and the seller. Barter is common in economies that are recovering from warfare or other catastrophic events and as such may be relatively underdeveloped. Barter can also be used to ensure that assets that will generate cash flow can be moved outside the country and thus can be used for debt recovery.
- *Offset* transactions are largely driven at an intergovernmental level and thus will have major political sensitivities associated with them. Direct offset is when there is a requirement of a large export transaction whereby a certain amount of domestic content provided by the importer forms part of the purchases that make up the exported items. This may require the establishment of local offices, production sites, and so on, and is commonly seen in defence contracts. The purchaser may require suppliers to enter into long-term cooperative agreements

---

[7] International Trade and Forfaiting Association website.
[8] IFA website.
[9] EU Federation Factoring and Commercial Finance (EUF) website.

including investment that are unrelated to the supply contract. This might include the provision of education and training for importer personnel, often in the country of the exporter. Finally, offset agreements may include technology transfer arrangements.

- *Counterpurchase* is when a seller undertakes to purchase goods from the buyer or from a company nominated by the buyer or to arrange for their purchase by a third party as part of a sale agreement. The contracts for the supply of goods and the counterpurchase are normally separated and the latter can take many forms from a declaration of intent to purchase, through to a binding contract with penalties. Normally, the value of the counterpurchase goods is a pre-agreed percentage of the price of the goods originally exported.
- *Tolling arrangements* occur when plant is sold but the purchaser may also have difficulty in sourcing the raw materials. In this arrangement, the supplier provides the raw material and rents the facility to produce the finished goods, in turn bought by a customer who pays the supplier. Title to the raw material remains with the supplier throughout the process.
- *Buyback* occurs when products from exported equipment are purchased by the equipment provider and often occur in large project financings. An example might be the sale of a refinery where part of the purchase price would be reimbursed in the form of refined products produced. Buyback contracts are often long-term.
- *Switch trading* occurs when a seller sells goods to a buyer who is the beneficiary of monies held in a blocked clearing account in a third country and wishes to use those funds to pay for the goods. The blocked funds are bought by the switch trader who uses the funds to purchase goods in the third country and finds a buyer willing to purchase those goods. The funds are then used to pay the seller.

   In all cases a valuation needs to be placed on the goods and services being exchanged (usually a monetary amount). There also needs to be rigorous documentation of the transaction, especially around specification of the goods.

Associations such as the Global Offset and Countertrade Association (GOCA)[10] and the Asia-Pacific Countertrade Association (APCA),[11]

---

[10] GOCA is now part of the larger Global Industrial Cooperation Association (GICA).
[11] See the APCA website.

a privatized organization, can act as lobbying bodies and also sources of information.

The Financial Action Task Force (FATF), also known as GAFI[12] seeks to "set standards and promote effective implementation of legal, regulatory and operational measures for combating money laundering, terrorist financing and other related threats to the integrity of the international financial system". It has 36 member countries and one observer, and its membership includes two regional organizations. There are also a number of regional associate members that are concerned with money laundering. It represents most major financial centres in all parts of the globe. A number of international organizations such as development banks and several central banks, the IMF and various UN organizations act as observers.

FATF makes recommendations at a country level seeking compliance with the Vienna Convention and the Palermo Convention that criminalize money laundering. In the language of these documents, reference is made to trade-based money laundering (TBML) and combating the financing of terrorism (CFT) but not to countertrade specifically.

This also touches on the murky area of incentive payments or even bribes. No provider of finance wants to be associated with such negative headlines, and this also relates to reputation risk, educating staff and setting the appropriate culture.

13.7. Case Study[13]

The port of Qingdao was established in 1892 in China.[14] It is an important hub of international trade in the West Pacific with routes to over 450 ports in over 130 countries as at the time of writing. It ranked as the seventh in total throughput and eighth in container throughput as well as sixth in metal ores throughput in the world in 2012.

The Qingdao Port International Co. Ltd. (QGGJ) handled 76.4% of the total cargo throughput of the port, some 365 million tons, and offered a wide range of port-related services including stevedoring and storage,

---

[12] FATF-GAFI website.

[13] A version of this case appeared in Carmel de Nahlik and Chris Jackson, *Project Finance in Practice: Case Studies.* London: Euromoney, 2014. The rights were reverted to Carmel de Nahlik and Chris Jackson and they grant permission to reproduce the case here.

[14] World Port Source has a page on Qingdao on its website: http://www.worldportsource.com/index.php.

through to logistics and financing-related services, such as secure storage of goods pledged to support loan. The port was also connected to a well-developed intermodal transportation system to allow it to move goods and services, as well as information, efficiently in support of customer logistics. It owned much of its own equipment. Port charges and regulation are heavily controlled by the state and observance of the latest rules, changes and permit requirements is an important activity for any port operator in China.

The corporate ownership structure was complex with equity interests in 14 subsidiaries largely established to handle the different activities of a port, such as shipping repair, bonded port area storage, insurance agency, and so on, and a further 17 joint ventures and associates and three entities with equity interests. Additionally, there were 11 branch operations. Just as a public share issue closed in May 2014, reports emerged of a probe into trade financing practices of some companies using Qingdao Port warehouses. As a result, the price weakened, and private investor appetite waned. Commodities stored in safekeeping in the port formed security for bank loans, in a long-established tradition of commodity financing. However, the economic downturn in China has led to a demand for commodities dropping in line with centrally sponsored investment, with the result that banks are looking at loans supported by commodities where the underlying value has fallen. One insider estimated in March 2014 that the value of transactions using commodities as collateral was about US$160 billion, or 31% of China's total short-term foreign exchange loans.

A US$270 million lawsuit emerged from the Qingdao debacle, between Citigroup and Mercuria and involving a repo or repurchasing facility, where metal is sold to a bank that provides the funds to the trading house with an agreement to repurchase it at a future date. According to reports, Mercuria and Citigroup entered into a series of such transactions involving metal stored in warehouses in Chinese ports. Once the problems in Qingdao became known (total amount estimated at US$3.2 billion) the authorities sealed all warehouses because it became apparent that some metal had been pledged multiple times by one Chinese trader, Decheng Resources. The port authorities estimated the fraud involved 400,000 tonnes of metal as at August 2014. Much metal in storage in China has since moved to other destinations.

Some of the metal subject to the multiple pledges and thus sealed had been sold by Mercuria to Citigroup, and without access to it, the buyback contract came into question. Citigroup demanded early repayment under a "bring forward event" clause as it had also short hedged the transaction and the hedge was showing a loss of US$24 million by the end of July 2014.

The UK court ruling, eventually published in late May 2015, has ramifications for many commodity traders who use repos to finance the day to day activities. It concluded that the early claim made by Citigroup was within its rights but the endorsed warehouse receipts did not represent good title to the metal and as such Mercuria did not have to repay Citigroup at that point. This raises questions about the allocation of oversight of the warehouse — was it Mercuria or Citigroup's responsibility? An undisclosed settlement was reached in late 2016.

This illustrates the challenges that can arise when it is possible to take advantage of legislation and less robust management practices and make multiple pledges of the same commodity. It also shows what can occur when a transaction is hedged and the repayment schedule on the underlying goes awry. While this case is more related to commodity repos, the underlying issue about secure warehouses has also caused concern in commodity circles. It has wider implications for the export of valuable commodities — we saw other issues in Chapter 4 in the Acacia case when the state intervened in the export of the gold and means that careful lenders or providers of finance also need to check that the arrangements for export will result in export and cash flow back in to the project.

Chapter 14

Funding Natural Resource Projects

Introduction

Reserves-oriented financing is based on the collateral value of oil reserves, gas reserves and mineral reserves, itself determined by the potential for cash flow. Some types of reserves-oriented financing are with recourse to the borrower and resemble a loan secured by a mortgage on real estate. In other types of reserves-oriented financing, the lender looks solely to the value of the reserves based on a conservative market price for production and the ability and undertakings of an operator as the source of funds for repayment of debt.

Many of the structures used in reserves-oriented financing were developed in the 1950s and 1960s. As the tax laws were changed to do away with perceived unjustified tax advantages, the structures nevertheless survived because of their usefulness in financing and particularly in achieving project financing objectives. This discussion will trace the early history of some of these structures to provide some perspective in their development. We include a number of structures that are not widely used today in order to provoke creative approaches to problem solving by drawing on lessons from the past.

It is important to keep in mind when reading this chapter that the ownership and taxation of oil and gas and indeed other minerals varies by country. In the US, for example, mineral rights can be owned by individuals — often the landowner may also own the mineral rights below ground, but it is not universally true. In many other jurisdictions, some or all of the rights are owned by the government, or in the case of the UK, by the Crown (and managed by the government). In the case of national ownership, the government

341

(usually via the appropriate ministry or department) grants exploration and development or production licenses, in essentially the form of concessions, for fixed terms with payments to the host government and often a revenue sharing agreement. This means that some US tax-driven project finance structures may not be applicable in all jurisdictions.

There are also national differences in the definition of various types of reserves, and of course the legal rights pertaining to their use as collateral. Many stock exchanges have rules relating to natural resource companies using this route to raise equity or debt funding from investors. An example is the JORC Code developed in Australia and New Zealand for the Reporting of Exploration Results, Mineral Resources and Ore Reserves.[1] The international accounting bodies are gradually engaging with this complex area though the IASB initiative has been subsumed into the wider area of intangible assets. These can have major impacts on the financial well-being of natural resource companies and their cash flows and local rulings should be checked. Of particular note are IFRS 9 (financial instruments concerned with hedging, classification, measurement and impairment), IFRS 15 (revenue recognition including its application to take-or-pay contracts) and IFRS 16 (leasing).

The renaissance of interest in oil and gas as a result of shale production has its own challenges in terms of environmental issues that are not to be underestimated! New technology may provide us with electric cars but we still require various elements to make the batteries and printed circuits work, so mining and natural resource stocks, now operating in harsher economic and political climates than before, remain important to each of us. However, greater scrutiny of the origins of natural resources mean that issues associated with child miners or unsafe mining conditions can rebound on all stakeholders including providers of funds.

14.1. Production Loans

Production loans are widely used to finance the development of reserves. In a production loan, an operator simply borrows money under a loan agreement, evidenced by a promissory note and secured by mortgage on the reserve and a security interest in the production.

Production loans are sometimes arranged as a line of credit against which the operator may borrow and repay so long as the total amount outstanding

---

[1] JORC website.

at any one time does not exceed a "borrowing base". Usually the borrowing base is determined by a pre-agreed percentage of reserve values as verified from time to time by petroleum engineers and is subject to overall limits.

These types of loans are sometimes called borrowing base loans. The liability of the borrower may be evidenced by a single note in the maximum amount which may be borrowed, or it may be evidenced by notes in the amounts actually outstanding. In some cases, the credit facility revolves as long as the borrowing base remains at or above the level agreed with the lenders and regularly reviewed by the petroleum engineers.

14.2. Non-Recourse Production Loans

A non-recourse production loan resembles a production loan, except that the lender agrees to make a loan based solely on the security of the oil or gas or mineral reserves, the ability or undertaking of the operator to produce the reserves, and a security interest in the production and proceeds of production which can be sold at an adequate price to service the debt. More specifically, the lender relies on the following security and undertakings for repayment of its loan:

- A take-or-pay contract, unless the lender is satisfied that expected market prices and customers for the production will exist.
- Placement of the project in a special project entity which will be restricted in liabilities other than to the lender.
- An undertaking by the special project entity and the sponsor or reputable operator to construct, complete and operate the project to certain standards of efficiency. In other words, a completion guarantee.
- First mortgage and security interest in all reserves and assets involved in the project.
- Assignment of all contractual rights of the borrower which relate to the project.

Clearly, the lender needs to have a strong sense of the dynamics of the geology of the area where the oil and gas is located — the first well to be drilled in a particular location that taps into a particular level of rock thought to be petroliferous is as risky as any venture capital investment. One of the challenges is that rock strata are not necessarily uniform in distribution and, of course, are invisible because they are located deep underground. Although seismic analysis has progressed enormously over the last 30 years — costs of computing have come down and imaging has become more sophisticated, aiding in the assessment of the reservoirs — unexpected events can still happen, and anticipated production levels fail to materialize.

14.3. Production Payments as Collateral to Obtain Financing

A mineral production payment is a right to either a specified share of the production from a certain mineral property or a sum of money in place of production. Stated another way, a production payment is a conveyance by a mineral owner of certain undivided interests in minerals to be produced and sold in the future. Production payments can be precisely calculated, albeit from forecasted data. This makes the use of production payments attractive as security in financial transactions. The production payment frequently bears interest payable out of future production. In other words, the value of a production payment is the present value of the expected future stream of production payments discounted at some interest rate.

Loans based on production payments are one of the earliest forms of project financings. Like many financing structures first used for oil and gas production financing, the structures were originally devised to achieve certain tax objectives. Although tax laws were changed to eliminate the real or imagined benefits of such arrangements, the structures survived because they were useful in arranging project financing.

A production payment is secured by an interest in the minerals in place. Payment is dischargeable only out of runs of oil or deliveries of gas or minerals accruing to certain property charged with production payments. It cannot be satisfied out of other production. The right to the production is for a shorter period than the expected life of the property. The owner of a production payment looks exclusively to proceeds from production for payment.

For a production payment to be valuable enough to use as collateral for a loan, the production payment must be generated from a proven mineral reserve. The nomenclature has changed so that reserves are now classified by probability rather than the older terminology of *proved*, *probable*, *possible* and so on (see section 6.1.2). Different countries may have different views on reserve definitions, so again this must be checked with local experts when putting together development and financing plans. An appraisal of the reserves must be obtained from one or more reputable appraisers, who analyze the nature and extent of the reserves. The feasibility of the production must be confirmed by an engineering study which analyzes the economies of obtaining the production, expected quality of production, probable cost of production, probable markets, cash flows expected to be generated and cash needs. Such studies are not inexpensive. Expected market prices for production are obviously very important in structuring a production payment loan.

A loan secured by a production payment is self-amortizing. Income from the sale of the oil, gas or other minerals is dedicated and used to pay back the loan. An illustration is provided in Figure 14.1. The following is assumed in the illustration:

1. The seller sells a mineral property for US$350,000, subject to a production payment in the primary sum of US$650,000, plus an amount equal to an interest factor on the unliquidated balance of the production payment.

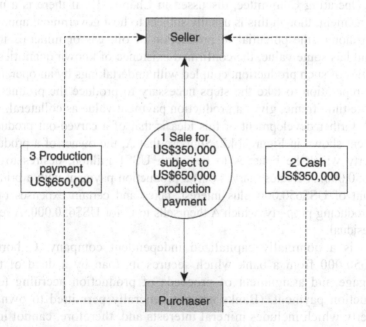

Figure 14.1: Loan Secured by a Reserved Production Payment
Prepared by Frank J. Fabozzi and Peter K. Nevitt.

2. At the time of the sale, the purchaser pays US$350,000 in cash.
3. As production is produced, the purchaser makes production payments of US$650,000, plus the agreed upon interest factor on the unliquidated balance.

Undertakings by an operator of good reputation and integrity are also needed if the production payment is to be used as collateral. Undertakings by the operator may include a completion guarantee to complete the well or mine within certain time limits, to provide the necessary equipment and make the necessary expenditures to achieve completion and to pay any cost over-runs. Completion means the well or mine will be constructed in a manner to permit certain specified production rates and production of a specified quality. The operator also undertakes to protect the property and keep it free from liens.

Since the undertakings of the operator are considerable, the operator is usually the major stakeholder in generating the cash flow to repay the proceeds of the loan secured by the production payment. Thus, the operator has the motivation and responsibility to perform and can be replaced by the Joint Operating Committee, discussed in Chapter 12, if there is a major disagreement, though this is usually subject to host government approval.

Although the potential of production of oil, gas or minerals in the ground has some value, the confirmed existence of known quantities and qualities of such production, coupled with undertakings by an operator of good reputation to take the steps necessary to produce the product in a definite time frame, gives a production payment value as collateral.

A further development of this idea is that of a carved-out production payment shown in Figure 14.2. Suppose that A, the owner of a producing property which he believes to be worth US$1 million, desires to raise US$650,000. A creates (carves out) a production payment with a principal amount of US$650,000 plus interest, taxes and certain expenses out of the producing property, which A then sells to C for US$650,000. A retains the residual.

C is a nominally capitalized independent company. C borrows US$650,000 from a bank which secures its loan by a deed of trust, mortgage and assignment of proceeds of production accruing to the production payment. (Banks are not generally permitted to own real property which includes mineral interests and, therefore, cannot invest directly in production payments — among other reasons, liabilities may attach to such ownership.) It is a method of borrowing against an oil,

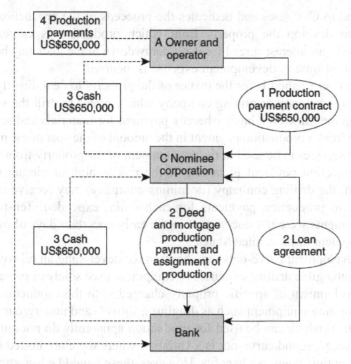

Figure 14.2:   Carved-Out Production Payment
Prepared by Frank J. Fabozzi and Peter K. Nevitt.

gas or mineral property on a non-recourse basis and not an acquisition of assets.

A development carve-out is a method whereby an owner raises capital to develop an oil, gas or mining property in exchange for a stated amount payable out of production. Clearly this is a high risk-transaction, even if it is a step out from an existing asset.

In one type of development carve-out, A, the owner of the mineral interest, estimates development costs and determines if such amount can be borrowed from a bank on the basis of an assignment of a production payment on a non-recourse basis. When this amount is determined, the production payment is sold to C, an independent and nominally capitalized company. C borrows the same amount from a bank and assigns to the bank a trust deed, mortgage and assignment of proceeds of production accruing to the production payment. The production payment must be sufficient to pay the principal amount of the loan, plus interest, local tax and a spread to C. C uses and dedicates the proceeds of the production payment to develop the property from which production is carved out. C reserves an interest spread for itself. Drawdown of the loan may be over a period of time as development expense is incurred.

Another method is for the owner of the property to deal directly with a drilling company or mining company which agrees to drill the well or develop the mine on a basis whereby payment for materials and services will be from a production payment in the amount of the cost of the materials and services to be used in the development of the property from which the production payment is carved. If the risk is high or circumstances warrant, the drilling company (or mining company) may receive several dollars in production payments for each dollar expended. Ten-for-one arrangements were not uncommon in the early uncertain days of oil well development in the United States.

Development carve-outs may be used for developing an oil well or a mine, intangible drilling expenses or equipment used solely or principally for development of specific property charged with the production payment; mining equipment such as draglines, shovels and underground face equipment which can be used for production apparently do not qualify.

A wrap-around carve-out is a variation where there are nested carve-outs to optimize any tax benefits. However, these would be less attractive to banks because of the higher financial reserve requirements associated with high risk transactions.

Nevertheless, the carve-out structure lives on outside of its original natural resource context and is used in highly leveraged buyouts, spinouts or other restructurings discussed in Chapter 15.

Finally, production portfolios can be created to lower the average borrowing cost. A corporation is formed, which is not consolidated for tax purposes, to hold properties located in three countries of which one is politically stable and two are politically unstable. An entity lends against the portfolio of properties on a non-recourse basis for development purposes. The income from the more stable country is used to underpin the finance development in the stable country and bring the cost of borrowing down. Typical projects include development of oil, gas and mineral deposits. Interest rates will be higher for development loans in the unstable countries because of expropriation and political risk, but will be lower for the stable country. By combining and diversifying the collateral, the overall borrowing rate for the high-risk countries can be lowered.

Advance payments for oil, gas or coal transactions involve the sale and the purchase of a mineral prior to its production. Typically, the sale is to an independent entity which borrows funds necessary to make the advance purchase. The purchaser agrees to purchase the mineral as it is produced. The purchase contract, the minerals and proceeds of the sale are assigned to the lender as security for the loans. As the mineral is produced and sold, the loan is repaid.

An example is shown in Figure 14.3. In the illustration (1) a public utility sponsor makes an advance of US$10 million to a drilling company in return for the drilling company giving the utility the right to purchase the production from the property to be developed and (2) production payments are made from proceeds of production in an amount equal to the advance, plus additional amounts to compensate the utility for the risk in making the advance.

14.3.1. *Example of an Advance Payment for Gas and Oil*

The sponsor, a public gas utility or pipeline, seeks a source of gas. A drilling company owns certain properties for development. The sponsor makes an advance of US$10 million to the drilling company to be used exclusively for exploration and development of a specified number of wells on certain

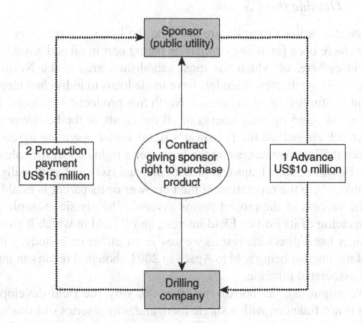

Figure 14.3: Advance Payment for Production

Prepared by Frank J. Fabozzi and Peter K. Nevitt.

of the drilling company's properties. The sponsor is to receive back US$15 million payable out of oil and gas production attributable to the wells and properties specified. The sponsor also acquires the right to purchase all gas from the properties, since its prime motive is to secure a source of gas for itself. The same arrangement might be made for oil or coal.

The drilling company can insulate itself from liability by placing the property to be developed in a subsidiary formed for purposes of the transaction. The property is developed using the advances which are repayable only out of production. Thus, the drilling company enjoys the benefits of a project financing repayable only out of production and non-recourse to the drilling company. While property is transferred to the project by the drilling company, the value of the property is greatly enhanced by development. Furthermore, in some cases advances might be used to acquire the property to be developed.

A typical project would be exploration and development of a source of gas, oil or coal.

14.3.2. *Oil and Gas Development Funding Outside the US*

Though the earlier examples are based in the US, since the early 1970s, lenders have been financing companies taking part in oil and gas development elsewhere, of which the most established area is the North Sea. Consortia or syndicates of lenders have made loans to individual members of joint ventures formed to develop North Sea production projects. These loans are secured by assignments of all the rights of the borrower in the project, which include the borrower's rights under operating agreements between the joint venturers and the borrower's rights under the sales contracts. However, such loans can present unusual risks and are usually only available where the reputation of the borrower or its parent is established and the success of the project seems assured. The classic example is the BP financing of its Forties Field interest, an oil field in which it currently no longer has a direct interest as we saw in an earlier case study, with the rest of the interest being sold to Apace in 2003, though it retains an interest in the associated pipeline.

We might ask, as borrowers often do, why the field development group is not financed with a single loan, and why a series of loans to different members of the development group are required. In a relatively new oil province with a mix of large experienced international companies and smaller, newer companies (often representing part of the host country share of the development although privately owned) there is a significant range of creditworthiness and experience. For the smaller company, with a smaller share of the field, this might be an attractive possibility because it would potentially gain from the umbrella effect of the credit worthiness of the larger companies. However, for a larger company (1) the field financing rate would be affected by the inclusion of smaller, often newer companies and thus indirectly point to an increase in loan spread paid by this borrower (albeit as part of a field) and (2) there is an implicit expectation that the large members will take care of the weakest members of the field in order to ensure the financing proceeds smoothly. Finally, the number of parties to such an agreement, especially, for example, in the early days of the North Sea, could be considerable because at some point government policy favoured the award of exploration and production licenses to consortia with significant "UK" content.

Hence, at the beginning, participation was financed individually and in the case of BP via a bank loan, with other early entrants offering equity-based incentives or royalty payments to lenders to enable finance to be raised.

The original financing of the Forties Field in the North Sea, as shown in Figure 14.4, was one of the largest production loan or advance payment schemes. The following information pertains to Figure 14.4:

1. British Petroleum forms two entities, British Petroleum Trading Company and British Petroleum Development.
2. Norex is formed by British Petroleum as a special purpose company to arrange financing.
3. British Petroleum Development assigns its production licence to Norex, and Norex borrows from banks on the basis of an assignment of the production licence. (The production licence can be assigned only with consent, which is revocable. No mortgage could be assigned since the British government owns the oil and gas.)
4. Funds are advanced by banks under the loan to Norex which, in turn, advances such funds to British Petroleum Development against production.
5. Oil is produced by British Petroleum Development and is marketed by British Petroleum Trading Company.
6. British Petroleum Trading pays Norex for the oil and Norex services the debt.

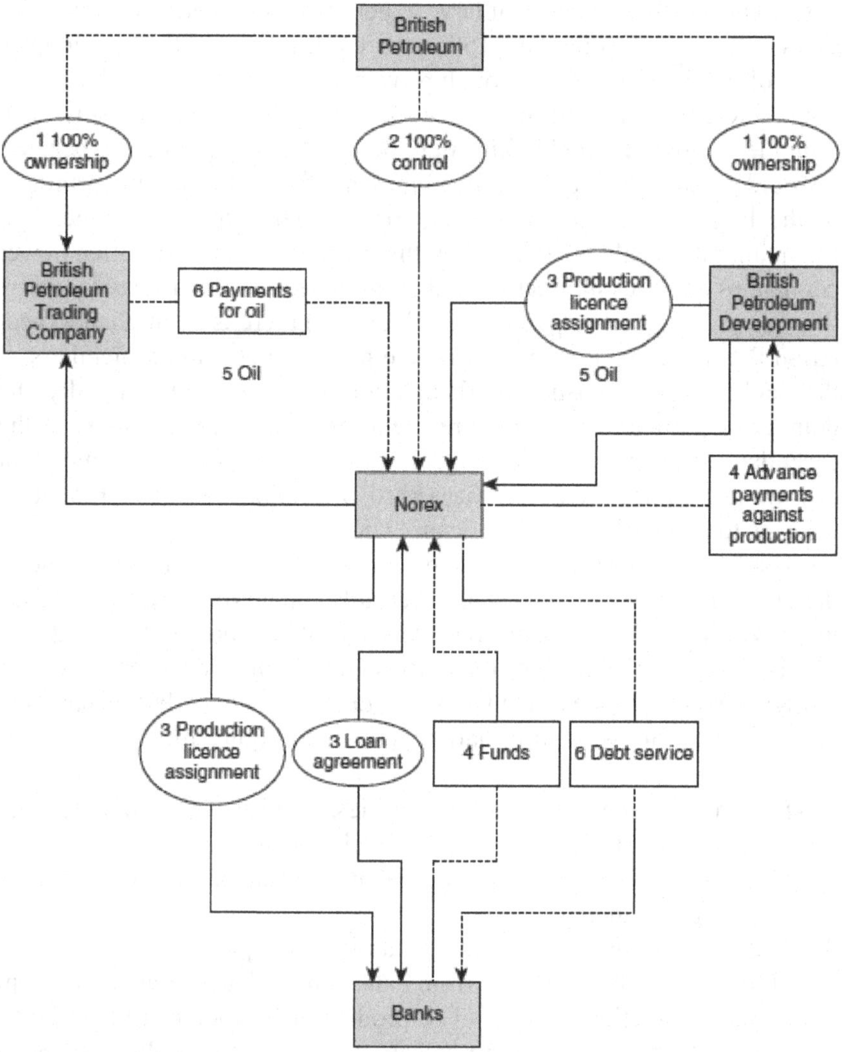

Figure 14.4:   Forties Field in the North Sea

Prepared by Frank J. Fabozzi and Peter K. Nevitt.

A total of US$900 million was advanced against the risk that the oil was there and that British Petroleum could produce the oil at reasonable costs. The usual security supports were not available to lenders. No mortgage or first lien on the oil in the ground (or sea) was available because the British Government owned the oil. The production licence could be assigned only with the consent of the government and such consent was revocable.

How many lenders understood the risks are open to conjecture? Fortunately, oil prices rose and the project has been successful, so much so that Apache, the company that bought BP's remaining interest has upgraded the recoverable reserve estimates.

14.3.3. *Supplier Project Facility Financing Supported by User-Sponsor's Advances*

An independent supplier of gas, crude oil, feedstocks or LNG, with limited credit and limited access to capital, finances a project facility by obtaining advances from a sponsor seeking a source of supply. Essentially this is a form of supplier credit, with the possibility of the supplier being able to optimize any tax allowances and pass them on. A typical project might be storage facilities, refineries, reforming facilities and pipelines.

14.3.4. *Using Financial Support from Other Group Members in a Consortium to Assist in Financing Through Carried Interests and Farm-In/Farm-Out Approaches*

Traditionally, before banks began to get involved, oil and gas wells were financed within the development group. The stronger partner offered to provide financing for the weaker partner in a number of ways. While these ideas have origins in petroleum finance, they have been taken and adapted in a number of other contexts to offer financing of projects based on well-developed legal structures and case law. These activities are specifically addressed in the new IFRS standards.

The three main concepts are a carried interest; a farm-in/farm-out; a net profits interest.

A carried interest: In a carried interest structure, a financially stronger partner (or indeed it may be shared across a group of partners) agrees to pick up (carry) all costs for that development associated with a weaker partner, which become a financial obligation secured by the weaker partner's interest in the project. The contract specifies the interest rate or other recompense for this, and the obligation is repaid out of the weaker partner's share of the project revenues once production begins. Once the costs are paid off, the full amount of the weaker partner's participation is restored to them.

The advantage of this structure is that it is fast because there is no need to wait for a weaker partner to find a bank or raise equity, which may cause significant delays. The disadvantage is that the provider of financial support may end up with a larger exposure to the project. The smaller company may threaten a "hold out" strategy to get a better deal, thus causing potential delays and bad feeling before the project starts.

A farm-in/farm-out: With the farm-in/farm-out structure, the interests change inside a consortium, possibly for a number of different reasons. A new partner may wish to enter the group and "farm-in" by paying for drilling a well; a group member may not have tax absorptive capacity in one year when wells are being drilled and so may "farm-out" to another party.

For example, suppose A has a 100% share of in the project Alpha. A would like to drill a new well but it is not a priority investment. B likes the economics of the Alpha investment and approaches A. A farms out 50% of its share to B in exchange for a well that is drilled on Alpha funded by B. Following completion of this work, A now has a 50% share and B has farmed in for a 50% share in Alpha. No money has changed hands, but value is delivered into the project as a result of the drilling of the well as a higher priority for B and the new information it yields.

The advantage of this structure is that it can often happen quickly without a need for public disclosure as opposed to a sale of an interest, which would require possibly revealing sensitive information in a data room to prospective buyers who may actually be "data window shoppers". This can be changed and reversed — farm-ins/-outs can be temporary.

The disadvantage of this structure is that although the group normally has to agree, this can cause difficult dynamics in a development group if all members are not happy with the choice of new entrants.

As for the tax treatment, clarification is always needed as this varies from jurisdiction to jurisdiction. Host governments usually need to give consent to any changes of interest.

Net profits interest: The net profits interest structure is more commonly seen in the US oil and gas, where it arose because landowners might not be interested in oil and gas development but still want to retain ownership. There are a few examples of this structure in early UK North Sea financing by smaller UK companies. However, this is the structure that has been widely adapted for use in other contexts. The owner of an asset essentially leases it to another party so that the asset can be exploited, in return for an interest in the profits after pre-agreed costs have been recovered. Variant forms of this structure appear in concession agreements and also in some host government mineral exploration and development contracts. It can also appear as a "carve out" of a working interest.

For example, A owns a farm under which is believed to be significant oil reserves. A's family has owned the land for generations and she does not wish to sell it. Instead, she leases the mineral rights for 10 years to B in exchange for a net profits interest of 10%. Each year, for 10 years, she receives a 10% participation in the net profits of the oil and gas activity. Note she does not share the losses. So this might also have been a route for Pat Wright in the Bula case study in Chapter 7.

The advantage of this structure is that A is able to benefit from the mineral exploitation without any investment, and the asset reverts to her at the end of the lease period. Provided the lessee is knowledgeable and experienced, this is an attractive investment.

The disadvantages are that B gains most of the tax allowances and A is limited to those allowances associated with the net profits interest she holds — but this may vary from country to country, especially where there may be specific tax treatment for oil and gas-related revenues. Alternatively, B might "enhance" the expenses, often a potential cause of bickering in deals of this type. Finally, if B is bankrupt, A may find she has another neighbour, depending on how the contract is drafted and if B is bankrupt or fails to observe best practice, A may face significant clean-up costs to in order to restore the land at the end of the license.

14.4. Limited Partnership Drilling Funds

Limited partnerships have long been an important source of funds for exploration and development of mineral properties. A great variety of limited partnership structures are used in the US and use of this approach has been attempted elsewhere in different industries. Some of these structures are discussed in this chapter.

It should be noted, however, that limited partnership drilling funds became popular as tax shelter investments for individuals. This unfortunately resulted in some poorly structured funds which were aggressively sold by securities dealers and promoters throughout the United States. The collapse in oil and gas prices as well as incompetence resulted in many individuals realizing nothing but tax losses on these schemes. Legitimate limited partnership drilling funds continue to be a potential source of capital, despite this bad experience of a few "bad apples".

14.4.1. *Example of a Limited Partnership Drilling Fund*

A sponsor seeks capital for exploration and development by forming a limited partnership within which the sponsor acts as general partner and individual investors are sought as limited partners.

Under this arrangement, shown in Figure 14.5, limited partners pay all non-capital costs which can be deducted for tax purposes immediately. The general partner pays all capital costs. Since the non-capital costs (intangibles) are incurred in exploration and drilling the well, much of the risk of the success of the venture is on the limited partners. The general

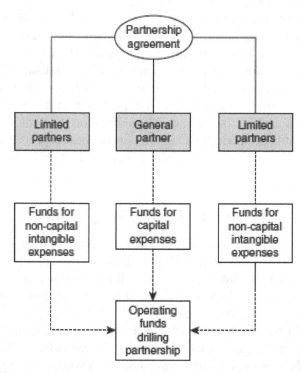

Figure 14.5:　Limited Partnerships to Finance Exploration and Development
Prepared by Frank J. Fabozzi and Peter K. Nevitt.

partner is liable only for capital expenses and these will not be incurred until the drilling is completed and tests indicate the likelihood of producing geological formations.

The general partner is entitled to a stated share of revenues from the well even though amounts which the general partner contributes for capital expenditures constitute a lesser percentage of total expenditures; examples may include up to 40% for the general partner and therefore 60% for the limited partners. This may include additional remuneration for the general partner for success fees, etc.

A typical project would be exploration and development of oil and gas wells, especially in the US and Canada, though forms of this structure also exist in other countries such as Norway and in other industries such as shipping.

14.4.1.1. *Income Tax*

Income tax benefits may be re-allocated in a partnership. In a typical limited partnership, the limited partners pay and claim deductions for non-capital expenses (intangible) which are immediately deductible. The general partner pays the capitalized costs and claims investment tax credits and depreciation.

There may be limits such as a requirement for a general partner to have at least 1% of every item of partnership income, credit, gain, loss or deduction, and that the aggregate tax deduction in the first two years of a limited partnership should not exceed the equity capital invested.

14.4.1.2. *Debt Rate and Balance Sheet*

Each partner raises its own capital. The liability of each limited partner is usually limited to its investment or subscription if it does not participate in the management of the partnership.

A general partner does not incur liability until wells are drilled and prospects look good. This concept enables a drilling company to develop properties with most of the risk of opening new wells placed on the limited partners.

As an example, the limited partnership structure exists in the US, UK, Japan, New Zealand, Germany and Denmark though it is seen in other areas such as film financing, discussed in Chapter 12.

All partnerships of this type are areas for up to date specialist legal and tax advice.

14.4.2. *Discussion of Special Tax Problems in Oil and Gas Limited Partnership Drilling Funds*

In a typical limited partnership formed for the purpose of developing oil and gas wells, the limited partners pay and claim deductions for most non-capital expenses which are immediately deductible and which include intangible drilling costs. A general partner pays the capitalized costs and claims tax depreciation.

Under tax laws where these structures flourish, partnerships are generally permitted to allocate shares of partnership income and loss to different partners. However, the tax authorities may disallow special partnership allocations if the principal purpose of such allocations is the avoidance of tax.

The limited partnership drilling fund constitutes an important method of raising capital for oil and gas exploration, including shale operations. The structures developed may have application for developing other extractive resources. Although the drilling limited partnership structure has been used for many years as a method of raising capital for development of oil and gas wells, recent changes in tax regulations in the US have resulted in some changes in their structure.

Care must be used to structure the limited partnership so that it will qualify as a partnership for tax purposes. Among the differences are (and these vary in different countries):

- mode of creation (intent may not be enough) and separate legal identity and written agreement;
- independent existence from its owners;
- continuity of life;
- centralized management;
- limited liability;
- free transferability of interest.

The most important thing to remember is that unless limited partners stay passive (or there is specific legislation that permits them to take an active interest) they may lose their advantageous tax status and incur liability for the partnerships obligations.

In addition to characteristics which distinguish a partnership from a corporation, a limited partnership must have certain specifically defined operating characteristics for the tax authority to rule that an organization is a partnership for tax purposes.

14.5. Case Study: Sent to Siberia

Following the political changes in what was the former Soviet Union, external investors began to look at this attractive natural resource province for investment opportunities. One such individual was a member of a well-known Scandinavian banking family and together with a Russian partner, in 1994 he established a venture to develop a gold project in the Amur region, close to the border with China. An iron ore mining venture followed and in 2010, the iron ore assets were listed separately as IRC limited on the Hong Kong stock exchange, with the original owners, now known as Petropavlovsk PLC, retaining a majority shareholding. IRC had a producing asset (Kuranakh) a magnetite and ilmenite mine and several other assets in development including Kimkan and Sutara (K&S) a magnetite project.

There is a need for steel inside China and only one other major supplier in the area. The iron ore deposits were close to the existing infrastructure provided by the Trans-Siberian Railway, but to enable faster transportation, a road and rail bridge across the river Amur and jointly sponsored by Russian and Chinese interests is being completed but has been delayed. This has meant that getting the ore out of Russia and into China has been affected by congestion and other problems with the existing infrastructure. The bridge is reported as completed and is expected to be fully operational by 2021/2.

The original offering of shares in IRC limited was planned to fund a staged development plan, but this was contingent on a US$340 million project loan facility to IRC to be provided by the ICBC bank that would cover 85% of the costs of stage 1 of the group development plan (the development of the K&S mine). The loan was guaranteed by Petropavlovsk, then a 60% shareholder. The project finance facility would support the export of iron ore to China and with a Chinese contractor handling the engineering, procurement and construction (EPC) contract attracted insurance from the Chinese Export Credit Bank. The loan agreement was signed in November 2010. The project loan was priced at LIBOR + 2.8%.

By 2018, both IRC and Petropavlovsk were making headlines once more. This occurred because several things affected the project:

1. There has been more than one reshuffle inside the board of Petropavlovsk, with consequent impact on market perception of the company and its subsidiaries. Some of this debate was conducted through shareholder notices about votes. These governance issues

have rumbled on into 2020 and directors and shareholders have come and gone. Family members in key positions have not helped the external image to shareholders. Press coverage suggests damage to computer systems by representatives of one concerned stakeholder group.[2]

2. The global iron ore market went through a restructuring as companies chased lower production costs through mergers, closures and relocations. While this project was relatively safe because of its location, the delays in completion of the trans-Amur bridge and aggressive sales into China by other producers made a reappraisal of the economics of the existing iron ore producing project necessary. The main project that was providing the cash flow to IRC pending the development of others (Kuranakh) is now in a care and maintenance basis and further capacity from the new K&S projects is not yet fully on stream, but is generating significant cash flow.

3. New capital was to be injected by two Chinese-based entities but has been delayed. One of these entities is now the subject of a winding up order in the Hong Kong courts but has made a payment of US$170 million (70% of the promised amount). In 2019, Petropavlovsk is said to hold 31% of IRC, General Nice Development has 14% and China Construction Bank Corporation's asset management arm has 6%. Public investors are believed to hold around 45%. In 2020, Petropavlovsk entered into an agreement with Stocken Board AG, a Liechtenstein holding company, to sell 29.9% of the IRC shares and remove the Petropavlovsk loan guarantee.[3]

4. The project loan has thus experienced challenges with the repayment schedule and a bridging loan was required. Negotiating this US$30 million loan to make the project loan repayment and satisfactory security arrangements with Petropavlovsk (given its board changes) has not been as swift as was anticipated.

5. Petropavlovsk is a Russian success story and is supported by Russian banks, but has been affected by the recent sanctions. Provision of the bridge finance has in turn affected Petropavlovsk's own financial arrangements and particularly bank covenants through cross-default provisions. There is now a Gazprombank facility in place replacing the ICBC loan and secured by charges over the assets of K&S and a series

---

[2]"Forceful Seizure of the Petropavlovsk Company Began" Amur Info website. 27 August 2020.

[3]IRC page on Petropavlovsk website.

of guarantees from Petropavlovsk. It is priced at US$160 million at LIBOR + 5.7%, equal quarterly repayment; US$80 million LIBOR + 7.7%, bullet repayment in 2026. This US$240 million facility was put in place in March 2019 to replace the ICBC loan and repay the bridging loan. Petropavlovsk is guaranteeing the debt through a series of five guarantee agreements.[4]

This highly simplified synopsis of a series of very complex events illustrates the challenges that can arise from stakeholder conflicts, joint venture partner issues, different attitudes towards decision-making and the impact of global events and political decisions in what may appear to be a sound natural resources project in a great location with a strong market nearby. It is a continuing story.

---

[4]Press release dated 15 Feb 2019 on Petropavlovsk website: The recommended proposal to guarantee the obligations of K & S, a wholly owned subsidiary of IRC Ltd, under two facility agreements with JSC Gazprom Bank.

Chapter 15

Corporate Changes and Restructuring

Introduction

The same techniques that apply to a project financing of a new road, factory or gas development can also be used when contemplating corporate restructuring. Once again there should be a distinct cash flow, a bundle of assets, and a risk environment and a network of contracts. In this chapter, we will consider how techniques from project financing are used in corporate restructuring. Different regulations about the use of assets to support corporate restructuring debt apply in different jurisdictions so while some systems may allow an acquirer to use the assets of the proposed acquisition to support the financial package to make the acquisition, this is not always permitted.

15.1. Asset Sales, Acquisitions and Mergers

As part of their stewardship obligation towards shareholders or stockholders, the management of companies should always be alert to opportunities to restructure activities to enhance shareholder value, including disposing of properties or operations that do not have the growth and profit potential offered by alternative new project opportunities, and acquiring and integrating new sources of revenue into their businesses. The present value of the potential cash flow from properties under consideration for disposal should be compared with the present sale value of such properties in a continuous dynamic review process. The effect upon the balance sheet, debt service, interest coverage and ratios should be considered. Apart from improving the working capital and financial statement by such disposals, management time may be freed to work on more productive ventures and significant reductions in the selling company's overheads may add to the gain. Getting rid of marginal operations is not an easy task, but few successful companies tolerate marginal operations where the invested capital can be better employed elsewhere.

A merger or an acquisition of companies or properties for stock or cash can sometimes be used as a method of improving the overall financial strength of the acquiring company through economies of scale or scope. A merger results in a single legal entity being created; an acquisition retains the discrete nature of one company as it enters the corporate structure of another. Both may use forms of project financing; depending on local regulations, properties of the acquired company may be used as collateral for additional borrowings. The balance sheet of the acquiring company may be substantially improved, and the overall borrowing capacity of the combined companies or properties greatly increased as a result of economies of scope and scale.

Acquisitions of the interests of other parties in joint venture projects of the acquiring company may sometimes be accomplished by stock securities with warrants rather than cash. The borrowing capacity of the project may then be improved because of greater concentration of control in one party. Accounting management and overhead expenses may be saved as a result of elimination of partners or investors in projects by the primary owner or sponsor. The management of a project with many partners with relatively small shareholdings can incur significant co-ordination costs, especially if the partners disagree. As mentioned in Chapter 14, in some oil and gas projects where there were larger numbers of smaller local participants, once the project matured, the numbers of partners fell in order to speed up decision-making processes and lower co-ordination costs.

The subject of sales of properties or mergers and acquisitions is a broad one, mentioned briefly in this chapter because it merits consideration along with other alternatives.

15.2. Leveraged Buyouts of Companies

Leveraged buyouts (LBOs) and management buyouts (MBOs) of companies and divisions of large companies are often accomplished as fairly pure project financings in which lenders are willing to advance funds for the purchase of a company or division on the basis of the projected earnings before interest, taxes, depreciation and amortization (EBITDA) — cash flows — available to service debt, the security of the underlying assets and personal guarantees from the key individuals concerned.

In many LBOs or MBOs the equity funds provided by the managers or promoters are modest compared to the funds required for the acquisition. In some MBO cases this modest capital contribution is justified by the unique expertise of the management team and the "sweat equity" they will contribute to making the company successful. These are typically buyouts of large company divisions that no longer fit in the parent's strategic plans, but other MBOs may be buyouts by employees of closely held companies owned and controlled by individuals who, because of advancing age or other reasons, are retiring from the business. (The term LBO is used hereafter to refer to both LBOs and MBOs.) The modest equity requirement is also a form of recognition of the astuteness of the sponsor purchasers in locating an acquisition with characteristics which permit an LBO with advantages for all parties to be structured so that lenders provide most of the cash required for the acquisition. The willingness of the seller to provide financing subordinate to other lenders will have a material effect on structuring especially if seller or vendor financing takes the form of subordinated equity (as opposed to subordinated debt).

Essential to an LBO is an excellent incoming management team who will be mainly concerned with reducing debt to more easily manageable levels. Lenders to LBOs do not want an empire builder in charge, or to be dependent on a single individual for the project's success. In practice, many LBOs are structured with insider management and external investors combining talents and expertise to structure a successful LBO, when they are also known as buy-in management buyout (BIMBO).

LBO structures are used by companies, private investors and managers of spun-off companies to finance acquisitions. Typically, those purchasers have limited financial resources and need to maximize the leverage of their capital through projected free cash flows, EBITDA or other measures[1] and/or using asset-based financing techniques, using the acquired assets as security, where this is possible.

---

[1] The area of EBITDA versus free cash flow or cash flow from operations is a thorny one. While there are standardized definitions of EBITDA, Free cash flow can include some specific adjustments. The solution is to always check exactly what basis is being used and what is included in the calculation, so the comparison is between apples and apples not apples and oranges when negotiating!

The usual ingredients for an LBO are:

1. The unit to be acquired must have a consistent history of positive cash flow.
2. The assets of the borrower (including value as a going concern) must have a liquid value which exceeds the amount of the senior debt.
3. The lender must be able to monitor the cash flow and the changing value of pledged assets during the loans.
4. The incoming management must have substantial experience in the business areas of the LBO target.
5. The incoming management needs to be sufficiently incentivized while allowing the major financiers the ability to take control should things go wrong.

15.2.1. *Cash is King*

"Cash is king" in structuring LBOs, since they are often typical project financings in which the acquisition debt is to be serviced and retired from the cash flows generated by the business.

Cash projections (as proxied by EBITDA or free cash flow) and financial projections are discussed elsewhere in this book. These projections and their robustness to change and their validity under scrutiny, comprise the most important information in analyzing, entering into or lending to an LBO. Special attention must be paid to contingencies as well as known future requirements (capital expenditures and debt service) and their impact on the expected future cash flows.

An equity investor with a deep pocket and a reputation for supporting investments in the case of difficulty is comforting to lenders. An equity investor with little interest in the transaction (except its own fees perhaps) is less comforting, because of the lack of an equity stake and the inability or reluctance such an investor may have to inject new capital should the need arise. Lenders are not being paid for the equity risk and do not want to be forced to assume that risk.

15.2.2. *Debt Structures*

Simply stated, the capital and debt structures in LBOs and MBOs usually fall into the following pattern:

- Equity (common stock)
- Subordinated debt (mezzanine debt)
- Senior secured debt
- Working capital loan

These are discussed in Chapter 6 in our companion book.

In some cases, there may be a bridging loan for the acquisition or buyout that would be the subject of a refinancing package once control of the assets had been gained. There are risks associated with bridging loans as we saw in the Petropavlovsk case in the previous chapter and shall see in the case at the end of this chapter, especially when there may be expectations of partial repayment from asset sales. There have been examples of such loans being adversely affected as the market for the proposed asset sales has fallen because of events in the external environment, leaving the lenders in an unhappy position.

The capital debt structure of a typical LBO or MBO typically may involve several tiers of debt or equity, such as the following:

- Common stock
- Preferred stock
- Subordinated debt (with warrants for common stock)
- Subordinated debt
- Senior secured bank debt
- Asset-based finance (inventory and accounts receivable)
- Equipment leases
- Working capital debt
- Trade credit

The categories of these financial instruments were discussed in earlier chapters. Debt structures in LBOs and MBOs are limited only by the imagination of the sponsor and the appetite of the market for such financial instruments.

15.2.3. *Senior Debt*

The senior debt for an LBO (like most project financings) is usually subdivided further into:

- secured debt;
- unsecured debt (with a negative pledge) or a subordinated loan; and
- revolving loan for current needs including working capital.

The providers of senior debt for LBOs are usually banks or insurance companies or finance companies. Such senior debt often has the following characteristics:

- Historically for a term of four to eight years, sometimes split into tranches some of which may have a balloon payment. More recent deals have been for shorter periods reflecting a significant refinancing debt overhang in the US markets.
- Interest may be fixed or floating.
- The senior debt may comprise up to 70% of the capitalization.
- The lenders do not get an "equity kicker" or equity linked reward.
- The risk is palatable to cash flow lenders — not balance sheet lenders.
- The senior debt has financial covenants which ensure cash flow will be used to retire debt.
- Revolving loans are for working capital and current needs rather than for the acquisition of assets.

A revolving loan is often secured by current assets of the acquired unit, such as accounts receivable and inventory.[2] The amount of the loan is based on a percent of the face value of current assets which represents their quick liquidation value. Since the amount of the inventory and accounts receivables varies with seasonal and other factors, the amount of the revolver varies. The loan can increase as well as decrease. There is no amortization schedule and the borrower pays down the loan as business conditions permit, unless the collateral base value falls.

A revolver which automatically renews each year is called an *evergreen revolver*. If a revolver is not renewed, the balance is typically then paid over a period like a short-term loan.

15.2.4. *Junior and Subordinated Debt*

The junior debt (mezzanine financing) for LBOs is usually a smaller layer of capitalization often consisting of up to 20% of total capitalization (though this has not always been the case). Such debt is provided by finance companies, risk capital companies, asset-based finance divisions

---

[2]A particular type of revolver structure secured by a basket of oil and gas properties has also been used in borrowing base loans (see Chapter 14).

of banks or insurance companies. It may also be provided by the selling company and perhaps be payable out of future earnings.

Junior debt is subordinated and holds a residual claim on any security as the senior debt is paid down. This debt generally has the following characteristics in an LBO:

- The debt is subordinated to senior debt but not necessarily other debt.
- For a term of six years but has historically been longer.
- Now likely to include warrants, payments in kind or to be convertible to common at an attractive price.
- Carries a higher interest rate than senior debt.
- May be zero coupon or stripped interest instruments.
- Interest may be fixed or floating.

In large LBOs, publicly issued so-called junk bonds have been used to finance such acquisitions. These bonds are more preferable to the promoters of the LBO because:

- They do not contain restrictive covenants such as would be required in private placements.
- The interest rate requirement is low in relation to the risk.
- Often, equity kickers such as stock warrants or convertible features are not required.

US savings and loan associations have been big buyers of these bonds with mixed success, and anecdotal reliance upon the presence of senior lenders to monitor the borrower's current and future viability.

15.2.5. *Equity*

The equity in an LBO is common stock purchased by the promoters — the key executives and managers — or the ultimate owner if it is a company acquiring the target company. In an LBO the equity may be only 10% or less of real capitalization. There can be different classes of equity designed to meet different investor requirements, but simple structures minimize co-ordination costs.

In recent years, there has been a proliferation of large investment funds formed for the purpose of investing equity in LBOs.

15.2.6. *Project Finance Structures Used in LBOs*

There are two basic structures which might be used for leveraged buy-outs. In the first structure, the purchaser arranges for the acquired entity to be housed in a subsidiary. In the second structure, the acquired entity is merged into the acquiring company. In either case, an asset-based financing can be used but the focus must be on cash flow to repay debt.

15.2.7. *Leveraged Buyout Housed in a Subsidiary*

1. Purchaser and seller agree to a purchase of a division of seller.
2. At a simultaneous closing, the following events take place:
   (a) The bank and subsidiary sign an asset-based loan and security agreement which covers the acquired assets.
   (b) Loan proceeds are advanced to the subsidiary by the bank.
   (c) The subsidiary pays a dividend (or makes a capital distribution) to the purchaser.
   (d) The purchaser (i) makes an equity investment in the subsidiary and (ii) pays the purchase price to the seller.

The seller transfers the assets of the sold division to the subsidiary. (If a subsidiary of the seller had been sold, the stock of the subsidiary would have been transferred to the purchaser.) This is shown in Figure 15.1.

15.2.8. *Leveraged Buyout in Which the Acquired Subsidiary or Division is Merged into the Acquiring Corporation*

1. The seller and purchaser enter into a contract whereby the purchaser is to acquire seller's subsidiary or division for a price.
2. At a simultaneous closing, the following events take place:
   (a) The bank and subsidiary sign an asset-based loan and security agreement, which covers the acquired assets as well as other assets of the purchaser.
   (b) The loan proceeds are advanced to the purchaser by the bank.
   (c) The purchaser pays the purchase price to the seller.
   (d) The seller transfers title to the stock and/or assets to the purchaser.

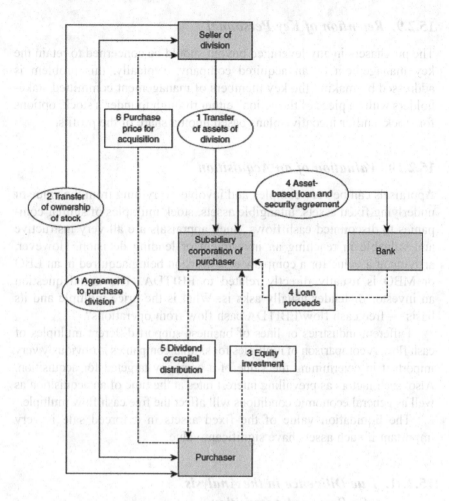

Figure 15.1: Leveraged Buyout Housed in a Subsidiary

Notes:

1. The seller agrees to the sale of a "division" to purchaser. The assets of the division are transferred to a subsidiary of seller. 2. The stock ownership in subsidiary is transferred by seller to owner, subject to receipt of purchase price (a simultaneous closing). 3. Purchaser makes an equity investment in the subsidiary. 4. The subsidiary borrows funds from a bank sufficient to cover the purchase price. 5. The subsidiary pays a dividend or makes a capital distribution sufficient to pay the purchase price to the purchaser. 6. Purchaser pays the seller the purchase price (all this occurs at a simultaneous closing). Prepared by Frank J. Fabozzi and Peter K. Nevitt.

15.2.9. *Retention of Key Personnel*

The purchasers in any leveraged buyout should be concerned to retain the key management of an acquired company. Typically, this problem is addressed by making the key members of management committed stakeholders with "a piece of the action" either through founder's stock, options for stock, and/or incentive plans based upon a share of the profits.

15.2.10. *Valuation of an Acquisition*

Appraisals can be very complex and involve everything from the value of underlying fixed assets, intangible assets, stock multiples of similar companies to discounted cash flows. Such appraisals are all very instructive and valuable in reaching an investment or lending decision. However, arriving at a value for a company or a division being acquired in an LBO or MBO is usually directly related to EBITDA. The initial question an investor or lender usually asks is: What is the price multiple and its basis — free cash flow/EBITDA/cash flow from operations?

Different industries or lines of business support different multiples of cash flow. A comparison of multiples for similar companies is obviously very important in determining the value of a company targeted for acquisition. Also, such factors as prevailing interest rates at the time of an acquisition as well as general economic conditions will affect the free cash flow multiple.

The liquidation value of the fixed assets in a forced sale is very important if such assets have significant value.

15.2.11. *Due Diligence in the Analysis of a Proposed Acquisition*

Investors or lenders to an LBO or MBO acquisition being financed largely as a project financing dependent upon future cash flows to service interest and repay debt, must conduct a thorough due diligence investigation of the company. This investigation supplements and must support, and be consistent with the financial projections for the entity proposed to be acquired.

If the entity proposed to be acquired or financed has had a previous history as an independent entity, the due diligence and credit examination falls into a familiar pattern. If, however, the acquisition has been operating as a division or subsidiary with overlapping accounting and accountabilities, the task is more difficult.

A sample due diligence checklist for the analysis of a prospective acquisition is provided in the appendix to this chapter. Not all items on the list will be available or appropriate in many cases. However, where an item is not available that fact should be noted and the reason it is not available. It obviously is not possible to construct a checklist applicable to all circumstances, so additional items to the example checklist are certainly appropriate in each case.

15.3. Employee Stock Ownership Plans

Employee stock ownership plans (ESOPs) are included in this chapter on restructuring because they offer a way for employees to participate in and even fund projects. ESOPs are similar to corporate pension and profit-sharing plans and trusts. In the US, ESOPs are controlled by the Employee Retirement Income Security Act (ERISA) and in the UK by the Companies Acts. The use of employee share ownership approaches has been slow outside the US other than in the UK, and the EC has launched several initiatives including four PEPPER (Promotion of employee participation in profits and enterprise results) reports spanning a 20-year period.[3] The latest report, PEPPER IV, published in 2009 suggests that while there appears to be a reported increase in employee participation across the 27 EC member states, further examination suggests this is limited to a small number of countries and concentrated in multinational companies. Increasing the adoption of employee ownership schemes will require changing or developing new legislation and/or fiscal rules across the EC states and in the education of employees.

An ESOP should be established by a company for the exclusive benefit of its employees. The structure has a number of characteristics which makes it an attractive mechanism for accomplishing project financing objectives for a tax-paying sponsor. Specifically, ESOPs may be used as the means of transferring ownership of closely held firms that for one reason or another do not wish to go public, or cannot go public, or merge. The ESOP structure has been used to achieve or assist in financing LBOs. An ESOP can also be used to cash out individual shareholders,

---

[3] European Foundation for the Improvement of Living and Working Conditions (EUROFOUND) is the parent site for the Pepper projects: https://www.eurofound.europa.eu/areas/participationatwork/pepperreports.

their estates and corporate shareholders in succession planning, and may be used to fund acquisitions and to finance new projects.

According to the National Center for Employee Ownership website,[4] in 2018 (the last year data were available) 14 million people were members of 6,416 ESOPs in the US, with total assets of US\$ 1.4 trillion. Some are forms of stock plans, in which the employers contribute stock into a trust for employees every year. The companies get tax deductions for the value of the stock contributed. The employees do not contribute. Others combine 401(K) plans with ESOPs to produce "KSOPs". Though the number of plans has decreased, the asset value has increased, reflecting acquisitions of companies with such plans and consolidation.

There are also leveraged ESOPs: the company sets up an ESOP that borrows money to buy stock either from the company or on the market. The company contributes money every year to the ESOP that uses the money to retire the debt. Both principal and interest on ESOP loans are tax deductible. However, principal payments may be legally limited to a percentage of the annual payroll, determined each year. So, although ESOPs do not in themselves constitute pure project financing structures, they can be used in some circumstances to accomplish objectives associated with project financing (e.g. obtaining the optimum use of a tax shelter and optimizing leverage).

ESOPs differ from profit-sharing plans and trusts in several ways:

- An ESOP may invest most of its assets in stock or property of its corporate sponsor, whereas most pension and profit-sharing trusts are limited in the amount they may invest in their sponsor company stock to offer employees diversification in the underlying portfolio.
- ESOPs may be permitted to leverage (borrow funds for) investments in the sponsor company stock or other investments, something many pension and profit-sharing trusts are not permitted to do.
- Sponsors of ESOPs are permitted to contribute stock of the sponsor to the ESOP and take a tax deduction equal to the fair market value of the stock contributed. Only cash can be contributed to a profit-sharing trust.
- Distributions by an ESOP to the employee participants must be in stock of the sponsor company, whereas profit-sharing plans usually distribute cash.
- An ESOP cannot create debt capacity which does not already exist. However, an ESOP for a company paying tax may increase debt capacity or permit a much more rapid repayment of debt out of pre-tax revenue.

---

[4]National Center for Employee Ownership: https://www.nceo.org/.

15.3.1. *Securitized ESOP Loans*

For example, a company using a conventional ESOP loan has decided to sell, say, 20% of its stock to an ESOP with the purchase price payable over seven years. It borrows the current value of that 20% stake and gives the borrowed funds to the ESOP to buy the stock. The company then pays the loan over seven years (or a shorter term if the company prefers). The shares of stock are allocated to employees as the loan is paid off. (An ESOP loan can be either to the company setting up the plan or to the plan with a guarantee from the company.)

A disadvantage is that the ESOP loan adds a significant loading of debt to the company. While this may not be a problem for a privately held company, it may be a serious drawback for a public company due to the accounting treatment of ESOP debt. This requires the ESOP debt to be shown on the company's balance sheet even though the ESOP's equity is not shown until it is allocated.

15.3.2. *Use of an ESOP to Cash Out a Shareholder Sponsor from a Project Company*

A project company is owned either by an individual shareholder or a corporate shareholder. The shareholder wishes to cash out his or its investment. The project company is profitable and has a substantial payroll. In our example, the project company establishes an ESOP and makes annual contributions to the ESOP equal to 25% of its payroll. The ESOP, in turn, purchases the project company stock from the stockholder sponsor for its fair market value and uses the proceeds from the cash contributions to pay for the stock.

The stockholder sponsor, thus, receives cash for his or its stock and pays capital gain tax on such sale. Depending upon the amount of stock sold, the stockholder sponsor may retain control over the project company after the sale is completed. The project company uses pre-tax cash to contribute to the ESOP, whereas dividends paid directly to the sponsoring stockholder would be after-tax and subject to ordinary income tax for an individual shareholder, or an effective tax of about 8% when received by the corporate stockholder.

Had the stockholder sold stock directly to the project company, the transaction might be treated as a dividend. If the sale was made to an outsider, anything less than majority control might be difficult if not impossible to sell at a reasonable price. This is shown in Figure 15.2.

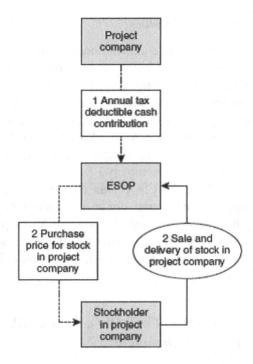

Figure 15.2:   Use of an ESOP to Cash Out a Shareholder

Notes:

1. The project company makes an annual tax deductible contribution to its ESOP which is equal to 25% of payroll. 2. The ESOP uses its cash to purchase stock of the project company from stockholders of the project company. ESOPs often also contain puts which enable retiring employees to put distributed stock to the ESOP for cash.

Prepared by Frank J. Fabozzi and Peter K. Nevitt.

ESOP deals in this category can include private equity firms who play a bridging role. If, for example, the employees may not be able to raise the money for the purchase price immediately, the private equity firm buys a stake in the company and ensures the owner receives the sale price quickly then selling the shares to the ESOP over time to allow for the purchase money to be raised.

15.3.3. *Use of an ESOP to Divest a Profitable Division*

The sponsor transfers the assets and operations of a profitable division to a newly established project corporation in exchange for all the stock of a project corporation.

The project corporation establishes an ESOP and makes annual tax-deductible contributions in cash to the ESOP equal to 25% of payroll. The ESOP then uses the cash to purchase project company stock from the sponsor. Further purchases of the stock held by the sponsor can be financed through a bank loan by the ESOP and the pledge of the project company stock as security. This is shown in Figure 15.3.

15.3.4. *Use of an ESOP to Acquire a Project Company or to Increase Stockholdings in a Project Company with Pre-Tax Dollars*

The sponsor company desires to acquire or increase its stockholdings in a project company. Once more the sponsor company makes a tax contribution to its ESOP, equal in this example to 25% of its eligible payroll. The ESOP then uses such cash to purchase stock either from the project company or from stockholders of the project company willing to sell their shares. The ESOP then exchanges the acquired stock of the project company with the sponsor company for sponsor company stock equal in fair market value to the project company stock.

15.3.5. *Use of an ESOP to Permit Repayment of a Bank Loan by the ESOP's Sponsor Company Using Pre-Tax Dollars*

The project corporation needs US$1 million for plant expansion and arranges a bank loan for that amount. The project company makes annual tax-deductible cash contributions to its ESOP equal to 15% of its payroll. The project company then sells shares of its own stock for fair market value to its ESOP for cash. The number of shares sold is such that the entire annual cash contribution to the ESOP is used to pay for the shares in cash. The cash received by the project company is then used to service the principal and interest payments on the bank debt.

15.3.6. *Converting Debt to Equity in a Leveraged Buyout*

Wesray used an innovative technique to solve a problem involved in selling a highly leveraged company, Avis Inc., to an ESOP. Banks were asked to participate in a one-day US$1 billion bridge loan. That loan

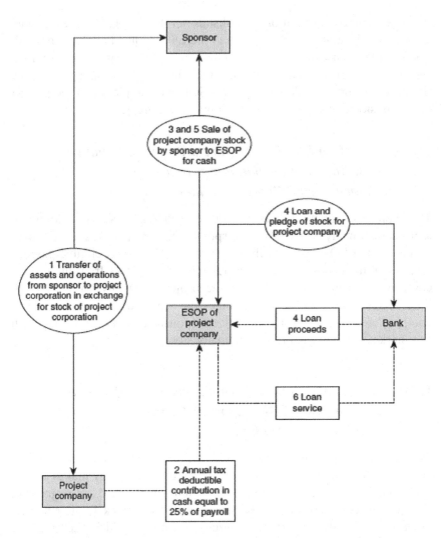

Figure 15.3:   Use of an ESOP to Divest a Profitable Division

Notes:

1. The sponsor company establishes a project company by transferring assets and operations of one of its profitable operating divisions to the project company in exchange for its stock. 2. The project company establishes an ESOP and makes annual tax deductible contributions in cash to the ESOP equal to 25% of payroll. 3. The ESOP uses cash to purchase stock in the project company from the sponsor. 4. The ESOP borrows from a bank using stock of the project company as security for the loan. 5. The loan proceeds are used to purchase additional stock of the project company from the sponsor for cash. 6. The ESOP pays the loan from earnings.

Prepared by Frank J. Fabozzi and Peter K. Nevitt.

was used to pay off Avis' high coupon debt and convert it to equity on Avis' books.

ESOPs can only buy stock. By converting the debt to equity, the ESOP was then able to pay for the new, higher equity value of the company. In effect, employee stock ownership plan financing with a lower interest rate was substituted for the high coupon debt, lowering Avis' debt service and allowing the employee stock ownership plan to pay more for Avis than other possible buyers.

15.3.7. *Downsides of ESOPs*

Scale — ESOPs are only suitable for medium-sized companies, not least because of the expensive set up costs. Fees of close to US$100,000 to set the ESOP up are not atypical.

If an employee leaves, the ESOP has to buy the shares back at a fair price, so the ESOP needs to buffer its liquidity and not to expect significant downsizing of the parent company.

High profile bankruptcies may have associated ESOPS with poor financial management in the minds of many people, conflating management of the operating company with employee benefit losses because the ESOP owned the shares. This illustrates the need to have clear separation of ownership and control transparency and good governance structures.

Linked to the last point is the need to offer a clear explanation to all stakeholders but especially employees about how the ESOP will work and their rights, benefits and any obligations or actions.

15.4. Case Study: Isosceles[5]

This case study is from the heyday of buyout fever in the 1980s but offers some cautionary lessons for today.

Isosceles was the largest hostile LBO[6] in the UK when it was completed in the spring of 1989. The target company was called Gateway Corporation Plc, "Gateway", and its core business was the Gateway supermarket business, the fifth largest food retailer in the UK, a mixture of small town centre sites, and larger out of town hypermarkets. Gateway had suffered from

---

[5]This case was inspired by an earlier shorter case prepared by Richard Wheatcroft of the Open University and expanded by CF de Nahlik.
[6]Technically it was a "buy-in"!

overambitious expansion plans, supported by a bull stock market, sacrificing profitability for the dash for growth. It had bought related businesses such as Herman's Sporting Goods in the US, the Medicare drugstore chain in the UK and Wellworth, a chain of food stores in Northern Ireland, and was diverting resources to try and manage them effectively.

The buyout group (Isosceles), led by David Smith, spotted an interesting business opportunity and believed that by tightening up on capital expenditure and disposing of some of the property and non-core activities, they could turn Gateway from a marginal player in the food retailing business, to a highly profitable one.

15.4.1. *Gateway*

Gateway had been built up from a smaller supermarkets group, by a charismatic individual who had revitalized it. His success in the City of London had been rewarded by support from institutional shareholders for rights issues to make the acquisitions into diversified areas. But as time went on, he and his colleagues came under pressure from the investors to match the performance of the larger multiple chains such as Sainsbury's or Tesco, and the diversifications were slow to deliver on their promise.

In late December 1988, the company was the subject of a hostile bid from Barker and Dobson, a confectionery company. This bid was worth 140.3 pence (p) in cash, and 77p in shares, making a total of 217.35p per share. The bid failed as a result of the difficulty of valuing the equity component.

The logic for this attempt to restructure Gateway was summarized as a return to the core business of supermarkets, including disposal of all non-core operations, and a disposal of the superstores, which were not trading as a successful chain, and therefore worth more to another entity. An offer of £750 million was made by a third party for the superstores, and an unsolicited bid from a third party of £200 million was made for Herman's.

Isosceles fought for control of Gateway in a messy battle for the publicly traded group. Isosceles ended up with 52% of the company, with a further 40% held by New Gateway, an alternative bidding group consisting of A&P, the German-owned American supermarket chain, and Wasserstein Perella (WP), its Wall street backers. This stalemate, in which Isosceles was unable to gain control of Gateway and merge with that company in order to offer the Gateway assets to its lenders as security for the indebtedness, was

Table 15.1: Initial Financing Structure for the Isosceles Buyout of Gateway Plc. (in £ millions)

Equity Capital	Total Equity	£200
Mezzanine debt	Senior mezzanine LIBOR + 3% + warrants, 9 years	100
	Junior mezzanine LIBOR + 3 1/2% + warrants, 10 years	150
	Term loan	125
	LIBOR + 2 1/2%, 8 years	
	Total Mezzanine	£375
Senior Debt	Bridge facility 1	600
	LIBOR + 2%, 1 year, (repaid on sale of superstore to ASDA)	
	Bridge facility 2	730
	LIBOR + 2%, 3 years	
	Term loan	195
	LIBOR + 2%, 7 years, (margin may drop to 1 1/2%)	
	Revolving credit	375
	LIBOR + 2%, 7 years, (margin may fall to 1 1/2 %)	
	Total Senior Debt	£1,900

Prepared by CF de Nahlik.

eventually resolved by A&P and WP converting their shareholdings into shares in Isosceles, as did the remaining minority shareholders.

The syndication process for the debt was not easy — 16 banks were reportedly left with 40% over and above their commitments (£550 million). These were not good omens for the future. The initial financing structure is shown in Table 15.1.

Isosceles saw the average cost of capital for the group of 17%, only a few points higher than its competitors, and lower than the target rate of return of food retailers in the UK at the time. It also felt that having a part of the debt in dollars matched well with Herman's revenue stream, even though this was one of the earliest candidates for disposal. There was also a cap and swap attached to £675 million of the sterling debt, fixing the rate for up to three years. However, the path was not to be smooth.

By mid-1990, the first refinancing was in place, and the company was refusing to pay a dividend, pending the amendment of the debt structure. Herman's had not been sold, and the company had decided not to sell Wellworth or a series of stores in the North of England. The consequence of this was a need to find an additional £75–200 million of equity, as well as additional debt to fund the £375 million gap.

The proposal was that the dividend on the cumulative preference shares would not be paid, but would earn an interim interest of 7%. (The majority of these shares were held by the company.) Further the company was warning that there was a possibility that some of the debt covenants would be breached in the autumn. The most sensitive of these was the interest cover ratio, measured quarterly, which needed to be over 1.75 to 1 in November 1990, rising to 3 to 1 three years later. Nevertheless, the spirit of optimism prevailed, and Isosceles was talking about a float of the shares back on to the stock exchange in the next two or three years.

As the year progressed, there was more news from Isosceles. The accounts for the year ended April 1990, published in Autumn 1990, were qualified by Ernst & Young. Isosceles believed that the company needed £100–200 million in new equity to survive, and the mezzanine lenders were under pressure to convert into equity. By December the restructuring was well in hand. A&P wanted more representation on the Isosceles board, and declined to participate in the new issue of equity. A total of £87 million of the Isosceles mezzanine debt had been converted, but the most interesting factor reported as a reason for the delays, was the reluctance of S.G. Warburg, the advising bank, to invest £15 million in new equity. S.G. Warburg made some £20 million in initial fees from putting the deal together, and the other investors, felt that the bank should also share in the losses.

The UK Stock Exchange takeover rules required WP, now the owner of over 30% of the shares, to make a bid for the balance. Clearly this was unacceptable to all the other shareholders, who wanted to merely put the company on a sound capital base with a rights issue. After discussions, a procedure, known as a "whitewash" was invoked, enabling Isosceles to poll independent shareholders, and a simple majority vote sufficed to allow the *status quo* to continue, and did not force WP to make the bid.

The rights issue was partially underwritten. WP underwrote £115 million, increasing its stake to 40% if all its underwriting was taken up. Another £107 million was underwritten by Isosceles' UK investors, led by Mercury Asset Management (a subsidiary of the Warburg's investment bank), which would end up with 46.5% of Isosceles if all their underwriting were taken up. The final £15 million was not underwritten, and was available on a demand basis. Additionally, lenders agreed to defer repayment of £592 million of senior debt due in August 1991 and 1992, and to spread it over the following three years at £100 million per annum, with the balance due in August 1996. S.G. Warburg contributed an additional £15 million in working capital, and mezzanine lenders deferred £48 million of interest over the next two years, to protect the senior lenders.

This easing of the company's debt burden, and improvement of the capital structure allowed Isosceles to make a profit for the year end 1990, a 40 week year. Astute commentators noticed that the accounts were again qualified, and the Herman's profits were taken "below the line", as it was carried as an investment held for disposal, valued at £194 million. Once again spirits soared, as the press rumours began of a flotation of the company in 1992. Sadly this was premature again. By October 1991, the original Isosceles team had gone, with a payoff of £1.8 million, following another disagreement about the adequacy of finance, and another appeal for more money. This new refinancing valued the shares at £12, potentially crystallizing losses. Several investors declined to participate in this fundraising, arguing that it only served to offer short-term relief to the Isosceles problem.

More departures in the Gateway operating company fuelled unease about the management of the situation. The stores were being rebadged and relaunched to try and capitalize on the smaller store sizes by adding perceived value — a strategy which was proving less than successful, as the UK retailing scene had moved on apace. Gateway was clearly suffering from a lack of capital for the expenditure to ensure that the company remained competitive, and was also being slowly starved of working capital as well. Analysts estimated that in a year, Gateway spent £30 million on all of its capital expenditure, the price that Tesco, one of the industry leaders spent on one supermarket, with a budget of £200 million plus per annum at that time.

In May 1992, the rumours resurfaced. Herman's had still not been sold; indeed the price was now expected to be some £80 million rather than the £200 million expected at the time of the original deal, and there was a hint that the property portfolio would need to be written down. The latest results were the subject of intense press speculation. The new chief executive, anxious to start with a clean slate, pointed out that the projections provided by the original buy-in team were based on the US supermarket market, and that they were not applicable to Gateway in the UK market. Hence, the problems had started with the original business plan.

The mezzanine debt had not been serviced, some £30 million was past due, and was being rolled up to be paid later, until a cap of £48 million was reached. The mezzanine lenders were able to insist that if things did not improve, and soon, then interest would be paid monthly from the start of 1993, subject to the agreement of the senior lenders. The two mezzanine lenders, GE Capital, and Standard and Chartered, were under pressure to convert their debt into equity. Meanwhile, the equity investors were writing off their investments. The loan covenants were being renegotiated yet again. This time the problem was with the requirement that operating profit should cover interest on the senior debt by 1.5 times. An anticipated rise to 1.75 due in August 1992 was completely out of the question. Another refinancing was clearly needed.

But what was the company worth at this point? Valuing on a 4 × cash flow multiple, one journalist estimated that the Gateway business was worth £720 million. Adding in Herman's at £200 million, gave £920 million, but the actual figure was clearly likely to be significantly lower, and more like £820 million, compared with debts of £1.1 billion to the senior lenders, and a further £400 million of equity, as well as £288 million of mezzanine debt.

The resolution was reported widely. The mezzanine lenders got some interest paid, and some warrants giving them 20% of the company once flotation took place. Incredibly, the latter was still a topic of discussion. The capital expenditure restrictions were lifted to £100 million, but no new money went into the company, now the owner of the fifth largest supermarket chain in the UK. The preference shares were converted to ordinary shares to simplify the capital structure.

But the company was not out of the woods yet. The year end results for 1991 revealed a £146 million loss after a write down of Herman's of £145 million. Despite this, the flotation plan, now on the stocks for 1995, was back in the press, and for the first time, the accounts were unqualified. Was the company safe at last?

The trading performance in 1992 was affected by the recession, and the operating profit forecast was gradually downgraded to £110 million, compared with £160 million in the budget. More rumbling began about interest deferrals. More write-offs of the equity by the institutions. Wellworth was in the frame as a disposal candidate once more, though at far from the original price of £150 million. In December 1992, it was finally sold for £122 million and Isosceles was permitted to keep £30 million of the sales proceeds for desperately needed capital expenditure. But with the last refinancing only completed in October 1992, there were hints of yet another to come.

The banks decided to scrap Isosceles, the holding company, and to concentrate on the cash-generating Gateway business. Herman's seemed close to being sold and the need for Isosceles, as a separate entity was declining. Then the latest Herman's sale attempt fell through.

The bankers became anxious, and speculated through the press that they felt that they were not getting the full picture. The chief executive at Gateway was forced to resign. New advisers to all the parties were chosen as S.G. Warburg was now seen to have a conflict of interest. There were additional fears that the complex share holding structure would still allow WP to veto any proposals. The trade creditors, sensing another crisis, began to get nervous, adding to the problem. The profit forecast fell to £105 million, with significant effects on forecast cash flow. On 19 December 1992, the company asked the banks for a standstill agreement on interest and on principal. Covenants were expected to be breached in January, as the payments for Christmas stock fell due, and the profit forecast was lowered further to £100 million. Some £600 million of debt was expected to be the subject of equity conversion discussions, as the banks tried to do something about their positions. WP declined to write down the value of its interest — a policy it had adhered to from the beginning, despite the other write downs by the other equity investors. The banks were also expecting to be asked to put up another £50 million as a high priority, in order to solve the working capital problem, and reassure the group's suppliers.

The outcome reached just before Christmas was for a radical restructuring. The standstill would stay in place until May 1993, and £90 million of "repayments" would be deferred. Additional working capital facilities were made available and though the amount was not been formally disclosed, it was thought to be about £30 million. And on 10 February 1993, the sale of Herman's was agreed for £26 million ($40 million), compared with the $300 million that Smith expected at the time of the buy-in, and the $500 million it had cost originally. Within days Herman's had gone into Chapter 11; a comment from the purchaser said that the systems were "so extensive they were better suited to a space shuttle than a retail chain".

The next stage was to be the merger of the two entities, Isosceles and Gateway, to eliminate the duplication of management resources, followed by a further debt/equity swap and a fresh injection of cash in three years' time. This time the proposal was for the swap of £600 million of senior debt, and about £318 million of the mezzanine debt into equity. After negotiation, the entire financial structure was rationalized into five new forms of debt and equity. Most importantly a £50 million two-year working capital facility was concerned, relieving the continued anxiety of suppliers to the group. The result would be that existing shareholders would now own 45% of the enlarged share capital, mezzanine and senior lenders, 45% and 10%, respectively, with senior lenders also receiving a special share to give them 51% of votes at a general meeting.

The new business plan suggested that Gateway would record an operating profit of £105 million for the year ending 1993, compared with £187.4 million in the previous year. The new management team expected that this would lay all Gateway's problems to rest. But the drama was still not over as one lender objected.

In May 1992, the restructuring, the third since the deal's inception, was finally signed by all parties. Bankruptcy was thus narrowly avoided. Fees involved were thought to be in the order of £15 million. Gateway was now ring-fenced from Isosceles and had assumed £500 million of debt, allowing a further £100 million of annual capital expenditure. The annual interest bill for Gateway was expected to be in the range of £37.5 million with a three-year principal holiday, and Gateway's newly transferred assets were valued at £525 million.

Isosceles retained some £949 million of debt to be serviced by cash passed up from Gateway, and has assets of the shareholding in Gateway, as well as a small golf course in Hertfordshire. A total of £256 million of the senior Isosceles debt is thought to be serviceable, but the rest, including the £400 million zero coupon bond due in 10 years time, and the ordinary shares were thought to have little if any value. Nevertheless, some shareholders subscribed for a 10-year option to buy up to 25% of the ordinary shares for £12.5 million, which allowed a value of its holding in Isosceles. The Chief Executive stood to make a £16.6 million bonus if Gateway ever returned to its value of £1.8 billion, repaid all debt and paid dividends.

Gateway was rebranded as Somerfield and eventually floated in 1996, with most of the money raised being used to pay down debt. In 1998, a merger with another supermarket chain resulted in further mis-estimations of the synergies as did a failed venture into home delivery from a catalogue. Finally, a five-year plan with an experienced new Chief Executive restored Somerfield's fortunes. In 2005, the company was taken private once more for £1.1 billion and restructuring began anew. In 2008, it became part of the Co-operative Group. The Co-op group also restructured following some issues with its banking subsidiary and 36 of the former

Somerfield stores were sold to the rival Budgens supermarket group. The former headquarters has been developed into 6,000 apartments.

This case study has been shortened but even in this version, it is possible to see what can go wrong when assumptions are overoptimistic and leverage is high. Just as we began with the Channel Tunnel case study and a forced conversion of debt to equity because the business plan was faulty, so we end with another example in a very different context. "Deal fever" probably drove both transactions and the operating detail was lost in the complexity of the structure and the numbers. The work-out costs associated with failing transactions are significant and all too often can be avoided. Sometimes, it is OK to say "No"!

Appendix: Due Diligence Checklist

The list is only intended as a starting place for construction of a due diligence questionnaire which must be tailored to a particular acquisition situation.

15.A. *Industry Reports and Analyses*

1. Industry reports, normally provided by external experts, describing prospects for the relevant industry and markets.
2. Recent analyses of the company or any subsidiaries and their business prospects, prepared by investment bankers, engineers, management consultants, accountants or others, including market studies, credit reports and other types of reports, financial or otherwise.
3. Detailed list of all competitors and strategic and financial analyses as well as estimated market share for each.

15.B. *Corporate Documents*

1. Charter documents for all group companies
   a. Certificate of incorporation, as amended to date.
   b. Bylaws.
   c. Long form good standing and tax certificates in state of incorporation.
   d. List of jurisdictions in which each company is qualified to do business or is otherwise operating.
   e. Form of stock certificates.

2. Corporate minutes and related materials for the last five years
   a. Minutes of board of directors' meetings.
   b. Minutes of shareholders' meetings.
   c. Minutes of committees of the board of directors.
   d. Materials (including financial projections) distributed to members of board of directors and committees thereof in connection with meetings.
3. Loan and other financing documents
   a. All documents and agreements evidencing borrowings, whether secured or unsecured, including loan and credit agreements, promissory notes and other evidence of indebtedness and all guarantees.
   b. Bank letters or agreements confirming lines of credit, including covenants thereto.
   c. Loans and guarantees of third-party obligations.
   d. Credit agreements and indentures.
   e. Correspondence with lenders or providers of funds, including all compliance reports submitted by the company or its independent public accountants.
   f. Trade financing agreements including letters of credit or other instruments.
   g. Islamic financing arrangements made by the group or individual company members.
   h. Any off-balance sheet or project financing arrangements entered into by any group members or related or associated companies.
4. Lease agreements
   a. Financing leases and sales, and lease-back agreements.
   b Conditional sale agreements.
   c. Equipment leases.
   d. Correspondence with landlords.
5. Capital stock
   a. Securities authorized and outstanding.
   b. Covenants of preferred stock, if any.
   c. Agreements relating to the purchase, sale or issuance of securities, including warrants.
   d. Agreements relating to voting of securities and restrictive share transfers.
   e. Agreements relating to preemptive rights.

    f.   Shareholder list indicating ownership by class of stock of all shares of the company.

    g.   Agreements relating to registration rights, if any.

6. All patents, trademarks, copyrights, licenses and other intellectual property rights and applications therefore and assignment and ownership documents relating thereto held by the company or its employees.

7. Personnel

    a.   Employment contracts.

    b.   Consulting contracts.

    c.   Contracts with unions, including collective bar gaining agreements.

    d.   Loans and guarantees to directors, officers or employees.

    e.   Employee benefits, including vacation pay and severance policies.

    f.   Employee stock option plans.

    g.   Employee size, turnover, absentee history and distribution reports.

    h.   Personnel manuals.

8. Pension fund-related data (e.g. ERISA if applicable)

    a.   Pension and profit-sharing plans.

    b.   Multi-employer plans.

    c.   Deferred compensation plans.

    d.   Other employee benefit plans.

    e.   Actuarial valuation reports for the last three years for each pension plan including multi-employer plans, to which the company currently contributes.

    f.   Any estimates of withdrawal liability that have been performed for the company that relate to multi-employer plans.

    g.   Current listing of benefit changes adopted or intended to be adopted by each of the pension plans since the last actuarial valuation.

    h.   Audited financial report for the last two years for each pension plan.

    i.   List of any non-qualified pension plans or employee compensation agreements showing the individuals covered, a description of the benefits provided, and the actuarial methodology and assumptions used for expense purposes.

    j.   Census of all employees showing date of birth, date of hire, sex, job classifications and current salary.

    k.   Defined contribution plans including audited financial report (for two years) and results of any tests performed for top-heavy status determination.

9. Management salaries, bonuses, and incentive pay.
10. Organization chart
    a. Management structure.
    b. Officers' and directors.
    c. A complete map of the current group structure showing all subsidiaries, affiliates and associated companies and detailing the relationships between the different entities.
11. Status of legal proceedings
    a. Schedule of all material pending litigation.
    b. Litigation, claims and other proceedings settled or concluded.
    c. Litigation, claims and proceedings threatened or pending.
    d. Consent decrees and injunctions.
    e. Regulatory compliance.
    f. Questionable payments.
    g. Attorney's letters to auditors.
    h. Environmental proceedings not covered elsewhere.
12. Compliance with laws
    a. Citations and notices received from government agencies.
    b. Pending investigations and governmental proceedings.
    c. Government permits and consents including Environmental Protection Agency, United States Department of Agriculture, state, local or foreign government regulatory approvals or applications for such approvals.
    d. Reports to and correspondence with government agencies.
13. Real property
    a. Deeds.
    b. Leases or subleases of real property.
    c. Zoning variances.
    d. Easements, restrictions and other encumbrances.
    e. Recent property surveys.
    f. Title insurance policies.
    g. Legal description of all real property owned.
14. Sales and marketing and contracts
    a. Sales commission plan, if any.
    b. Sales allowance and return policies.
    c. Warranty or consignment policies.
15. Other agreements, as applicable, including:
    a. Marketing agreements, including sales agent, dealer and distributor agreements, original equipment manufacturer (OEM) agreements and pricing agreements.

b. Government contracts and subcontracts.
c. Supply agreements.
d. Purchase and requirements contracts.
e. Joint venture and partnership agreements.
f. License agreements.
g. Franchise agreements.
h. Management, service and tax sharing agreements.
i. Construction agreements and performing guarantees.
j. Advertising agreements.
k. Agreements associated with acquisition and disposition of companies, significant assets or operations.
l. Secrecy, confidentiality and non-disclosure agreements.
m. Commission, brokerage and agency agreements.
n. Contracts outside the ordinary course of business.
o. Samples of forms of purchase orders and invoices.
p. Indemnification contracts and similar arrangements for officers and directors.
q. Intercompany documents relating to the relationship and conduct of business among the company, its corporate parent or significant shareholders and any subsidiary or affiliated companies, and any of their divisions, departments or affiliated entities.
r. Agreements with insiders including interested director transactions and stock options granted to officers and directors.
s. Form of product warranties of the company.
t. All other agreements material to the business of the company.

16. Schedule of major suppliers and customers, setting forth annual dollar amounts purchased or sold.
17. Structure of purchasing organization, purchasing practices and accountability.

15.C. *Insurance*

1. Personal property.
2. Real property, including hazardous waste and flood, if required.
3. General liability.
4. Business interruption.
5. Workers' compensation.
6. Product liability.
7. Key man insurance.
8. Automobile insurance.

9. Loss experience for the last three to five years for property, general liability, business interruption, workers' compensation, product liability, automobile fleet and any other insurance coverage.

15.D. *Group Insurance and Welfare Benefits*

1. Comprehensive listing of all welfare/insurance programmes including post-retirement life and health insurance, if applicable.
2. Summary plan description for all programmes.
3. Descriptions of insurance financing arrangements for all programmes.
4. Claim experience and premium history for the last three years for all programmes.
5. Current listing of any medical claims in excess of, or anticipated to be in excess of a limit such as US$50,000.
6. A separate listing of any non-qualified or executive medical reimbursement programmes showing the individuals covered and a description of benefits offered.

15.E. *Environmental/OSHA Compliance*

1. A list of all waste treatment, storage or disposal sites relating to the operations of the company.
2. Copies of any permits received under the Resource Conservation and Recovery Act (RCRA) or financial compliance filings made there under.
3. Copies of any notices of violations or warnings received from any authoritative body.
4. Information as to generation of hazardous wastes as defined in Section 3002 of RCRA. What kinds and where have these wastes been stored or disposed? What is the annual volume of waste generated?
5. Written estimates, if available, of future expenditures for environmental programmes and their effect on the company's business (prepared for the internal purposes or filed with governmental agencies).
6. Information about any accidents that have taken place in the last five years.
7. Information about policies and procedures adopted and testing schedules and reports for compliance with industry and other health and safety codes of conduct and/or standards.

15.F. *Product Development*

1. R&D cost by project for the last three years and projections for the next three years.
2. Sources of outside R&D funds including any joint venture agreements.
3. Complete list of any patents or trademarks held and registration details.
4. Information on expected intellectual property resulting from these activities.

15.G. *Manufacturing Inputs and Costs*

1. Five-year historical analysis of per-hour direct wage rate and fringe benefit cost.
2. Five-year historical analysis of manufacturing productivity by equivalent unit of measurement.
3. Three-year historical analysis of components of fixed overhead and fixed burden rate.
4. Three-year historical analysis of components of variable overhead and variable burden rate.

15.H. *Financial Information*

1. Balance sheets and income statements for the last five years as included in the consolidated financial statements of the company.
2. Quarterly balance sheets and income statements for the last two years as included in the consolidated financial statements of the company.
3. Balance sheet and income statement for the most recent fiscal quarter as included in the consolidated financial statements of the company.
4. Budget for current fiscal year.
5. The most recent available general ledger(s).
6. A chart of accounts.
7. Inventory valuation and pricing policies.
8. Accounts receivable analysis and ageing as of the most recent practicable date.
9. Accounts payable analysis and ageing, including trial balance as of the most recent practicable data.
10. Most recent business plan of the company (i.e. five-year plan) including projected financial statements.

11. Copies of the calendarised business plans for the last three years.
12. Firm sales order backlog data for the last three years through the most recent practicable date.
13. A copy of the accounting policy and procedures manual.
14. A summary of changes in accounting principles or estimates made in the last five years that had the effect of increasing or decreasing earnings.
15. Copies of accountants' management letter comments for the last three years.
16. Correspondence with independent accountants.
17. Reports and studies prepared by outside consultants on the company's business or financial condition.
18. Reports and materials prepared for the board of directors or committees thereof.
19. A summary of all extraordinary and non-recurring expenses for the last five years.
20. A summary of bad debt experience for the last five years and most recent fiscal quarter and management's explanation.
21. The most recent available aged inventory summary (preferably by location).
22. A summary of obsolete inventories written off during the last five years and management's explanation.
23. A summary of book to physical adjustments for the last three years including management explanations.
24. A fixed asset listing by location including date of acquisition, cost, useful life and accumulated depreciation.
25. A summary by location of significant acquisitions and disposals of property, plant and equipment for the last three years.
26. Appraisals of fixed assets or tax assessment valuations.
27. List of all material contracts in progress, including total contract price, costs incurred to date, estimated cost to complete and estimated profit margin.
28. A list of all open sales and purchases commitments, including terms.
29. List of accounting costs of all land and buildings.
30. Three-years historical analysis of scrap factor or reject rate.
31. As of the most recent practicable date, an analysis listing the components of:
    a. Other income (expense).
    b. Prepaid expenses.

    c.   Deferred charters.
    d.   Other assets.
    e.   Accrued liabilities.
    f.   Other liabilities.
32. An analysis of the following expenses for the past three fiscal years and the most recent fiscal quarter:
    a.   Warranties outstanding and claims history.
    b.   Research and development.
    c.   Advertising and promotion.
    d.   Bonus and profit sharing.
    e.   Pension and retirement benefit plans.
    f.   Repairs and maintenance.
    g.   Workers' compensation.
    h.   post-retirement benefit obligations.

15.I. *Tax Matters*

1. Federal, state and local tax returns for the last three years for all corporate entities.
2. Audit adjustments proposed by the Internal Revenue Service or equivalent national taxation authorities and state and local tax authorities since 1986.

15.J. *Projections*

1. Assumptions underlying sales projections, including unit volumes and prices, product line extensions or cutbacks, new product introductions, industry demand and projected economic cycles.
2. Assumptions underlying cost of sales and gross profit projections, including raw material costs, direct and indirect labour, and variable and fixed manufacturing overhead.
3. Assumptions underlying operating expense projections.
4. Assumptions underlying balance sheet projections.

15.K. *Miscellaneous*

1. Press clippings and releases relating to the company or its subsidiaries, if any, for the past five years.

2. Copies of company newsletters, if any for a similar period.
3. List of all miscellaneous benefit programmes including educational assistance, jury duty, employee service awards, healthcare, housing, travel concessions, company discounts, etc., including the approximate annual cost of each programme.
4. Any salary administration studies that have been performed.
5. List of key employees who have left the company during the last five years.
6. Work safety reports that have been performed.
7. Any other documents or information which, in your judgement, are significant with respect to the business of the company or which should be considered and reviewed in making disclosures regarding the business and financial condition of the company to prospective investors.

Afterword

In this book we have taken you on a journey from the Himalayas and Bhutan to a supermarket in the UK via mines, oilfield tax, tuna fishing was not quite as described, schools, roads and airports and via China, Russia, Africa and North America to see the different ways project financing techniques can be applied. These cases are very brief because each of them could probably take up a book to describe and analyze. What a good stakeholder in a project financing needs is to understand the basics and look at the different ways techniques can be applied to enable them to think creatively about solving the problems they are facing: how to structure the financing of the project so that it fits with project management and with the expected cash that will be generated. They also need an understanding of where cost numbers come from and where the numbers go in the financial models.

This is a brief taste of project financing and we wish you every success as you apply the techniques in your professional lives.

Index